# The Best American Travel Writing 2005

# The Best American Travel Writing 2005

*Edited and with an Introduction*
*by* Jamaica Kincaid

Jason Wilson, Series Editor

HOUGHTON MIFFLIN COMPANY

BOSTON · NEW YORK 2005

ISSN: 1530-1516
ISBN-13: 978-0-618-36951-5      ISBN-10: 0-618-36951-1
ISBN-13: 978-0-618-36952-2 (pbk.)      ISBN-10: 0-618-36952-X (pbk.)

Printed in the United States of America

MP 10 9 8 7 6 5 4 3 2 1

# Contents

# Foreword

I HESITATE to open a collection of the best travel writing with an example of the worst travel writing, but here goes:

*Iceland is a land of fire and ice.*

Whoever first used this infamous, less-than-inspiring sentence in print can breathe easy; his identity will remain anonymous here. But only because I cannot finger the culprit. In my imagination, however, I can clearly picture this wordsmith. He's sitting in a hotel bar in Reykjavík, scribbling away in his black leather-bound journal, probably with a fountain pen, as the deadline nears. He is wearing a fedora and one of those tan vests with lots of pockets, and he's smoking a pipe or a skinny, pungent cigar. He scratches his thick Hemingway-esque beard, musing over all the wonders he has witnessed during his weeklong tour of Iceland. Suddenly, just as the barmaid delivers the afternoon's third cocktail, a eureka moment occurs. He thinks: Volcanoes! He thinks: Glaciers! Fire. Ice. Egads, man. Iceland is *indeed* a land of fire and ice! Innkeeper, I must wire my editor in New York at once!

However it happened, the original composition of the line "Iceland is a land of fire and ice" has proved to be a seminal moment in the travel literature of Iceland. From that time on, the description has proved irresistible to travel writers; it has found its way into countless articles, guidebooks, and television documentaries.

During one recent evening when I couldn't sleep, I was flipping through late-night television and came upon a program about Iceland on a channel devoted to golf. In the show, a group of middle-aged American men had been brought to Iceland to play in a summer golf tournament in the midnight sun near the Arctic Circle. Their tee time was 1 A.M.

Sandwiched between footage of the men shooting a rather mediocre round of golf was documentary footage of Iceland's sights — steaming hot springs, pastoral sheep farms, idyllic fishing villages, and the discos of Reykjavík — narrated by a perky young female host. Soon enough came the requisite shots of volcanoes and glaciers. And even in my half-sleep, I knew what was coming next.

"Iceland is *truly* a land of fire and ice," cooed the host, as if she were the first person in the world to ever utter such profundity.

Allow me to be candid: The process of searching an entire year's worth of travel stories — in order to choose the two dozen or so exemplary ones that appear in *The Best American Travel Writing* — can often be as mind-numbing as watching that Icelandic golfing adventure in the middle of an insomnious night.

Thomas Swick, travel editor of the *South Florida Sun-Sentinel*, calls bad travel writing the "tiramisu of journalism." In a recent article for the *Columbia Journalism Review*, Swick asks, "Why do the travel magazines, lavish with tips and sumptuous photographs, leave us feeling so empty?"

I often agree. I would be more than happy, for instance, never to read another Sunday travel article about "my wife Barbie and I" traipsing about trendy design shops or taking cooking classes in villas. I might be moved to tears if I made it through a year without hearing about another city or region that's currently "on the verge." (This year, by the way, it's Puglia that's "on the verge," recently described as "the New Tuscany.") And if I had the power, I would instruct the Travel Writing Police to lock up anyone who described any place as a "land of contrasts."

What is this love of cliché and banality that afflicts so much travel writing? Why does so much of it end up being so aggressively positive? From where comes a travel writer's impulse toward overwhelming politeness and away from honest opinion? On one level, such writing reinforces the old idea of the travel writer as a hack, a freeloader who has simply found a cheap way to travel. On a deeper level, such writing misinforms the reader about the world through false good cheer. It's the equivalent of an insincere smile

— the one people from other countries often accuse Americans of wearing.

Seth Stevenson, in his contribution to this edition of *The Best American Travel Writing*, takes the opposite tack. "Travel writers can be so afraid to make judgments," he writes. "You end up with these gauzy tributes to the 'magic' of some far-off spot. But honestly, not every spot is magical for everyone. Sometimes you get somewhere, look around, and think, 'Hey, this place is a squalid rat hole. I'd really rather be in the Netherlands.' And that's OK." The title of Stevenson's very funny essay: "Trying Really Hard to Like India."

It is essays like Stevenson's that keep me reading through pile after pile of mediocre travel writing. I know great stuff is out there, and I rejoice each time I find something notable. Some pieces — such as Ian Frazier's or John McPhee's dispatches from *The New Yorker* — are easy to find. Others, such as Charles Martin Kearney's evocative account of his overland journey through Asia (from *The Missouri Review*) or William Blundell's warm memoir of his visits to Florida (from the *American Scholar*), take a little more digging through smaller, less-read magazines. But every year the digging is worth it.

This year's edition concludes with Simon Winchester's wonderful essay "Welcome to Nowhere," in which he recounts a brief encounter on the impossibly remote Ascension Island that almost defies the imagination. When he returns home to England, he's told, "You know, you are a very, very lucky man indeed. Lucky to be in such a place. Lucky to see such things. And luckiest of all to meet such very kind people."

Each year, as I find the great travel writing for this anthology, I feel lucky in the same sort of way.

The stories included in this anthology are selected from among hundreds of pieces in hundreds of diverse publications — from mainstream and specialty magazines to Sunday newspaper travel sections to literary journals. I've done my best to be fair and representative, and in my opinion the best one hundred travel stories from 2004 were forwarded to Jamaica Kincaid, who made our final selections.

I now begin anew by reading the hundreds of stories published in 2005. I am once again asking editors and writers to submit the best of whatever it is they define as travel writing. These submissions must be nonfiction, published in the United States during the 2005 calendar year. They must not be reprints or excerpts from published books. They must include the author's name, date of publication, and publication name and must be tearsheets, the complete publication, or a clear photocopy of the piece as it originally appeared. I must receive all submissions by January 15, 2006, in order to ensure full consideration for the next collection. Further, publications wanting to make certain that their contributions will be considered for the next edition should make sure to include this anthology on their subscription list. Submissions or subscriptions should be sent to Jason Wilson, The Best American Travel Writing, P.O. Box 260, Haddonfield, NJ 08033.

I would like to thank Jamaica Kincaid for all her diligent work on this year's anthology, as well as Ryan Mann and Heidi Pitlor, among others at Houghton Mifflin.

JASON WILSON

# Introduction

THE TRAVEL WRITER: She is not a refugee. Refugees don't do that, write travel narratives. No, they don't. It is the Travel Writer who does that. The Travel Writer is a dignified refugee, but a dignified refugee is no refugee at all. A refugee is usually fleeing the place where the Travel Writer is going to enjoy herself—but later, for the Travel Writer tends to enjoy traveling most when not doing so at all, when sitting at home comfortably and reflecting on the journey that has been taken.

The Travel Writer doesn't get up one morning and throw a dart at a map of the world, a map that is just lying on the floor at her feet, and decide to journey to the place exactly where the dart lands. Not so at all. These journeys that the Travel Writer makes begin with a broken heart sometimes, a tender heart fractured, its sweet matter bejeweled with the sharp slivers of a special pain. Or these journeys that the Travel Writer makes begin in curiosity but not of the Joseph Dalton Hooker kind (Imperial Acts of Conquests) or of the Lewis and Clark kind (Imperial Acts of Conquests) or of the William Wells Brown kind (an African American slave who freed himself and then traveled in Europe and wrote about it). No, not that kind of curiosity but another kind, a curiosity that comes from a supreme contentment, comfort, and satisfaction with your place in the world and this benevolent situation, so perfect and so just, it should be universally distributed, it should be endemic to individual human existence, and would lead an unexpected anyone to go somewhere and write about it. In this case, everyone who goes anywhere and notices her surroundings and finds them of interest will be a Travel Writer.

*

This person I have been describing, the Travel Writer, almost certainly is myself. And also this person I have been describing reflects the writers of these essays in this anthology. Especially because I have selected these essays, I see the writers and their motives in much the same way I see my own. I will not be disturbed when they object. I will only continue to see them in this way.

At the beginning of the travel narrative is much confusion, for even though when sitting down to write, to give an account of what has recently transpired, the outcome is known, has been a success; the Travel Writer must begin at the beginning. The beginning is a cauldron of anxiety (the passport is lost, the visa might be denied, the funds to finance the journey are late in coming, a child comes down with a childhood disease). Things all work out, she is on the boat or the airplane or the train. Or he is in the restaurant, eating something that is delicious (that would be William Least Heat-Moon?), but even so there is no respite. For the traveler (who will eventually become the Travel Writer) is in a state of displacement, not in the here of the familiar (home), not in the there of destination (a place that has been made familiar by imagining being in it in the first place). That time between the here that is truly familiar and the here that has come through imagining, and therefore forcibly made familiar, is dangerous, for the possibility of loss of every kind is so real. Yet the Travel Writer, travel narrator, will persist. Nothing can stop her, only death, the unexpected failure of the human body, the airplane falls out of the sky, the ship sinks, the train bolts from its rails and falls headlong into the deepest part of the river. She eventually arrives at her destination; she begins to collect the experience that will constitute the work of the Travel Writer. She gathers herself up, a vulnerable bundle of a human being, a mass of nerves, and she begins.

The first time I traveled anywhere, I was not yet a writer, but I can now see that I must have been in the process of becoming one. I was nine years old and had been the only child in my family until then, when, suddenly it seemed to me, my first brother was born. My mother no longer paid any attention to me; she seemed to care only about my new brother. One day, I was asked to hold him and he fell out of my arms. My mother said that I had dropped him, and as a punishment, she sent me off to live with her sister and her parents, all of whom she hated. They lived in Dominica, an island, one night's distance by steamer boat away. The boat I sailed on was called *M. V. Rippon,* and it traveled up and down the British Caribbean with a cargo of people, goods, and letters. No one I knew personally had ever sailed on it, but it often brought to our home angry exchanges of letters from my mother's family. And sometimes it also brought to us packages of cocoa, cured coffee beans, castor oil, unusually large grapefruits, almonds, and dasheen, all of these things my mother's family grew on their plantation. The angry letters and the produce came from the same place and from the same people.

It was to this place and these people that my mother sent me as a punishment for dropping my new and first brother on his head. The *M. V. Rippon,* which had until then been so mysterious, a great big, black hulk, with a band of deep red running all around its upper part, appearing every two weeks, resting in a deep part offshore from Rat Island for a day or two and then disappearing for another two weeks, soon became so well known to me that I have never forgotten it. My mother took me on board, abandoned me in a cabin that I was to share with another passenger, a woman she and I did not know, and then left. Even before the *Rippon* set sail my stomach began to heave. It never stopped; my stomach heaved all night. My nine-year-old self thought I would die, of course, but I didn't. After eternity (and I did not experience this as an eternity; I experienced it as the thing itself, Eternity), it was morning and I looked out through a porthole and saw a massive green height in front of me. It was Dominica. Slowly the *Rippon* pulled into port. It was raining, and it was raining as if it had been doing so for a long time and planned to continue doing so for even longer than that. All the passengers got off the boat. I could not. There was no one to greet me. In my nine years I had never known this feeling, a feeling with which I am now, at fifty-six, quite familiar: displacement, the feeling that I had lost my memory because what I could remember had no meaning right then; I could not apply it to anything in front of me; I did not know who I was. I remembered that I was my mother's daughter, but between that and the place I was then, the jetty in Roseau, Dominica, that person had been lost or modified or transformed, and there was nothing and no one on the jetty in Roseau, Dominica, to help me be myself again, the daughter of my mother.

I believe it was the captain of the *Rippon,* or someone like that,

someone in charge of things, who got a car with a driver to take me
to the village of Mahaut, which was where my mother grew up and
where her family still lived. But the voyage from the jetty in Roseau
to the village of Mahaut was as difficult a journey in its way as had
been the voyage from Antigua to Dominica. This new landscape of
an everlasting green, broken up into lighter green and darker
green, was not even in my imagination. I had never read a description of it. Perhaps I had read about it and thought it not believable.
Perhaps my mother had told me about it, for she told me so many
things about her childhood and this place in which she grew up,
but such a detail as this, the way the land lay, the look of things, did
not make an impression, not a lasting, memorable one. In any case,
I had thought that mountains were something in my geography
book, not something in real life. I had thought that constant rainfall was something in a chapter of unusual natural occurrences, not
something everyday. My mother did not tell me that in her growing
up, it rained nine months of the entire year. It explained much
about her, but I could not have put it into words then; I didn't
know her really then. And then the roads were winding but in a
dangerous way. They wound around the sides of the mountain,
sharply. On one side of the road was the side of the mountain,
which went up to a height that I did not know existed, for Antigua
is a flat island with some hills here and there; on the other side of
the road was always a precipice, a sharp deep drop to the bottom.
My aunt, my mother's sister, was made lame while riding a bicycle
on one of these roads, and she went around a sharp turn incor-
rectly and fell into one of these precipices on the road between
Roseau and Mahaut when she was young. I arrived at the house,
the home where my mother grew up. Her sister had not been opening her letters for a while now (this is a tradition that I have kept
up, not opening letters from people with whom I am having a quarrel) and so had no idea that my mother had decided to send me to
live with her family. She seemed glad to see me. She had never seen
me in real life; she only knew of me through my mother's letters. I
almost attended her wedding, but then my family couldn't afford
to send me to it. She seemed glad to see me. But I didn't like her,
my aunt, for she didn't like my mother. I immediately began to
plan to leave. My stay with them, my mother's family, was open-
ended. I think it was meant to last until I grew up, and no longer

wanted to see my little brother dead. By the time I got to Mahaut, I had forgotten that I wanted him dead. I only wanted to go home to my mother.

I went to school in Mahaut. I learned how to walk in the rain. In Antigua, it rained so infrequently that when such a thing did happen, rain, the streets became empty of people. It was as if we didn't know how to exist normally with such a thing as rain. People would say, I wanted to do such and such a thing, but I couldn't because it was raining, and such a statement was always met with incredible sympathy and understanding. We did nothing, when it was raining, in Antigua. In Dominica, the rain falling was the same as the sun shining; it was all met with indifference. I learned how to use a cutlass. I learned the meaning of the word *homesickness*. At the end of each day, when the sun was about to drop suddenly into the depths beneath the horizon and the onset of the blackest of nights would dramatically come on, I did not think I would lose my mind; I did not think I would die. I thought I would live in this way, in this blackness, this place where in the dark everything lost its shape even when you touched it and could run your hands over its contours, forever, that night would never end.

From the beginning, I began to think of ways to get out of this place. But I could not find a solution. There was nothing wrong. My mother's father was of no interest to me, but my mother's mother was very special. She quarreled with the rest of her family and so never had anything to do with them. She cooked her own food and ate it all by herself. After a while, I liked her so much that I was allowed to be with her all the time. I would squat with her over a fire as she roasted coffee beans and then ground them and then made us little cups of coffee that had a small mound of sugar at the bottom of the cup. I liked her green figs with flying fish cooked in coconut milk better than I liked my mother's. She and I even slept in the same bed. That was the wonderful part. Still, I wanted to go home; I wanted to go back to my mother.

I wrote to my mother the usual sorts of letters: How are you? I am well. I miss you very much. But in my school notebook, the one that had a picture of the Queen of England and her husband on the cover, I wrote another kind of letter, and these had some very harsh and untrue things about my daily life as I lived it with my mother's family. In that notebook, I wrote that my aunt hated me and often beat me harshly. I wrote that she sent me to bed without my dinner. I wrote that she did not allow me to bathe properly, leaving my private parts unclean and that my unwashed body smelled in a way that made my classmates avoid me. I wrote those things over and over again in that notebook, but after I wrote them down, I would tear out the page from the book, fold it up, and hide it in under a large stone outside near the hedge of periwinkle that grew in the garden. I did not mean for these letters to be found; I did not mean that anyone else should read them. All the same—inevitably, no doubt—my aunt found them and after she read them became ablaze with anger, and my mother and I became one to her, a despicable duo to be banished forever from her presence, and she placed me on the *M. V. Rippon* the next time it was due back in Dominica to make a voyage to Antigua.

No detail of my return to Antigua is clear to me now; I only wanted to arrive there. I did, of course, and found my mother even more lost to me than before. She had given birth to another son, my second brother, and she loved me even less, as she loved my brothers even more. It was at eleven years of age that I began to wish for the journey out that led to my life now. I did not know then that it would be possible; I most certainly did not know of the sharp turns and deep precipices that existed and continue to exist to this day.

And what of the essays here? Every one of them reminds me of two of the many sentiments attached to the travel narrative: curiosity and displacement. None of them are about a night's stay in a nice hotel anywhere; none of them chronicle a day at a beach. They were not chosen to say something about the state of American travel writing; they were chosen because I simply liked them. And I chose these travel narratives: John McPhee's "Tight-Assed River," Ian Frazier's "Route 3," Jim Harrison's "A Really Big Lunch," Thomas Keneally's "Romancing the Abyss," Bucky McMahon's "Adrift," Robert Young Pelton's "Into the Land of bin Laden," Tom Ireland's "My Thai Girlfriends," Peter Hessler's "Kindergarten," Kira Salak's "The Vision Seekers," Timothy Bascom's "A Vocabulary for my Senses," Tom Bissell's "War Wounds," Charles Martin Kearney's "Maps and Dreaming," Seth Stevenson's "Trying Really Hard to Like India," William E. Blundell's "My Florida," and Pam Houston's "The Vertigo Girls Do the East Tonto Trail," and the rest of the entire table of contents, for they all hold an idea that is so central to my own understanding of the world I have inherited. These essays stimulate my curiosity; they underline my sense of my displacement.

How I like that, the feeling of being out of place. And again, what of the essays here? Reading John McPhee's "Tight-Assed River" and Ian Frazier's "Route 3" again and again, for the pleasure of the writing itself, and this pleasure is a sort of journey too. For as I read these two essays, I kept saying to myself, how did he do that, in wonder at the beauty of the sentences. And then there is the deliciously funny "Trying Really Hard to Like India" by Seth Stevenson and the truly hilarious "The Vision Seekers" by Kira Salak. I will stop here.

But before I do, here is this: Not so long ago, I was in Nepal, walking about in the foothills around Makalu and Kanchenjunga, collecting seeds for my flower garden. The journey was full of the usual difficulties: avoiding being killed by Maoist guerillas, avoiding being killed by the constantly shifting landscape. I was not killed by anything, and I also collected the seeds of many different plant specimens. While there, I liked being in that place, and I liked what I was doing. I returned home and to this day, the memory of it pleases me.

Read these essays, close the book, sit back, and just wait, but you won't have to wait for too long.

JAMAICA KINCAID

# The Best American
# Travel Writing 2005

TIMOTHY BASCOM

# A Vocabulary for My Senses

FROM *The Missouri Review*

AFTER SIX MONTHS at language school in northern Ethiopia, we finally moved south to our first mission station. Father, whose career as a doctor had been on hold, was posted to a hospital near the town of Soddo, in Wallayta district. There, we occupied a real house instead of a temporary apartment. The suitcases could stop masquerading as dressers, and though my older brother was still away at boarding school in Addis Ababa, I had my younger brother, Nat, to distract me. Plus, I now had a yard to gallop in, with grass kept short by a tethered donkey.

Out back, a huge avocado tree spread over the lawn, and this tree was a wonderful leafy world unto itself. Though barely five, I found that I was able to clamber up inside the green dome of leaves. Once there — where heavy limbs reached out parallel to the ground — I prowled in secret, like my pet chameleon, holding thinner branches as handrails. From hidden perches, I monitored the whole mission compound, seeing into the countryside all around.

The Wallayta region was lush compared to the cold, grassy plateau at Debre Birhan. Farm plots covered the terrain, stitched together in green and yellow squares and rectangles and trapezoids, blanketing the valleys and even the gentle sloping mountains. Banana trees flourished behind each thatched house, with leaves big as elephant ears. Papaya trees shot skyward too, looking like telephone poles that had sprouted green footballs.

A red dirt road split the fifteen acres owned by the mission. To the south, where the road entered the compound, four whitewashed classrooms boxed in an open field that served as a parade ground and soccer pitch for the mission's elementary school. I could see tin flashing through a row of trees and hear Ethiopian children calling out to each other at recess. Across from these classrooms, a series of long, narrow buildings stretched out in parallel rows, linked by roofed walkways. This was the clinic and patient wards. Made of *chicka*, an Ethiopian adobe of mud and straw and dung, these walls were whitewashed like all walls on the compound. And the roofs were made of tin, so they shimmered with silver light at midday. Through the leaves of the avocado tree, I could spy into open windows, where the wooden shutters had been thrown open and patients lay on their iron beds, motionless — black silhouettes waiting to feel better.

About fifteen missionaries worked at Soddo, and their houses were spread out along the remaining dirt drive. Across from us was the Andersons' squat, blocky house, with a spray of banana trees covering one corner. Then came the Schmidts and the Bergens, and the road petered out fifty yards up the slope, where old Selma lived next to her beloved bookshop full of ink-scented gospel tracts and Amharic New Testaments.

I clambered around in the dark foliage of our avocado tree every day, spying on this new world and picking the wrinkled fruit and squeezing it to feel if it was ripe. Mom made me avocado sandwiches on request, spreading the slick green pulp like butter or adding sliced egg and salt. Then I climbed right back into the tree with half a sandwich clamped in my mouth, to hide up there under the green umbrella, happily watching the mousebirds as they came and went, pirouetting on their thin tail feathers. I even dreamed at night that I could scramble out on the giant limbs until they bent down and delivered me to lower branches, so that I'd slip-slide clear to the ground. Like my chameleon, which I kept in a box of avocado leaves, I felt safest in this dark green refuge.

The only Ethiopian I encountered daily was Marta, the house worker, with her hair bound up in a blue turban, firm as a soccer ball, and her face turned gentle by a smile. As she stoked the wood stove and wrung out the wet sheets, she hummed hypnotic tunes. She murmured the same word over and over — *Yesus*.

I felt at ease around Marta, but take me elsewhere and I became as cautious as my chameleon. If Mom brought me along to fetch Dad from the hospital, I turned my face into her skirts and froze as soon as we entered the waiting room. Dozens of Ethiopian patients were there, perched on wooden benches or lying on the cement floor. These sick strangers with veined woodsmoke eyes and callused skin always wanted to finger my crewcut and cup my arms, as if weighing the soft white flesh. They spat on Nat's cornsilk hair to show their appreciation. *"Betam taruno,"* they whispered in awe, as if looking at a remarkable painting or a large diamond. I found them weird and frightening, so I hid and refused to answer questions. As far as I was concerned, they didn't exist.

The avocado tree, the chameleon, the sky, these were my only companions, aside from Marta, Nat, and my parents. As a result, what I learned about Ethiopian culture came to me slowly. One morning as Mother planned the Bible lesson she would teach to a women's group, cutting out a cardboard figure of little Zaccheus the tax collector (high in his lookout tree searching for Jesus), she burst out uncharacteristically, "If they wanted us to work with the Wallayta people, then why didn't they teach us Wallayta?"

It had never occurred to me that in Ethiopia there might be more languages than the one Mom and Dad had wrestled with at Debre Birhan. Stunned, I asked, "Momma, don't they speak Amharic?"

She sighed. "Only a few. And it's not the women."

Because of this language gap, Mom often had trouble being understood by Marta. She would bite her lips in exasperation as she tried to pantomime yet another foreign task, such as how to mix the ingredients for an angel food cake — beating only the egg whites and beating them until they were stiff enough to stand, then adding sifted flour and confectioner's sugar bit by bit.

She became so desperate about managing Marta that she resorted to a pictograph drawn in colored pencil. First, she rendered our kitchen clock with an oversized hand pointing to nine; then she penned in the black iron stove with red flames blazing from its open door, implying that Marta should refuel it at this time. She drew clock hands pointing to ten and paired this with a blue checkered dress over a basin of sudsy water: time for laundry. Then she drew pots and pans on the stove and a clock with both hands pointing to noon. Lunch!

When Dad came home from the hospital, he too seemed befuddled sometimes.

"I had a man jump out the window today," he announced.

"Charles!" Mom gasped. "He didn't!"

"Headfirst. When I told him I needed to take his blood, he dove."

Curious as always, I broke in, "But, Daddy, why would you take his blood?"

"To see what was wrong with him."

"Then why did he run away?"

Dad grinned. "Now that's the million-dollar question. I guess he thought I was going to steal his soul."

"That's crazy," I replied.

Mom chastised me. "Timmy, don't say crazy."

"Mom's right," Dad added. "He probably didn't know anything about microbes. Some people in Soddo think that our spirits live in our blood, so maybe he thought I would take *his* spirit."

My picture of Ethiopia was my parents' picture, except for rare, weird glimpses stolen from the safety of my crow's-nest high in the avocado tree. Sometimes, when I had found the right roost, I would spy on incoming patients. A group of farmers came along, walking two abreast with their callused toes splayed as they strained under a stretcher of eucalyptus poles and strapped cloth. The woman they carried, pregnant and weary to death, lay buried under white cotton shawls. Only her hands showed, clamping the poles of the litter in a clawlike grip. And all I could hear, besides the muffled footfalls in the dust, was her labored breathing, which came out in sudden moaning bursts like air forced from a bellows.

They passed; then along came a blind man led by a little girl who held on to the opposite end of his staff, guiding him down the road. They went very slowly because his legs were swollen up thick as an elephant's legs and covered with bloody bandages. Then came a boy a bit older than me, maybe even the age of my brother Johnathan, who swung himself along on a single T-shaped crutch. The leg next to the crutch ended at the knee in a brown stump. When he stopped and looked up, he spotted me. He just stood there and gawked, mouth open in a happy gap.

I had seen this boy lurching by our house before, and I imagined he attended the mission's elementary school, where Mom taught English classes. I had overheard Dad muttering once when he noticed the boy: "All they had to do was to bring him to us!"

He meant the words for Mom, who was standing next to him carving a loaf of bread, but I blurted out, "Who didn't bring him?"

So Dad explained. The boy had fallen out of a tree and broken his leg, but the healer in his village insisted no one should go to the foreign doctors. He splinted the leg himself, tying the splints so tightly the blood couldn't flow. The boy's leg didn't improve. On the contrary, it began to smell like dead fish.

"He had gangrene," Dad said. "And once you get gangrene, there's nothing anyone can do, except cut away the ruined part."

"You cut off his leg?"

"We had to . . ."

"But, Timmy," Mom interrupted, and she adopted her Sunday-school voice, "do you see how he smiles? He learned about Jesus while he was here. That's why he comes back so much."

Now, as I stared down from the avocado tree, the crippled boy waved. I put my finger over my lips. He put his own finger over his lips. I pointed down the road, meaning for him to go on. He gestured back the same way, pointing as if I should walk away from my perch into midair. Then I laughed, unable to help myself, and he laughed too. He pivoted on his crutch and swung away, still smiling that enigmatic smile, so unexpected from a boy with only one leg.

The Wallayta Christians, all of them, had this "something" that the boy had, something that I didn't have, and that not even Mom and Dad had, despite all their spiritual yearning. They seemed to carry secret wells inside themselves that bubbled over in the very throes of pain. When evening descended, they would comfort each other by breaking into spontaneous song, chanting strange antiphonal tunes that quavered in minor keys, tender to my unaccustomed ears.

"Yesus was poor," the lead singer called out in a tremulous voice, letting the words lift high into the dim, tin-covered rafters of the hospital ward.

"Yesus was poor," all the other patients chanted back.

"We are poor too," she sang, and they echoed, "We are poor too."

"But God took care of Yesus."

"Yes, God took care of Yesus," they replied.

"And God will take care of us . . ."

Sometimes the lead singer even made up new verses — "Yesus was lonely. We are lonely too." Or "Yesus was sick. We are sick too." On and on she went, and the other patients faithfully followed, lying back in their metal cots, full of aches and pains but chanting out this strange, sweet trust.

Their voices drifted out the paneless windows of the mud-walled hospital and across the red dirt road, hanging in the lowering dark, then wafting through our screen door on the evening breeze. The sound drifted through the dimming rooms of our house, then out the back door into the dusky yard and the shadowed avocado. I felt something deeply holy about such words and music, even though I understood so little.

At this hour, Dad would also go out and start the generator in the little shed behind our house. He yanked at the cord of the antique machine until slowly, patiently, it pumped to life, puttering like the submerged motor on a trawler. This faithful engine, after it had steadied itself on its oil-stained cement pad, settled into a deep, thumping rhythm — pucka, pucka, pucka, pucka — and I always thrilled at the sound. With it came electricity, the invisible stuff that snaked its way into the house in wires and woke up all the light bulbs. With it came light itself.

What a wonderful, consistent sound — the pumping of that sturdy old generator. It was time itself, moving predictably, not rushed or spastic. It meant a range of calm things. It meant the coming of the night. It meant the North Star already bright on the horizon. It meant the moon.

Sometimes Mother would heat the cast-iron kettle on the wood stove and scrub me down in the kitchen. She plopped me into a galvanized washbasin next to my one-year-old brother, Nat. If the water went cold, she pulled us out like laundry that needed to be rinsed. Then she added scalding water from the kettle, stirred it a bit, and lifted us back in, to be deliciously warmed.

I could hear the distant tremolo of the singing patients over the steady pumping of the generator, and I sang my own unconscious song — *Jesus was a child too, just like me. But God took care of Jesus, and God will take care of me.*

I fooled around, tickling Nat, because I knew that if we could prolong the whole wet and slippery process until 9:00, the generator would be turned off to save fuel. Then the two of us boys might get dried off in the warm yellow light of a candle, which was magical in its own way. Maybe we could even escape Mom's grip, to race through the flickering house chasing our giant shadows. If we could just keep her in a good mood, then we might get one last minute of abandonment, delirious with our own clean skin and wet hair.

Eventually, though, we were captured. We went to our beds and said our prayers, careful to include brother Johnathan at Bingham Academy and Sisoni Doeki, the Indonesian orphan we sponsored through World Vision. I thought of the crippled boy too, whose name I did not know. "Lord, take care of the boy with one leg and everybody else in the whole world. In Jesus' name, amen."

Then I did what all children must do: I went to sleep and grew older.

MADISON SMARTT BELL

# Mine of Stones

FROM *Harper's Magazine*

SOUSONNÉ (as I will call him) had slowly been planting trees on his flat patch of land at Morne Rouge since he acquired it from the previous owner, who'd stripped this acre of all but one of its trees for charcoal, then turned it into a manioc field. The place was set high enough in the hills to be cool, if one could find a little shade, and almost always there was some movement of the air.

Last summer we sat together at an outdoor table under the sole surviving mango tree, drinking bottles of beer that I had imported from a gas station on La Route Nationale 1, Haiti's most passable thoroughfare, itself about a mile down a road that more resembled a ravine but that could be traversed with a four-wheel-drive vehicle and sufficient will to arrive. Sousonné was a carpenter, woodworker, and maker of drums; he'd retreated here from the nearby coastal town of Cap-Haïtien when the tourist trade there dried up in the late nineties. From where we sat we could see the young trees — bananas, coconut palms, *bwa blan*, pineapple, sweet orange — he'd arranged, along with cotton, aloe, and hibiscus, around the one-room wattle-and-daub house that served him as a workshop. With water, what was left of the land remained astonishingly fertile, and although it was now the dry season (indeed, in Haiti nowadays, thanks to deforestation and the attendant climate change, it is almost always the dry season), Sousonné had kept the trees alive by hauling water from a nearby spring. In ten years' time there'd be an acre of paradise here, if he could manage to keep it going. If every landowner in the country could plant and nourish as many trees, a decade would realize the dream of a flowering, flourishing Haiti: *Haïti Fleuri.*

In place of the two-story concrete walls that his neighbors lower on the road had erected to ensure the privacy of the small feudal states within, Sousonné had only a slatted wooden gate and a fence variously composed of cactus, barbed wire, bamboo, and a few cunning arrangements of thorny dry brush that seemed to have fallen by accident where they lay but were in fact impossible to penetrate. The fence was just good enough to keep people and animals from wandering into the compound, but it did nothing to interrupt the view. Above us, the nearest peaks of Morne du Cap were mostly bare; a thin verdure covered the earth that still clung to the rock, but trees were few, and in many places the rock was exposed, quarried into open mouths from which erosion gullies drooled. A huge truck lumbered down the road, hauling rock to the plain for construction. When it had passed, all was quiet except for the occasional clink of picks on the ledges above, where men exploited individual claims in the mine of stones. Behind us, the sun was sinking through a Tiepolo sky toward the great *mapou* of Bwa Kayman, where in 1791 the ceremony that started the first explosion of the Haitian Revolution had been held. Although wounded by the drought and under persistent attack from the Protestants, the enormous, ancient tree hung on.

In Vodou, the *mapou* is a sacred tree, understood to be attractive to spirits. Sousonné had planted a couple of *mapou* saplings in his compound, and now their yellow-green, spade-shaped leaves turned in the wind, and all the garden seemed to take a great inhalation. I let myself go out into the movement of the leaves and felt something like the building of a trance. Informed First Worlders would have recognized it as the first phase of hypnosis, whereas Haitians might see in it the nearness of a spirit. I had come, a long time ago, to prefer the Haitian version. In the First World, I was stuck with the resources of my own psyche; in Haiti, a spirit might volunteer to walk with me as a guide.

For fifteen years I had been writing a series of novels about Toussaint Louverture, the first national leader of the Haitian Revolution, which began with the overthrow of slavery in 1791. A Vodouisant would say that Toussaint's spirit was quite near, invisibly present, breathing in the wind that moved the leaves of Sousonné's young trees, exhaled from the pool of souls of the innumerable Haitian dead, that great reservoir of spirit energy: *Les Morts et les Mystères*. Here in the north of Haiti, time seemed to collapse; the two hundred years that had passed since the death of Toussaint were summoned into the present by the spiraling leaves. It was the ninth year in which I had traveled to Haiti, and each time, it seemed, the effect grew stronger.

For years I had been trying to complete a transit of the old Cordon de l'Ouest, across the mountain range that divides the north of Haiti, where Sousonné had planted his trees, from Port-au-Prince and the rest of the country. During the revolution, a string of posts along that range had been the root of Toussaint's power, allowing him to make an isolated fortress of Cap-Haïtien and the entire northern region, from Fort Liberté to Môle Saint Nicolas. Napoleon's best soldiers had broken themselves on those rocks. Two hundred years later the terrain remained forbidding. From the interior, I had covered the range as far as the town of Dondon, and from the coast as far as Marmelade, but thus far the passage between those towns had been impassable to me. I dreamed of the rain forests that had been there in Toussaint's time, and I wanted very much to see what might be up there now.

I always wanted to do this or that when I came to Haiti, but I had learned that completely different things might ensue; it was necessary to accept those transformations, for a too stubborn insistence on one's own program — *têt bèf,* as Haitian Kreyol succinctly has it, "bull head" — can be almost suicidal here. Better to yield up my own will and let the spirits lead. That was the main thing Haiti had taught me, and it was also a point that most of American officialdom seemed to miss.

In Haitian Vodou, it is said that most priests of the religion "work with both hands." The right hand is for grace and healing and harmony, for giving rather than seizing; work of the right hand is done less by the individual will of the operator than by the spirit that spontaneously moves him. The left hand is sinister and operates for power and money and gain, using the forces of spirits trapped in objects, enslaved to do magical work for their purchasers. One can guess which gets employed more often, and at a higher price. This pattern repeats itself across the whole course of American involvement here.

Haiti has neither oil nor anything else of glaringly obvious economic or strategic interest to the United States, so when the

Clinton administration sent the U.S. military to restore the elected government in 1994, it looked like a purely idealistic democratization project. But anyone who took a longer, closer look would be likely to notice that the idealistic right hand of American influence was being countered by less visible movements of the far less well-intentioned left hand. In the last decade of the twentieth century, Haiti might have done a better job of harvesting the flowers of democracy without our interference or help.

The legitimate president, Jean-Bertrand Aristide, was a Salesian priest and liberation theologian who came to political prominence in the late eighties, mainly through a series of broadcasts on Radio Soleil whose populist rhetoric irritated the increasingly shaky government. Those were years of unusual instability in Haiti, following the collapse of the dictatorship begun when "Papa Doc" Duvalier took the presidency in 1957 and ended when his son, Jean-Claude, abdicated in 1986. In the ensuing confusion, the Haitian hard right kept asserting its authority via a rapidly shifting series of juntas, and political violence escalated with events like the massacre of landless peasants near Jean Rabel on the Northwest Peninsula in 1987, the slaughter of voters in a Port-au-Prince polling station later the same year, and in 1988 an attempt to assassinate Aristide himself as he celebrated mass in the church of Saint Jean Bosco in the capital.

The Saint Jean Bosco massacre was actually the third attempt on Aristide's life, and his escape looked almost miraculous; indeed, these brushes with martyrdom gave the young priest a mystical aura in the eyes of the Haitian people. He won widespread grassroots support through a network of small churches called Ti Legliz. In 1990, late in the campaign, he yielded to popular pressure and became a candidate for president. The rallying cry, *Nou sé Lavalas* ("We are the Flood"), made Lavalas the name of the movement that swept Aristide into the presidential palace.

In the United States, the Bush I regime took a dim view of these developments. Liberation theology requires its subscribers to work for the betterment, even the empowerment, of the poor. Inspected through the lens of the lingering cold war mentality of the American right, Lavalas populism looked a lot like socialism — and in a country cheek by jowl with Cuba. From the start, Aristide's program was to move the mass of the Haitian people from misery to a dignified poverty and to do so in a manner promoting national self-sufficiency — a goal incongruent with the practical implementation of Bush's "New World Order." Bush administration officials in Haiti conducted polls to convince themselves that Aristide could not win the presidency and were appalled when in fact he did. Most Haitians believed that the American officials there, if they had not actually instigated the coup that catapulted Aristide into exile in 1991, had known it was coming and done nothing to stop it.

Even as the Clinton administration embargoed Haiti and fulminated about the *defaktos,* as the military junta was most often called, the CIA was sending payments to one of its collaborators: Emmanuel "Toto" Constant. During the *defakto* period, Constant was chief of the "Front for the Advancement and Progress of Haiti" (FRAPH), a paramilitary adjunct of the Haitian army responsible for the main menu of terroristic atrocities, including the massacre of Aristide supporters in the Raboteau area of the coastal town of Gonaives in 1994. Although Constant has been convicted in absentia of complicity in the Raboteau killings and is entitled to a new trial if he should be returned to Haiti, he lives peacefully in Brooklyn nowadays, apparently immune to extradition.

When U.S. forces headed for Haiti in September 1994, Jimmy Carter was in Port-au-Prince, working for a peaceful resolution up to the eleventh hour and fifty-ninth minute; the story was that the *defaktos* did not start cooperating with Carter until one of them was notified by a call from Washington that the American planes had taken off. The result, vastly confusing to our boys in the military as well as to the Haitian people who had lived under systematic state terror since Aristide went into exile, was that the "invasion" morphed into an "intervention" while the planes were still in the air. Journalists on the Haiti beat invented the hybrid "intervasion" to denote it. Originally advised that FRAPH was the enemy, the soldiers were told as they deployed across Haiti that FRAPH should now be treated as a loyal opposition party. Toto Constant made a fleeting public appearance to that end (in the company of a spokesman for the American embassy), though soon afterward he departed for the United States. This transformation permitted most of the death squad members to vanish somewhere up-country, weapons in hand.

*

Ground travel in Haiti is hindered by the catastrophic disrepair of the road system — on a bad day it can take up to eight hours to drive the hundred-odd miles from Port-au Prince to Cap-Haïtien — and by a perennial state of life-threatening hazard, which makes a lot of people afraid to drive. Banditry, reduced to a nocturnal activity when the U.S. military arrived in Haiti in 1994, had leaked back into the daylight hours by 2000; for remnants of the *defakto* period paramilitary and for the masses of soldiers dismissed when Aristide abolished the Haitian army soon after his return, the gun had turned into the meal ticket. Politically motivated roadblocks were another impediment; in turbulent times, demonstrators might raise barricades from chunks of old masonry and derelict car parts and, invariably, burning tires to shut down traffic within and between the principal towns and freeze anyone's effort to accomplish anything. For these reasons, after my first few visits, I began riding a small plane from Fort Lauderdale directly to Cap-Haïtien, avoiding the road back and forth from the capital.

The presidential election scheduled for the fall of 2000 was preceded by parliamentary elections that took place in May. As a rule, I prefer to arrive in Haiti just after elections, when tension and turbulence usually give way to calm, so that spring I took the direct flight to Cap-Haïtien, and for double insurance I booked my return for a Sunday; road-blocking demonstrations seldom occur on the weekends in Haiti, when there is little traffic to interrupt. The day before I was scheduled to depart, however, I was driving into Cap from Bréda Plantation, on the plain outside the city gate, and found La Route Nationale 1 closed by burning tires and barricades. Since there was a $2,000 deductible on my car-rental insurance specifically in case of *"mouvements de foule,"* I pulled the 4 × 4 into a bootleg turn and went off-road, cutting across a wedge of the plain to the only other road into town, La Route Nationale 3. The tires were already burning high when I reached the point of entry into the slum of La Fossette, but the demonstrators had not yet dragged the barricade across the intersection, so I hit the gas and ran it. Ten minutes later I was safely back in the quiet colonial part of town where I stayed, though, less fortunately, on the wrong side of the barricades from the airport whence I was supposed to depart the next morning.

As luck would have it, all the other occupants of my small hotel

were Organization of American States election observers, who had
come in from their posts around the north of Haiti for R&R. Before, they had always kept to themselves, but now they were interested in talking to me, since I had actually seen what was happening. For their part, they were suddenly willing to tell me why.
During a night of slightly anxious drinking, the head of their team
sketched the math for me on a paper napkin. In several multi-
candidate elections the candidates of Fanmi Lavalas, Aristide's
party, had come through with a plurality of between 40 and 50 percent, while the other candidates, six or seven of them, split the difference more or less evenly. The trouble was that the Haitian constitution required a majority, not a plurality, to decide a winner. To
save the bother of a runoff, the supervisors had simply dropped the
bottom four candidates from all these elections and recalculated
the remainder as if it were 100 percent of the vote. Then the whistles began to blow.

The people now blockading Cap-Haïtien were involved in an ostensibly popular outcry demanding that the election results be af-
firmed in favor of the Fanmi Lavalas candidates without delay or
equivocation. But the OAS people I was talking to believed that the
whole thing had been instigated by a relatively small, professionally
organized group that had done the same thing around Port-au-
Prince a few days before. And they were serious. During the night,
we could see flames shooting into the sky along the road from
La Fossette to the airport gate. Moreover, the OAS team learned
through their satellite phones that the demonstrators had welded
the bridge shut at Limbé on the coast and felled trees across the
crossroads of Dondon in the mountains — thus sealing off the
whole north of Haiti from the rest of the country, just like Toussaint used to do.

In the event, I made my way to the airport by departing at dawn,
supposing correctly that the people manning the barricades would
be inattentive at that hour. But the repercussions of the jiggered
election went on and on. Why had the Lavalas people done it? It
seemed clear enough that their candidates would have won the
runoff elections the constitution required, and by manipulating
the results they had put a powerful tool into the hands of their
indefatigable enemies, who now could claim that Aristide and
Lavalas were out to establish a one-party, winner-take-all system,
tantamount to a dictatorship and likely to evolve into one. The

rejoinder from Lavalas sympathizers was that Aristide absolutely needed an overwhelming majority in parliament to break the deadlock that had paralyzed almost all legislation since 1995, that the outcome of the questioned elections was obvious anyway (in fact, neither side much disputed this point), and that Lavalas had grown wary of foreign advisers (by which they meant us) rerunning elections over and over on whatever pretext until they got a result they liked.

Regardless of motive, the cost was high. Whatever international aid had been seeping through was now completely shut off, pending resolution of the disputed elections. Even strictly humanitarian aid was blocked, and as Paul Farmer, the doctor renowned for his human-rights activism, pointed out in the press and in e-mail and to anyone who might listen, the result was a brutal punishment of the poorest of the poor, now denied funds that might have provided them with basic health care and water-purification systems. Still worse, anti-Aristide propagandists managed to spread the taint of the May elections to the presidential election in November — though in fact there were no such irregularities in the November elections. The opposition, now somewhat queasily clustered under the umbrella of Convergence Démocratique, proclaimed its own president, Gerard Gourgues, who despite his credibility as a human-rights activist made a call for the restoration of the Haitian army on the day of Aristide's inauguration. No one seemed to take the Convergence shadow government too seriously, but there was a plausible coup attempt by a small commando force that attacked the Presidential Palace on the night of December 17, 2000. Aristide's detractors claimed that the coup was a hoax perpetrated by Fanmi Lavalas itself, in order to justify retaliation against the opposition. Although there were violent, ostensibly popular counterdemonstrations following the foiled coup (Convergence headquarters were burned), that conspiracy theory seemed about as likely as the one holding that the Bush administration was responsible for the events of September 11. Certainly the Bush administration had gotten more headway for its initiatives out of that catastrophe than Aristide ever got out of the coup attempt.

I went to Haiti for the first time in the summer of 1995, soon after the American "intervasion" and Aristide's return to the Presidential Palace. It was popular at that time to refer to Aristide's arrival in

power as "The Second Revolution," fulfilling the forestalled promise of the first. In an oral-history culture like Haiti's, the most distant events seem to have taken place in the time of one's grandparents, and the spirit of Toussaint Louverture appeared to be present
like a wise elder at Aristide's shoulder — there to complete the mission of liberation that had been frustrated back in 1802, when
Toussaint was betrayed by Napoleon's generals and deported to die
in a prison in France.

But Haiti's problems with the outside world had their origins in
the revolution that Toussaint had helped to begin. When Haiti declared independence from France in 1804, it instantly became a
pariah state. The United States and the surviving colonial powers
were still running slave systems all over the Western Hemisphere,
so the Haitian example was anathema to them. For the next hundred years, the country was drastically unstable, its government
changing hands by violence more often than not. Most of the population had reverted to African village ways, living without much
need for government services and comfortably out of the government's reach. The *lakou,* or extended family compound, was the
basic social unit, within which members of the group cooperated to
supply their material needs and to serve their ancestral spirits. The
people en masse would emerge from their *lakous* in the jungled
hills to support or oppose the overthrow of the current government and then, once the matter was settled, disappear back into
them.

In the early years of his rule, Papa Doc Duvalier put an end to
this relatively cheerful anarchy by installing a system of state terror
inspired by his admiring study of Adolf Hitler. Having observed
that changes of government in Haiti occurred most often through
military coup, Duvalier created a nationwide paramilitary organization; modeled on Hitler's Brown Shirts, the "Tontons Macoutes,"
as the people soon christened them, checked and balanced the
army through a relationship of mutual paranoia. This strategy was
so successful that President-for-Life Duvalier became the first Haitian head of state since the revolution to die in office of natural
causes. His heir, Jean-Claude, was not so fortunate, though he did
manage to hang on to power for a couple of years longer than his
father had done. There followed a period of distinctly less cheerful
and much bloodier anarchy, until the 1990 election of Aristide.

In 1995 the wind of reform was everywhere; the regeneration of

Haiti felt like a tremendous thing of which to be part. Like many foreign visitors there, I yielded to the country's dreamlike enchantment. Every year I returned once or twice, and in the midst of my revolutionary research I got involved in some small-scale reforestation projects and efforts to revive tourism in the north. I helped a couple of Port-au-Prince writers get their books published in France and (pending the return of the tourists) bought paintings from a Cap-Haïtien artists' cooperative and tried to market them in the States. But *Haïti Fleuri* did not materialize.

The Haitian constitution under which Aristide was first elected permits no president to succeed himself — Haiti wants no more presidents for life. In 1994 he returned to office with only a few months remaining on his term, most of which had been spent in exile, though he had just enough time to abolish the army and, with the help of U.S. and UN advisers and trainers, establish the Haitian National Police as the first civilian, human-rights-respecting law-enforcement body the country had ever known. Then Réné Préval — a member of the Lavalas movement so close to Aristide that graffiti around Port-au-Prince at the time of his election read *Préval = Aristide pou 5 ans anko* ("Préval = Aristide for five more years") — won the presidency in 1995 and found himself in an essentially impossible situation. Parliament was deadlocked to the point that no legislation could be passed, while much of the aid money needed to build a working society was contingent on the passage of laws to implement then-fashionable IMF and World Bank "structural adjustment" policies. The paralyzed government and the blockage of the international-aid pipeline kept most of the promised reforms from occurring. The lot of the average Haitian got worse instead of better, as the local currency collapsed vis-à-vis the U.S. dollar, in which imported foodstuffs were priced. The mood of the populace, discouraged by the spiraling cost of living — *la vie chère* — grew increasingly dark.

Préval, originally trained as an agronomist, had some notable successes with land reform, especially in the still-fertile Artibonite region, but the general feeling was that the country had gone into a holding pattern, awaiting Aristide's inevitable reelection to the presidency, which could legally take place in the year 2000. Because of the numinosity of the date, the prospect of his return got draped in millenarian expectations, even by me.

\*

I hadn't passed through Port-au-Prince since 1999, and before I headed up north, I wanted to find out how things felt in the capital since Aristide's reelection. A domestic flight to Cap-Haïtien would spare me the difficulties and dangers of the road when it was time to go north. My Port-au-Prince base was the Hotel Oloffson, a rambling, tropical gingerbread fantasy, reputed to be the model for the gothic structures of Charles Adams's cartoons, and more certainly the original of the "Hotel Trianon" in Graham Greene's *The Comedians.*

In the old days, Greene is said to have done his Haitian reporting by sitting beside the Oloffson pool, and probably that could still be done, because everyone showed up here, and they all liked to talk. Word was that 2003 had been a bad year, a year of no evident progress. Insecurity and impunity were flourishing. The murder of Jean Dominique, the founder of Radio Haiti Inter, slain in the station compound in April 2000, remained unsolved, and some believed that the state was protecting the assassin. No one in the Haitian press had a higher stature — Dominique's long career of gadfly commentary had won him the name of the "conscience of Haitian journalism" — so his assassin's impunity seemed especially ominous for the freedom of speech so recently restored.

The international crew that hung around the Oloffson was glumly inclined to agree that the Haitian National Police was a good idea gone wrong for a number of reasons: The U.S. and UN support staff had been terminated too soon; the training period had been too brief and on-the-job experience was very thin; since the HNP was now the only legitimate armed force in the country, the behind-the-scenes struggle to control it was ferocious; the force was too easily infiltrated by former army men and death squad members, and perhaps also by the American CIA. Worse, the HNP was outgunned from the start. In 1997, I could still have bought an assault rifle on the street for about $20 U.S., and in 2003, I sometimes wished I had done it, for the price had gone up to about $3,000. One of the rumors going around was that HNP officers were themselves importing weapons for resale, so as to supplement their often unpaid salaries. The rank and file of the army had been in the same shape: poorly paid and often obliged to furnish their own uniforms and equipment. Once the army was disbanded, the common soldiers began to starve, and those who did not sell their weapons early had little disincentive, in an economy featuring near-total unemployment even before they were dumped into it, to resort to entrepreneurial crime (hitherto almost unknown in Haiti) or to sell their services on an alarmingly open market. Under similar circumstances, the HNP was vulnerable to corruption. An honest officer had no hope of promotion in the system that obtained. I had been stopped on the road and meticulously searched on several occasions, and although the officers were civil and professional every time, I was always told afterward that if they had found the drugs they were looking for, they would have kept them to sell for themselves.

Street violence and intimidation had become endemic, perpetrated by gangs known under the general rubric of the Chimè, in support of Fanmi Lavalas, though not necessarily with Aristide's blessing. Even Aristide's detractors did not claim that he controlled the Chimè completely — or could — for although the Chimè served political purposes, they did not much resemble the organized paramilitary wings of the Duvalier or *defakto* regimes. Insubstantial as their name implied, the Chimè came and went as occasions demanded; they weren't any kind of a standing force.

The old and new dragons of the Haitian far right had not been idle; there was a lot of spooky activity on the Central Plateau involving old army types who were supposed to be training for another coup attempt in the mountains across the Dominican border. Persistent rumor had it that these efforts were sponsored and encouraged by the International Republican Institute, an organization affiliated with the U.S. Republican Party and commonly associated with Jesse Helms. The IRI acronym is, with a strange suitability, pronounced in Haiti to rhyme with "eerie." Perhaps those theories were paranoid, but a few weeks before I arrived, attackers dressed in army fatigues had sabotaged the renovation of the hydroelectric plant at Peligre Dam, just before it was supposed to have put thousands more kilowatts online to Port-au-Prince. Paul Farmer felt ripples of the assault at Zanmi Lasanté, the hospital he runs not far from Peligre; five of his Haitian colleagues were held hostage for several hours by the saboteurs, who later made off with an ambulance, and one of the two Peligre security guards killed in the attack had been Farmer's patient. More recently still, saboteurs had demolished road-building equipment intended to restore the ruined road between Saint Marc and Gonaives: more than $500,000 of damage. Of course you could always find someone to tell you that the sabotage was really carried out by the party in power, to create an excuse for its failure to restore the country's infrastructure.

Tim Pershing, an occasional regular at the Hotel Oloffson, was not buying that story. Although he had also not signed on to the extreme opposite version, which held that U.S. right-wingers were out-and-out running a neocontra operation in the hills on the frontier, he did suspect that they were doing a decent amount of winking and nudging. Destabilization efforts were easy, after all, especially in the provinces, where the police were spread extremely thin.

Pershing would not say whether he was really a relative of the famous general, though he did sport the same lush handlebar mustache. He was working the opposite side of the street from IRI, teaching a version of high school civics to grass-roots organizations on the Lavalas end of the spectrum, on behalf of something called the National Democratic Institution, which was a reverse image of the IRI. Oddly, both organizations were being funded by the National Endowment for Democracy — itself a tentacle of USAID. That IRI and NDI persistently worked against each other only confused matters more, and not only for their Haitian advisees; Pershing told me that he found the exportation of American partisan politics to Haiti to be downright bizarre.

I was tempted to see IRI and NDI in Vodouisant terms: as the sinister left and beneficent right hand, respectively, of American foreign policy. From a Haitian perspective, it was hard not to notice that both hands extended from the same organism. Leslie Voltaire saw no difference between NDI and IRI; to him they were fingers of the very same hand, groping for Aristide's overthrow. I called on Voltaire, unannounced and unexpected, at the Ministry of Haitians Living Abroad, in downtown Port-au-Prince, not much thinking he'd receive me, but it happened that he had read and liked my Haitian novels, so maybe it was the spirit of Toussaint Louverture that got me in the door. Outside it was sweltering, the noon sun high, the street breathless with gasoline fumes fixed in the dense humidity. The two anterooms of Voltaire's ministry, where I briefly waited to be passed along to the next level, were each progressively more air-conditioned, and I think these pauses were for the benefit of one's health — so that the frostiness of the inner sanctum would not be too great a shock to the system.

Voltaire was a self-contained man, with a quiet catlike poise; his voice was light and his manner had the charged calm of someone who has recognized at some point in the past that raving and screaming are useless. A staunch Aristide loyalist who had shared the president's exile in Washington and played some role in the government ever since, he undoubtedly had also shared many of Aristide's frustrations, both in and out of the country. Now he ran the bureau that dealt with what is informally known as the Tenth Department: the millions of diaspora Haitians, most of whom live in Canada or the United States. That is a very significant group, if only because of their remittances; Voltaire estimated that $800 million came back to Haiti every year from the diaspora, while the annual value of exports was only $250 million. With the aid embargo almost total, the Tenth Department had become Haiti's most viable resource.

The problem, as it appeared to me, was that the diaspora money reinforced the feudal practices that had constituted Haiti's political system, *faute de mieux,* since independence in 1804: Those who could pay built walled compounds, installed generators, and purchased 4 × 4 vehicles that could navigate the ruined or nonexistent roads, thus compensating (at least for those within their walls) for the state's inability to provide basic security and services. (Richard Morse — host, proprietor, and resident rock star of the Hotel Oloffson, who had been a Lavalas hero during the *defakto* period — cast a jaundiced eye on the unrest beyond the hotel's cinder-block frontier, muttering, "If you don't permit democratic means of opposition, then you should prepare for alternative forms of opposition." In the months following the murder of Jean Dominique, his remarks had been more openly pointed, but lately something seemed to have restrained him — perhaps the killings of other journalists — and his comments had grown more opaque. As early as 1997, Morse had said that he was trying to build a separate state inside the hotel compound. It was what everybody had to do, at some level, to survive.)

Another vicissitude of the endless economic crisis, Voltaire told me, was brain drain; the intellectual and political classes were pouring out of the country and, increasingly, skilled laborers were, too. This exodus was a severe impediment to the development of democracy on the American plan; Haiti was capable of creating the kind of middle class that is democracy's breeding ground, but it was not capable of keeping it in the country. Meanwhile, tens of thousands of people were abandoning the exhausted countryside to flood the city slums, where, since there was next to no legal work for them, many would drift into the shadowy arms of the Chimè.

Entrepreneurial criminality, familiar and tolerated in most big cities of the United States, was a new and frightening thing in Haiti. Many were feeling nostalgic for the stability that Duvalier's totalitarian state had furnished, including two men I knew whose fathers had been assassinated by the regime. One of them, a Cap-Haïtien restaurateur, had told me in tones of real regret, "Life was more sure for me under Duvalier" — the Duvaliers had kept Haiti safe for tourists, if not for its own people. In June 2002, when a European friend and I were strolling along the Cap-Haïtien waterfront by night, a burly Haitian man walking alone sized us up and suddenly shouted, "Vive Duvalier!" It would have been unthinkable even one year before, but that night no one objected or even paid much attention. Meanwhile, Jean-Claude Duvalier was broke in France and looking for work and explaining to anyone who would listen that his only profession was politics.

When Aristide was first elected, Lavalas really did sweep all before it, and when he was restored in 1995, there was more than enough euphoria to go around. In 1996 and 1997, I thought I understood what was going on — it had seemed easier then to find a side and take it — but in 2003, I didn't even think I had a right to an opinion. There seemed to be no solid foundation on which an opinion could be based. The more I talked to people in Port-au-Prince, the cloudier things got, until it seemed that the most obvious fact was always embraced by its dark, contradictory inversion. Up north, in the region of Cap-Haïtien, it was another world, which often seemed to me a simpler one.

Sometimes I spent a night in Sousonné's compound near Bwa Kayman. He gave me use of the little house: one bare room under the tin roof, a mat, a mosquito net, and a candle. When I risked an excursion outdoors at night, the stars above were brightly fixed, the bamboo whispered in the ravine, and I felt that the new trees around the house were growing. In this atmosphere, certain fundamentals recovered their truth. Haiti still owned remarkably fertile soil and an amazingly vital culture. If trees were watered, they would take hold, and if the trees came back, so would the rain. With trees to hold the land in place, *lavalas* — the seasonal floods — would nourish the earth instead of stripping it off the bare rock. If one had a clear intention and the patience to let it happen, beneficent spirits would surely come to inhabit Sousonné's young *mapous*, there where they quickened, silvered by the starlight. *Haïti Fleuri* was still possible.

Also, staying at Sousonné's place gave me a solid head start toward that hard-to-reach stretch of the Cordon de l'Ouest: the new road connecting Marmelade and Dondon. At dawn, he and I pushed my rented 4 × 4 to start it and began the passage across the plain toward La Route Nationale 3, which would take us up to Dondon. At the car rental I'd had the choice of a truck with good tires or one that you could start with the key, and the tires were plainly more important. In 1995, Route 3 had offered a passable stretch of pavement as far as Fort Liberté, but now, once past the airport, no vestige of that remained; instead we zigzagged over washboards and potholes so deep they would send our heads smacking against the roof of the cabin. At Dondon we forded the Bouyaha River, thanks to four-wheel drive, and found the new road that crossed the dizzying mountain peaks toward Marmelade.

In places numinous as this, Sousonné was wont to say that the air was full of spirits, and I did feel that I was inhaling something extraordinary as we climbed. We were running the backbone of Toussaint Louverture's ancient power. These mountains, heavily forested in the days of the revolution, had been ideal for guerrilla tactics, and so long as Toussaint controlled them he had access to a seaport at Gonaives and to the Spanish side of the island via the Central Plateau. He could also seal off the Northern Department from the rest of the country, a tactic still useful to some in the twenty-first century.

Toussaint did not live to see the result of his struggle: the emergence of Haiti as an independent black state, founded by slaves who had broken their own chains and driven off their masters. After his deportation to France, the torch he'd carried was passed to Jean-Jacques Dessalines, a man of more ferocious spirit, whose watchword was *Koupé têt, boulé kay* — "Cut off heads and burn down houses." Papa Doc Duvalier had systematically associated himself and his regime with the spirit of Dessalines, as he deployed Dessalinien tactics on his own people: ruthless application of overwhelming force. Aristide seemed more attracted to the spirit of Toussaint, who had a real distaste for useless bloodshed, political and diplomatic skills to match or surpass his remarkable military talent, a delicately evolved sense of Haiti's relationship with the surrounding colonial powers, a devout Catholicism able to coexist with the Vodou he also practiced, and a social vision, based on harmonious cooperation among the races, a good two hundred years ahead of his time. Perhaps it was those similarities that encouraged Haitians to regard Aristide's rise to power as a Second Revolution that would complete the process begun two centuries before and finally set them altogether free.

In Haiti the influence of a forebear can be more tangible than elsewhere; the spirits of Dessalines and Toussaint were part of the community of ancestral souls available to mount the heads of the living. It had long seemed plausible to me that the spirit of Toussaint Louverture walked with Aristide, at least for part of the road he had taken, but why then was there such frustration now? It was likely that Toussaint himself had served more than one spirit, for he had some extremely ruthless capacities alongside his more benevolent traits; among other things, the Haitian notion of leadership for life was first proposed in Toussaint's constitution of 1801. In the end, though, Toussaint was undone by foreign powers, and Aristide also had suffered plenty of vexation from outside interference; maybe he too was destined to be a "Precursor," Toussaint's title in the pantheon of Haitian heroes; it was Dessalines who got to be called "Liberator." Either way, Toussaint's spirit would somehow persist: A Haitian spirit may abandon one *serviteur* and move on to another, if it feels it has not been well served.

The road from Dondon to Marmelade was, as Sousonné had predicted, "a little rocky," or, to be more precise, it was a rock slide that required me to keep the truck in first-gear four-wheel drive for the whole transit, thanking the spirits for every micron of rubber on the tires. The engine had just barely enough juice to clear the steepest crests. But certainly it was better than no road at all. The surrounding vistas were silent and vast; although all the peaks and most of the valleys were heartbreakingly bare, these mountains beyond mountains retained an unearthly beauty. I had flown over other ranges on the plane from Port-au-Prince and seen how the shallows of the bay south of Cap-Haïtien were brown with earth eroded from the wasted hills. Here, deeper into the interior, it really was no better; there were no trees left to burn for charcoal, and the people had abandoned a landscape that could no longer nurture them. There was next to no sign of human habitation, though we did pass a couple of gangs of men with hoes.

The environmental crisis in Haiti was at the bottom of everything else; if it was not reversed extremely soon, these mountains would be desert, and the rest of the country would feel the shock. On the Northwest Peninsula, according to reports, it had already happened; there the people had already eaten all their dogs. A rumor ran around the Oloffson of an American plan to evacuate the Northwest Peninsula entirely and ship the remaining inhabitants down to the cities, a scheme that would have the merit of providing the U.S. military with a clear field of fire from Môle Saint Nicolas, whose deep-water harbor controlled the Windward Passage between Haiti and the eastern tip of Cuba, all the way to Port de Paix.

We struggled on through the vacant landscape, now and then slipping on the shoals of loose rock. Apart from the engine and the sound of the wheels, we moved through a whistling high-altitude quiet, until on the outskirts of Marmelade the bustle of human life recommenced. Cautiously I nosed the truck through a street market until we reached the central square, where Toussaint had bid farewell to his troops two hundred years before. I had arranged this point as a meeting place with a friend from Port-au-Prince, but we saw no sign of him; once again I reminded myself of the fragility of all expectations in Haiti. The square was small but pretty, decorated with red-blooming flamboyant trees and iron benches that looked brand-new. I was just taking in how much better maintained the area looked than the last time I had been there when a man came out of a neighboring house whose resemblance to the former president, Réné Préval, seemed an odd coincidence, until it was borne in on us that it really was Préval.

I had forgotten that Préval is a native of Marmelade and hadn't known that he'd retired there from the presidency. Despite the unexpectedness of the encounter, he immediately took us in hand, offered to feed us and give us a bed and show us everything. With the ravaged peaks of the mountains between Dondon and Marmelade fresh in my mind, I asked him if he thought there was still hope for reforestation. Préval told a parable about an acquaintance of his who had returned to Marmelade after years of absence; she was horrified at the clear-cut hills and thought the peasant charcoal manufacturers should all be flung into prison. Préval asked her what she cooked with at home and got the expected answer. Haitian peasants cannot afford to use charcoal themselves; to them it is a cash crop, and almost all of it is sent down to the towns and cities. It was a matter of demand rather than supply. Haitian peasants are neither stupid nor improvident; they know the value of the trees on the land, Préval said, but they also know the value of their children. The production of charcoal, with its ruinous consequences, was a last resort to pay educational expenses or simply to keep the children alive. For reforestation ever to succeed, the peasant would have to be able to find a living in the trees.

Préval drove us (effortlessly and expertly, over complications in the road that would have given me far more serious pause) up to Habitation Baucher, an old colonial coffee plantation alongside the ruins of which a new coffee and bamboo operation had recently been started with seed money of a million dollars annually for five years from the Taiwanese government. The operation had the air of success. Fast-growing bamboo is excellent for soil conservation and is becoming increasingly popular as a construction material in Haiti; most of the buildings in the coffee plant involved bamboo in their construction, and there was also a furniture factory attached. The coffee operation was still more promising; coffee trees need shade to prosper, which means that shade trees also must be protected and encouraged, and everywhere the bushes with their brilliant red berries stood in the shadow of mango, almond, and orange trees. When Préval took us outside the compound of the new plant to give us a tour of the colonial ruins of Habitation Baucher, he greeted a little old man who had built his mud hut on remnants of a two-hundred-year-old foundation. Adjacent grew a couple of dozen knee-high coffee trees, carefully shaded by a burlap arbor until the covering trees could grow: Here was a man who had been furnished a motive.

The coffee produced here is of sufficiently high quality to elude, Préval hoped, the current coffee crisis, in which prices have collapsed due to stockpiling by big corporations like Nestlé. The plantation bought coffee from 4,500 small growers self-organized into groups of fifteen each, acquiring their beans on a fair-trade basis at between eighteen and twenty-one Haitian gourdes per pound, as opposed to the traditional eight. The force of this incentive was palpable — enough projects like this one, and the Haitian hinterlands might again become viable for the population. Most promising of all, the goal of the Taiwanese grant had been to render the project autonomous at the end of five years. This kind of self-sufficiency was what Lavalas had always striven for, and it was also what globalization, on the American plan, wanted least, though Préval did not want to talk about that.

Toussaint Louverture had certainly ridden these roads in his era, Préval told us, and I again felt the curious foreshortening of time in Haiti, where all past events are held just on the edge of living memory, not much further back than yesterday. The new coffee and bamboo plantation sprang from the colonial ruins like a green shoot from the trunk of a severed tree. Perhaps the spirit of Toussaint walked with Préval. Toward the end of his rule, as legend had it, the people had addressed him as Papa Toussaint, and Préval's comportment with the people he met had that same feeling of kinship. It was not a baby-kissing exercise. Préval had rooted himself in the whole community of Marmelade as in a vastly extended family. Indeed he seemed to have successfully extended the cooperative principles of the traditional *lakou* to embrace the whole town and the region around it.

Due to insecurity and the fact that our headlights were not working, it was advisable to get off the road before dark, though I was sorry to leave Marmelade. As I unlocked the door to the truck, a woman slipped up to me and displayed the suppurating wound on her arm. "*Mêt,*" she said, in a piteous tone. "Master."

By that I was genuinely appalled. "*Sé pa mêt ou mwen yé,*" I told her. "I'm not your master." Préval had told us he never gave money, and we had seen for ourselves what he offered in its place: services, education, jobs, grain after grain of hope for the future; when we arrived he had been giving a math lesson to a local schoolboy about ten years old. I knew he was right, but I could not help myself. I gave her a dollar, though I couldn't look her in the eye.

The moon was full when we returned from Marmelade; moonlight and a measure of rum moved Sousonné to philosophize a little. "The problem that we have in Haiti," he told me, "is that mortality and natality are poorly controlled. There are too many births and not enough deaths. It is the poorest people who have the most children, and since these children cannot be educated, they become Chimè." He was describing, though in the abstract, the conditions that surrounded him here. Sousonné sent his own children down the road to school, at the price of the sort of sacrifices Préval had described, and at the same time he fed as many of the less fortunate children in the zone as he could afford and taught the boys martial arts. Without him, those children spent their time scavenging for food or work (both very difficult to obtain) and amused themselves by killing songbirds on the wing with stones (at which their skill was remarkable). In time, if fortune smiled, Sousonné hoped to start a real school for them here, but he had no help other than his own thin resources; there was no outside aid.

One word usually means many things in Haiti, and Sousonné's use of the word "Chimè" carried me toward a deeper meaning. Before that term was coined, Haitian delinquent youths were called *malélevé* ("ill brought up") or, still more tellingly, *sansmaman* ("the motherless ones"). They were people who'd somehow reached adulthood without the nurture of the traditional *lakou* — communities that the combined forces of poverty and globalization had been shattering here for the last few decades. That was what made them so dangerous. The Chimè were indeed chimeras; ill fortune left them as unrealized shadows. With better luck they might have been human beings, but they weren't. These were the people Aristide had originally been out to salvage; *"Tout moun sé moun"* was his earliest motto ("Every man is a man").

In the beginning, Aristide had seemed to intend to build a *lakou* as large as the country. Something had thwarted the project, and the Second Revolution had gone into a kind of suspended animation, like the first. And yet Réné Préval had shown us that it was possible, after all, to build a *lakou* at least as large as Marmelade. What it took was patience, a clear and undivided intention, and a modicum of material aid with no globalization strings attached. *Haïti Fleuri* was still possible.

"It should have been easy here," Tim Pershing had said, looking over his shoulder in the direction of Iraq. "Here you had a democratically elected government and a sympathetic population. And you didn't really have an armed opposition willing to confront the U.S." In 2003, just one year from the Bicentennial of Haitian Independence, when the fruits of the Second Revolution were expected to ripen, it no longer looked easy. Far from the spirit of Toussaint Louverture, more and more people were muttering Dessalines's slogan, *Koupé têt, boulé kay.* Another aphorism making the rounds was *Zonbi goutté sel, li pa vlé reté,* applied to the centuries-old Haitian addiction to power: "Once the zombie tastes the salt, he does not want to stop."

If Haiti can fairly be blamed for a few pernicious political habits, these are matched, if not overshadowed, by the American genius for getting it wrong — for example, the notorious USAID program to exterminate the Haitian pigs in the wholly erroneous belief that they were infected with swine fever and somehow capable of communicating the disease to pigs in the United States. The *kochon kreyol* is a black-haired, long-eared razorback capable of prospering on what it can scavenge. It glows with a historical numinosity, since one such pig was sacrificed to the spirits of the thousands of slaves who had died in French Saint Domingue during the legendary Vodou ceremony that launched the Revolution at Bwa Kayman in 1791. The pigs were what the average Haitian *paysan* had in place of a bank account; their annual sale paid school fees for his children. USAID had a replacement program, but because the Stateside emigrant hogs required a standard of living higher than that of the average Haitian human being, it was ludicrously unsuccessful. In the course of this debacle, innumerable Haitian hearts and minds went permanently AWOL. Fifteen years later, an Italian veterinary volunteer I ran into in one of the upmarket Cap-Haïtien hotels said with frustrated bewilderment, "I don't understand what's wrong with these people — they don't want to show me their pigs!"

Even on the nongovernmental end of the U.S. aid spectrum, pig-headedness is abundant. Haiti's Institut de Sauvegarde du Patrimoine National (ISPAN) had a well-thought-through plan to turn the area surrounding Bwa Kayman into a national park, and they had the skill and the experience to do it, but no resources; their hope for money had vanished into the aid embargo. What they are getting instead is an evangelical missionary project from a Stateside organization called Men for Missions International, whose intention is to extirpate the Devil from Haiti within fifty years. ISPAN regional director Eddy Lubin showed me a page of their publication winningly entitled "Recon Report"; the plan was as military as the title suggested. First they would soften up the mentality of the population by giving away thousands of solar-powered radios locked to the frequency of the evangelical station, 4VEH. Then they would mount crusades to destroy all the traditional Vodouisant communities in the country: Souvenance, Soukri, Nan Kanpèch. The brochures are illustrated with photos of the target sites, including the ancient *mapou* of Bwa Kayman, which, since it is inhabited by Satan, would presumably have to be uprooted.

Next morning, the clink of mattocks resumed in the treeless hills above Sousonné's compound, and here and there smoke rose from charcoal makers' fires, though I could not quite figure out where they'd found wood to burn. At dawn I climbed the shaly slope to one of the mines of stones. The heat had not yet risen, but I was sweat-drenched halfway through the climb and had to stop three times for breath before I reached the summit. Below, the spring from which most people in this zone hauled their water was shaded by substantial trees. Before the last stage of desperation, Haitians will not cut trees around a spring, and this one was also a sacred source, the *reposwa* of a spirit.

When I reached the height, the view was panoramic; to the north I could see across the whole Northern Plain to the smoky haze above the sea, and westward, beyond the lowlands of Bwa Kayman, the Baie d'Acul glittered in the morning light. There one of Columbus's first three ships had sunk, and his men had used the timbers to build their first New World settlement.

At my back, a lone miner was exploiting his claim. His tools were a pick, a sledgehammer, and three pieces of blunt iron that looked like broken mower blades. In the twenty minutes I stayed there, he managed to dislodge a handful of gray gravel. On a good day, he told me, he might earn as much as 200 gourdes by selling rock to the men on the trucks that arrived below — the equivalent, at the currently vicious exchange rate, of about five U.S. dollars, but he did not expect this to be a good day, because one of his feet was hurt. In fact, this sum was substantially higher than the minimum wage paid for light assembly by the foreign textile factories near the Port-au-Prince airport — a mere 66 gourdes, though there was talk that the state meant to raise it to 120.

I needed another twenty minutes to crawl back down the rock-slide. One false step would start a little avalanche. Every rainfall rips the tear still deeper into the mountainside. I had thought that there was nothing worse than charcoal, but the mine of stones was definitely worse. It was the end of desperation. From somewhere below came the tap of a drum, resonant in the morning calm; it might have been Sousonné trying his handiwork. A voice sang in the back of my mind:

> *Figyè, mapou yo*
> *Yo tout fin peri-o . . .*
> *Pa gen koté anko*
> *Pou lwa yo reté.*

It came from the chant by the traditional group Wawa, and it had all the force of an old Vodou song.

> The figs and the *mapou*
> Have just finished dying . . .
> No place left any more
> For the spirits to stay.

TOM BISSELL

# War Wounds

FROM *Harper's Magazine*

IN THE BEGINNING was the war. Many children of Vietnam veterans, when they look back on their adolescence, feel this with appropriately biblical conviction. *In the beginning was the war.* It sits there, in our fathers' pasts, a dying star that annihilates anything that strays too close. For the growing-up children of many vets, the war's remoteness was all but impossible to gauge because it had happened pre-you, before you had come to grasp the sheer accident of your own placement in time, before you recognized that your reality — your bedroom, your toys and comic books — had nothing to do with the reality of your father. Despite its remoteness, however, the war's aftereffects were inescapably intimate. At every meal Vietnam sat down, invisibly, with our families.

My mother, who divorced my father when I was three, and whose father, a Marine Corps bird colonel, had introduced them, eventually could no longer handle the nightmares, the daymares, the never knowing which husband she would be experiencing at any given moment. My mother descends from a long medaled procession of military men. She understood men who had been to war. It was what men *did.* Whatever shadows war threw across the minds of its survivors — and it did, of course it did; she knew that — were to be borne stoically. But the war hero she married was capable of only fitful stoicism. This place he had returned from was not Normandy but a country that throughout the early years of their marriage became a tacit synonym for failure, savagery. Wars were supposed to end. And yet her war hero remained at war.

When I was a boy, I would dread the evenings my father had too much to drink, stole into my bedroom, woke me up, and for an hour at a time would try to explain to me, his ten-year-old son, why the decisions he made — decisions, he would mercilessly remind himself, that got his best friends killed — were the only decisions he could have made. Other nights he would remember fondly the various women he had courted in Vietnam, of which there seemed an extraordinary number, bringing to my still unformed imagination bizarre images of myself as an Asian boy. With my school friends I would tell elaborate stories about my father. How he single-handedly fought off an entire garrison of "gooners." The day he got lost rafting down a river and survived a waterfall plunge. The time he was wounded and how a heroic black soldier dragged him to safety. Some were true; most were not. The war had not ended for him, and now it was alive in me.

Sometimes it feels as though Vietnam is all my father and I have ever talked about; sometimes it feels as though we have never really talked about it. My father trained as an officer at Quantico with the writer Philip Caputo, with whom he has remained close and who ultimately became my literary mentor. My father even makes a brief appearance in Phil's *A Rumor of War,* which is commonly regarded as one of the finest memoirs of the conflict and was the first Vietnam book to become a major bestseller. When in *A Rumor of War* Phil learns of the death of his and my father's friend Walter Levy, who survived all of two weeks in Vietnam, he remembers a night in Georgetown when he, Levy, and some others went to a bar "to drink and look at girls and pretend we were still civilians." And then this: "We sat down and filled the glasses, all of us laughing, probably at something Jack Bissell said. Was Bissell there that night? He must have been, because we were all laughing very hard and Bissell was always funny." I still remember the first time I read that sentence and how my heart had convulsed. Here was the man of whom I had never had as much as a glimpse, whose life had not yet been hewn by so much darkness, the man I did not find in bluish 2:00 A.M. darkness drinking wine and watching *Gettysburg* or *Platoon* for the fortieth time. In *A Rumor of War* I saw the still normal man my father could have become, a man with the average sadnesses.

When I was young, I used to stare at his framed purple heart ("the dumb medal," he calls it) and, next to it, a photo of my father from his training at Quantico. BISSELL is stenciled across his left breast. Friendly Virginia greenery hovers behind him. He looks a little like a young Harrison Ford and is smiling, holding his rifle, his eyes unaccountably soft. I wanted to find that man. I believed I could find him in Vietnam, where he had been made and unmade, killed and resurrected. When over the phone I told my father I had tickets, we could leave in a few months, he was quiet, as quiet as I had ever heard him. "Gosh," he said.

We have been driving for several hours, down the coast, along surprisingly well-maintained roads, through what feels like lush green tunnels of Vietnamese countryside. My father is making satisfied little mouth noises as he pores over a copy of the *Viet Nam News* he picked up in Ho Chi Minh City's airport, where we spent a few hours upon our arrival before lighting off for Hué in central Vietnam.

"Interesting article?" I ask.

His head lifts with birdlike alertness, and he looks over at me. "I'm just enjoying this cultural exchange." When he finishes memorizing the contents of the *Viet Nam News,* he peppers our translator, Hien, with questions such as, "Is that a pigeon?" "Are those tea farmers?" "Is that sugarcane?" "When was this road built?" "Do the Vietnamese use much solar power?"

"So how do you feel?" I ask him, after Hien has debriefed him on the overall impact of rice exports upon the Vietnamese economy.

"Marvelous," he tells me. "Super. I'm having a ball."

"You're sure you're up for seeing some of your old stomping grounds?"

He fixes upon me a crumply eyed look, his mouth cast in the same emotionally undecided frown that I have noticed, with increasing frequency, in recent photographs of myself. "It was a long time ago. I'll be fine."

We pass through the rural sprawl of several villages. I see women wearing conical peasant hats, huge vase-shaped wicker baskets full of rice, all the stage-dressing clichés of the Vietnam War. Yet these are not VC women, and no GI will be along to bayonet the rice baskets in search of hidden ordnance. The clichés mean nothing. They are not even clichés but rather staples of Vietnamese life. I have discerned already that the war informs much here but defines little, and it suddenly seems very strange that we refer to the Vietnam War, a phrase whose adjectivelessness grows more bizarre as I ponder it. It manages to take an entire nation and plunge it into perpetual conflict.

"Where are we?" I ask after a while.

"We are nearing the Hai Van Pass," Hien says, pointing ahead to where the bus-clogged road corkscrews up into the Truong Son mountain range. To our left the wall of thick, long-needled pine trees suddenly breaks to reveal a steep drop. Beyond the cliff's edge is the blue infinity of the South China Sea, a whitecapped chaos so astonishingly choppy I half expect to see the face of Yahweh moving across it.

At the top of the pass we are stopped in a mild traffic jam, and my father gets out of the car to take pictures. I follow him. It feels cold enough up here to snow, the clouds soppingly low. When he wants some photos of himself he hands me his camera.

I stare at this relic, called a Yashica FX-7.

"I had that camera with me," he announces proudly, "the first time I came to Vietnam."

"*This* is the camera you took all those slides with?" The John C. Bissell Vietnam Slide Show was a staple of my Michigan childhood. "Dad, this camera is thirty-eight years old!"

He looks at me. "No it isn't." His hand lifts and bats about frivolously. "It's . . . what? Thirty-two years old."

"It's thirty-eight years old, Dad. Almost *forty.*"

"No, it's not, because 1960 plus forty years is 2000. I arrived in 1965, so —"

"So 2005 minus two is today."

My father is silent. Then all at once his color goes. "Oh my God. Holy shit."

"Kinda incredible, isn't it?"

"I didn't know I was that old until just now."

He is worriedly touching his face as I line him up in the viewfinder.

On the other side of the Hai Van Pass, Vietnam grows more tropical, a great rotting chromatic extravagance of jungle and rice paddies. A thick mist hovers above these calm, endless reaches of standing water. Water buffalo the size of small dinosaurs are sunk to their flanks in the mud nearby, while rice farmers wearing con-domlike body bags wade through chest-deep water holding bun-dled nets above their heads.

After a while we stop, at my insistence, at the Son My Memorial, which is a few miles outside the city of Quang Ngai. Son My is a sub-district that is divided into several hamlets, the most famous of which is My Lai. It was in a part of My Lai where, in 1968, the most notorious U.S. war crimes against Vietnamese villagers took place: Anywhere between 150 and 570 unarmed civilians were butchered with astonishingly versatile brutality. My father did not want to come here, for various reasons, some easily grasped, others less so. One of the "less so" reasons is my father's somewhat unaccount-able friendliness with Captain Ernest Medina, who commanded Company C, the unit within the 11th Brigade, 23rd Infantry Divi-sion, responsible for the majority of the My Lai killings. Medina, a Mexican-American whose promising military career was garroted by My Lai, eventually wound up settling in northern Wisconsin, and my father would see him occasionally. My father maintains that Medina is a "great guy" who claims to have given no order for what happened and has no explanation for it. On the way here my father grumpily said that what I did not understand was that things like My Lai happened all the time, only on a much smaller scale. I looked at him, astonished. I knew what he meant, and he knew that I knew what he meant, but to hear him say those words — their buried tolerance for murder — was very nearly too much. I could have asked, and almost did: *Did you ever do anything like that?* But I did not ask, because no father should be lightly posed such a ques-tion by his son. Because no father should think, even for a mo-ment, that his son believes him capable of such a thing. Because I know my father is not capable of such a thing. So I am telling my-self as we pull up to Son My.

Two tour buses are already parked here, both decorated with a splashy porpoise motif. I walk up to a large wooden sign that lists "The Regulations of Son My Vestige Area": "Visitors are not al-lowed to bring explosive powder, flaming, heating substances, poi-son or weapons into the museum. Also you should inform and stop any anti-attitudes toward this historical relic." The grounds are marked by a series of tall, wind-hissing palm trees, cobbled paths, and cubically sheared evergreen hedges and statuary, harrowing statuary: staggering gut-shot peasant women, beseeching children, defiant raised fists. These are the first instances of Communist sculpture that I have ever seen that do not produce an instant impulse to have at them with a jackhammer. Meanwhile my father is studying a headstone that lists the names and ages of some Son My victims.

"What don't you see?" he asks me as I join him.

One column of victims' ages works out like this: 12, 10, 8, 6, 5, 46, 14, 45. Most are women. "I don't see any young men."

"That's because none of the young men were around. This was a VC village."

"Dad. *Dad.*"

"It's just an observation. This whole thing was probably a revenge mission. Actually, I know it was. They probably said, 'We're gonna teach 'em a lesson,' so they massacred everyone. Which is a slight violation of every rule and regulation both moral, written, military, and civilian."

As we walk over to the museum, I notice that the palm trees are marked with little plaques to denote the still visible bullet holes the soldiers fired into them during the massacre. ("Kill some trees!" was, among American soldiers in Vietnam, the equivalent of "Fire at will!") "Good Christ," my father says quietly, stopping to finger one palm tree's spiderwebbed bullet hole. His face is suddenly spectral. "Five hundred people . . ."

The museum is filled with tourists, most of them older Europeans, all of whom are walking around, looking at the exhibits, with something like cosmic dread splashed across their faces. I look at a photo of a man who has been thrown into a well, his shiny brain visible through the hole in his skull, and feel that same dread take up residence upon my own face. More photos: a skinny man cut in two by machine-gun fire, a woman with her brains neatly piled beside her. In an adjacent room is a rogues' gallery of My Lai perpetrators, huge blowups of badly Xeroxed photocopies, the pixels as big as dimes. Let their last names stand: Calley, Hodges, Reid, Widmer, Simpson, and Medina, at his court-martial, at which he was acquitted. (Most of the men directly responsible for the My Lai massacres had been discharged by the time the story broke; the arm of military justice is particularly short, and they were never brought to trial at all.) There are also photos of Lawrence Colburn and

Hugh Thompson and Herbert Carter. The former two were helicopter crewmen who managed to maintain a grip on their humanity and choppered out a handful of civilians during the slaughter. The latter is said to have pumped a round into his own foot during the massacre to avoid taking part — the operation's only casualty. Colburn's and Thompson's Soldier's Medals for heroism are also on display here, though far less conspicuously.

I see my father ducking out with Hien, both of them gray and punched-looking, and I begin to follow after them when behind me I hear a heavily accented German voice declaim, "I have been to Auschwitz, and it is moving, but this is so much *more* moving, *ja?*" I turn. The people this German woman is speaking to are Canadians.

"Excuse me?" I less say than hear myself saying.

She looks at me unapologetically. She is wearing a chunky jade necklace I have seen being sold on the streets. "More moving. Because of the life. The life around this place." She is waving her hands, which are long and thin skeleton hands, while the Canadians stealthily take their leave.

Although I am fairly sure this constitutes some form of "antiattitude," I do not report her. I do not say anything and stalk off outside. I find Hien and my father standing by the ditch in which many of the victims of the My Lai massacre were dumped. Nearby is a *Guernica*-style mural with death-spraying choppers and wicked-faced American soldiers looming over defenseless Vietnamese women and children. The ditch itself is not very big, long, or wide and is largely grown over with scrub.

"Why would one man," Hien is saying, "like Calley, kill, while another man, like Colburn, try to prevent it? What is the difference?"

My father is staring into the ditch. "It's just . . . war," he tells Hien. Hien nods, but I know he is not satisfied by this. I am not satisfied by this. Neither, it seems, is my father. "I guess what it comes down to," he goes on, searchingly, "is discipline." After Hien leaves, my father rubs his chest through his shirt. "My heart hurts."

"Yeah," I say.

"I've seen American Marines take revenge, but they just killed men, not women and children. It's horrible. When I came here, we were . . . we were like crusaders! We were going to help people. We were going to make their lives better, give them democracy. And the way we did it was so morally . . ." He sighs, rubs his mouth, shakes his head, all the willful gestures of sense-making. My Lai happened two years after my father left Vietnam. The Vietnam War of 1966 was not the Vietnam War of 1968, which had by then scythed down whole fields of men and goodwill, including that of the war's own planners and originators. Kennedy, McNamara, Johnson: By 1968 all had fallen. I think about the story my father once told me about how he had been asked to transport a Vietcong prisoner by helicopter to the village of Tam Ky. He described this prisoner as "a little guy who's terrified, frightened to death, tied up, but still bucking and heaving. And he fought and he fought and he fought for forty-five minutes. He knew he was going to be thrown out of the helicopter. He *knew* that. So we arrived in Tam Ky, and they asked me, 'What'd you learn?' I said, 'I learned that this little guy wants to kill me because he thought I was going to pitch him out of the helicopter!' And goddamnit, at one point I was about to." We had both laughed, grimly. War stories. My father would not have been capable of throwing a bound man from a helicopter, under any circumstances. But I imagine him — I imagine myself — here in My Lai during those first moments of that day's terrible momentum, the evil freedom of the trigger availing itself upon the minds of friends and comrades, and I do not like the range of possibilities that I see.

My father suddenly looks up across this miserable ditch into a verdant neighboring pasture. "I wish Hien were here." Did he have, finally, a better answer for him as to why only some men kill while others think to save? No, actually. He wants to know if that is corn or wheat growing over there or what.

"What does your father do?"

A question young men are asked all the time. Women in particular ask it of young men, I suppose in the spirit of a kind of secular astrology. Who will you be in ten years, and do I want to be involved? The common belief is that every young man, like the weeping Jesus of Gethsemane, has two choices when it comes to his father: rejection or emulation. In some ways my father and I could not be more different. While I have inherited his sense of humor, his love of loyalty, and his lycanthropically hairy back, I am my mother's child in all matters of commerce and emotion. I am terrible with money, weep over nothing, and typically feel before I think. I can anticipate my mother because her heart is mine. My father remains more mysterious.

What does my father do? I have always answered it thus: "My father is a Marine." This typically results in a pinch-faced look of sympathy. But the truth is, my father and I get along. We have not always gotten along — I maintained a solid D average in high school, he viewed my determination to be a writer (at least initially) as a dreamer's errand, and marooned in our history are various wrecked Chevys and uncovered marijuana caches — but we have always been close. As I get older, I have noticed the troubles many of my friends have with their fathers: the animosities and disappointments, held so long in the arrears of late adolescence, suddenly coming up due on both ends. But my father and I, if anything, have gotten closer, even as I understand him less and less.

My father is a Marine. But how poorly that captures him. He is not a tall man, but he is so thin he appears tall. His head is perfectly egg-shaped, which accounts for my brother's and my nickname for him: Egghead. (Although nothing explains his nicknames for us: Ringworm and Remus.) His ducklike gait, a strange combination of the goofy and the determined, sees his big floppy feet inclined outward at forty-five-degree angles. (I used to make fun of him for this until a girlfriend pointed out to me that I walk precisely the same way.) My father, then, was no Great Santini, no Knight Templar of bruising manhood. During the neighborhood basketball games of my childhood, which were played in our driveway, my father, for instance, unforgivably shot granny-style free throws. "Hugs and kisses" is how he used to announce that he was putting me to bed. I unselfconsciously kissed my father until I was in high school, when some friends busted me for it: "You kiss your *dad?*" But we fought all the time. I do not mean argue. I mean we *fought.* I would often announce my presence by punching him hard on the shoulder, whereupon he would put me in a full nelson until I sang the following song, which for years I believed he had made up: "Why this feeling?/Why this joy?/Because you're near me, oh you fool./Mister Wonderful, that's you." The torment was not just physical. When I was very young, my father would tell me he invented trees and fought in the Civil War and would laugh until he had tears in his eyes when my teachers called home to upbraid him. In return my brother and I simply besieged the poor man, pouring liquid Ex-Lax into his coffee before work, loading his cigarettes with tiny slivers of treated pine that exploded after a few drags. One went off in a board meeting at his bank, another while he was on his way to church, sending him up onto the curb. He always got us back. In high school I brought a date over and was showing off with my smart-aleckry, only to be knocked to the floor by my father and held down while he rubbed pizza all over my face and called our dogs over to lick it off. There was, needless to say, no second date.

But my father is a Marine. He could be cruel. After a high school party that left his house demolished and our Christmas presents stolen, I sought him out to tell him I was sorry, that I loved him. "No," he said, not even looking at me as he swept up the glass from a broken picture frame. "I don't think you do." We owned a large stuffed diplodocus named Dino, which became a kind of makeshift couch we used to prop ourselves against while watching television, for my father was the kind of father who got down on the floor with his children. Once, resting against Dino while we watched *Sands of Iwo Jima*, I asked my father what it felt like to get wounded. He looked at me, grabbed the flesh of my forearm, and pinched me so hard sudden tears slickened my eyes. I returned fire by callously asking him if he had ever killed anyone. I was ten or eleven, and my cold, hurt little stare drilled into his, sheer will being one of the few human passions ungoverned by age. He looked away first.

He is a Marine. To this I attributed much of the sheer insanity of growing up with him. He once shot a flaming arrow into his brother's front door, just for instance. Every July Fourth he would take it upon himself to destroy his neighbor's garbage cans by filling them with fireworks and a splash of gasoline, always igniting the concoction by daintily tossing in a cigarette smoked down to its filter. Another neighbor deposited half a dozen garter snakes into our bathtub; my father responded by taking the snakes over to the neighbor's house and calmly stuffing them under his bedspread. Once, at dinner, Phil Caputo recounted a story of my father drunkenly commandeering a tour bus in Key West, Florida, flooring it across a crowded parking lot while his passengers, about seventy touring seniors, screamed. Only later did I realize that Phil did not live in Key West until the early 1980s — which would have made my father a forty-year-old bus thief.

I joined the Peace Corps after college and quickly washed out. The mansion of my father's disappointment had many rooms, and even now I cannot much stand to reread the letters he sent me as I was preparing to come home. They are loving, they are cruel, they are the letters of a man who fiercely loves his son and whose own past is so painful he forgets, sometimes, that suffering is a misfortune some of us are forced to experience rather than a human requirement. But what have I done with my life? I have become a writer greatly interested in sites of human suffering. And lately it occurs to me that this has been my own attempt to approximate something of what my father went through.

During the war in Afghanistan, I got stuck in Mazar-i-Sharif with dangerously low funds and one friend, Michael, a Danish journalist I had followed into the war. Even though I had all the proper credentials, the Uzbek border patrol turned us back three times in a row. We had brought only enough money for a few days, and, at fifty dollars a cab ride from Mazar to the border, we were running out of options. I called my father on the borrowed satellite phone of an Associated Press journalist. It was Christmas Eve in Michigan, and he and my stepmother were alone, probably waiting for my brother or me to call. He had no idea I was in Afghanistan, since I had promised I was going to stay in Uzbekistan. My father picked up after one ring, his voice edged with joy.

"Dad, please listen because I don't have much time. I'm stuck in Afghanistan. I don't have any money. I may need you to make some calls. Did you hear me?"

The link was quiet but for a faint, cold static.

"Dad?"

"I heard you," he said quietly.

At this, at hearing him, my eyes went hot. "I'm in trouble, I think."

"Have they hurt you?"

In a moment I went from boyishly sniveling to nearly laughing. "No one's hurt me, Dad. I'm just worried."

"Are you speaking code? Tell me where you are." His panic, preserved perfectly after its journey through cloud and space and the digital guts of some tiny metal moon, beamed down and hit me with all the force of an actual voice.

"Dad, I'm not a *captive*, I'm —" But he was gone. The line was

silent, the satellite having glided into some nebula of link-termi-
nating interference. I chose not to ponder the state in which my father would spend the remainder of his Christmas, though I later
learned he spent it falling apart. And for a short while, at least,
the unimaginable had become my life, not his. I was him, and he
was me.

My father and I make our way down a bright beach in the city of
Qui Nhon. The previous night we drank gallons of Tiger beer, and
I find myself comparing my constitution to his. My father imbibes a
fraction of what he used to, but he still possesses the iron disposi-
tion every alcoholic needs if he or she seeks to make a life out of it.
I look and smell as though I have endured a night in a halfway-
house urinal, whereas he looks and smells as though he has just
slept fifteen hours in some enchanted flowerbed. I am reminded of
the various times I had, while growing up, seen my father triumphantly insensate after a bottle of Johnnie Walker Red, wearing
only underwear and a winter jacket, off to do some 3:00 A.M. snow
shoveling. Mere hours later he would be rosy pink and whistling as
he knotted his tie before work. Constitutionally, I am not this man's
spawn, and here on the beach he pats my back as I dry heave into
some bushes.

   Qui Nhon is where my father washed ashore with a thousand
other Marines in April 1965, one month after the deployment,
in Danang, of the first American Marines sent to Southeast Asia
explicitly as combat troops. The April battalions were dispatched
at the bidding of General William Westmoreland, who sought to
bring the war to the Vietcong. Marines would no longer stand im-
potent guard beside airports and radio towers and hospitals but
would hunt down and kill Vietcong insurgents. (This plan did not
work. One estimate holds that almost 90 percent of the skirmishes
that resulted from search-and-destroy tactics were initiated by enemy troops.) Many expected a quick victory, since everyone knew
the VC and North Vietnamese Army could not withstand America's
superior firepower. Others braced themselves for a long, ugly fight.
My father, like nearly all young Marines of the time, possessed the
former belief.

   It takes us fifteen minutes' worth of beachcombing to find the
site of his landing: A thin stand of coastline palm trees, miracu-

lously unaltered since 1965, hardens his memory into place. We stand looking out on the endless sea in a black grid of shadows cast by the cranes and scaffolds of the resort being built a few dozen yards away. I begin asking him questions, but very gently he asks if I might not give him a moment. Instantly I realize my error. He cannot talk right now, and he stares out at the ocean in both confusion and recognition. I fall silent. This is where the man I know as my father was born. It is as though he is looking upon himself through a bloody veil of memory.

"They told us this was going to be a combat landing," he says after a while. "To expect the very worst. The ships we were in flooded themselves, and the landing craft and amphibious vehicles swam off. We came ashore, heavily armed, locked, cocked, ready to go to war. We had tanks and trucks and Ontos."

"Ontos?"

"Lightly armored vehicles mounted with six recoilless rifles. They shot all kinds of ammunition. Armor-piercing. Antipersonnel ammunition. Willy Peter, which is white phosphorus, one of the most deadly things you could ever get hit with. When the shell explodes, it sprays white phosphorus, and if you put water on it, it flares right up. It's oxygen-fed, and you have to take mud and smother it. Lovely weapon."

"How old were you with all this at your disposal?"

"I was twenty-three years old. A platoon leader. But I was also the company commander, and I had all of the infantry and supply people under me. I was probably one of the youngest company commanders in Vietnam — if not the youngest." Of this, I can tell, he is still proud. "Everyone was cheering us. It was glorious. That's my biggest frustration when I talk to people who weren't here. They'll say, 'Nobody really wanted us to come to Vietnam.' Well, they sure as hell welcomed us with open arms."

"When did it start to go bad?"

He points to the hills beyond Qui Nhon — an arcadia of rough, beautiful triangles of fuzzy jade and sharp spurs of exposed white rock, a few white waterfalls pouring sparklingly down the hills' faces. "Those look beautiful, but the VC were there, as we found out. It took only two days before we were fired on. We were so inexperienced, we were shooting ourselves at first. One guy, tragically, fell asleep on watch and turned himself around in his foxhole. He woke up, saw people, and opened fire. Killed the rest of his fire team."

In Vietnam, and especially during the war's opening innings, American soldiers experienced chaotic fighting unlike any they had ever seen before. There was no land to take, no front to hold, and few opportunities to glory in the routing of the enemy. All-out battles were few and far between, and enemy combatants perpetually melted away into the forest only to reappear, in the minds of increasingly (and understandably) jittery American soldiers, in the form of putatively innocent villagers.

As we drive on to the village of Tuy Phuoc, I ask my father about this severance between the kind of fighting he was trained to do and the kind of fighting the VC forced him to engage in. "The VC," he says, "would not close with us. They didn't have the firepower. And we knew that if they made a stand against us, they would lose ass, hat, and fixtures. So they would pick on our patrols." He is agitated now and stares with cool determination out his window. Tuy Phuoc, the village we are headed to, is where my father was wounded.

He points out the window at the railroad track that runs contiguous to the road, found on an elevated mound of packed sod perhaps eight feet high. "See that? That's what we used to hide behind, as a fortified position." At this he enjoys a chuckle.

"How many firefights were you in?"

"A dozen, twenty. They would last anywhere from ten seconds to two hours. Then the VC would break off and disappear. We lost a tremendous number of people trying to save our wounded and retrieve our bodies. And they knew it. They knew we would. That's how Walt Levy died, you know: trying to haul someone out of a rice paddy who was wounded."

"I'm sensing some anxiety here. You're sweating."

"Really?" He touches his temple, a lagoon of perspiration. He quickly wipes his fingers on his shirt. "Well, maybe a little."

"How do you feel about the Vietcong now?"

He looks at his camera as he turns it over in his hands. "We were all soldiers. They suffered terribly, you know, compared to us. Brave people. Committed. To their country. We sort of . . . lost that."

"I'm sorry," I say, surprising myself.

"Yeah," he says. "Me too."

Tuy Phuoc is less a village than a series of islands spread across a large plain now completely flooded by the seasonal rains. We ride among these islands along a long straight road that clears the greedy waterline by only a few inches. Each island is a little node of Swiss Family Robinson–type existence: a modest house, a collapsing wooden fence, a damp sandy yard, a small dock, a wooden boat tied up to it. Plastic bags and limp old bicycle-tire linings hang with obscure meaning from the branches of several trees. My father mentions that forty years ago all of these houses were thatched huts. Hien jumps in to say, with some pride, that the government has been building and modernizing all of Vietnam's villages since the war ended in 1975.

The road is narrow and crammed with pedestrians; above, the sky seems a spacious gray cemetery of dead clouds. The surrounding floodwater is tea-colored where it is deep and green where it is shallow. "Vietcong villages," my father suddenly says, looking around at Tuy Phuoc's islands. "All of these." We finally park when the road is too flooded out to continue and stand next to the car. My father was wounded, he thinks, perhaps a hundred yards ahead of where we have been forced to stop. He is visibly rattled and lights up a cigarette to distract himself. On either side of the road stands a crowd of Vietnamese. They call to one another across the water, waving and laughing. Every few minutes some brave soul mounts a scooter charge through the flood, the water parting before his tires with Mosaic instantaneity.

Tuy Phuoc, I gather, is not much of a tourist town, and for the most part we are left alone. But nearly everyone is looking at us. The people of Tuy Phuoc are short and damp and suntanned in a vaguely unhealthy way. The women smile, the men nod civilly, and the children rush at us before thinking better of it and retreat behind their mothers' legs.

"You want to tell me what happened?" This is mostly a courtesy, since I know what happened. My father was shot — in the back, buttock, arm, and shoulder — at the beginning of a roadside melee and was dragged to safety by a black soldier. One of the things I had long admired about my father was his absence of racial animosity — a fairly uncommon trait among the men of rural Michigan. I always attributed this to the black Marine who saved his life. I identically credited my youthful stridency on racial matters — I was forever jumping down the throats of my parents' dinner guests or high school friends whenever the word "nigger" made its unlovely entrance from stage right — to this same mysterious savior.

"We were on a search-and-destroy mission," my father explains. "We entered Tuy Phuoc in a convoy. After twenty minutes of driving we found the road was cut by a huge earthen mound. The VC obviously knew we were coming, so we were all very suspicious. I was at the head of the convoy and called up the engineers. They were going to blow up the mound and rebuild the road so we could continue. About fifteen men came up, and I turned around to talk to the gunnery sergeant from the lead infantry company, and the mound exploded. Inside the dirt they'd packed a bunch of steel and shrapnel. The only reason I'm here is that I turned around to speak to the gunnery sergeant. I remember saying, 'Gunny, I'll go back and get some more equipment.' You know, shovels, stuff like that. The bomb caught Gunny in the face, and I went flying through the air. Then I tried to get up. Couldn't. There were people lying all over the place. I think fifteen were wounded. Gunny was the only guy killed. My platoon sergeant hauled me into a ditch, and they field-dressed me and jammed me full of morphine and then flew in the choppers. I was very fucked up, in total shock. I had two hundred separate wounds. They counted 'em. My left arm caught the brunt of the blast. I thought they were going to have to take it off. So that ended my war for a while."

"Wait a minute," I say. "I thought you were shot."

"No, I never got shot. Which is fine by me."

"But that's not the story you told me."

He looks at me. "I don't think I ever told you that story."

"Then why do I remember you being shot and a black Marine dragging you to safety?"

"I have no idea."

"Was the sergeant who pulled you into the ditch black?"

"I don't think so. I honestly don't remember."

My father's sleeve is rolled up, and I am now looking at his left arm. Incredibly, I have never before noticed the scoring of cross-hatched scar tissue running up and down his forearm or how thinner his left arm seems compared with his right. I have, however, many times noticed the bright, pink nickel-sized scars on his bicep and his shoulder blade, the small keloidal lightning bolt on his neck. When I was young, I used to stare at these obvious wounds and, sometimes, even touch them, my tiny fingers freshly alive to their rubbery difference in texture. But I have to admit, now, that I do not actually remember my father ever telling me he was shot or that a black man had saved his life. I remember telling that story myself, but I do not remember being told that story. At some point the story simply appears in my mind. Why did I create this story? Because it made my father heroic? In the emergency of growing up, we all need heroes. But the father I grew up with was no hero to me, not then. He was too wounded in the head, too endlessly and terribly sad. Too funny, too explosive, too confusing. Heroes are uncomplicated. *This* makes them do *that*. The active heroism of my imaginary black Marine made a passive hero of my father; they huddled together, alongside a road in the Vietnam of my mind, shrouded in nitroglycerin, the cordite of gallantry. The story made sense of the senseless. But war does not make sense. War senselessly wounds everyone right down the line. A body bag fits more than just its intended corpse. Take the 58,000 American soldiers lost in Vietnam and multiply by four, five, six — and only then does one begin to realize the damage this war has done. (Project outward from the two million slain Vietnamese and see, for the first time, an entire continent of loss.) War, when necessary, is unspeakable. When unnecessary, it is unforgivable. It is not an occasion for heroism. It is an occasion only for survival and death. To regard war in any other way only guarantees its inevitable reappearance.

I look at my father, who is still smoking and peering around. Suddenly he appears very old. He does not look bad. He is in fact in better physical shape than I, but he is older-looking than I have ever seen him before. His neck has begun to give up and sag, his eyes are bigger and more yellowy, the long wolfish hair at the base of his throat is gray. I am twenty-nine, six years older than my father was when he was wounded. Can I really know the young man who went flying through the air, ripped apart by a booby trap? Can I even know this man, still flying, and in some ways still ripped apart? Ultimately our lives are only partially ours. The parts of our lives that change most are those that intrude with mythic vividness into the lives of those we love: our parents, our children, our brothers and sisters. As these stories overlap they change, but we have no voice in how or why. One by one our stories are dragged away from us, pulled into the ditches of shared human memory. They are saved, but they are changed. One day my father will be gone except for the parts of him I remember and the stories he has told me. How much else about him have I gotten wrong? How much of him have I not properly understood? What have I not asked? And looking at him I want him never to go. I want him always to be here. There is too much left for us to talk about.

At last, a lone Vietnamese man shoelessly wanders over to say hello. His hairless legs and arms are so thin and brown they look made of teak. As he and my father shake hands and (with Hien's assistance) chat, I realize that this man is around my father's age. It is in fact not at all beyond possibility that this man personally wired the booby trap that nearly killed my father. But his solar friendliness is not feigned, and beneath its insistent emotional heat I can see my father's discomfort soften and wilt. Within moments the man and my father are laughing over something together.

I listen to my father and his new Vietnamese friend talk respectfully around the small matter of having taken up arms against each other as young men: Yes, my father *has* been to Vietnam before; no, the Vietnamese man did not always live in the south. Their conversation slides into a respectful silence, and they nod and look at each other. With a smile, the man suddenly asks my father what brings him to Tuy Phoc, since it is so far away from anything of note. For a long time my father thinks about how to answer, looking up at the low gray clouds, a few small trapezoids of blue showing through. To Hien he finally says, "Tell him . . . tell him that, a very long time ago, I got hurt here."

Once, while hunting partridge, which I did not like to do, my father abandoned me after I maintained I was not going another step until he gave me a granola bar. He refused, I stopped, and off he went. I was probably twelve years old. It was a cold fall day, witchy orange-yellow leaves blew all around me, and, as the moments turned to minutes and the minutes to hours, I sat down on a log and began to despair. Trees grew taller, the air colder; the forest was an endless organic mirror of my fear. I do not remember how long I was alone. After the sky had darkened, after I had turned up my collar and drawn myself into a defenseless ball on the forest floor, my father burst through some bushes on a different path than that by which he had left me and gathered me up into his arms. He was crying. He had gotten "turned around," he said quickly. Not lost. My father never got lost. He was a Marine. He said nothing else; neither did I. I held him, and he held me, and he carried me out of the forest.

WILLIAM E. BLUNDELL

# My Florida

FROM *The American Scholar*

SARTORIALLY SPEAKING, my father was a man of almost spectacular dullness. During the later decades of his working life in New York, he bought two suits a year, one navy and one brown. He never went to work in anything but a white shirt so starched it almost cut his throat. His ties were all dark and so timid in pattern that you pictured them cowering in the closet, each praying it would not have to hang around his neck that day and suffer the agony of public exposure.

If Monday through Friday he looked like a businessman, on Saturday and Sunday he looked like a businessman who had been fired months before and had gone to seed. In spring and fall his uniform for working in the garden never varied: a fedora, retired from business service, that appeared to have been trampled by a herd of buffalo; dress pants, also retired, shiny in the seat; collared shirt; brown zip-up gabardine jacket that I believe was manufactured during the Coolidge administration. Blue denim never touched my father's body. Canvas never touched his feet. He wore shoes with laces.

With a couple of dreary sports jackets standing in for the suits, he maintained this style even after he retired, my mother died, and — desperately lonely, for he had loved my mother more than he knew — he married a widow they had known through mutual friends. I still have a picture of him and me together after the ceremony, at which I was best man. It was the seventies and I looked awful: way too much hair, knit suit, tie a yard wide, foolish grin. My father looked as he might have twenty years before. I had moved to

California by then and saw him seldom, but when I did, his ward-
robe comforted me. Big pieces of his world and mine had crum-
bled away beneath our feet, but his clothes spoke to me of a perma-
nence lying like a shelf of rock beneath the roiled surfaces of our
lives.

Then word came that he and my new stepmother were moving to
Florida. This seemed to make sense. They were among the Cold
Old, and Florida's soaking heat would do them good. And they
could play more golf, which they both liked in a nonobsessive way. I
didn't know much about Florida except that it was warm and exotic, that its right coast was lined with walnut-colored Jews and its
left with beet-colored Christians, and that there were a lot of alligators in between. I thought of it as just a place, albeit an odd one. I
didn't know any better then.

My father and stepmother bought a modest two-bedroom condominium at the north end of Naples, which lies far down the Gulf
Coast. Naples is a pseudopod extended southward by the Midwest,
my stepmother's milieu, and I do not believe my father was ever
fully comfortable there. The inhabitants were, in the main, Anglo-
corporate golfers who had brought their bigotries southward. The
best Gulfside apartment towers, the best condo developments by
the shore, were organized as private clubs, a legalism that allowed
residents to exclude people who were Not Like Them. In Naples,
you would have had to mount an expedition to uncover a black or
brown person who wasn't making somebody's bed.

The condominium my father and stepmother bought was not a
club and it was not by the shore. It was unfashionably inland, on
the third, or top, floor of one of several white wedding-cake buildings that huddled disconsolately around a small golf course spiked
here and there by a scraggly palm. It was a "senior executive"
course, which meant only that it was so short and so easy that no
oldster playing it was likely to drop dead from either fatigue or frustration, an event that might have created disposal problems for
management. The only water hazard was a pond that contained the
inevitable alligator. He was later hustled off to the Everglades in
disgrace after eating a resident's poodle.

In most of the promotional literature, developments like this are
billed as hotbeds of physical activity, with vigorous oldsters de-

picted swimming, bicycling, playing tennis, jogging. In twenty-five years of visits, I never saw anyone playing tennis — there were two courts — or jogging. I never saw anyone, much less anyone with gray hair, on a bicycle. Only once did I see anyone swimming. Most of the time people just played golf or drank.

There are thought to be inflection points in everyone's life, moments when a single event can profoundly influence the future. I am convinced that one of these occurred on an early visit I made to Naples. I rang the bell at the condominium, the door opened — and I was confronted by a figure in a bright yellow short-sleeved jumpsuit with a big plastic zipper up the front, topped by a pull ring that must have been two inches in diameter. This apparition was, incredibly, my father.

Few people find themselves suddenly facing a two-hundred-pound canary, particularly one to whom they are related, and I'm very much afraid that I uttered an involuntary cry as I tottered back a step. I could see that the poor man was hideously embarrassed, and so, pulling myself together, I greeted him as if nothing had happened, walked in, and began babbling inanities to my stepmother. He disappeared into the bedroom and came out wearing a drab short-sleeved shirt and dark pants. I never saw the jumpsuit again.

We didn't talk about the incident, of course. Though my father and I both had a gift for bullshit — as a sales executive he lived on the stuff, and as a journalist I was not unfamiliar with it — we were at bottom reserved people. But I couldn't help wondering: What force on heaven or earth could have compelled a man like him to put on a yellow jumpsuit? It was only after many years of visits to his adopted state, for reasons personal and professional, that I could formulate an answer: Florida had made a snatch at my father and almost got him. I had saved his life.

Fan out the brochures on the dining room table. You will never find in them the faintest hint of Florida as the nation's cloaca, where predigested lives, the nourishment pretty much sucked out of them, await final extrusion. You see instead a hustling, bustling state, youthful and energetic, one in which the *alter kockers* of Miami Beach legend are an embarrassment to be airbrushed out of existence and replaced by images of tanned cleavage and pastel hotels at South Beach, phallic rockets thrusting upward on gouts of flame at Cape Kennedy, wholesome white-toothed families at Disney World. Not a wrinkle in sight. Come to Florida and play. Come to Florida and work. Come to Florida and live. But absolutely nothing about coming to Florida to die. Does Iowa deny its corn? Does Kansas disavow its wheat? Is Texas ashamed of its oil? Florida may be the only state that would rather not talk about one of its major industries.

I cannot let this happen. My Florida is the Florida of the bad old stereotypes realized, a nation of the elderly and near-elderly colorfully disporting themselves as twilight falls. They are strangely garbed, my Floridians, given to raspberry slacks and hunks of jewelry the size of golf balls. They drive luxury Detroit iron as a matter of patriotism — executives of Lincoln and Cadillac should fall on their knees every night in thanks for South Florida — and passion, as exemplified by one Winter Haven resident who murdered his wife of sixty-one years because she refused to let him buy a Cadillac.

In my Florida, American flags flutter over superwide boulevards lined with businesses charting the downward spiral that is every retiree's lot. Over here, at the beginning of that spiral, are golf shops, clothing stores, car lots, and, above all, furniture stores peddling the Florida look, which rests heavily on lime greens, flamingo pinks, acres of painted wicker, gold-veined mirrors, and huge fake plants that look like browse for brontosaurs. In Naples, my favorite among these shops was called Not Just Futons and Bar Stools! — a name that neatly captured two favorite pursuits of its target clientele.

As the resident settles in and begins to worry about the old nest egg, he or she is targeted by what might be called level-two businesses: law and accounting firms specializing in estate matters, and rank upon rank of banks and brokerages. Skinny old men in white shoes haunt these palaces of Mammon. They pester the staff, drink the free coffee, check interest rates every hour, and watch stock quotes scroll by. They are the Jacob Marleys of Florida, clanking their chains in warning to the rest of us.

And, at the end, we have the climactic Florida, the one no one wants to acknowledge: hospitals, clinics, doctors' offices, nursing homes with pleasing names (who makes them up?), and funeral homes, their crematoria sending a fine ash into the evening sky.

No chamber of commerce in the hustling new Florida wants to

touch this demographic with a hundred-foot pole, reasoning that you can't lure a new semiconductor factory to town by boasting about how many old people live there. But like the elephant in the living room, the reality squats on the rug and grins at us even as we try to ignore it — Florida as the predictor of what, if we're not careful, may befall the rest of us before we die.

Golf may befall us. In my Florida, golf is not a sport. It is a sacrament. Some of my most excruciating evenings have been spent listening to men of real accomplishment in the world tell me exactly how they played the seventeenth at Numbnuts Moors or Diddledock Downs. In their circle, the ultimate compliment paid to a deceased player is to say, with head bowed respectfully, that he shot his age nearly up to the end.

Accidents may befall us. Anybody who can fog a mirror can get a driver's license in Florida and keep it long after he can read what's printed on it. Aside from Boston, every insurer's nightmare, and Montana, where fourteen-year-old ranch kids rocket along at flank speed in daddy's pickup, Florida is the place I least like to drive in. Once, motoring along in the southbound lane on Route 41 in Naples, I froze as a saucer-eyed old gentleman in a Lincoln crept toward me head-on. I had to stop traffic to turn him around. On other occasions I've been ripping along the state's 70-mph freeways, rivers of concrete lined by flattened raccoons and the scorched peelings of blown-out truck tires, and have nearly obliterated a senior citizen's vehicle meandering along in front of me at about 30 mph.

Finally, booze may befall us. Some of the hardest drinkers I have ever seen were Florida retirees. They drank straight-up martinis and double blackjacks on the rocks, and they kept them coming until they were barely able to stand. Then they wanted to drive home. Their wives would flutter around them, chirping like exotic birds, trying to get the car keys.

Florida, with its heat and lassitude and loosening of standards, promotes such abuse. Potentially alcoholic men who maintained self-control all their lives because their work structures demanded it, men whose behavior was tempered by their responsibilities, come to Florida in retirement and fall apart. *Nobody needs you now,* the state croons to them. *You don't have to pretend anymore. Put your feet up, have a drink, have two or three or five.*

My father, a controlled alcoholic himself, was tempted but did not succumb. He drank precisely one and a half martinis at the cocktail hour (rigidly observed) every night — never less but never more, though it was plain to me that he wanted more. I think he knew what Florida had in mind for him and would have none of it.

In the rest of the country, people wake in the morning with jobs to do and all manner of possibilities before them. They might get promoted, get fired, fall in love, get dumped, take a trip, conceive a child, buy a Porsche. But in my Florida, people wake up and know they will do none of these things. And they are a lot less certain than the rest of us that they'll wake up at all. Courage is required to live this way. My Floridians are up to it. Whatever else they may be, they are brave and clear-eyed about death.

On several occasions I have asked people I knew about friends of theirs I had met on a previous visit. "Died last spring," they'd say briskly. "Heart. Say, have you ever eaten at Casablanca?" Nobody sat around reminiscing about what a great guy old Harry had been. The dead seemed to be forgotten almost instantly. At first I thought this unfeeling, but I don't see it that way now. I believe it to be practical, wise, and adaptive. Young people often think about death, talk about death, fear death, and in doing so give death power over them. In my Florida, the old, surrounded by it, learn to spit in its eye and save themselves from fear.

But not from anger. Once, walking across the broiling tarmac of the condominium parking lot, my father suddenly whirled on me and, apropos of nothing at all, said in a near snarl, "This getting-old business is the shits. Inside, I'm still eighteen." Apparently this had been on his mind for some time. As usual, he issued the statement as a simple declaration, not as an opening to further discussion. He had had what for him was an emotional outburst — something thought by the males of our family to border on bad taste — and it would have been unforgivable if I had pressed him further. So we walked, silent, under the sun.

But what he said stuck in my mind. If he was any example, millions of men and women up and down his adopted state were not, as their heirs devoutly hoped, "growing old gracefully." They were angry. They were trapped in weak, failing bodies that every day betrayed the germ of youth still vigorous within them. Some, like my father, accepted the unfairness of this without forgiving it and soldiered on into old age with some dignity. But Florida seduced many of the others. Its fragrant air and vivid colors, its warmth, its night whispers hinting at impossible rejuvenations — these snuffed out realistic anger at the dying of the light and replaced it with a hormonal silliness. These people came to think they *were* eighteen.

One night, in the bar of an intimate and well-regarded Palm Beach hotel, I watched as a young woman suffering from an excess of silicone and naked except for pasties and thong, lap-danced for a man in tasseled loafers who appeared to be at least eighty. His wife and graying daughter looked on, beaming. This, the stripper told me later, was his birthday present.

Was this not . . . unusual? No, she said, and gave thanks for the Social Security set. She made a good part of her living, she added, dispensing gifts such as this to men who, in another part of America, would be off to bed after *Wheel of Fortune,* their dentures soaking in a glass.

After this display I was approached by a woman who could not have been much younger than the birthday celebrant. She had watched me from the bar, she said coyly. Would I like to buy her a drink? She wore a red tube dress and troweled-on makeup. I fled all the way to Charley's Crab, where aging men in huaraches, white canvas pants, and shirts cut low to show gold chains and chest hair — was it, I wondered, *real* chest hair? — told each other about their alleged conquests.

Granted, this was Palm Beach, one of the weirdest venues in the state, a place where dog walkers on the beach may pass bales of marijuana washed ashore from smugglers' boats or even the occasional body of a drowned Haitian. Musk is always in the air here. Billows of it have risen from the more spectacular infidelities of the celebrity rich and the caperings of the Kennedys, but not a small amount emanates from the oversexed elderly. In Palm Beach, you are a long, long way from Columbus, Ohio.

Across the peninsula, around Naples, you might as well be *in* Columbus. Half the population seems to hail from Ohio. In the seventies you were far more likely to find the style of dress known as "the full Cleveland" — white shoes, belt, and tie; colored shirt; clashing polyester jacket and pants — in Naples than in the Buckeye State.

In more recent years, men and women have gone to big straw hats with gaudy bands, tight white pants or pedal pushers, and sandals that expose toes better left hidden.

My stepmother was more subdued. Though to my knowledge she had never set foot on a boat, she wore tailored clothes of a faintly nautical bent, as if she expected to board a yacht at any moment. As for my father, when he was feeling particularly raffish in his later years, he might concede enough to the heat to wear a subdued pair of shorts — with, alas, dark socks and laced shoes. He would have stood before a firing squad before wearing anything that revealed his toes. I like to think that the jumpsuit incident had restored him to sanity and that if he was doomed to remain a New York sparrow among Florida peacocks, he accepted the role.

He was set apart still further by an indifference to football. A hush would fall over Naples when Ohio State University ("*The* Ohio State University," as my stepmother insisted, reminding me of its correct and hopelessly pretentious name) was playing football on television. While my father did the crossword puzzle, thousands of ex-Ohioans were closeted in their condominiums, clutching OSU banners, wearing OSU colors, worshiping Woody Hayes (who today would be hustled into anger counseling), and, later, grumbling about his insufficiently ferocious successors. Nobody cared what the Florida teams were doing.

Which, I later came to see, was not surprising. In my Florida, the last thing the residents concern themselves with is Florida itself. To them this pancake-flat shelf of limestone jutting into the sea is a good platform for golf courses but otherwise a *tabula rasa* upon which they are entitled to inscribe their dreams. Just as the lecturer never gives a thought to the blackboard he writes on, so they don't give a thought to the state they live in. What they have ordered up is Ohio with palm trees and no snow, and they are getting it.

Much of today's Florida is, in a manner of speaking, not Florida at all. Over the years, landscapers have introduced a horde of alien species that are competing with native plants over broad reaches of land. Introduced animals are having a similar effect. No state, with the possible exception of Hawaii, has been so altered by imports, and no import has devastated the natural ecosystem more than the retiree. For his or her sake, landscapes not covered by alien species are covered by lawns and concrete. In county after county, coastal wetlands and swamps have been drained and doused with insecticides to make way for subdivisions, golf courses, shopping malls, condo towers, and strips of cheesy shops. The novels of Carl Hiaasen, chronicler of the awful new Florida, have as a recurring character a former governor who, being decent and honest, was driven from office by a cabal of developers and now, half-mad, lives in the Everglades and subsists on road kill. I have looked for him there, half-expecting to find him.

When I think of my father now, I never see him in Florida. I see him in a boat on a lake in the Adirondack Mountains, a place he loved all his life. He camped, fished, and hiked there as a boy and as a young man, and for many years all our family vacations were taken on Lake George, to me still one of the most beautiful lakes in the world. When we arrived there every summer, he seemed to expand and at the same time to relax. My sister and I would trap crayfish at the water's edge and later watch him send them down at the end of a fly line to tempt the smallmouths in the sun-dappled rocks below. We stood on the dock to watch a northern pike dart from the weeds, quick as thought, to seize a yellow perch.

When he moved to Florida, my father, instructed by the Adirondacks, took with him an enduring interest in the natural world. He went with my wife and me to track down the endangered snail kite, a rare bird of the central Everglades. He and I often went to Corkscrew Swamp, a haunted domain. Another time, walking on an Everglades hammock, we roused such a cloud of mosquitoes that we could barely breathe, and fled, frantically slapping and brushing at exposed flesh. My father was laughing. Suddenly I remembered him a quarter-century before, in a boat in the middle of Lake George in a sudden squall that raised sizable waves. I was uneasy — we had only a seven-horse motor — but he relished it all, grinning and facing into the wind and rain the whole way home.

In my Florida he was an oddity. My stepmother showed not the slightest interest in anything around her that was not built by man; my father said she wouldn't walk around the corner to look at the Grand Canyon. Nobody else seemed interested, either. When I would visit unique natural areas in Florida, which I did often (the Adirondacks had worked their way with me too), I noticed few cars with Florida plates that didn't carry rental stickers. On the trails, I encountered few older people who weren't accompanied by young adults or kids, presumably visiting children and grandchildren. If it were not for the burdens of hospitality, my Floridians would stay in their compounds, breathing chilled air, looking out their windows at shaved lawns. Hot, buggy, and anarchically overgrown, the wild Florida surrounding their enclaves is a threatening presence, better left to tourists.

In his midseventies, my father began to descend into the Final Florida. He first suffered TIAs, transient ischemic attacks that robbed him momentarily of adequate blood flow to the basal brain, where, among other things, the sense of balance resides. He fell down. He suffered tremors of the tongue, which frightened him. Then came a more serious stroke, a wheelchair, and, briefly, a convalescent home (where, in one of those lightning strikes of comedy that often illumine the gloomiest scene, he formed a bridge foursome with one partner who was nearly blind, another who was nearly deaf, and a third who forgot her point count the moment she computed it).

I was there for part of this period and several times took my father to his specialists, all of them assembly-line workers in that vast, clanking factory called Medicare. They warehoused patients in their waiting rooms the way Ford might warehouse fuel pumps, and with about as much feeling. We waited an hour every visit and never got an apology or even an acknowledgment of our inconvenience. The doctors were hurried and detached, treating my father and the others as units of illness to be dealt with and/or placated in the least amount of time possible because Medicare won't finance the Beemer or the house in Maine if you spend more than a few minutes actually talking to these old people. Keep eye contact to a minimum. They're going to die soon anyway.

This made my father angry. He was a difficult patient at best and sheer hell at home, where my stepmother tried to nurse him. She left behind queerly dispassionate notes of this experience that made me wince when I read them. He was furious at the world, furious at her, outraged at becoming a cripple, and savagely sarcastic in a manner that must have hurt her greatly. But it was his rage that healed him. He moved out of his wheelchair into a walker before he was supposed to. Then, day after day, he tried to walk — first to the door, then partway down the corridor toward the elevator, then all the way to the elevator about a hundred feet away. Sweating and breathing hard, he did it again and then again. In eight months he was completely recovered and for a brief time had relatively good health before another stroke felled him. He died in 1984, at age seventy-nine.

I took his clothes to a thrift shop operated by a charity. There were only a couple of cardboard boxes and perhaps a half-dozen hangers. I looked for the jumpsuit, but it wasn't there.

My stepmother survived my father by sixteen years, and they were not good ones. Year by year, Florida drew its net around her. She saw fewer people, did fewer things, went out less. She told everyone not to send her any gifts for any reason. When I visited, she would not allow me to take her to dinner; she ate nothing but frozen meals. Her life got smaller and smaller until finally there was nothing left of it but a solitaire hand laid out on a kitchen table next to a cheap little transistor radio playing the old songs she had known as a girl. She grew more and more insubstantial, a Florida ghost, and her eventual passing seemed less a death than the tail end of a gradual disappearance.

When my father died, my stepmother had his ashes buried in the memorial garden of an Episcopal church in Naples they had fitfully attended (she was the Episcopalian; he went along). She had a small tree bearing exotic yellow flowers, very much a Florida kind of tree, planted in a corner of the garden. The tree struggled for years. Finally, well before her ashes came to join my father's, it died and was cut down.

The garden is built around a square of flagstones with, at its center, a fine bronze of an angel bearing the soul of man to heaven. The huddled, defeated man is unutterably weary, his head resting on the angel's shoulder, his legs drawn up like a child's, the angel's strong arm beneath them and supporting them. I have sat on a bench in the garden many times over the past sixteen years, admiring the statue, enjoying the peace of the place, and wishing my father were somewhere else.

Perhaps this is because the tree died. Perhaps it is because my father had never been an Episcopalian. Whatever the reasons, I do know this lush little garden is not where he belongs. I cannot argue Florida's claims on my stepmother. By the end she had surrendered everything to the place, all her interests, her initiative, her very life, and so belongs here. But my father does not. All unconscious of it, he resisted Florida's blandishments and remained outside its power — which is only to say that he remained entirely himself. So it is time now, I think, to take him north, to colder country he could call home. He earned that much.

J. MICHAEL FAY

# In the Land of the Surfing Hippos

FROM *National Geographic*

## Christmas Hippo

WHEN I FIRST STOOD on the beach in Gabon, I took off my clothes and contemplated writing home to say: "Don't worry, Ma, I'm OK. Just don't come looking for me — you'll never see me again, ever." Christmas morning a decade later, and here I was back on that same beach, where hippos surf and buffalo sunbathe. Lounging half naked in front of my little tent as deep as you can get on the shores of what is now Loango National Park, gazing out on the vast, empty Atlantic, I thought: "You dog, Fay, how is it possible that you're the chosen one who gets to hang out here?"

This was a reunion. Nick Nichols, his wife, Reba Peck, and two sons, Ian (twenty-two) and Eli (fourteen), were here, along with our old friend Jane Sievert and her seven-year-old daughter, Malia. Our campsite was a closely grazed patch of grasses and sedges amid a grove of manilkara trees and hyphaene palms. When we humans sleep, elephants and buffalo come to the clearing to feed. Olive ridley turtles bob their heads in the sea, munching on the algae growing on the coastal reefs, and tarpon roll in the surf, while humpback dolphins and bull sharks patrol the edge of the shore. This spot at the Moubani Creek Inlet is just up the beach from where, three years earlier, we'd popped out of the forest at the end of my long walk from the interior. Today Jane, Malia, and I had a more modest plan. We'd decided to make a kayak trip up the Moubani, which winds about three miles inland through the mangroves. Yesterday we'd seen a hippo's tracks emerging from the sea, heading for the upper reaches of the creek, and we thought we might find him up there in some backwater.

It was a year since I had taken on Operation Loango, a partnership between the Society for Conservation and Development, an ecotourism company formed by the visionary Dutch entrepreneur Rombout Swanborn, and my employer, the Wildlife Conservation Society (WCS). The aim is to develop an economic base for Loango National Park (lodges, safaris, sport-fishing, whale and turtle watching) and to assist the government in managing the park. In June 2003 we finished building Loango Lodge about thirty miles north of here, providing income that's being pumped into jobs for local Gabonese youth, equipping them to be everything from game wardens and ecoguides to auto mechanics. Our conservation projects ("operations," as we call them) include satellite tracking of elephants, whale research, prevention of poaching and illegal fishing, turtle monitoring, beach cleanup, and the day-to-day running of the park.

As Jane, Malia, and I shoved the kayak off, the resident goliath heron was knee-deep in the inlet, where he stands for hours, perfectly still, waiting for a mullet or baby tarpon. When we passed, he opened his enormous wings (seven feet from tip to tip) and took off like a jumbo jet, slow and steady.

We cruised along the narrow spit that separates the Atlantic from the hidden lagoon world and entered the dark, mangrove-lined creek beyond. The water was a mix of turquoise and black. At high tide the ocean spills over the spit into the lagoon, creeping up the inlet as the pressure from the sea builds, pushing the black, tannic water back upstream.

The mangroves here are big trees, their stilt roots forming an impenetrable tangle like some kind of hideous — or maybe wondrous — jungle gym. We passed a little grassy patch neatly mowed by the hippo the night before. It was now occupied by egrets, greenshanks (a long-legged sandpiper), and thick knees (a strange nocturnal shorebird somewhere between a coot and a plover), either stalking insects or just dozing upright.

We hugged the banks to watch the mangrove crabs that inhabit the stilt roots. Exquisite little creatures, they look like tiny carved ebony boxes with inlays of yellow and purple. Just below the tide line were masses of white shells — luscious oysters packed thick on every mangrove root. I thought about the village that had existed at the inlet until maybe a century ago. It was the northern outpost of the Loango kingdom, whose throne was near the Congo River some 250 miles to the south. The people of Loango came here for padauk wood (prized for its hardness and bright red color), for elephant ivory, and to acquire slaves from the neighboring tribes. It's clear from the abundant shell middens that oysters supplied the villagers with a steady source of food over many generations. I imagined the naked kids paddling up the Moubani in their dugouts, collecting oysters and catching fish and land crabs.

As likely as not, paddling conditions were as perfect then as now — slight breeze coming off the ocean, cumulus clouds shading the sun (no more than 80°F), and not a tsetse fly to be seen. As we rounded the sharp bend leading us inland, the kayak leaving a silvery wake on the dark surface, some fruit bats scared up a biggish bird. We got into position for a look, and my eyes met with what looked like an overdressed clown with a sharp beak. Its breast was a rich rusty brown, the throat a bright white, the back and wings a crisp blackish brown. But the eyes: Wow, what eyes! In a bird the size of a raven they were about as big as a human's and lined with a thick white ring. This thing was the most wonderful avian delight I'd ever seen. A look in *A Guide to the Birds of Western Africa*, by Nik Borrow and Ron Demey, revealed the bird to be the white-backed night heron *(Gorsachius leuconotus)*. "Largely nocturnal; secretive and very shy by day," the book said. Hardly an adequate description of such a gem. The authors might have added: "Yet another little-known and unbelievably beautiful product of nature that can be seen on any day in Loango National Park."

Pushing on, we came to a spot devoid of mangroves — an elephant trail that crossed the creek — like a gateway leading directly into the heart of darkness. I noticed a patch of blue in the shallows and on closer examination realized it was the dorsal fin, in full regalia, of a lunker male mudskipper. He must have weighed half a pound. Just like elephant seals, these amazing amphibious fish have gruesome fights for territory. When the battles get heated, they present their almost sailfishlike dorsal fin, with its daunting show of iridescent blue spots.

This guy, however, wasn't in a tangled fight with a competitor but in the clutches of a predatory blue swimming crab. These eight-legged killers dig themselves into the sand and wait for a fish to pass above. When the moment is right, *whap!* — like a mousetrap going off — the prey is gripped in needle-sharp pincers. I'd watched crabs catching tiny fish fry before but nothing as big as this mudskipper. He was still alive but nearly inert, writhing half-heartedly. I leaned over to take a picture, which must have distracted the crab. It relaxed for a split second, and with a flip of the tail the mudskipper was out of there. Empty-pincered, the crab dug itself into the sand and vanished.

We landed on a bed of round volcanic rocks: geodes. How different this place must have looked hundreds of millions of years ago when there were active volcanoes, and dinosaurs roamed amid giant ferns. Today's megafauna are forest elephants, but as the now vague trail leading into the dark forest showed, their fortunes have risen and fallen with human activity. Several hundred years ago, when slavery and European diseases decimated people in the area, thus leaving the elephants largely to themselves, the trail would have been a well-trodden pachyderm highway. But in the 1900s when the French began a century of exploiting timber, ivory, crocodiles, and other wildlife, elephant numbers ebbed, and nature began reclaiming the trail. Still, I estimate there are a few thousand elephants in and around Loango today.

Our next excitement came from above — a movement in the trees followed by repeated kissing sounds. We spied a mustached guenon, a monkey about the size of a large tomcat with a bright white bar across his upper lip, staring at us, raising his head as he chirped an alert to others. The chirps intensified, and some bigger gray-cheeked mangabeys started barking — *ah! ah! ah!* — on the opposite side of the stream. Then red-capped mangabeys joined the primate orchestra: *kako! kako!* In the distance the boom of a greater white-nosed monkey sounded through the forest: *niao! niao!*

As we advanced upstream, the river narrowed, and snags began to block our progress. My eyes scanned the muddy bank, which suddenly began to surge. So did my heart, as the form of a massive hippo materialized no more than twenty-five feet in front of the boat. Face-on to us, he plunged into the water like a battleship released from dry dock full speed ahead. He'd been sleeping under a tree, and we'd scared the bejeezus out of him in what he may have judged a surprise attack. We paddled frantically for the mangroves on the opposite bank, which seemed a mile away.

"Go, go, go," shouted Jane, "he's coming. He's right behind the boat." The theme music of *Jaws* popped into my head, along with visions of this behemoth chomping our chunk of plastic kayak right in half.

When we reached a tangle of mangrove roots — slippery like spaghetti and virtually ungrippable — I tossed the paddle aside and catapulted Malia up into the tree. Jane and I followed, clambering and slithering over the spaghetti branches until we had about ten feet of jungle gym between us and the water's edge. We looked back only to see a boil of water erupting just behind the bobbing, now empty, kayak. The hippo had plunged into the black depths.

We perched motionless for the better part of an hour, eyes fixed on the water like spooked prey. Because passage on foot through the mangrove maze wasn't an option, we'd have to hop back in that boat and get ourselves downstream without stirring the now invisible beast. All was quiet. Would it stay that way?

Jane and Malia struggled through the mangrove roots until they were about a hundred feet downstream. I jumped on the bow of the kayak, tipping it hard from side to side to call the hippo's bluff. The water stayed calm. No bubbles, no movement. That was good. I recovered the paddle and lost no time in zipping downstream to fetch the ladies, slipping as quietly as possible past every swirl and bubble.

It was midafternoon when we finally heard the crash of surf again. Otherwise all was calm, with the goliath heron back at his post, master of all he surveyed. Feeling a bit guilty about our close call, but giggling to myself, I thought: "Heck of a Christmas for a seven-year-old."

## Fish Pirates

It was 6:15 A.M. at the Iguela Inlet on Loango's northern boundary. Water flowing into this milewide estuary from the interior travels about seventy-five miles down the Nioungou River, through an enormous unpeopled basin of papyrus swamps, flooded forests, and raffia palms. As it crosses this plain, the water picks up nutrients, which are released into the sea, attracting concentrations of fish as thick as bouillabaisse.

I'd been based at the inlet for weeks, building our trawler surveillance camp and overseeing other operations. Gil Domb, who was filming our work for National Geographic Television, and I were drinking our morning coffee when he blurted out, "Wow, that's a big boat." I looked up, and damned if there wasn't a trawler just north of the inlet, so close in as to be, as we say, "zero meters from the beach." Checking it out with my binoculars, I saw an all-too-familiar shark-fin stripe on the bow. That would make her either *Le Pêcheur I* or *Le Pêcheur II* — the same lot who were here a couple of weeks ago, fishing inside the three-nautical-mile legal limit. Over the past ten months we'd become familiar with most of the rogue fishing trawlers off this stretch of the Gabon coast, and there was no mistaking the Pêcheur clan.

Our spotter team of three Gabonese included a new recruit, Basil Maganga, who was on duty that morning. His job was to watch for vessels fishing in restricted zones and, the moment he saw one, to alert the national authorities.

Scanning the beach, I saw no sign of Basil. Maybe he was still in bed. Maybe he was making breakfast. But wherever he was, I feared he was oblivious to the presence of the trawler right in front of his nose. Gil and I jumped in the skiff and sped off to "crab island," where I left him to film the daily fiddler crab migration. I then made tracks along the shore to find Basil. Instead of wearing his standard-issue ecoguide uniform, he was sporting Hawaiian-style trunks with a white T-shirt and was inspecting the blank horizon with his binoculars, the trawler having disappeared beyond the point to the north.

I greeted Basil lightly and asked about boats. The coast was clear, he replied proudly. Stifling my feelings (I felt like strangling him), I calmly but firmly informed him that less than an hour earlier there was a trawler right in front of the camp. How could he miss it? What was he doing? It would, I said, be like missing an elephant in your living room.

Without saying another word, I sprinted north up the beach to record the trawler on video. Basil followed close behind. I stopped and scolded him again: Where were his spotting scope, tripod, GPS, notebook, pencil, video camera, and range finder — all of which should have been in his backpack?

As Basil ran back for his equipment, I approached the rocky point a few hundred yards up the beach and rounded the bend. There she was, with the shark fin and a hideous Spiderman painting on her bow: *Le Pêcheur I*, not even half a mile offshore in thirty feet of water, now cruising south toward the inlet, scraping the bottom with her trawl nets. I got video of the trawler with the surf in the foreground; she looked as if she were going to plow right onto the beach. The video images are crucial evidence, which we send in an e-mail report to the authorities, with the time, date, GPS location, and name of the boat.

But this was the weekend, and I was on a desolate beach in Gabon. How could I get this mechanical monster clear of the inlet before it scooped up the fish soup?

I reached for my secret weapon — the satellite phone in my sack. About twenty seconds later Jean Ampari, my collaborator in Libreville, answered his cell phone. Jean works for the Forestry Ministry, which is also responsible for the environment, water, and fisheries. He's in charge of controlling all trawlers — and with a green light from President Bongo, we're helping him clean up industrial fishing in Gabon.

"*Bonjour,* Mike." Jean knew my voice.

"We have *Le Pêcheur I*, serial number 010311601, fishing illegally again in the same spot where we busted her two weeks ago, five hundred meters off the coast, two kilometers north of the Iguela Inlet, first noted at 6:30 in the morning and still fishing."

Jean said he'd call *Le Pêcheur*'s parent company, APG, right away. I repeated the details, excused myself for calling on the weekend, and thanked him for his action. I went back to filming the trawler, while Basil, who had caught up with me, was making observations through his spotting scope and furiously writing down the details.

As my camera rolled, *Le Pêcheur*'s twin nets came up, and the crew came alive. The catch spilled onto the deck, and the men immediately started sorting the fish into baskets. The prize fish here are snapper, jack, barracuda, threadfin, and drum — Gabonese favorites that fetch ever higher prices as supplies dwindle.

We couldn't see much behind the high steel gunwales except for arms flailing, the occasional fish flying through the air into a sorting basket or overboard, and countless dead fish being swept back into the sea through exit holes. The sanitized term for these rejected fish — young ones too small to sell for a profit — is bycatch.

What happens to bycatch fish is akin to taking a herd of beef cattle, killing them all at once, and throwing away the calves. This bycatch represents the next generation of the very fish *Le Pêcheur*'s crewmen will need to live on, and here they were converting them into tern snacks.

When Basil saw this carnage, he flipped. He couldn't believe they'd just throw fish away like that — enough to feed a large village, he said. This was the moment he became a militant; I could see it in his eyes. He was so angry I thought he was going to swim out and turn the fishermen themselves into bycatch. Most of our ecoguides experience such an epiphany. When we hired Loic Mackaga, for instance, he was a convicted elephant poacher. His conversion came from working with Gil Domb, filming elephants and hippos on the beach. Seeing these animals through a long lens rather than the sights of a gun — mothers caring for their young, infants crying for milk and playing with their siblings — gave him a whole new appreciation of them. (Of course, Loic also recognized that the benefits of a steady job outweigh the stigma of being a convicted felon.)

About half an hour after my call to Jean, *Le Pêcheur I* turned offshore and stopped about two miles out. Better, but not good enough. I called Jean again; an hour later the trawler was gone.

Walking back down the beach, I thought about the owner of the *Pêcheurs*, among the most flagrant poachers off Loango. When I see his boats stealing fish day after day, I wonder if he believes he has the right to plunder the natural resources of a country that can ill afford to lose them. In the past year we've recorded dozens of instances of trawlers poaching fish inside the legal limit, mostly at inlets. These boats, though registered in Gabon and flying the Gabonese flag, are run almost exclusively by foreigners, predominantly Asians, Europeans, and West Africans. I also thought about all the other resource extractors I've met in central Africa over the years — loggers, hunters, miners — all taking, taking, taking.

European nations have a long tradition of pillaging Africa, with no responsible limits. Now the European Union has a fishing deal, last renewed in 2001, with Gabon — one of fifteen such agreements the EU has with African nations. At least another eleven are being negotiated. The treaty with Gabon includes provision for sixty-four tuna seiners and surface long-liners belonging to private companies (primarily French and Spanish), which can take 10,500 tons of tuna a year. Add to that another flotilla of European freezer trawlers, which have the rights to 14,400 tons of crustaceans and cephalopods, and you have a yearly grand total of 24,900 tons of seafood the EU can extract legally from Gabonese waters. For this haul Gabon receives a minimal payment. (In practice there are no limits: The fine print permits catches in excess of quotas at the same price.)

Critics say these agreements are market driven rather than based on scientific studies of sustainable fishing. They're designed only to supply European markets and to secure employment for EU fishery workers. And they fail to meet the objectives of international treaties under which EU members (and other First World nations) have committed to help develop, and reduce poverty in, poor countries like Gabon.

It makes me angry. The EU boats never put in at Gabonese ports, don't employ a single Gabonese (although Spain is now considering building a tuna-processing plant in Gabon), and never sell a single fish on the local market. No wonder Gabon, a country that eats less fish than it produces, still needs to import more than 10,000 tons of fish annually to meet its own domestic consumption. You'd think that in 2004, in a globalizing world with diminishing natural resources, wealthy nations like those in the EU would be more responsible. You'd think that by now prudent management and sustainable fishing would be more of a reality.

My hope is that the EU will soon become a strong force for fisheries in Gabon and that we'll succeed in getting a marine extension to Loango National Park. For now I was just very happy we'd cleared the coast of *Le Pêcheur I* — and that the incident had woken the sleeping giant in Basil Maganga. Gabon needs all the foot soldiers it can get.

## Turtle Quest

Through the sea mist I was drawn by the refracted light of three headlamps. Then Clement Moukoula, the head of our sea turtle team, materialized. I couldn't make out exactly what he said over the crash of the high-tide breakers, but it was something like, "It's 21:07, and you, sir, are seven minutes late. Let's go!"

Every year from October to March, Clement is a nocturnal creature. His job is to count, observe, tag, and otherwise gather up all
the information he can about the sea turtles that come ashore at
night to lay their eggs. I'd joined him and two others, Serge "Feree"
Ogoula and Jean-François Babicka, to survey a three-mile stretch
along the northern limit of the park, just beyond the St. Catherine
ecoguide camp. Our coastal patrols actually extend about eight
miles up the beach in an effort not only to stop human predators
from pilfering turtle eggs but also to allow mammals to return to
Loango's shore. It seemed miraculous, but in the past six months
turtle-nest pillaging had dropped to virtually zero (although turtle
numbers overall were mysteriously down), and we now had elephants and sitatungas (large striped antelope) strolling the beach.

Mature female leatherbacks come ashore every three or four
years but lay several clutches of eggs in that one season. This was
the peak of the egg-laying season, and although I'd been out with
the team on four consecutive nights, I still hadn't seen a turtle. I
told Clement, who was poker-faced as usual, that if we didn't succeed tonight, he and the others would all be fired. That got a smile
out of him.

We followed normal operating procedure: headlamps out, walking just above the tide line in a close search for fresh turtle tracks, a
search facilitated by the glow from the flare of an enormous offshore oil platform. I go into a trancelike state on these walks, but
Clement, who has done turtle counts all over Gabon for years,
never stops making notes. He was obsessed with figuring out why
turtle numbers were suddenly so low. He wondered if accelerated
beach erosion had something to do with it. Or was it the new oil
flare or perhaps trawler fishing? I suggested global warming, the
catchall excuse for collapsing ecosystems everywhere. Or could it
be another frequently cited phenomenon, El Niño?

By rights this should have been a good night for leatherbacks,
with a waning moon and the tide incoming, but by the time we
reached the stick marking the three-mile limit of the study beach,
we hadn't found a single one. So we had a bit of a snooze on the
moist sand, then headed back down the beach. By now I'd gone
from my trance to doing incantations to see a turtle.

When we were about half a mile from our starting point, an ominous black thing loomed ahead of us like an apparition in a hor-

ror movie. A leatherback! She was head-to-land about twenty feet above the tide line on a nice wide patch of beach. Clement instructed us to stand back while he checked how far along she was in the nesting process. "She's dug the egg chamber," he whispered. Just behind her was a perfectly cylindrical hole about six inches in diameter and a foot deep. "Sit quiet for a minute until she lays, then we can approach, no problem."

I heard the turtle make what sounded like a gasp, and Clement was up in a flash. Huddling up behind her, the low beam from his headlamp defining the chamber, we could see that she'd dropped several eggs. Clement looked distressed. "The hole isn't nearly deep enough," he said, pointing to the turtle's back right flipper, most of which was missing. The loss must have handicapped her ability to excavate, a task that calls for all her strength and dexterity.

I watched spellbound. This old girl was pushing hard, and she already looked exhausted. *Bloop* — more eggs fell. They were the size of billiard balls, round and white. Every time mom pushed, out came eggs, up to four at once, covered with a gooey mucus. As the hole filled, we counted: 30, 50, 80, and, finally, 84 eggs. Clement was right — the egg mass overflowed the hole.

As soon as she'd finished, the turtle team hopped into action to record her vital statistics. Her carapace was measured: 143 centimeters (56 inches) long and 105 centimeters (41 inches) wide. Clement estimated her weight at 300 kilograms (660 pounds), suggesting she was no more than twenty years old. (Leatherbacks, which range widely in the open ocean, feeding on jellyfish, their staple food, can reach more than a ton and live fifty years.) Loading a stainless steel ID tag into his pliers, Clement grabbed the skin between the carapace and the damaged flipper and squeezed hard. She didn't even flinch. The turtle was duly christened ASF2637, according to the tag number. Because tags sometimes fall off, Feree then applied a second one to the opposite flipper. Seemingly oblivious to all this activity, the turtle started covering the eggs by alternately scooping sand over the pile with one hind flipper and tamping it down with the top side of the other.

I glanced at Clement questioningly. He nodded. I touched her flipper, and my heart stopped when she almost grabbed my wrist with it — that flipper seemed prehensile! I'd expected the limb to be hard and scaly, but it was fleshy and supple as a seal's. The baby-soft skin was slate gray, with what looked like sponged-on blotches of white latex. Diligently, she continued sweeping and tamping, working with such eerie dexterity that she struck me not as a turtle at all but as a person dressed up in a turtle costume. Any second now she would start talking: "Hey, Mike, can you push that egg into the hole for me?"

I thought about all the things ASF2637 must have seen in her decades at sea: giant passenger ships, trawler nets, sharks, manta rays, humpback whales, oil spills, and tons of garbage. Where had she been, and what had injured her flipper?

She finished tamping, but two eggs remained exposed. Clement grabbed them and removed them far from the nest, lest they alert predators like civets, ghost crabs, or monitor lizards to the nest's location. The covered eggs would incubate, unattended, for sixty to seventy days. The hatchlings would break through the nest chamber at night and head for the water. Crabs would be lurking on the beach, and for the tiny turtles that made it to the sea, jacks and mackerel, not to mention trawler nets, would be waiting.

Now the turtle's front flippers — paddles nearly as long as her body — went back into action, throwing bucketloads of concealing sand all over the egg chamber and surrounding area. With each throw she pushed slightly forward and to the side, cutting a deep swath in the sand. After a bout of scooping she rested her head, closed her teary eyes, and gasped for more air, her carapace glistening in the moonlight. As I slid my fingers along it, it felt like the curve of a finely polished marble sculpture. Indifferent to our presence, the turtle was following an innate program encoded millions of years ago. If anything, I felt she somehow knew we were on her side.

After forty-five minutes of huffing and puffing and chucking sand, she was fifteen feet from the nest and forty or so from the surf. A ghost crab would be hard-pressed to find turtle eggs around here: The sand was so churned up, it looked as if someone had Rototilled the beach. Clement and crew measured the exact distance between the nest, the high-tide line, and the surf and drew a map of the tracks to and from the nest site. A GPS position was taken, so they'd be able to visit the nest in a few months to see if the eggs had hatched.

Her work done, ASF2637 lumbered toward the water, as we silently urged her on. At last she made it to the pounding surf, and — now you see her, now you don't — disappeared home into what seemed a lonely and foreboding sea.

## Trash Dudes

The sun was already showing signs of being evil as the trash crew readied for action. An early riser, Serge Nkala Y'Eteno, the trash chief, was way down the beach at the work site, having some quiet time to himself. The other five were busy making a thick slurry of instant mashed potatoes mixed with Nestlés cocoa powder and heaps of sugar. I opted for coffee and a bowl of oats.

By seven o'clock we were all walking toward the site about fifteen miles south of Iguela Inlet, where the cleanup operation had begun about a month before. Roughly thirty more miles to go (five months of work) before all of Loango's waterfront is junk free. Today's section was in a strong tidal zone, and the shape of the beach made for a good (or rather, bad) concentration of trash. I was hanging out with Serge Gnogomie, whom I call "Nogomi" to avoid confusion with Serge Y'Eteno. Nogomi described the work. Every night, he said, Chief Serge assigns each team member a one-hundred-meter stretch of shoreline from the water's edge to the high beach. Next day the team scours five hundred meters of beach, making trash piles at five-meter intervals — a hundred separate heaps of garbage to be cataloged and disposed of. The pay is nominal, about six dollars a day plus all the rice, corned beef, and breakfast mush they can eat.

It wasn't long before we came across an amorphous blob of plastic the size of a large beach ball. It looked like a meteorite from space, black and hard. Turning it over, I noted a protruding label that included the words "well number." That told me exactly what our object was: a large bundle of the bags used by oil companies to hold mud or rock samples. Someone should have incinerated it but had done only half the job, dumping the blackened remains into the ocean. We find a lot of oil industry trash on Loango's beaches.

I walked down the beach to join Chief Serge and the others. The accumulated trash covered the sand as far as the eye could see. This stuff has been washing ashore for decades, and cleaning it up is just one piece of the conservation puzzle we're attempting to solve with Operation Loango. You can't expect to have vibrant ecotourism here with dirty beaches, can you?

The most widespread eyesore was a relatively recent product: the plastic water bottle. In just the past decade billions of these things have invaded the earth. Most countries now produce bottled water, and hundreds of millions of people drink only that. Seeing all the bottles on this remote beach, I thought: This can't go on. The world just can't afford to burn this much energy to make bottles from fossil carbon that we fill with spring water, ship halfway round the world, sell for more than the price of gasoline, and then chuck out. It's *nuts*.

Chief Serge was busy banging the top out of a fifty-five-gallon steel drum. This one had had some kind of corrosive material in it, a chemical soup long since leaked from the rusty shell into the ocean. We dispose of these by removing the top and bottom so they don't float, then throwing the hulk into the sea. The saltwater does the rest. To document items like this, every fifty meters Serge takes two GPS readings to demarcate an area where the density of trash will be calculated. Then he sits down at each pile and makes a note of every intact object.

What's to be done with mountains of trash turned into mountains of data? We'll use the statistics as weapons of mass awareness to convince oil companies, cities, and other offenders we identify that they're part of the problem and need to become part of the solution. We'll show the mayor of Pointe-Noire, the main port of neighboring Congo, all the Congolese trash we've found. We'll talk to oil company executives, encouraging them to be more careful about incinerating waste. We'll urge the general public to demand locally produced drinking water. Who knows, we might even persuade water-bottling companies to use more eco-friendly containers.

It was now about 10:30 in the morning. Sweltering. Already, the hundred trash piles had been amassed, and Chief Serge was sitting in front of pile three. Dimitri Mouvoungou had begun marking off tomorrow's beach assignment, and Nogomi had gone back to camp to fetch drinking water fresh out of the local creek. I watched Serge as he meticulously cataloged the pile, which included a 1.5-liter plastic soda bottle, three nicely stacked foam cups, a fishing float made from three motor-oil containers bundled in a piece of trawling net, five intact flip-flops (three right and two left), an unopened Sprite can labeled in a language he (and I) didn't understand but which he copied down faithfully, a 500-gram Olma margarine tub, the top to a can of Quaker Oats, a little white doll's shoe, a dozen 1.5-liter water bottles, a syringe, a Johnnie Walker Red Label bottle, a plastic shopping bag . . .

The sun was burning me up, and I decided to take a dip in the ocean. When I caught up with Serge again, he was at pile ten, assiduous as ever with his logbook but now getting help from Gisele Mabiala, the only female in the crew. Around 11:30 the youngsters Karl Remanda and Youri Rognoundou passed by, doing a sweep of the lower beach and making sure they hadn't missed a single item in their two hundred meters. These two always work together ("We do a more thorough job that way"), and for them to be satisfied, the eye has to be able to scan a completed section of beach and not be distracted by a man-made *anything*.

Tagging along with Karl and Youri, I asked what was the most striking thing they'd found. A few weeks ago, they said, they'd come across a brick-shaped object wrapped in many layers of what looked like commercial Scotch tape. Peeling it off, layer by layer, they finally came to a thick white paste that "heated" and discolored the tips of their fingers when they touched it. It had a chemical smell, like soap. I wondered: Was it heroin or cocaine? This wasn't the first time the crew had found such objects. I joked with Karl and Youri that if I were they, I'd be looking out for the valise containing the payment for those little packages — we could use it to start up another operation. They had no idea what I was talking about.

I looked down the beach, then up the shore, past a buffalo in the distance, as far as I could see, and the magnitude of what these six people were accomplishing with just their bare hands struck me. I ran through some quick calculations. With a thousand such volunteers we could clean the beach all the way to Cape Town, 2,500 miles to the south, in forty-eight days, for about $385,000.

By the afternoon the crew (except for Chief Serge, who was still hostage to his data collection) had begun digging incineration holes at roughly ten-meter intervals. At 1:22 the first disposal fire was lit. The mix of a stiff onshore breeze and the flammable trash made for a serious blaze, which soon sounded like a big pot of popcorn, crackling and exploding and releasing little whistles of gas. I watched as the Olma margarine tub slipped into the flames and a pressurized soda bottle jumped as if in a death throe. Black smoke billowed into the air, and soon all that was left was a cauldron of burning metal and plastic. In these infernos the volume of the trash is reduced by more than 99 percent; glass bottles crack and melt, aluminum fishing floats burn, even entire TVs are reduced to ash, silicon, and copper.

A second hole was now ablaze, primed by lumps of tar from the frequent oil slicks that wash ashore. Burning the trash this way, which causes its own pollution, seems drastic, but our fires are probably equivalent to about two seconds' worth of the gigantic gas flares that burn continuously a few miles off Gabon's coast.

By 6 P.M. Chief Serge, his recordkeeping finished, was helping load stuff into the last burn hole. The sun was setting behind us as we strolled back to the camp for a hearty meal of corned beef and luncheon meat on oily rice. We sat around the campfire, recounting the catch of the day: 535 plastic bottles, 560 intact flip-flops, a 55-gallon drum, 4 refrigerators, 4 hard hats, a 20-liter pressurized Freon bottle, and 2,240 other sundry bits and pieces.

About 50,000 water bottles from now, we should be done cleaning Loango National Park. Who knows? Maybe we'll take Operation Loango all the way to Cape Town.

IAN FRAZIER

# Route 3

FROM *The New Yorker*

BETWEEN ME IN A New Jersey suburb and New York City, fifteen-
some miles to the east, runs a highway called Route 3. For many
bus and car commuters, it is essentially the only direct road from
here (and other suburbs) to there. To say that billions of vehicles
use it daily is an exaggeration, traffic experts will tell you. People
have written songs about the fabled Route 66, and the phrase "New
Jersey Turnpike" has a metrical neatness that fits it into certain
rock-and-roll tunes; but as far as I know nobody has sung about
Route 3. Its unavoidable, traffic-packed, unalluring, grimly lifelike
quality defeats the lyric impulse, probably. Route 3 starts on the low
north-south New Jersey ridges where many suburbs are, crosses the
miles-wide swamp that developers started referring to as the Meadowlands some years ago, rises to another ridge near the Hudson
River, and joins an artery bringing an accumulation of traffic down
the spinning drain into the Lincoln Tunnel and, at the other end,
the vast retort of Manhattan.

An eastbound traveler on Route 3 sometimes has the serrated
skyline of midtown straight ahead. At certain times of the year during the morning commute, the sun comes up right behind the city;
the shadows of the buildings theoretically stretch the whole length
of the highway and slide backward gradually, like tide. When the
road reaches the Meadowlands, the sky opens out, with the tall
light poles of the Giants Stadium parking lot receding to a remote
vanishing point and the pools of swamp water perfectly reflecting
the reeds along their edges, the radio towers, the clouds, and the
intricate undersides of cautious airplanes descending to Newark

Airport. Along much of the road on either side, the landscape is as ordinary as ordinary America can be: conventioneers' hotels and discount stores and fast-food restaurants and office complexes and Home Depot and Best Buy and Ethan Allen, most of the buildings long and low, distributed in the spread-out style of American highway architecture. And then suddenly, just before the Lincoln Tunnel, that ordinariness ends, and you're in jostling, close-up surroundings about to become New York. At no other entry to the city is the transition between it and everyday, anywhere U.S.A. so quick.

I usually travel to and from the city by bus. The one I take to go home leaves from the fourth floor of the Port Authority Bus Terminal. Most bus commuters sensibly occupy themselves with newspapers, laptops, CD players, and so on. I always try to get a window seat and then look at the scenery. If this were a ride at an amusement park, I would pay to go on it. The bus comes out of the terminal on a high ramp above Tenth Avenue. For just a moment you can see clear down Tenth, a deep ravine usually filled at the bottom with taxicabs. From the ramp, the bus descends into the tunnel, either straight or in a loop, depending on traffic and time of day. Once in the tunnel, it can be there forever. Brake lights on vehicles ahead reflect on the bus ceiling and tint people's faces. During an evening rush hour, my son and I observed a foot sticking up from the narrow electric tram cart that runs on a track along the tunnel wall. The foot had on a work boot and the shin was wearing work pants. We decided that it must belong to a tunnel worker who was out of sight down in the cart taking a nap.

When the bus leaves the tunnel, it is in Weehawken, New Jersey. It climbs the elevated spiral of highway that people call the helix, and then for a mile or so there's a complicated section of road where traffic bound in different directions sorts itself out. Then the bus turns northwest onto Route 3. At this point, it is in Secaucus. A newspaper story some years ago said that state police had seized about a ton and a quarter of cocaine in a truck just as it left a warehouse in Secaucus off Route 3. I'm not sure which warehouse it was, but I have some likely ones in mind. Route 3 in Secaucus is where the transition to ordinary America occurs; prominent on your right are two large signs that say ROYAL MOTEL.

What fixed the Royal Motel in my mind, and what makes me glad, somehow, every time I pass it, was a story that appeared in the

*News* in 2000. The story said that one morning, at 2:13 A.M., New York City police arrested a woman for soliciting prostitution at the corner of Tenth Avenue and Forty-sixth Street. The woman gave her name as Tacoma Hopps. The police handcuffed her, put her in the back of a Ford minivan they were using to transport suspects, and left her there while they went to make another arrest. Tacoma Hopps squeezed her hands through the handcuffs, got in the van's driver seat, and sped off downtown. Before the police, suddenly left afoot, could radio ahead to stop her, she had driven to the tunnel and through it. She then left the vehicle in Secaucus and began walking along Route 3, barefoot and carrying a green duffel bag. Secaucus police spotted her. In the duffel bag were two bulletproof vests, a pistol clip containing twenty-five hollow-point bullets, and a New York City Police radio, parking permit, and vehicle keys. When the New York police arrested her, she had given her home address as the Royal Motel. When the Secaucus police arrested her, that was apparently where she was going.

Beyond Secaucus, the bus crosses the wide Hackensack River; the fact that there are no other vehicle bridges over the Hackensack for miles upstream and down contributes to Route 3's congestion. West of the river, on the bus's right, you see the Continental Airlines Arena and Giants Stadium. Recently, developers announced that behind the stadium they're going to build a 104-acre recreation complex, with indoor ski slopes and a surfing pool, to be called Xanadu. Beyond the stadium is swamp and another big river, the Passaic. Then come hills and houses, and trees instead of reeds. In some places here, the road's shoulders glitter with a boa of trash; in others, the right lane merges almost undetectably with large, vague parking lots around commercial enterprises. One of these is the Tick Tock Diner, a chrome Art Deco structure outlined in four colors of neon and surmounted by clocks. When Sean J. Richard, a labor racketeer associated with New Jersey's DeCavalcante family, heard a while back that he was to meet with a capo (alleged) from New York's Lucchese family named Dominic Truscello in a van outside the Tick Tock Diner, Mr. Richard became so frightened that he soon decided to turn state's evidence. His testimony is expected to put a few people in jail.

Across from the Tick Tock, the 127-acre factory and laboratory compound of Hoffman–La Roche Pharmaceuticals rises in buildings of utopian whiteness, one upon the next. On the top of the highest building is the lighted logo of the company — ROCHE, inside a capsule-shaped border. Valium, the company's famous sedative, introduced in 1963, earned a lot of the money that built this Acropolis of pharmaceuticals. Anxiety sufferers of that era probably remember the Valium pill. It was small and round, of a color between yellow and white. On one side a thin, fine score divided the pill into halves; on the other was the word ROCHE and beneath it the number 5 (meaning milligrams). A friend who works as a statistician for the company tells me that although the formula for Valium went out of patent a long time ago and cheaper versions exist, the company still sells a lot of it. Evidently, the name and the look of the Roche pill have acquired a magic that transcends chemistry. Leo H. Sternbach, Valium's inventor, is ninety-five years old and lives not far from me. My friend says that when Mr. Sternbach stops by the lab, as he still occasionally does, he is treated like a king.

Past Hoffman–La Roche on the same side of the street, at the top of a hill with a lawn, the Holy Face Monastery sits half out of sight behind trees. At the foot of the driveway, right beside Route 3, the monastery has erected a shrine. It is a statue of Jesus on a white brick pedestal with concrete tablets nearby bearing the Ten Commandments. Jesus' arms are raised as if in benediction of the traffic; the position of one hand is such that a beer can just fits in it, a coincidence that jokesters take advantage of. I have often seen people, usually alone, praying before the shrine in the mornings and later in the day. They stand with heads bared and bowed and hands clasped at their waists, sometimes so deep in prayer that they seem to be in another dimension.

Now the bus turns off Route 3 at the Grove Street, Montclair/ Paterson exit. It proceeds along Grove, stopping occasionally to let passengers out. When it pulls over, the branches of trees along the street brush the bus's top and side. To a suburbanite just come from the city, the scratching of branches and leaves on metal is the sound of being home.

As a grownup, I have lived in Manhattan, Brooklyn, and Montana. Now I live in the New Jersey town of Montclair. Recently, a friend who's a rancher in Wyoming sent me a card saying he finds it hard to believe that he has a friend who lives in New Jersey. Sometimes I find it hard to believe I'm here, myself. When I lived in the city, I had the usual New Yorker's disdain for this state. Oddly, though, I was attracted to it, too. I used to come over to Jersey a lot, maybe because it reminded me of Ohio and other places I love in the middle of the country. I like being on the continent, rather than slightly offshore. I get a sense that I'm more connected to it; when there's a big snowstorm, for example, I imagine the snow stretching from here back across the Alleghenies to Ohio in unbroken white. And I like the feeling that I'm near the city but also just out of its range.

Suburban New Jersey is a bunch of different stuff mixed up like a garage sale. George Washington kept his army in this area throughout a year of the Revolutionary War; the British held the city, and he wanted to be close to it yet strategically hard for them to get to. His ally the Marquis de Lafayette stayed in a farmhouse on Valley Road in Upper Montclair. A local chapter of the D.A.R. has preserved the farmhouse's flat stone doorstep near the spot where the house was. The memorial, with the stone, a small plaque, and a flagpole, is in a little niche in the town's business district. On one side of the niche is a photo-finishing-and-retouching store; on the other a place called the Backrub Shoppe (recently closed), which offered backrubs lasting from ten minutes up to an hour.

On long walks through suburbs whose names I sometimes can't keep straight — Glen Ridge, Bloomfield, Brookside, Nutley, Passaic, Garfield, Lodi, Hasbrouck Heights, Hackensack, Teaneck, Leonia — I've encountered the New Jersey miscellany up close. Giant oil tanks cluster below expensive houses surrounded by hedges not far from abandoned factories with high brick smokestacks; a Spanish-speaking store that sells live chickens is near a Polish night club off a teeming eight-lane highway; a Greek church on a festival day roasts goats in fifty-five-gallon drums in its parking lot down the road from tall white Presbyterian churches that were built when everything around was countryside. Neighborhoods go from fancy to industrial to shabby without apparent reason, and you can't predict what the next corner will be.

From a car on a highway, though, suburban New Jersey looks so nondescript and ordinary as to be invisible. The eye, in passing, registers not this specific place but a generic likeness that has reproduced itself all across the country. In the Montclair Art Museum is a room of landscape paintings by the artist George Inness, who lived in Montclair from 1885 to 1894. They show the land before it was developed and paved. Inness's winter-gray hilltop tree lines, his ridges sloping underfoot, and his high sky lit by the presence of the ocean over the horizon are all still here, somewhere among the roads and buildings and wires now obscuring them.

That invisibility may explain, partly, why commuters on the bus don't bother to look out the window: Everything there has been seen and reseen and accounted for until it might as well be a blank wall. The only people who regularly look out the bus window are young children. Except during traffic delays, the one time the adult passengers all sit up and stare out en masse is when the bus is driven by a man named Sal. Sal is short and has a boyish (though graying) shock of hair. His movements are more antic than usual for a bus driver. Sal is the only bus driver I know of who seems to notice what's along the road. When he sees something that interests him, he takes up the microphone and announces it to the passengers. Colorful Halloween displays, Christmas lights, a yard full of yellow and purple crocuses, the Goodyear blimp over Giants Stadium — all rate an excited mention by Sal, followed by his usual exclamation: "Oh-boy-oh-boy-oh-boy-oh-boy!"

When the bus gets to the Port Authority and is going up the ramp, Sal always says, "Ladies and gentlemen, boys and girls, I'd like to welcome you to the beautiful Caribbean island of Aruba" — or St. Martin, Barbuda, St. Thomas, etc. — "where the temperature is a sunny seventy-eight degrees. Complimentary beverages will be served upon arrival, don't forget to put on your sunblock, and have a happy day! Cha-cha-cha!" Inside the terminal, when he opens the bus door in the line of buses that are disembarking passengers, he says, "Ahh, smell that fresh Caribbean air!"

For a while after September 11, Sal quit doing his announcements. His bus pulled into the station in silence, with the passengers waiting expectantly but in vain. The loss of Sal's announcements, minor as it was, saddened me out of proportion. Without some silliness, what is life for? Later, though, to general relief, Sal went back to giving what he calls his "spiels."

Although I shouldn't, I often let New Jersey traffic get to me. When I drive here, I am often beeped at for coming to a complete stop at stop signs, not running yellow lights, yielding the right of way at intersections, and following other rules of the road that local practice has discarded. At each beep, I jump and swear. After the relatively easygoing traffic of Montana, New Jersey driving had a predatory fierceness I wasn't ready for. Also, not long after we moved, a man in Englewood was run over and killed in a Starbucks while sitting at a table near the window and working on his laptop. That increased my fears.

New Jersey is the fourth-smallest state in the country and the most densely populated. Especially in areas where traffic is at its worst, room for new roads can't be found. About five and a half million people in New Jersey have driver's licenses, and they drive more than seven million registered vehicles. Traffic planners sometimes mention tepid-sounding solutions like new toll systems to encourage off-peak travel or high-tech ways of alerting drivers to jams.

In fact, the main method for dealing with so many cars in so small a space is the traditional one of ad hoc free-for-all. A few years ago, in a survey of New Jersey drivers done by the Insurance Council of New Jersey and the state's AAA, 52 percent said that they are very angry or moderately angry when they drive. About 40 percent admitted that they are likely to curse or make gestures at other drivers or to use their vehicles to punish them by tailgating, flashing high beams, slowing down to block them in a lane, etc.

The morning rush hour into the city has been getting earlier every year, newspapers say. It used to begin between six o'clock and seven and now begins between five and six. Nearly a million vehicles cross into Manhattan from various directions every day. The *News* says that if a similar number of vehicles were lined up single file, they would stretch from New York City to Los Angeles. And yet no New Jersey highway is among the worst ten places for traffic congestion in the nation, as drivers in Atlanta or Seattle or Los Angeles can testify. To further add to Route 3's averageness, the traffic on it is not much different from traffic anywhere.

Recently, I decided to walk to the city along Route 3. Observing scenery makes me imagine going out in it, and I wanted to see the road other than through glass. From the bus, walking on the shoulder appeared to be possible. Twelve miles from the Grove Street exit to the Lincoln Tunnel did not seem far, and once there I would take the Weehawken ferry, because the tunnel does not have a walkway open to pedestrians. I hadn't been on a long ramble for a while. I put on broken-in shoes and brought a map, in case I had to detour. At about noon of a mild day in late fall, I set out.

From the railing of the Grove Street bridge, Route 3 curved out of sight to the east amid a dwindling succession of multiarmed towers carrying high-tension lines. At this off-peak hour, the road was, as usual, full of cars going fast. I chose the right-hand, eastbound lanes, because that side seemed to have more room. I came down the ramp, along the margin. Of course there was no sidewalk, but neither were there signs forbidding pedestrians. I passed the Holy Face Monastery and shrine. The shoulder was so irregular that I had to keep climbing over the guardrail and back again and tromping through weeds. The traffic blew by, thrumming with the dull rubber thumps of tires hitting pavement seams.

The earth beside this kind of highway is like no earth that ever was. Neither cultivated nor natural, it's beside-the-point, completely unnoticed, and slightly blurred from being passed so often and so fast. And yet plants still grow in it, luxuriantly — ailanthus, and sumac, and milkweed, and lots of others that know how to accommodate themselves to us. In the swampy parts, the common reed would take over the roadway in a blink if the traffic stopped.

The tangled brush and the reeds collect an omnium-gatherum of trash. I saw broken CDs, hubcaps, coils of wire, patient-consent forms for various acupuncture procedures, pieces of aluminum siding, fragments of chrome, shards of safety glass, Dunkin' Donuts coffee cups, condom wrappers, knocked-over road signs, burned-out highway flares, a highlighter pen, a surgical glove, nameless pieces of discarded rusty machinery, a yellow rain slicker with MACY'S STUDIO on the back . . . Scattered through the grass and weeds for miles were large, bright-colored plastic sequins. Oddly, I knew where they had come from. Once, while on the bus, I saw a parade float — probably from the Puerto Rican Day Parade, held in the city — pull up alongside and then speed by. A car must have been towing it, though I don't remember the car. The float was going at least seventy, shimmying and wobbling, banners flapping, and these sequins were blowing off it in handfuls and billowing behind.

Sometimes, walking beside Route 3 got to be too much, owing to the narrowness of the shoulder or the thickness of the undergrowth, and then I would cut over to one or another smaller road nearby. In the Meadowlands, there are some no-place avenues you might expect to find in a Florida swamp where the developers have given up; on an access-type road, an eight-story office building of Smith Barney stands all by itself in the reeds. Farther on, Route 3 has the aspect of a parkway, running through expanses of grass that are easy to stroll across. Nothing occupies this short-grass region but occasional Canada geese keeping one eye on the traffic, like bartenders watching a drunk.

The challenging part of my journey would be crossing the Hackensack River. I had two choices, the westbound bridge or the eastbound bridge. Both are narrow and lack walkways, though they do have little ledges like wide curbs at the sides where a walkway should be. The westbound bridge offered the safety advantage of traffic coming at me rather than from behind; at that proximity to cars, however, it's better not to see. Also, the westbound bridge is a half mile long, and its railing is not high. I whacked through the reeds in the median to the eastbound bridge. It is shorter, because the river here is narrower. Here, at least, the bridge's other side was in sight. I put on the Macy's Studio slicker for increased visibility and started across. Walking on the curb ledge required a one-foot-in-front-of-the-other gait as the trucks and cars went by at sixty-five mph an arm's length away. I held the gritty railing with my right hand. Below, the brown Hackensack swirled around the wooden pilings of a former bridge. In these narrow confines, the traffic noise was a top-volume roar. After a long several minutes, I made it to the other side.

From there my way became complicated — now on Route 3, now detouring around an impassable part, now backtracking after a shoulder I'd been following dead-ended at a fence. In no-man's regions I sometimes found foot trails leading through the grass but no clue about who had made them. By sunset, I was walking up a sloping sidewalk in Union City above approach lanes for the tunnel and going faster than the traffic inbound. I went down to Boulevard East, turned onto a lane under the elevated span, crossed a road running along the river, and sat down to rest on a bench in a little waterfront park. Across the river was a recompense for five hours of walking: the city, its lights diffusing in the mist of faint clouds above it, the whole varied sequence of glittering buildings cropped ruler-straight at the bottom by the Hudson's dark waterline.

I walked to the ferry, paid five dollars for a ticket, got on, and in six minutes crossed to the pier at Thirty-eighth Street. At the Port Authority, I caught a 6:30 bus, wedging myself in the very back row among four other middle-aged guys. The one next to me had a high forehead and a loosened tie. He was fooling with his laptop, and as the bus came through the tunnel he put on a DVD of a Bruce Springsteen concert and began to listen to it with earphones. He had it turned up so loud that the rest of us could hear, and he occasionally hummed tone-deafly along. We could have objected — but we were in New Jersey and it was Bruce, after all. The back seat, and the whole bus, with its closed-in, comfortably crowded atmosphere of people going home, seemed without any connection at all to the highway howling inaudibly just outside.

That night, I was shook up and couldn't sleep — as if walking beside so much noise and speed had rearranged my molecules. I thought of the commuter buses nose-to-tail in line for the tunnel and the mass of idling cars converging. To live by the internal-combustion engine is to live on top of fire; a cyclone of explosions carries us along.

Aaron Burr and Alexander Hamilton fought their famous duel on the New Jersey side of the Hudson River, in the town of Weehawken, two hundred years ago this July. Aside from the construction of the Lincoln Tunnel, the duel is the biggest thing that ever happened in Weehawken or nearby. The town is not large, and the tunnel's toll plaza and approaches take up a lot of it; sometimes as the bus climbs through Weehawken I wonder if the duel site might be close, or even under the wheels. History books say the duel was held "on the Weehawken dueling grounds," which sounds specific. When I called the Weehawken Public Library and asked the librarian if she knew where the site was, she immediately referred me to the town's expert on local history, Edward A. Fleckenstein.

Mr. Fleckenstein lives atop the Weehawken cliff, in a house with a view across the Hudson River and straight down Forty-second Street. He kindly agreed to see me, and met me at the door with his brother George. Both men are taller than average, hale, genial, and formal; though it was a Saturday morning, both had on jackets and ties. Edward is a semiretired attorney specializing in estates and corporate law, and George used to run the family meatpacking business. Edward is eighty-four and George is eighty-two. Both are bachelors and have lived in this house all their lives.

In a study lined with pictures of their ancestors, Edward and George sketched a time-lapse picture of Weehawken and surroundings. The midtown skyline opposite had only one notable skyscraper, the Paramount Building on Forty-third Street, when they were young boys. By the time the boys were teenagers, the Chrysler Building, the Empire State, and Rockefeller Center had all gone up, and midtown looked a lot like it does now. The Lincoln Tunnel came in in 1937; Edward, a boy of sixteen, was among the first to walk through it at the opening ceremony. Heading west from the tunnel, you could not go anyplace very directly, because that way was the swamp, which people called just "the swamp" and not the Meadowlands. Edward remembers looking across the swamp while on a family outing and predicting that one day a road would go straight across it. His words were prophetic; when he was just out of law school, construction started on Route 3. The road was finished across the Hackensack and Passaic Rivers by 1950, and by 1951 it was a busy highway with traffic jams.

Traffic had always been bad around here, Edward Fleckenstein pointed out. "Before the tunnel, there were long lines of wagons and cars, clear up to the top of the cliff, waiting to get on the ferry to the city," he said. "The tunnel was supposed to take care of that. In those days, we had an ambitious mayor, J. G. Meister, and he was a big booster for the tunnel. He said it would be such an honor for the town. One of the original ideas for the tunnel was for it to emerge on the other side of the next ridge, in Secaucus. And that probably would have been better, in hindsight, because of course it's more open over there and you wouldn't have the congestion of being confined in these hills. But Mayor Meister and other Weehawken supporters prevailed, and the tunnel came out in Weehawken. They said they would name it the Weehawken Midtown Tunnel, but, once there was the George Washington Bridge, naturally this had to be the Lincoln Tunnel."

Conversation soon turned to the town's other great event, the

Burr-Hamilton duel. Referring to photocopies of historical documents, Edward Fleckenstein said where he thought the dueling grounds were and why he thought so. His brother excused himself to go to church services. Edward said he would show me where the site was, and he put on his fedora and topcoat and we got in my car. First, we stopped at the Hamilton memorial, a bust on a column at the cliff's edge. Whether Hamilton fired at Burr or deliberately into the air is unclear; he missed, in any event, and Burr's shot hit him in the abdomen. Hamilton knew at once that the wound was mortal. He fell against a large rock; the rock is now next to the column, part of the memorial. Hamilton was rowed back across the river to a friend's house in Greenwich Village, where he said good-bye to his wife and children and died the next day.

The site of the dueling grounds — about a hundred feet south of the end of the cliff, by Mr. Fleckenstein's estimation — takes some effort to visualize. In the car, he directed me to a street under the elevated highway and then onto a cinder lane near the waterfront. This place used to be a bay, he said. A cliff, roughly parallel to the present cliff but not as high, enclosed the bay at one end. There was a gravel beach accessible only by water, and above the beach, at the base of the cliff, a ledge about fifty feet long. Duelers used to row over from the city, pull their boats up on the beach, and fight their duels on the ledge. Construction of a county road leveled the cliff and ledge in 1859, and afterward railroad builders put tracks through. The landfill that buried the bay disguised the spot further.

Mr. Fleckenstein did not want to walk around in the 11° cold and the wind, so after I took him home and thanked him a lot I came back. At least seventy duels were fought on this spot, he had told me. The combatants came here because dueling was illegal in New York. (New Jersey did not outlaw it until later in the 1800s.) Hamilton and Burr were not the only famous duelers. DeWitt Clinton, governor of New York and father of the Erie Canal, fought a John Swartwout here and wounded him in the left leg about five inches above the ankle on the fifth shot. Commodore Oliver Hazard Perry, the hero of the Battle of Lake Erie ("We have met the enemy, and they are ours"), dueled Captain John Heath, neither man injured; Perry's second in that duel was Commodore Stephen Decatur ("Our country, right or wrong"), who was himself later killed in a duel in Maryland. Before Burr dueled Hamilton, he fought John Barker Church, Hamilton's brother-in-law, on this ground, neither man injured; and a Burr supporter fought and killed Hamilton's nineteen-year-old son, Philip, three years before the Burr-Hamilton duel. In all, at least thirty-six men died on the Weehawken dueling grounds.

Now the place is a construction side lot for the Lincoln Tunnel. There's an office trailer, a heap of pipe lengths, a portable john, some road-building stone, a chain-link fence, weeds, little orange plastic flags warning of buried cable. The long-ago life-and-death dramas I'd been picturing could not fit here; enterprise and time had painted out the past.

Then I looked across the river. You would have sat in the boat with your second, your pistols in their case on his lap, while someone rowed. For the twenty minutes or half an hour the journey took, you would have wondered, or tried not to wonder, about the condition in which you might come back. The far shore would grow closer; New York would diminish behind. The great city, the river in between, and this shore of scary possibility haven't changed. For questions of honor that we would find trivial or hard to understand, the touchy white men who founded our country sometimes shot each other to death within a thousand feet or so of where the Lincoln Tunnel toll booths are now.

JIM HARRISON

# A Really Big Lunch

FROM *The New Yorker*

ON OUR FREQUENT American road trips, my friend Guy de la
Valdène has invariably said at lunch, "These French fries are filthy,"
but he always eats them anyway, and some of mine, too. Another
friend, the painter Russell Chatham, likes to remind me that we pi-
oneered the idea of ordering multiple entrées in restaurants back
in the seventies — the theory being that if you order several entrées you can then avoid the terrible disappointment of having ordered the wrong thing while others at the table have inevitably ordered the right thing. The results can't have been all that bad,
since both of us are still more or less alive, though neither of us
owns any spandex.

Is there an interior logic to overeating, or does gluttony, like sex,
wander around in a messy void, utterly resistant to our attempts to
make sense of it? Not very deep within us, the hungry heart howls,
"Supersize me." When I was a boy, in northern Michigan, feeding
my grandfather's pigs, I was amazed at their capacity. Before I was
caught in the act and chided by my elders, I had empirically determined that the appetite of pigs was limitless. As I dawdled in the
barnyard, the animals gazed at me as fondly as many of us do at
great chefs. Life is brutishly short and we wish to eat well, and for
this we must generally travel to large cities or, better yet, to France.

Never before have the American people had their noses so
deeply in one another's business. If I announce that I and eleven
other diners shared a thirty-seven-course lunch that likely cost as
much as a new Volvo station wagon, those of a critical nature will let
their minds run in tiny, aghast circles of condemnation. My re-

sponse to them is that none of us twelve disciples of gourmandise wanted a new Volvo. We wanted only lunch, and since lunch lasted approximately eleven hours, we saved money by not having to buy dinner. The defense rests.

Some would also think it excessive to travel all the way from Montana to Marc Meneau's L'Espérance, in Burgundy, for lunch, but I don't. Although there are signs of a culinary revolution in the United States, this much bandied renaissance is for people in cities such as New York, San Francisco, Seattle, and Chicago. When traveling across America over the past forty years, I've repeatedly sought extreme unction of a sort while in the midst of digestive death in the parking lots of restaurants. I've found it best, in these situations, to get some distance — to drive for a while, pull over, take a walk, fall to my knees, and pray for better food in the future.

I suspect that it's inappropriate to strand myself on a high horse when it comes to what people eat. We have proved ourselves inept fools on so many mortal fronts — from our utter disregard of the natural world to our notions of ethnic virtue to the hellish marriage of politics and war — that perhaps we should be allowed to pick at garbage like happy crows. When I was growing up in the Calvinist Midwest, the assumption that we eat to live, not live to eat, was part of the Gospels. (With the exception, of course, of holiday feasts. Certain women were famous for their pie-making abilities, while certain men, like my father, were admired for being able to barbecue two hundred chickens at once for a church picnic.) I recall that working in the fields for ten hours a day required an ample breakfast and three big sandwiches for lunch. At the time, I don't think I believed I was all that different from the other farm animals.

It's a long road from a childhood in rural Michigan to being the sort of man who gets invited to a thirty-seven course lunch. But, above all, a gourmand is one who is able to keep eating when no longer hungry, and a gourmand without a rich sense of the comic is a pathetic piggy, indeed. Once, at Taillevent, in Paris (a restaurant that is always referred to as a "temple of gastronomy"), I had the uncomfortable sense that I was in a funeral parlor. I heard no laughter except from my own table. And when I wanted a taste of Calvados as an entremets, the waiter actually told me that I'd have to be patient until after the cheese course, an hour distant. Luckily,

an intemperate French count who was at my table told the waiter to
bring my Calvados immediately or he would slap his face; at those
prices, you don't want to be schooled. Haute cuisine has rules for
those who love rules. Those rules have, for the most part, driven
me into the arms of bistros. If I were given the dreary six months to
live, I'd head at once to Lyons and make my way from bistro to bistro in a big stroller pushed by a vegetarian.

The thirty-seven-course lunch, which was held on November 17 of
2003, was based on recipes by the great cooks and food writers
of the past (among them Le Maréchal de Richelieu, Nicolas de
Bonnefons, Pierre de Lune, Massialot, La Varenne, Marin, Grimod
de La Reynière, Brillat-Savarin, Mercier, La Chapelle, Menon, and
Carême) and drawn from seventeen cookbooks published between
1654 and 1823. It was food with a precise and determinable history. My host for the lunch was Gérard Oberlé, a man of unques-
tionable genius, whom I had met a decade earlier at a wine-and-
book festival near Saumur, on the Loire. I don't recall seeing any
books at the three-day party, where I was a wine judge, along with
Alain Robbe-Grillet and Gérard Depardieu. (None of us was particularly startled when we were told that the wines had been "pre-
judged" and were there for decoration only.) Early one morning, I
discovered Oberlé eating a sturdy platter of charcuterie on the
patio of the château where we were staying. It took me a number of
years to uncover all the aspects of his character — as if I were peeling the laminae from a giant Bermuda onion (which Gérard somewhat physically resembles, but then so does the Buddha). Gérard is
a book collector and a dealer in illuminated manuscripts, a musi-
cologist with a weekly program on Radio France, a novelist and an
essayist, an "expert of experts" dealing with insurance fraud (assess-
ing the actual value of private libraries destroyed by fire), a coun-
tertenor who once sang Purcell's "Come Ye Sons of Art" while
woodcock hunting in Michigan's Upper Peninsula, a student of the
history of French food who has produced a couple of what he calls
"two-kilo" bibliographies on the subject, a wine and salami scholar,
a former officer in a society for the protection of the integrity of
*fromages de tête* (headcheese), a culinary eccentric, and a grand
cook. Once, in Cancale, on the Brittany coast, where we were eating the rare and enormous seventy-year-old oysters known as *pieds*

*de cheval* (horse's feet), he remarked, "These would be difficult to eat in a car."

Soon after I met Gérard, I visited his manor, in Burgundy, where he prepared a particularly interesting dish of ancient origin — a torte of fifty baby pigs' noses. "Really a simple dish," he said. As he explained it, you soak the pigs' noses overnight in clear water, then simmer them for about two hours in red wine, herbs, and garlic. Later, you add potatoes and bake the dish, with the upturned noses forming a delightful mosaic on the surface. Such dishes are usually only for the extremely curious or those with an agricultural background. I recall both of my grandmothers boiling pigs' heads with herbs and onions to make a headcheese, for which the especially toothsome cheek, tongue, and neck meat was extracted, covered with the cooking liquid, and gelatinized in a glass dish.

By the time I met Gérard, I had already been exposed to excesses of every sort, including those of the film industry, and I had known a number of big eaters, myself included. But I had never met a truly refined big eater. Not long afterward, Gérard threw a dinner with fifty courses. Why? Because it was his fiftieth birthday. Why else? When I first read the menu, it seemed incomprehensible to me, though there was an interior logic — the meal was designed after one described in Petronius' *Satyricon.*

This is not to say that Gérard concentrates on the arcane and the frivolous. In my dozen or so visits to his home, I've experienced many French standards, in versions better than any I'd had before. You know you are not in a restaurant when you enter Gérard's kitchen and notice a wooden bowl with a kilo of black truffles waiting to be added to your all-time favorite dish, *poulet demi-deuil,* or "chicken in half-mourning." The dead fowl has been honored by so many truffle slices, slid under its skin, that it appears to be wearing black (not to mention the large truffle stuffed in the bird's cavity, to comfort its inner chicken). When I said, "Gérard, you shouldn't have," he replied, "I'm a bachelor. I have no heirs."

Over the years, on my visits to France, Guy de la Valdène, Gérard, and I had discussed the possibilities for a "theme" meal, and we had read the menus of several that Gérard had already given. At a certain point, it began to seem entirely reasonable to plan a lunch that began with twenty-four courses and then urged itself upward. And no restaurant was more logical a location than L'Espérance, in

the village of Saint-Père-sous-Vézelay, a scant hour and a half from
Gérard's home, in the Morvan. Of all the great chefs in France,
Marc Meneau, a very tall man who looms above his employees as
did de Gaulle above his citizenry, is one of the least aggressive,
apparently devoid of any interest in becoming a public figure. His
restaurant, long a required destination for gourmands, is pure
country French, elegantly set in a grand garden, with nothing
whatsoever in its decor to intimidate the customer. (And it would
soon regain the third Michelin star that it had lost in 1999.)

Gérard had known Meneau for years, and with Guy and me
safely at home in the United States, he proceeded to plan the feast,
using his improbable library as the source. Having once sat in on
an after-lunch confab on the *"vrai ancien coq au vin"* (reduce seven
liters of Merlot down to one, whisk in the rooster blood, etc.), I can
only imagine the countless hours of discussion that ensued between Gérard and Meneau.

When the morning of the event finally arrived, I wasn't particularly
hungry. This didn't alarm me — many professional athletes before
a big game feel that they would prefer to spend the day with their
Tinkertoys or in the arms of Lucrezia Borgia. I had already been off
my diet for two weeks, touring the French countryside with Guy
and Peter Lewis, a Seattle restaurateur. Everywhere we went, we ate
the best food available, with the excuse, not totally accurate, that
we'd worked hard, saved our pennies, and had it coming. (The
novelist Tom McGuane once noted that in the course of thirty-five
years of correspondence between us, I had lost a total of eighteen
hundred pounds — so I was really "getting down there.")

The day dawned cool and misty. There was a certain anxiety
in the air at the manor, with Gérard watching to make sure that
I didn't partake of the breakfast that I thought I needed. All I
wanted was a simple slab of the game pâté from the evening before,
but when I tried to sneak into the kitchen from the outside pantry
door, he was there in front of the fridge like a three-hundred-
pound albino cat.

I've always felt that there is no lovelier village in France than
Vézelay and no lovelier religious building than its cathedral on the
hill, the Madeleine of Vézelay. I'm not Catholic, but I've lit candles
in that church in prayer for troubled friends, and it has always

worked. At least, they're all still showing vital signs. But I had no
time to run up the steep hill and light a candle for my own diges-
tion. The twelve of us sat down at noon. To my left was the vint-
ner Didier Dagueneau, whose exquisite Pouilly-Fumé we had been
drinking since our initial Krug Grande Cuvée. The first time I met
Didier, I was startled by his appearance, which is that of a Minneso-
tan pulp cutter. During the winter downtime at his vineyard, in
Pouilly, he travels far north, toward the Arctic, to run the dozens of
sled dogs that he owns and whose racket irritates his neighbors. To
my right was Gilles Brézol, Gérard's business partner and a man of
sophisticated intelligence, who taught French for a year in Alabama and Nevada during the civil rights upheaval. I've had dozens
of meals with Gilles, who eats as much as I do but remains irri-
tatingly slender. In fact, in this group of mostly book collectors
and journalists sworn to secrecy, no one was technically obese. Although the lunch had originally been planned for eleven, a twelfth
guest, a beautifully tailored, elderly French gentleman, unknown
to all of us, had been invited by Meneau, in accordance with the superstitious notion that any large group should include a stranger,
who might very well be an angel in disguise.

Meneau came out of the kitchen; his only advice was *"Courage"*
(or "coo-rahj," as my phrase book likes to say). We began with a girl-
ish delicacy — a clear soup made from poultry, diced vegetables,
and crayfish — followed by tartines of foie gras, truffles, and lard.
The next soup was a velvety cream of squab with cucumbers, served
with cock-crest fritters. Then there was a soothing crayfish bisque,
and I began to wonder how long we would be pursuing the soup
motif.

But, oddly, I felt squeamish about the first of the hors d'oeuvres
— oysters and cream of Camembert on toast, which proved to be
the only course I couldn't eat. (We all have our own food pho-
bias, and a mixture of pungent cheese and oysters makes my little
tummy recoil.) Next came a chilled jellied loaf of poultry on sorrel
cream, followed by a private joke on me — fresh Baltic herring
with mayonnaise. (According to my late mother, I was wild about
herring from the age of two. Her family was Swedish, and the fish
was a staple.) I loved the tart of calf's brains with shelled peas but
was not terribly fond of the omelet with sea urchin, a dish that
Louis XV liked to prepare for himself — though it was certainly

better than the cottage cheese with ketchup that Richard Nixon favored as a snack. (There is a well-founded rumor that George W.
Bush nibbles on bologna with marshmallow bonbons.) A filet of
sole with champagne sauce accompanied by monkfish livers was
wonderful, as was the roasted pike spiked with parsley. I did pause
to consider whether all of these hors d'oeuvres might dampen my
appetite for the main courses. The wine steward noted my unrest,
and a quick goblet of Montrachet tickled my enthusiasm upward.
There were only two pure-blood Americans at the table, Peter
Lewis and I, and we had agreed not to shame our own holy empire.

We headed into the "second service" without an appropriate
break — say, a five-mile march through the mountains and an
eight-hour nap. The courses, naturally, became more substantial.
First came an oven-glazed brill served with fennel cream, ancho-
vies, and roasted currants, then a stew of suckling pig that had been
slow-cooked in a red-wine sauce thickened with its own blood, onions, and bacon. I leaped forward from this into a warm terrine of
hare with preserved plums, and a poached eel with chicken wing
tips and testicles in a pool of tarragon butter. But I only picked at
my glazed partridge breasts, which were followed by a savory of
eggs poached in Chimay ale, and then a mille-feuille of puff pastry
sandwiched with sardines and leeks.

Now it was halftime, though there were no prancing cheerleaders.
The menu advised us to "languish" in the salon and nibble on ravi-
oli with carrots and cumin and thick slices of "Noirs eggs of puff
pastry with squab hearts." Instead, I went outside, where the grass
was wet and my feet seemed to sink in even farther than usual. In
the walled herb garden, I began to reflect that this kind of eating
might not be a wise choice in the late autumn of my life. Perhaps I
should fax the menu to my cardiologist in the States before pro-
ceeding? I soon realized that this was one of the ten million insincere impulses I've had in my life. I began to walk faster for a dozen
yards and almost jumped a creek but then thought better of it.

The "third service" loaded even bigger guns, or so it seemed,
with its concentration on denser, heavier specialties that tried the
patience of my long-fled appetite. From Massialot, we were offered
a "light" stew of veal breast in a purée of ham and oysters in a
pastry-covered casserole, and a not-so-light gratin of beef cheeks.

La Varenne's gray squab was boned; stuffed with sweetbreads, squab livers, and scallions; and spit-roasted. It was the Prince des Dombes who said, "Nothing arouses me but taste" (*"Je ne me pique que de goût"*). He would have been a disappointing match for a vigorous girl. You can imagine her hanging a rope ladder from her tower bedroom for knights-errant — or, better yet, woodchoppers and stable hands — to climb, while the Prince aroused himself in the kitchen. From his files, we had wild duck with black olives and orange zest, a *buisson* (bush) of crayfish with little slabs of grilled goose liver, a terrine of the tips of calves' ears, hare cooked in port wine inside a calf's bladder, crispy breaded asparagus, a sponge cake with fruit preserves, and cucumbers stewed in wine.

It was consoling to begin winding down with a swirl of turnips in sweetened wine, radishes preserved in vinegar, a warm salad with almonds, cream of grilled pistachios, meringues, macaroons, and chocolate cigarettes. These were simple warm-ups to the medley of desserts served to us in the salon: a rosette of almond milk with almonds; a soft cheese of fresh cream with quince jelly; rice whipped with sweetened egg whites and lemon peel; a grand ring-shaped cake, a savarin, flamed with Old Havana rum and served with preserved pineapple; little molds of various ice creams; and a "towering structure of every fruit imaginable in every manner imaginable."

Sad to say, my notes from the meal are blurred and smeared by the cooked exudates of flora and fauna and the wines that rained down on us as if from the world's best garden sprinkler. Reading through the veil of grease, I see that my favorites among the wines served were Chablis Les Clos, Montrachet 1989, Volnay-Champans 1969, Château Latour 1989, and Côte Rôtie. Of course, any fool would love these great wines as he felt his wallet vaporize.

There. Time to do dishes. As Diderot said of a lunch at the fabulously wealthy Baron of Holbach's home, "After lunch, one takes a little walk, or one digests, if it's even possible." Night had long since fallen, and I reflected that lunch had taken the same amount of time as a Varig flight from New York to São Paulo.

In the salon, my fellow diners were yawning rather than gasping or sobbing. Was this another example of the banality of evil: a grievous sin committed — in this case, gluttony — and no one squirm-

ing with guilt? I have noticed that Frenchmen are far less suscepti-
ble to heart disease, in part because they don't seem to experience
the stress of self-doubt or regret. My mother, a Swedish Lutheran,
liked to ask her five children, "What have you accomplished today?" If I'd told her, "I have eaten thirty-seven courses and drunk
thirteen wines," I would have been cast into outer darkness. But
then this was the Iron Mom, who also said, with a tiny smile, in reference to my life's work, "You've made quite a living out of your
fibs."

At midnight, while sipping a paltry brandy from the nineteen-
twenties and smoking a Havana Churchill, I reflected that this was
not the time to ponder eternal values. I was sitting next to Gérard,
who was cherubically discussing the historical subtleties of certain
courses. In a way, we were forensic anthropologists, doing arduous
historical field work. How could we possibly understand the present without knowing what certain of our ancestors had consumed?
Marc Meneau, his lovely wife, Françoise, and thirty-nine members
of his staff had led us on a somber and all-consuming journey into
the past.

At dawn or a few hours thereafter, I felt relieved, on stepping out
of the bathtub, that I hadn't fallen on a hard surface and broken
open like an overly mature muskmelon.

No question looms larger on a daily basis for many of us than
"What's for lunch?" and, when that has been resolved, "What's for
dinner?" There have been mutterings that the whole food thing
has gone too far in America, but I think not. Good food is a benign
weapon against the sodden way we live.

By the time I reached Paris the next afternoon and took a three-
hour stroll, I was feeling a little peckish. I'd heard that certain
quarrels had already arisen over our lunch, and I felt lucky that my
capacity for the French language was limited to understanding
only the gist of conversations — sort of the way the average American comprehends our government. On the phone, the natives
were restless to the point of "scandal," and from the tornado of
rumors (everyone knows that men, not women, are the masters
of gossip) I learned that many had found both the food and the
service disappointing, the lack of "theater" sad. (As for myself, I
couldn't make a judgment. I once helped to cook a whole steer and

a barrel of corn for a picnic in Michigan and have eaten many ten-course dinners, but our French lunch had left those occasions in the numbered dust.) The most interesting rumor I heard was that the tab for the lunch had been picked up by a Louisiana billionaire, who couldn't attend because a pelican had been sucked into an engine of his Gulfstream. This detail was so extraordinary that it seemed likely to be true.

That last evening in Paris, before my flight and the tonic Chicago-style hot dog that awaited me at O'Hare, Peter and I dined at Thoumieux, my old standby restaurant, near the Invalides. We had a simple Gigondas, and I ordered two vegetable courses, then relented at the last moment and added a duck confit. Long flights are physically exhausting, and good nutrition lays the foundation of life. On Air France, I was sunk in profound thought, or so I felt at the time. Like sex, bathing, sleeping, and drinking, the effects of food don't last. The patterns are repeated but finite. Life is a near-death experience, and our devious minds will do anything to make it interesting.

WILLIAM LEAST HEAT-MOON

# By the Big Sea Water

FROM *Gourmet*

IN THE SUMMER OF 1949, just before my tenth birthday, I was serving as navigator aboard my father's tub of an automobile, a large black machine actually more like a hearse — a fit simile given that a year later he would nearly die in it when a drunken corn farmer drove into him on a Missouri highway. But in the July before the crash, we were passing through the eastern edge of the dark North Woods of upper Minnesota. With a topographical abruptness hardly typical of the state, the road seemed to fall away as it rolled down a cliff; ahead was a distant horizon, not of dark trees but of a pencil line linking two radiant shades of blue. It was impossible to discern which reflected the other. There I had my first glimpse ever of a body of water showing no opposite shore.

With a road map before me, I knew it had to be Lake Superior, but how could a lake so far inland have a shore beyond the horizon? I was about to learn the Ojibwa name for it: Kitchigami, "big sea water," or, in Longfellow's less correct if more famous version, Gitche Gumee. That lake was the largest body of entirely fresh water in the world, big enough for seventeenth-century *voyageurs* to consider it a sea.

I was also about to learn that the Empire State Building would all but disappear in the deepest part of Lake Superior. Here was a realm more awesome than the somber forest lying behind, a watery world a boy from Kansas City could fill with creatures escaped from his imagination. The blueness, its depths, the wind having at it, all bespoke remoteness and cold even in midsummer. I couldn't then have articulated it, but I felt I was on the brink of a wilderness, an intimidating mysteriousness.

Almost as soon as we turned southward from Minnesota Route 1 onto U.S. 61, the lake showed more of its strangeness. Every few miles small hand-painted signs cropped up, each advertising in one wording or the other: AHEAD: SMOKED CISCOES.

What a cisco was — smoked or unsmoked — I had no idea. My father, who had just taught me how to catch a northern pike and who seemed to know northern waters, had no answer either. A cisco must be a creature from the deep, some rarity, maybe a freak of nature like those a traveler back then might find on exhibition along rural highways: jackalopes, two-headed alligators, mermen.

One of the few things that could move my father to stop and get out from behind a steering wheel was the scent of barbecue smoke across a road. In Kansas City, such a whiff usually led us to brisket of beef or so-called burnt ends laid over a slice of white bread. But along the bouldery shore of Superior a little north of Two Harbors, Minnesota, the occasional wooden cafés hanging along its high edge and showing SMOKED CISCO signs didn't look like the smokeries we knew. Here was promise of unknown fare, the kind that can make the labor of travel worth its undertaking.

We pulled into a rickety café held up by wooden posts seemingly insufficient in number and diameter to keep the place above the lake then banging ominously far beneath. The buckled floor was manifest warning that one diner too many could send the entire enterprise into the water. My father, a cautious man who sometimes wore a belt with his suspenders, stepped as gingerly as a heavy person can toward a table by a bank of windows giving onto the lake and a fog coming toward us. Pasted to the walls here and about were menus. Under one heading, FROM THE LAKE, between the herring and trout, the café offered several WHEN AVAILABLES, among them smoked cisco. So, we nodded, a cisco was not a beast but a fish. My hope for an alien tale to take home vanished.

I knew from my father's example that a jolly equatorial amplitude, a fulsome girth, does not guarantee an adventuresome eater; yet he could be bold — provided there were certain assurances like "Anything smoked probably won't kill you — unless it's turned green." He ordered up two plates of smoked ciscoes to demonstrate a belief to which he usually gave more utterance than practice: From a mere vacation, one goes home older, but from true travel, one returns changed by challenge. To him, an exotic dish could provide the happiest of challenges. I was about to learn something else: Of the highest order among travelers are those moments when a place and a comestible indelibly link to write themselves deeply into one's memory. That day, Lake Superior wrote itself into me.

The remembrance took me again to the North Shore of Superior in Minnesota early last summer. I'd heard the little cisco was not faring well in the Great Lakes and that to find a plate of them was increasingly difficult. As I made my way toward the Canadian border along U.S. 61, the North Shore Highway, a fine 150 miles opened only in 1924, I wasn't expecting AHEAD: SMOKED CIS-COES signs so much as impetrating the lake deities to offer up a couple — just two or three for old time's sake. The miles came and went, the roadside becoming less and less developed as I neared the last county before the Canadian border. I wasn't far from leaving the country, and I'd turned up not a single smoked fish of any sort. The coastal road opened frequently to splendid lacustrine scenery, and the hues of Superior, modulated by sky and proximity to shore, might have been decocted from gemstones: here flowing sapphire, there aquamarine; at night there would be black opal; when I stopped to walk the shore and looked into a small catchment, I saw liquid chalcedony vibrating from the thump of the surf.

Superior, like its region, is an expression of water and weather working over rocks — hard rocks: granite, basalt, gabbro. The coast is a concatenation of steep and high headlands dropping to beaches strewn with stone from boulders to pebbles, the smaller pieces often indeed gemlike under the wash of the waves. The gleaming rocks are spheres and ovoids, globets and orbs, colorful rotundities turned to cabochons a beach walker can almost string into a necklace right there. One also finds irregularities in sometimes startling shapes. In fact, at the decrepit café where I first tasted smoked cisco, behind a glass counter under the cash register, lay a small beach stone shaped by water and weather into an old man's head that, had it been excavated from a cave or midden, a seasoned archaeologist would swear was craft from a human hand.

The Superior of our time was probably created by incomprehensibly massive lobes of glacier ice moving southward and gouging out stone softer than the adamantine igneous rock around portions of its margin. The lake today is the outcome of fire and ice, a place relinquishing its fierce origins but slowly. Once, its waterline was almost twice its present height above sea level, a fact one can readily see in downtown Duluth in the steep, stairsteplike former shores of the ancient Superior.

The earliest *voyageurs* called it Lac Supérieur, a name having nothing to do with altitude, size, depth, excellence, or (these days) comparative cleanliness. Rather, Superior refers to its position "above" its four sisters: Its uppermost coast is five hundred miles north of the southern shore of Lake Erie, nearly enough longitudinal space to hold France from the Mediterranean to the Channel. For many residents of the Superior shore, its finest aspect is a coast free from cities — except for Duluth (population 86,000) — which means that fishermen working beyond breakwaters still drink straight from the lake, a detail I hoped would mean that somewhere yet swam a cisco.

As the miles rolled under me with no sign of the fish—smoked, grilled, steamed, boiled, fried, chowdered, fresh — I at last fetched up in Grand Marais. Not far across the city line, in a collection of brightly painted buildings rambling down to a small harbor, I made out a fading sign: FRESH LAKE SUPERIOR FISH. When I pulled over, in front of me was a much newer one:

DOCKSIDE FISH MARKET
FRESH & SMOKED

Painted on the window of the market door were two golden herrings, smiling, and beyond them, inside, behind the counter, lay rows of the actual fish accompanied by other species, some not native to Superior. "Any ciscoes?" I asked. "No," the clerk said with a kindness elicited, I think, by my crestfallen expression.

At the market, the only commercial smokehouse on the upper North Shore, I bought two herrings and walked toward the dock, stopping on the way to look into a fish shed where Harley Toftey, bright in orange waders, was cutting his morning catch, eighty pounds of herring, each about twelve inches long and weighing about a pound. He deftly and nearly bloodlessly opened the bellies of the sleek and fulgent fish, removed innards while leaving head and tail, and tossed each into a bin ready for twelve hours in his small smokehouse, the next-to-last stop on a voyage from 150 feet down in frigid Superior to a warm dinner plate.

I said I was looking for ciscoes, and he said, "I am too." He shook his head. "They've just kind of disappeared. I take out herring, Menominee, whitefish, and trout — but ciscoes, no."

Next door was Tom Eckel's cutting house, where he, too, in orange waders was preparing his morning harvest, this one primarily lake trout. He grew up on a Superior island, something harder to do these days, and he was old enough to remember the area before World War II. His Gitche Gumee pedigree was pure. I rephrased my question to reflect the sad news I was finding: "Did you ever catch a cisco?" He looked at me as if I'd asked, "Did you ever catch a cold?"

With North Country politeness he said, "A long time ago," and returned to a big trout under his knife. Then, "I don't think you'll ever see the ciscoes come back — not in this area. Too many predators." When he put the fillet knife down a moment later, he said, "But then I didn't think we'd ever see the lake trout back like this." Halfway through the next filleting (in Minnesota, one learns conversational patience), he mused, "The lampreys are under control, I'd say, and I've heard 90 percent of our fish right here are natives again."

Everyone's commentary about ciscoes was historical, about what had been. Worse, in less than an hour, I'd just talked to two thirds of the commercial fishermen remaining in Grand Marais. As I left the cutting house, I asked about a stretched-out black sock tacked to the wall. "Found it in the belly of an eight-pound trout," said Eckel. When I reached the door, he added, "Don't know what happened to the rest of the guy."

I sat on the dock in an easy lake breeze and opened my smoked-herring lunch. Two details gave me hope yet for finding a cisco: Eckel had said he preferred to go after larger species and mentioned a couple of fish stands along the southern end of the North Shore, down near Knife River, places closer to the café where I'd first tasted cisco.

After two days of wandering around Grand Marais and exploring the coast all the way to the border at the Pigeon River, I headed southwest, my hopes further raised by a growing awareness that part of the difficulty in my search might be linguistic: One person's cisco might just be another's chub (a name loosely applied) or blind robin or (even more loosely) whitefish. Where was there a commercial fisherman who uses genus-species nomenclature to describe what comes up in the net?

I was looking for *Coregonus artedi*. I liked the Latin version because of a story attached to it: The latter term refers to a Swede, Petrus Artedi, father of ichthyology. After Artedi fell into a canal and drowned, Carl Linnaeus, coincidentally the creator of binomial taxonomy, wrote of his colleague, "Thus did the most distinguished of ichthyologists perish in the waters, having devoted his life to the discovery of their inhabitants."

I was about to learn that a cisco is also known as a lake herring, even though it isn't a true herring but rather a member of the salmon family, along with lake trout and various so-named whitefish of the Great Lakes.

Overharvesting, pollution, and the spread of foreigners like lampreys and alewives have all affected smaller fish such as ciscoes and the larger species that depend on them, so that certain fish today have declined precipitously from their populations in, say, 1949. I also began suspecting that my quest would have gone better had I arrived in the autumn, when ciscoes rise from the depths and cluster to spawn in warmer shallows. Like a fellow whose inamorata slyly eludes him, I was drawn on by the challenge of the pursuit.

Late one afternoon, near Knife River, Minnesota, I came upon a beat-up tavern with a worn sign promising smoked fish. The place was closed — it looked like for days — but I managed to raise Betty Kendall, the proprietor, who lived next door in a trailer. The airless and dark bar, redolent of years of cigarettes and spilled beer, was abundant with reds — carpets, chairs, curtains — and hanging baseball caps and dozens of representations of Betty Boop, a character from an era Betty Kendall shared. Also a sign: TO HELL WITH THE DOG — BEWARE THE OWNER. By the look of things, I thought I should heed it. Diffidently, I asked my question, "Any ciscoes?"

She said, "How many do you want?" Half expecting a laugh of derision to chase me out, I said, "Three or four — enough to make a dinner." She disappeared into what I took for a closet and returned with several sheets of newspaper cradling golden ciscoes. She wrapped them. I asked were they fresh. "These were smoked yesterday at four o'clock. They come from over on the Wisconsin side." I recited a nutshell rendition of my quest, and she said about her late husband, Smokey, "He used to eat three or four while he was smoking them. You would have thought they were popcorn. Now, only a couple of fishermen in Knife River still go after them."

When I left, my wrapped ciscoes snug under my arm as if rare first editions of books I'd long sought, I noticed across the road another fish stand, this one shut down; but only a little farther on was yet another. I was in a hotbed of smokeries. Russ Kendall, brother of Smokey, had built his place as a proper market, small but with appropriate glass-fronted cases, refrigeration, and a happy spread of smoked fish. He knew the cisco story through the whole of the twentieth century, from abundance, when a cisco stand popped up about every fifteen miles, to the near scarcity I'd been encountering. A local Indian had shown Kendall's father how to build a smokehouse. He said, "People don't fish them so much now because ciscoes are the most trouble and least money, but I'll tell you this: They're good enough that, years ago, when this place was just a roadside stand and our catch was out in the open air before government regulations, a cow wandered up one morning and ate a couple ciscoes right off the table. Later the owner complained his milk tasted fishy."

That evening I unwrapped packages from three different vendors and began a celebration of a memory, a fulfillment of what Lake Superior had written in me some half century earlier. On the table lay slender, streamlined creatures, fish of classic lines, their round eyes blanched from the oven. I cut along the back and pulled free the scaled skin once nearly luminescent, now turned golden by smoke. Flesh, the color of parchment, lifted easily from insubstantial bones almost invisible. The ciscoes — lake herrings — were so delicate I wondered how they could survive in the dark and cold, eat-and-be-eaten deeps in which they spent most of their lives. They were tender and moist — "oily," people say on the North Shore — and reportedly rich in salutary omega-3 fatty acids. Their sweet delectability made finishing one almost a regret; even having a dozen others iced down, enough for several more lunches and dinners, didn't relieve my sense of impending cisco deprivation. But, beyond that, in mind was a wobbly café, a smiling father freed from a steering wheel, a smudgy window opening to a lake reaching out till it disappeared in distant fog. I felt I'd followed a small, silvery fish into a long corridor back toward 1949.

PETER HESSLER

# Kindergarten

FROM *The New Yorker*

THE NIGHT BEFORE his first day of kindergarten, Wei Jia refused to talk about it. He was five years old, and he had spent the summer playing in Sancha, wearing nothing but a dirty tank top and a pair of underpants. Sancha is a small village in the mountains north of Beijing, and, along with a Chinese-American friend named Mimi Kuo, I rent a weekend house there from Wei Jia's relatives. The village is home to around a 150 peasants, who make their living primarily from orchards. That Sunday evening, while we were eating dinner, I asked Wei Jia if he was excited about going to school the next day. He ignored the question.

Earlier in the day, Mimi and I had made the two-hour drive from Beijing. It was the first week of September, and the walnuts had come into season; peasants carried long sticks that they used to knock the nuts onto the ground. Along the road we saw dozens of men, some on bicycles, their sticks poised as if for a joust. We also passed a topless elderly woman. Her silver hair was well groomed, and she walked at a determined pace. I pulled over to the side of the road.

"Leave me alone!" the woman shouted when Mimi stepped out of the car. "There's nothing wrong!" Tears shined on her cheeks; she clutched her shirt in one hand. When the woman stormed past, we could see fresh bruises across her back.

We drove a bit farther and tried again. She began screaming the moment Mimi opened the door. "I'm not going back there!" the woman shouted. "I'm not going back!" She veered out into the road, causing an oncoming car to slow down. Perhaps in the next village there would be somebody who knew her and would help. It was only two miles; surely she would make it that far. This kind of thing happens in the countryside, and sometimes an outsider's attempt to help only does more harm. *"Mei banfa"* the Chinese say — nothing can be done.

At seven o'clock the following morning, we left for school. Wei Jia wore khaki trousers and a red T-shirt. I had given him a new Mickey Mouse backpack, and his mother had put a pencil box in one of the pockets. Inside the box was a single pencil. The pencil was newly sharpened; the trousers still had a crease. It was the first time I had ever seen Wei Jia in clean clothes.

I'd known the boy's family since 2001, when Mimi and I began spending time in Sancha. I went to the village because it was quiet — there were no restaurants, no shops, no bus service. When I sat at my desk to write, I usually heard only the sounds of rural life: the bray of a mule, the wind in the walnut trees. Three or four times a week, a flatbed truck rumbled up the hill to sell basic groceries. Twice a day, in the morning and just before sunset, the government propaganda speakers on the telephone poles screeched to life. Village announcements, national news, Communist Party slogans — all of it echoed off the valley's high rock walls. But rarely in Sancha did I hear the sound of children playing. The local elementary school closed years ago because young families tended to move away; all across China, peasants have been leaving rural areas for the economic opportunity of the cities. The few families that remained in Sancha were small, because of the government's planned-birth policies, and the children attended schools in the more heavily populated villages down in the valley, ten miles away, where they either boarded or lived with relatives.

That year, Wei Jia was the only kindergartner from Sancha. He was going to live with his grandparents in Xingying, a village with an elementary school. On the morning of his first day, Mimi drove the car and the boy sat on my lap, in the front seat. Wei Ziqi, his father, and Cao Chunmei, his mother, rode in the back. Between them sat Wei Ziqi's older brother — the Idiot.

Once, I asked Cao Chunmei what the Idiot's real name was, but she didn't know. Everybody simply called him the *shazi*, which means "idiot." He was in his forties. Most villages in China seem to have a *shazi* or two from that generation, because in the past the peasant diet often lacked iodine. A pregnant woman who does not consume enough iodine runs the risk of bearing a mentally handicapped child. Nowadays, the widespread distribution of iodized salt has dramatically reduced such birth defects in rural China.

Generally, the Idiot seemed as happy as anybody in Sancha. He ate well, and he spent his days on the Weis's front porch, high on the mountain. From the porch, one could see for miles: the tile-roofed village, the winding road, the ruined traces of the Great Wall atop the mountain peaks. These were the boundaries of the Idiot's world. He couldn't do much work in the fields, and he couldn't talk. Whenever he wanted to say something, he contorted his face with such passion that it seemed as if the power of speech had fled precisely at that moment and he was just beginning to grapple with its loss. But in fact he had never spoken. The villagers ignored his attempts to communicate.

This was the first time I had seen the Idiot leave Sancha, and I asked Wei Ziqi why he was coming with us. "We have a little problem to take care of at the government office," he said.

Wei Jia leaned forward with both hands on the dashboard as we drove out of the village. He rarely got to ride in an automobile, and the experience for him was anything but passive. At every turn, I felt him edging toward the windshield, trying to see what was around the bend. He lurched forward whenever we reached the crest of a hill. I have never seen a child's car seat in China, and I was keenly aware of the fact that I should put Wei Jia in the back; but it would have broken his heart. And so I held him tightly.

We came down from the mountains, past the freshly cut stalks of wheat and corn in the valley. The men with sticks were going at the walnuts; husks crunched beneath our tires. Children walked along the road. "See, they have backpacks, too," Cao Chunmei said. "They're going to school just like you." Wei Jia's arms were stiff against the dash.

As we approached Bohai Township, Wei Ziqi asked Mimi to stop at the government office. Then he explained why the Idiot had come along.

"The government is supposed to pay a monthly fee to help us take care of him," he said. "That's the law. I've asked the Party Secretary in Sancha about it, but she hasn't helped. So the only thing to do is to come here ourselves. I'll ask them to pay the fee now, and if they don't, then I'll leave the Idiot until they're willing to pay it. It's their responsibility."

"You're going to leave him at the government office?" Mimi asked.

"Yes," Wei Ziqi said. "It's the only way to get their attention."

Mimi asked how much the monthly fee should be.

"Fifty yuan at the very least," Wei Ziqi said. It was the equivalent of about six dollars.

We parked outside the government compound. In front, there was a sculpture consisting of a shiny steel ball and an enormous twisted rod. Many of the local townships had recently erected sculptures in a similar style, accompanied by slogans intended to inspire images of modernity and prosperity. The Bohai Township slogan was "The Star of the Century." The sculpture was hideous. Wei Ziqi walked through the gate, followed by his brother. The Idiot's face had been blank all morning.

Wei Jia kept his hands on the dash. Five minutes later, his father returned. He was alone. We kept driving.

Wei Jia was the smallest five-year-old I have ever known. His mother often worried about his health; he was a finicky eater, and he weighed only thirty pounds. Four-year-olds towered over him; a child of three was often nearly as big. Wei Jia's mind was sharp, but he had a speech impediment, and even his parents had difficulty understanding him. Yet he had a wiry strength, and his sense of balance was remarkable. For the last year, he had been allowed to roam free in the village, and he moved easily along the mountain paths above his home. It was impossible to wear him out. He almost never cried. His capacity for roughhousing was infinite: It was as if the toughness and dexterity of a nine-year-old had been squeezed into a three-year-old's body. Over time, he came to call me Mogui Shushu (Uncle Monster), a play on the traditional term of respect used by Chinese children for adults. I was the first foreigner he had ever met.

Wei Jia's face was a perfect oval. His hair was cropped short, and his eyes glowed with mischief. But his parents could set him straight at a moment's notice. They avoided praising him — like traditional Chinese parents, they had a deep fear of flattery. Partly it was modesty, but there was also the superstition that pride would attract misfortune.

Occasionally, if I wanted to annoy Mimi with my Western ways, I would relentlessly praise the boy to Cao Chunmei: "Wei Jia is so good-looking."

"He's ugly," his mother would say immediately.

"He's so smart."

"He's stupid. Not a bit smart."

"What a nice child."

"Cut it out," Mimi said, in English.

"He's a bad boy," the mother said.

The only praise that I ever heard the parents give Wei Jia was a single adjective: *laoshi*. The dictionary defines it as "honest," but the term is difficult to translate. It also means obedient, as well as having a certain sense of propriety that is characteristic of people in the countryside. "Wei Jia is *laoshi*," his parents would say, and that was the closest they came to pride.

We parked by the back gate of the Xingying Elementary School. A teacher greeted us and led us inside. Wei Jia's face was blank. He walked into the classroom, stopped dead, and announced, loudly, "This place is no good!"

His parents tried to grab him, but he squirmed free and ran out the door. He was crying now, rushing back through the gate to the car. "I'm going home!" he said. "I don't want to be here!"

His mother followed him. The other children looked up and then lost interest. The classroom was dirty, and there was a hole in the ceiling. The blackboard was chipped and scarred. Twenty children sat at their desks; each of them played with a pile of Lego-like blocks. There were only three girls. Bohai isn't strictly a one-child township — like many parts of China that are mountainous and less populated, this area allows peasants in some villages to have a second child if the first is a girl. But it's not unusual in China for people to bribe doctors for ultrasound information, which is restricted by law. Locals told me that the majority of babies born in Xingying are boys.

Outside, Wei Jia stood in the dust beside the car, crying. He struggled against anybody who tried to lead him back into the school. Usually, Wei Ziqi is strict with his son, but he seemed to sympathize with this fear, and now he tried to reason with him. "Everybody goes to school," Wei Ziqi said patiently. "I did, and so did your mother. Aunt Mimi went to school, and so did Uncle Monster."

The schoolyard's loudspeakers crackled, and music came on for the flag raising. The older children, wearing the red kerchiefs of the Young Pioneers, marched in place while the national anthem played. Wei Jia's face was creased with panic. Until now, he had never seen more than a handful of children together at once.

It took nearly forty-five minutes to calm him down. His father carried him into the classroom; his mother sat him down behind a desk. After ten minutes, he made another move for the door, but this time they caught him. He cried again, another hard burst, and then he calmed down. Resignation furrowed his forehead.

We left as quietly as we could. I asked Wei Ziqi where the bathroom was, and he told me just to use the schoolyard fence on the way out. I could hear the children's voices — talking, laughing, chanting lessons — while I pissed in the weeds. We had been at the school for almost an hour. The car seemed empty on the way home.

That day, the Idiot escaped twice from the government office. The first time, the cadres caught him just outside the gate. The second time, he made it into Bohai Township. It took a while for them to find him.

The officials telephoned Wei Ziqi and told him to pick up his brother; Wei Ziqi requested the subsidy. Neither side would budge, and finally, late in the afternoon, the cadres put the Idiot in a car and drove into the mountains. They dropped him off two miles outside Sancha. It was a steep climb, and the Idiot was not accustomed to such distances; he was fortunate to find his way back.

I heard all of this later, from Wei Ziqi, who was more or less satisfied with the exchange. The county government — a higher level than the township — had agreed to review the issue of the subsidy.

The next time I visited Sancha, the Idiot greeted me with an enormous grin and pointed at my parked automobile. He kept grunting and gesturing. I realized that he was telling the story of our trip into the valley. "I know," I said. "I remember." I wanted to tell him that I hadn't understood that situation until it was too late — *mei banfa*. But there was no way to communicate my regret, and the Idiot continued his gestures. He seemed thrilled to see me again.

During the National Day school holiday, Wei Jia returned home with a series of purple bruises across his legs and back. It was the first week of October, and the corn had come into season; the Weis had piled their harvested crop on the porch. Wei Jia spent an afternoon playing on it. Afterward, his parents noticed that the bruises had darkened. They decided that the boy should see a doctor.

Mimi and I had come to Sancha for the holiday, and I offered to drive Wei Jia and his father down to Huairou, the nearest city. From the mountains, Huairou is roughly halfway to Beijing, and in recent years it has grown from a small town into a satellite city of the capital. At the hospital, a nurse performed a blood test and told us that the boy's *xuexiaoban* count was low. I was unfamiliar with the term, and I didn't have my dictionary.

"His count is only 17,000," the nurse said. "It should be more than a 150,000." She recommended that we immediately go to the Children's Hospital in Beijing for further tests.

Wei Jia had been born at a hospital in the capital, but this was his first time back. He was quiet during the drive to Beijing, as if sensing that something important was happening. Once we arrived at the hospital, I felt as if everybody was staring at us — the obvious foreigner, the obvious peasants. Wei Ziqi wore a surplus security-guard-uniform vest — it's a common garment for men in the countryside — and the boy was dressed in a filthy green sweatshirt. His cloth shoes had holes in the toes.

We joined a line for another blood test. There were about thirty other children, and all of them looked like city kids — pampered products of China's urban one-child policy, which, along with rising living standards, has undermined the traditional strictness in child rearing. At the hospital, most children were accompanied by both parents and often at least two grandparents as well. The adults bickered and shoved in the queue; the children whined and cried. Near my feet, a small child vomited on the floor. Inside the lab area, a little girl slipped out of the line to tinker with a tray of test tubes and slides. "Stop that!" a nurse shouted, slapping the child's hand. A sign on the wall proclaimed WITH YOUR COOPERATION AND OUR EXPERIENCE, WE WILL TAKE GOOD CARE OF YOUR PRECIOUS.

When Wei Jia's turn finally came, his face twisted as if he were going to cry. "Be *laoshi!*" Wei Ziqi said firmly, and the boy calmed down. But he was shaking after the blood test was finished.

The doctor on duty — dressed in a dirty white coat, with a look of exhaustion on his face — recommended Vitamin C and said that the boy just needed to rest at home. It wasn't until almost a day and a half later, after I had taken them back to Sancha and then returned to my apartment in Beijing, that I was able to look up *xuexiaoban* in the dictionary: "platelet."

I went online and searched for childhood diseases with low platelet counts and bruising. Leukemia kept coming up. In a panic, I sent e-mails to three doctor friends in the United States, copying Wei Jia's blood-test printout.

The e-mails arrived early the next morning. All three doctors said that leukemia seemed unlikely; independently, they all guessed that it was a condition known as ITP — immune thrombocytopenic purpura. ITP is a disease with unknown causes that is rarely chronic in children; generally, if the patient rests and eats well, it resolves itself within two months. But Wei Jia's platelet count was so dangerously low that there was a risk of bleeding in the brain. "I'd give him steroids or immune globulin," one doctor wrote. My friend Eileen Kavanagh, who was then finishing medical school in New Jersey, responded, "The thing that bothers me the most is that they didn't put him in the hospital to figure all of this out."

I telephoned Sancha, and Cao Chunmei answered. "He's been fine," she said. "But for the last half hour he's had a nosebleed that won't stop."

She put her husband on the phone.

"He's OK as long as he's lying down," Wei Ziqi said. "But if he sits up it starts bleeding again."

"He should be in the hospital," I said. "The doctor made a mistake."

I had already called Mimi, who was contacting friends in order to find a better hospital in Beijing. But the only transport available in Sancha was the Weis's motorbike, which was too rough for the boy's condition. I told Wei Ziqi that I'd borrow Mimi's car and drive out to the village.

\*

Wei Ziqi and I had been born exactly two weeks apart, in June of 1969 — the Year of the Rooster. One evening in Sancha, we discussed our educational experiences through junior high school, which represented the end of Wei Ziqi's formal education. After comparing the years that we had entered various grades, Wei Ziqi looked at me shrewdly. "Did you flunk?" he asked.

Back in 1974, my parents had referred to it as "being held back," and they had always stressed that I had been undersized rather than stupid — at the age of five, I weighed only thirty-five pounds. But there was no such euphemism in the Chinese spoken by the peasants of Sancha.

"Yes," I said. "I flunked nursery school."

"I figured you must have flunked a year," Wei Ziqi said with a grin.

He was different from the other villagers. His mind was quicker, and he seemed to be the only one who realized that the path of progress might eventually return to Sancha, which stands at the terminus of a dead-end road. Back when Wei Ziqi was born, the road had been nothing more than a dirt track that passed beneath a magnificent entrance gate to the Great Wall. The villagers tore down the gate in the 1970s, because they wanted to use the stones to build a road out. Not long after they finished the road, people started to leave. Nowadays, a number of houses are uninhabited, and many residents are elderly people who never had the option of going elsewhere. There are still two women, in their eighties, with bound feet.

Even the history of the village seems to have slipped away. There are no official ancient written records in Sancha, although one can find a few lonely paragraphs carved in stone high in the mountains. Along the peaks, which are too remote for villagers to forage in for stones, the Wall is mostly intact. If you follow it eastward, you eventually come to a cracked stone stele lying amid the rubble. The inscription notes that this section of the Wall was completed in the forty-third year of the reign of the Ming-dynasty emperor Wanli — in 1615. But there is no mention of the village, and nobody in Sancha knows for certain when it was first settled.

In the lower section of Sancha, where most residents are named Yan, the early morning sunlight comes through a gap in the mountains and shines on the last remaining corner of the ruined en-

trance gate. Our part of the village is situated on a higher shelf —
because of the mountains, the sun doesn't reach us until late morning. Nearly everybody here is named Wei. Wei Ziqi believes that his
ancestors settled here during the nineteenth century, possibly after
fleeing a famine in the northern province of Shanxi, but he isn't
certain. All he knows is that he is the fifth generation of his family
to live in Sancha.

Wei Ziqi is short and barrel-chested, and he rarely talks about the
past; his few sentimental streaks run in other directions. He appre-
ciates Sancha's natural beauty; he says that's one reason that he
hasn't moved to the city. If I ask about a hike in the mountains, his
directions reflect how much of his world is botanical — turn left at
the big pine, take a right at the walnut grove. Once, he told me that
he wished the villagers hadn't torn down the entrance gate, because it might have attracted visitors. Wei Ziqi is one of the few
Sancha residents who collect books; he has more than thirty volumes, many of which are college texts for courses in Chinese law.
For somebody like Wei Ziqi — pragmatic as well as literate — law is
a natural subject of interest. When Mimi and I first rented the
house, Wei Ziqi used one of his books, *Modern Economic Contracts*,
to draw up a three-page handwritten agreement. He proudly explained the eleven clauses, one of which prohibited the use of the
house to "store contraband explosives." The rent was the equivalent of forty dollars a month.

Wei Ziqi farms about an acre of land, and when I first came to
know him, the Wei family earned about five hundred dollars in the
average year. By local standards, their situation was good — they
owned a motorbike, a telephone, and a black-and-white TV. But
they weren't necessarily satisfied, and Wei Ziqi kept an old blue
notebook that he referred to as his "Information." The Information consisted of simple sketched maps, as well as statistics on local
altitudes and seasonal temperatures. On one page, he had written
ten potential names for a tourist business that he hoped to start in
Sancha. They included Mountain Peace and Happiness Village and
Sweet Water Farmyard Villa (Sancha is known for having good
spring water). Other pages contained long drafts of potential ad-
vertisements: "If each household uses a small amount of money
and big developers invest, we can change our village into a paradise
where tourists can appreciate the plants, climb the Great Wall, and
enjoy peasant family meals."

In 2002, Wei Ziqi had his first business cards printed up in Huairou. He settled on a humble name: A Small Post on the Great Wall. The back of the card invited tourists to "return to the simple nature of the past." In recent years, even as rural migration accelerated, upper-class Beijing residents with cars have started taking pleasure trips to the countryside. By the summer of 2002, it seemed that almost every weekend somebody found his way to Sancha, usually by chance. When they saw Wei Ziqi's hand-painted advertisement beside the road, they often stopped at his house for a meal cooked by Cao Chunmei. Wei Ziqi told me that if he were able to advertise in the cities, he could triple his income.

He liked talking with Mimi and me, and often he asked us about life in America. He was amused by my inability to fix even the simplest electrical or mechanical problem, and he liked the fact that I was a writer. The other villagers were also interested; sometimes I turned around from my computer and saw a peasant standing in my living room, watching in rapt enjoyment. Nobody in Sancha knocks when they visit a neighbor.

I parked the car and walked directly inside. Wei Jia lay on the *kang,* the traditional northern-Chinese brick bed that can be heated by a wood fire. His face was pale, and flecks of blood had dried dark around his nostrils. He didn't say anything when I touched his forehead.

"It's a lot of trouble for you," Cao Chunmei said. She is a heavyset woman with short hair, and usually she has a lovely smile. But now her face was drawn; on the phone she had told me that her son might have a fever. "Will you eat some lunch?" she said politely.

"I already ate," I said. "I think we should go now."

Cao Chunmei had put a change of clothes and a roll of toilet paper in the Mickey Mouse backpack. They had decided that she would stay behind until Wei Jia was settled in the hospital. Wei Ziqi carried him down the hill and put him in the back seat of the car. The boy lay with his head in his father's lap.

The road from the village is steeply switchbacked, and I drove slowly, so the car wouldn't bounce. After ten minutes, Wei Jia said that he felt sick, and I pulled over. He made gagging noises but nothing came up. As soon as he sat up, twin trails of blood trickled down from his nostrils. Wei Ziqi dabbed at them with the toilet paper. We kept driving.

Fall is the best season in northern China, and it was a beautiful clear day. The peasants had come to the final crop of the year, the soybeans, and they were threshing the haylike stalks along the road. I knew that we had an hour of mountain driving before we reached the highway, and I tried to keep calm by concentrating on the details. We came to Nine-Crossings River — the orange-painted rails of the bridge, the white-streaked bark of the waterside poplars. At Black Mountain Stockade, we had to stop again; this time the boy vomited. There was a long descent from the last blue line of the mountains, and then we reached the plain, where the Ming-dynasty emperors are buried. We passed the faded yellow roof of the tomb of Xuande, the fifth Ming ruler. According to legend, he had killed three Mongols with his own bow. Next, we drove by the tomb of his grandfather, Yongle, the great ruler who had moved the capital north from Nanjing to Beijing, in 1421. Just beyond that tomb, Wei Ziqi asked me to stop again.

The boy spat something up and murmured that he had to go to the bathroom. I couldn't tell how much of it was due to car sickness — it's a common ailment among rural people, who are unaccustomed to automobile travel. Wei Ziqi took down the boy's pants, and he produced a sickly stream of diarrhea. He was very pale now, and there was no expression in his eyes. The back of the car was strewn with bloodstained tissues.

"I think we should keep moving," I said.

"Give him a minute," Wei Ziqi said. We stood in a ditch next to a harvested apple orchard; tour buses streamed past on their way to the Ming tombs. I wondered if any tourists noticed the scene: the car with its lights flashing, the father cradling his son. The bare trees in the stark autumn light. The driver in the ditch, waiting.

Wei Jia ran a fever for most of that week. Mimi had arranged for him to be in the children's ward of a Beijing hospital where the blood specialists are supposed to be good. On the fifth day, Wei Jia's temperature reached 104°. His platelet count dipped beneath 15,000 — if it went much lower, there was a serious risk of bleeding in the brain.

Mimi and I visited daily, and she generally handled any direct interaction with the doctors. It was safer that way — her spoken Chinese was better than mine, and she didn't look like a foreigner.

Nevertheless, there had been some difficulties in dealing with the staff. When we had first arrived at the hospital, after the drive from Sancha, one of the nurses brusquely informed us that Wei Ziqi couldn't stay with his son, because only "female comrades" are allowed to spend the night in the ward. Mimi begged for a one-night exception, because the Weis lived so far away, but the nurse refused. In the end, I had to make another four-hour drive, late that night, to pick up Cao Chunmei.

Chinese hospitals have a reputation for mistreating peasants. Whenever we visited, Mimi and I tried to monitor the boy's care, and we had advised the parents to avoid a transfusion, if possible. The blood supply in China isn't safe; donors are in short supply, and the system relies primarily on people who are paid for giving blood. Testing practices vary widely from region to region, blood bank to blood bank. In China, an estimated one million people have been infected with HIV; the epidemic has been particularly severe in Henan Province, just south of Beijing, because of unsanitary donor conditions. Even in cities like Beijing, hospitals usually rely on antibody tests, which are cheaper and less reliable than the molecular diagnostics used by blood banks in developed countries.

In the evenings, after visiting the hospital, I often e-mailed my doctor friends in the United States with questions. On the morning of the seventh day, the Beijing doctors performed a bone-marrow test for leukemia. Immediately after the procedure, Wei Ziqi telephoned me and asked to borrow eight thousand yuan — nearly a thousand dollars. The doctors had decided that the boy needed a transfusion, which had to be paid for in advance. In China, most peasants have no medical insurance, but the Weis had taken the unusual step of purchasing a private policy when their son entered kindergarten. It would cover about half of his bills, but the money could be claimed only after the fact.

That day, Mimi was preparing to leave on a trip, so I went to the hospital alone. When I arrived, Wei Jia was sleeping fitfully. His mother told me that he had been bleeding from the mouth. Accompanied by Wei Ziqi, I introduced myself to one of the doctors on duty. I asked her if the transfusion was critical.

"Who is this?" she said sharply to Wei Ziqi. "Why is he asking questions?"

"He's a writer," Wei Ziqi said proudly.

"I'm a friend, as I just explained," I said quickly. "I have some simple questions about what we should do."

"This isn't his affair!" the doctor said to Wei Ziqi. "You're the parents, and you have responsibility for the child. He has nothing to do with it."

"I just want to make sure we make the right decision," I said.

"The decision has already been made!" I had assumed that the hospital staff would be patient with me just because I was showing concern for a Chinese child. But now they glared at me: three nurses and two doctors, all women.

"Who can I talk to about this?" I said, but the women ignored me. I repeated the question — silence. Finally, one of the nurses whispered something, and the others laughed. I felt my face turn red.

"It's very simple," I said. "I'm paying for this. I have to know why he needs a transfusion before I pay the money."

One of the doctors, a middle-aged woman named Zhao, turned to me. "He needs immune globulin," she said tersely. "If he doesn't get it, there's a risk that he'll have brain damage from internal bleeding. Already he is bleeding inside his mouth. We know what to do, and you don't understand anything about it."

"I'm trying to understand as much as I can," I said. "If you speak slowly, it helps. I'm only asking these questions because I care about the boy."

"If you care, then let us give him the transfusion."

I asked if it might be better to wait for the test results to come back, but Dr. Zhao said that the lab was too slow. Finally, I asked if there was a risk that the immune globulin might be infected with a disease.

"Of course there's a risk!" she said. "It could be infected with HIV or hepatitis or something else!"

"Don't they test the blood?" I asked.

"You can't test blood completely," she said.

"I think you can, actually."

"Believe me, you can't!"

"Where does the blood come from?"

"How am I supposed to know?" She was practically shouting now. I backed out of the room with Wei Ziqi. I told him that the blood supply was my main concern, and he nodded calmly.

I used my cell phone to call an American I knew who worked in medicine in Beijing. She was familiar with one local organization that followed international testing standards for blood. After checking with the organization, she called back to tell me they could sell a clean unit for 378 American dollars. They could have the blood delivered, but I'd have to get the hospital to accept it.

I took a deep breath and walked back into the staff room. "I'm sorry to bother you again," I said to Dr. Zhao. "But if we find guaranteed clean blood, can we use that?"

"There's no guaranteed clean blood in Beijing," she said.

I told her that the other organization performs thorough HIV tests.

"There's no test like that," she said.

It sounded like a lie, but I realized that it might simply mean *mei banfa* — nothing can be done. I said, "If I buy clean blood from them and have them deliver it, can we use it?"

"We won't accept it!" she shouted. "It's against hospital policy. Who do you think you are?"

I stepped outside again. At the time, I didn't realize that Dr. Zhao was actually in the right — such a sale of blood was strictly illegal. My American contact also hadn't known. In China, pragmatism often blurs such regulations, and a foreigner can find himself operating in shady territory without even knowing it. I called the American again to see if she had any ideas.

"I know some Chinese doctors who used to work at your hospital," she said. "I'll ask them to check on the blood supply, and then I'll call you back."

I waited in the hospital room with Wei Jia and his parents. During everything that had happened in the past week, they had remained completely calm: no tears, no raised voices. Life in Sancha had taught them that there were limits to what you could control and understand. During my argument with Dr. Zhao, Wei Ziqi had stood in the background, as if it were not his affair. He had a deep respect for my doctor friends in America.

The only decoration in the hospital room was a clock featuring Mickey Mouse and Donald Duck. There were two other patients: a teenager with a heart problem and an eight-year-old with an ailing kidney. The kidney treatment involved large amounts of hormones, and since June the eight-year-old's weight had increased by 50 percent. Everything about his body, especially his face, appeared stretched and swollen. My phone rang.

"It's pretty good news," the woman said. She told me that the hospital that was treating Wei Jia used the same blood bank as the medical organization that followed international testing standards. "They haven't ever come up with a positive for HIV. That blood bank has been safe so far."

On impulse, I tried to call a doctor friend in San Francisco, but his answering machine clicked on. I stared at my cell phone. "I think it's OK," I said finally to Wei Ziqi.

We went downstairs to the hospital's payment division. Clerks sat behind windows, and money was everywhere: strewn across tables, spinning in counting machines, bound into red bricks. From my bag, I took out a thick wad of cash. Without a word, the clerk tossed it into a counting machine.

After the immune globulin was given, Wei Jia's fever broke, and within two days his platelet count was back to normal. It held steady for the rest of the week. The bone-marrow examination showed no leukemia; the doctors decided that the condition was in fact ITP. Five days after the treatment, a group of Wei Jia's relatives came to visit.

There were four men: a grandfather, a great-uncle, an uncle, and a distant cousin named Li Ziwen, a peasant who had joined the military and then moved to the city a few years ago. The rest of the men had come in from the countryside. The great-uncle told me that he hadn't been to Beijing in almost thirty years.

The men gathered around Wei Jia's hospital bed. Cao Jifu, the grandfather, put his hand on the boy's back and spoke softly to him. But the sudden attention had made Wei Jia shy, and he sat in silence at the head of the bed. The sheets had red-brown stains on them from blood tests.

After ten minutes, somebody mentioned lunch. Li Ziwen reached into his pocket and pulled out a wad of bills. He dropped the money onto the bed.

"Use this for the child," he said.

Wei Ziqi tried to give the money back, but Li refused. For a minute, they argued gently, and then Wei nodded his head in thanks.

The uncle was next and then the grandfather. The great-uncle went last. He was poorer than the others, and his stack included some tens and twenties. The money lay in four bright piles on the sheets. The boy looked very small, and now he leaned back, away from the bills. There was an awkward silence, and finally somebody mentioned lunch again. Cao Chunmei pushed the money out of sight, under the boy's pillow. The men filed out of the room.

We went to a restaurant across the street. Wei Ziqi studied the menu intently. When the waitress brought a bottle of grain alcohol, he examined the seal. "Can you guarantee that this bottle isn't counterfeit?"

The waitress seemed surprised by the question. "I'm pretty sure," she said. "But I guess I can't say for certain."

Wei Ziqi sent back that bottle, and the next one as well. Finally, the third one satisfied him. When the food arrived, he commented that the iron-plate beef wasn't so good. Carefully, he monitored the dishes, and for a moment I had trouble believing that this was the same man who had stood in the background during the arguments about his son's treatment. But, as a farmer, Wei Ziqi knew food; he was the expert at the restaurant.

The men drank steadily. The grandfather's face was the first to turn red with the grain alcohol. He stood up and gave me a formal toast: "We appreciate all of your help with Wei Jia."

Everybody downed a shot. Wei Ziqi told the story of our drive into Beijing, and the men began discussing the boy's health. Wei Ziqi turned to me.

"You know," he said quietly, "I was frightened during that drive."

I told him that I had been scared, too.

Winter is the quietest season in Sancha. There are no crops; apart from some pruning, there is little work in the orchards. The villagers often remain in bed until midmorning, and they eat two meals a day instead of three. Everything slows down.

Wei Jia stayed home from school most of that winter. For two months, he hardly left the house, and his parents were careful with his meals. The doctors gave him a month's worth of steroids. There was a brief period during which Wei Jia whined and cried easily — his parents said that he had learned to act this way from his neighbor in the hospital, the city boy with kidney problems. Whenever Wei Jia cried, his parents mocked him for looking ridiculous, and soon he stopped. Over the winter he gained nine pounds. His father taught him how to write some simple Chinese characters, and together they listened to English-language tapes.

Wei Ziqi kept busy that winter. He enlarged his front porch and part of his home, to prepare for summer tourists, and he made up a new business card. The name changed from A Small Post on the Great Wall to A Post on the Great Wall. Wei Ziqi acquired a cell phone; it didn't work in the village, because the mountains were too high, but he could use it in Huairou, where he increasingly spent time on business — meeting people, buying construction materials. For thirty yuan, he purchased a pair of black leather shoes that he reserved strictly for trips to the city. At home, he kept the shoebox in good condition. A brand name had been printed on the box: "Italy." Later that year, the government agreed to pay the subsidy for the Idiot.

Over the winter, I made a trip back to America, where a friend asked me if I planned to have Wei Jia tested for HIV. I knew that I would never suggest such a test, because I didn't trust the hospitals, and the parents would find the request strange. With every step that I took — from the United States to Beijing, from Beijing to the village — familiar rules slipped away. Like everyone else, in a crisis I simply reacted. But after the emergency had passed, I sometimes felt an emptiness that reminded me that I was far from home and that it was not my village, not my child.

Mimi and I returned to Sancha for Qing Ming, the Day of Clear Brightness. It was the first week of April and the apricot trees had just begun to bloom; a thin pink color was brushed across the lower hills. Qing Ming is the Chinese holiday for the dead and is celebrated by tending the tombs of ancestors. In the countryside, it also marks the start of the busy season. In Sancha, only the adult men perform the tomb sweeping. We awoke at dawn and hiked into the hills behind the village.

Each tomb is nothing more than a mound of dirt, and the villagers cover the piles with fresh earth. Mimi took photographs — because she was an outsider, it was fine for her to come along. The tombs were arranged in neat rows, according to generation, and Wei Ziqi started with a single mound at the back. "This is the Laozu," he said as he shoveled dirt onto the pile. The word means

"Old Ancestor." When I asked about the dead man's name, Wei Ziqi shrugged. "I've never heard it," he said. "But he was the first one to be buried here."

The next line of tombs was the generation of his great-grandparents, and then he heaped dirt onto his grandparents' grave. The men chatted idly while they worked. It was communal: A man took particular care with the tombs of his own ancestors, but everybody added a little dirt to every tomb. After the shoveling, they burned money for the dead to use in the afterlife. The bills looked like official Chinese currency, but they were labeled, in English, "The Bank of Heaven Company, Ltd."

The cemetery had run out of space for Wei Ziqi's parents' generation. We hiked down the mountain to his parents' gravesite, which was next to a small plot of farmland. Wei Ziqi paused to examine a tangle of fur that was strewn across the path. "Rabbit," he said. "A hawk got it, probably."

As we walked, I asked him what his father had been like.

"He was a peasant," Wei Ziqi said simply.

I pressed him, asking what he remembered most about his father.

"He liked to play cards," Wei Ziqi said. We continued down the hill. A moment later, he said, "I remember that my father had a bad temper."

That evening, I was finishing dinner with the Weis when a neighbor stopped by and said that his grandson was running a fever. He wanted to go down to the valley to Shayu, twenty minutes away, where there is a small clinic.

I agreed to drive, and we piled into the car that I had rented for the week. Wei Jia sat on his father's lap in the front seat. The sick child, a four-year-old named Huang Hongyu, sat in the back with his grandparents.

At the clinic, a doctor examined the child. He said that the problem wasn't serious, and he prepared to give the boy an injection.

"I have an idea," I said to Wei Jia, pulling him outside. "Do you want to drive the car?"

I put him on my lap, behind the wheel. We pulled away just as the child in the clinic started screaming.

"I don't cry when I get a shot," Wei Jia said.

We made a loop around the village. By the time we returned, the rest of them were ready to leave. Huang Hongyu had calmed down, and the grandparents seemed relieved at the doctor's words. Halfway back to Sancha, I allowed Wei Jia to sit on my lap again. He held the wheel tightly as we took the switchbacks up the mountain. The boy in the back was carsick and began to vomit.

"Do you want me to stop?" I asked.

"It's not necessary," the grandfather said. He had come prepared with plastic bags.

I rolled down the window and kept driving. We came to the lower village, and Wei Jia leaned forward in order to see more clearly. Electric lights glowed a soft orange against the brick of the homes, and then, high above, there was a dark line where the mountains gave way to stars and the great emptiness. The boy in the back had stopped throwing up. I kept telling myself that the children were fine and we were almost home.

JACK HITT

# Say No More

FROM THE *New York Times Magazine*

LANGUAGES DIE the way many people do — at home, in silence, attended by loved ones straining to make idle conversation. "Did you sell any baskets?" Gabriela Paterito asks her neighbor Francisco Arroyo in her vowelly Spanish. She's in her two-room shack in Puerto Eden, a tiny fishing village on Wellington Island in the Patagonia region of southern Chile. There is a long, long silence. She's a short woman, dense from some seventy years of life but with a girl's head of beautiful black hair. In the room are Francisco and a few others, among the last six speakers of Kawesqar, the language native to these parts since the last ice age.

Linguists now estimate that half of the more than six thousand languages currently spoken in the world will become extinct by the end of this century. In reaction, there are numerous efforts to slow the die-off — from graduate students heading into the field to compile dictionaries; to charitable foundations devoted to the cause, like the Endangered Language Fund; to transnational agencies, some with melancholic names appropriate to the task, like the European Bureau for Lesser Used Languages. Chile started a modest program, not long after the ugly debates surrounding Christopher Columbus in 1992, to save Kawesqar (Ka-WES-kar) and Yaghan, the last two native languages of southern Chile. But how does one salvage an ailing language when the economic advantages of, say, Spanish are all around you? And is it possible to step inside a dying language to learn whether it can be saved and, more rudely, whether it should be?

Gabriela crams another stick into her wood stove to keep us dry and warm. The rain is coming now like nails, as it does most days. The silence stretches out. You begin to feel it, like a cold draft. Three or four aching minutes of it. My boots need some examining.

"*Canastos,*" mutters Francisco, repeating the Spanish word for baskets, his grunting tone suggesting a bad day. When languages die under the pressure of a dominant tongue like Spanish, there is a familiar path of retreat. The language will withdraw from the public sphere first, hiding out in the living rooms and kitchens of the fluent, where it becomes increasingly private and intimate and frail. Francisco takes a two-foot length of reedy grass and softens it by rubbing it against the stove. All around weaving begins — the distinctive Kawesqar baskets, small with long grassy handles.

"It's been raining all day," Francisco adds, again in Spanish. Juan Carlos, who is thirty-nine and my guide, motions me to give him a cigarette. Juan Carlos was born and grew up here but left at fifteen for school. Now college-educated, he has devoted his life and work to helping the Kawesqar community. (He has just finished a documentary film about the Kawesqar.) He doesn't smoke, he told me, except here. For the last few days, smoking and enduring long silences have pretty much accounted for our social life. I haven't smoked seriously for fifteen years. I'm blowing through two packs a day.

Every window here frames a magnificent photo op. Outside Gabriela's is a curving line of shacks hugging the shore of a small bay, bright red-and-yellow fishing boats beached in front, and behind, a dramatic ascent of mountains capped in white — gushing here and there with little snow-melt waterfalls. Full-spectrum rainbows break out so frequently that no one notices but me and the tourists. They, too, are visible out the window, all wearing their orange cruise-ship-issue rain slickers, their cameras aimed aloft. To get here, it's a three-day chug by boat through the cold, uninhabited island channels of Patagonia. Once a week, the tourists come. They have less than an hour onshore to feel the intensity of its remote beauty — and maybe buy a native basket — before motoring out to the anchored cruise ship and a night of pisco sours.

"A lot of rain," announces Juan Carlos. The fire crackles and hisses. The rain continues, staccato.

"Rain," Gabriela adds.

I sit quietly, smoking my way through their Samuel Beckett dialogue.

"Not many baskets," Francisco says, offering his full report. I wonder if I should ask them to speak Kawesqar, but I don't want to intrude. I want to get a sense of when they naturally converse in their language. Later, Juan Carlos tells me that the elder Kawesqar feel awkward speaking their moribund language around me. It's a combination of embarrassment and a sense that they don't want to make me feel uncomfortable. As the rain pours down, I light up a cigarette. My very presence here to observe this thing, difficult to see, has made it disappear.

The Kawesqar are famous for their adaptation to this cold, rainy world of islands and channels. The first Europeans were stunned. The Kawesqar and the other natives of the region traveled in canoes, naked, oiled with blubber, occasionally wearing an animal skin. The men sat at the front and hunted sea lions with spears. The women paddled. The children stayed in the sanctuary between their parents, maintaining fire in a sand pit built in the middle of the canoe. Keeping fire going in a land of water was the most critical and singular adaptation of the Kawesqar. As a result, fire blazed continuously in canoes and at the occasional landfall. The first European explorers marveled at the sight of so much fire in a wet and cold climate, and the Spanish named the southernmost archipelago the land of fire, Tierra del Fuego.

When Charles Darwin first encountered the Kawesqar and the Yaghans, years before he wrote *The Origin of Species,* he is said to have realized that man was just another animal cunningly adapting to local environmental conditions. But that contact and the centuries to follow diminished the Kawesqar, in the twentieth century, to a few dozen individuals. In the 1930s, the remaining Kawesqar settled near a remote military installation — Puerto Eden, now inhabited mostly by about two hundred Chileans from the mainland who moved here to fish.

The pathology of a dying language shifts to another stage once the language has retreated to the living room. You can almost hear it disappearing. There is Grandma, fluent in the old tongue. Her son might understand her, but he also learned Spanish and grew up in it. The grandchildren all learn Spanish exclusively and giggle at Grandma's funny chatter.

In two generations, a healthy language — even one with hundreds of thousands of speakers — can collapse entirely, sometimes without anyone noticing. This process is happening everywhere. In North America, the arrival of Columbus and the Europeans who followed him whittled down the roughly 300 native languages to only about 170 in the twentieth century. According to Marianne Mithun, a linguist at the University of California at Santa Barbara, the recent evolution of English as a global language has taken an even greater toll. "Only one of those 170 languages is not officially endangered today," Mithun said. "Greenlandic Eskimo."

Without the revitalization of youth, a language can go from being alive to endangered (declining speakers among the young), then moribund (only elderly speakers left alive), then dead (the last known speaker dies) — all linguistic terms of art. William Sutherland, the author of a study in *Nature* magazine last spring, compared the die-off to an environmental catastrophe. According to Sutherland, 438 languages are in the condition of Kawesqar, that is, with fewer than fifty speakers, making them "critically endangered" — a category that in the animal world includes 182 birds and 180 mammals. Languages "seem to follow the same patterns" as animals, Sutherland told a reporter for *Bloomberg News*. "Stability and isolation seem to breed abundance in the number of bird and animal species, and they do the same for languages." Conversely, the instability and homogenization of the global economy is creating a juggernaut of monoculture, threatening plants and animals. But, Sutherland makes clear, the one life form even more endangered is human culture.

According to Daniel Nettle and Suzanne Romaine, authors of *Vanishing Voices,* the last time human language faced such a crisis of collapse was when we invented farming, around 8000 B.C., during the switchover from highly mobile hunting and gathering to sedentary agriculture. Then the multitude of idioms developed on the run cohered into language families, like Indo-European, Sino-Tibetan, and Elamo-Dravidian. The difference this time is that with each language gone, we may also lose whatever knowledge and history were locked up in its stories and myths, along with the human consciousness embedded in its grammatical structure and vocabulary.

One often hears the apocryphal story about the Inuit and their forty words for "snow." True or not, it acknowledges the inherent human sense that each language, developed over a certain time and geography, is a revelation of what we call "a sense of place." To

let languages die out, en masse, is to permit the phrase "terra in-
cognita" to creep back onto our environmental maps. One organization of linguists, biologists, and anthropologists, known as Terralingua, is working to keep languages alive by highlighting what gets
lost when they fade away. "I remember when I was doing fieldwork
in Mexico," said Luisa Maffi, Terralingua's president. She encountered a man whose native Mayan was already blurred with Mexican
Spanish. He had traveled with his two-year-old daughter to a health
clinic because she was sick with serious diarrhea. "He no longer
knew the word for *yakan k'ulub wamal,*" she said, using the Mayan
term for a plant long known to cure the problem. "It was probably
growing in his backyard."

A handful of linguists dismiss salvage efforts like Terralingua's as
futile exercises. They say languages just die, as spoken Latin did,
and then are reborn as French, Spanish, and Italian. No big deal.
Or more bluntly, all this sentimentality about dying languages is
just another symptom of academe's mewling, politically correct mi-
nority-mongering. In the magazine *Prospect,* the writer Kenan Malik
summarized this position in an essay titled "Let Them Die." "There
is nothing noble or authentic about local ways of life; they are often
simply degrading and backbreaking," Malik argued. "What if half
the world's languages are on the verge of extinction? Let them die
in peace."

Linguists counter that yes, there is a natural process of language
death; but the order of magnitude of the current die-off is what
should create concern. What's happening with human culture
now, they say, should shock people the way the Cuyahoga River
catching fire in 1969 radically changed how many thought about
the environment.

To general linguists, the dismissive position is just deliberate ignorance. But they also argue that the utilitarian case is too narrow.
In peril is not just knowledge but also the importance of diversity
and the beauty of grammar. They will tell you that every language
has its own unique theology and philosophy buried in its very sin-
ews. For example, because of the Kawesqar's nomadic past, they
rarely use the future tense; given the contingency of moving constantly by canoe, it was all but unnecessary. The past tense, however, has fine gradations. You can say, "A bird flew by." And by the
use of different tenses, you can mean a few seconds ago, a few days
ago, a time so long ago that you were not the original observer of

the bird (but you know the observer yourself), and, finally, a mythological past, a tense the Kawesqar use to suggest that the story is so old that it no longer possesses fresh descriptive truth but rather that other truth that emerges from stories that retain their narrative power despite constant repetition.

"There was once a man and a woman who killed a sacred deer," Gabriela began, translating into Spanish a Kawesqar tale told in the mythological tense. "Afterward a great flood came. The waters rose until they were standing in it up to their waist. Everyone died but the man and the woman." Then, in time, she went on, from just these last two Kawesqar, they figured out a way to endure, repopulate the land, and revive the life of the Kawesqar among the channel islands.

Outside, the rain kept coming down.

The rhythm of Puerto Eden became easier after a few days. The fishermen headed out in the morning, and the rest of us made social calls. In time, I got to hear some actual Kawesqar spoken, and it sounded a lot like Hollywood's generic Apache but with a few unique and impossible sounds. I learned to say *"Aes ktael sa Jack, akuókat cáuks ktael?"* ("My name is Jack, what's yours?") That second word, *ktael*, means "name" and is (sort of) pronounced *ka-tull*. It happens entirely in the back of the mouth, in a really challenging way. But during these visits, always and constantly, dominant-culture television hollered at us from a corner. Besides meeting the Kawesqar in Puerto Eden, I have to say, I caught up on a lot of missed episodes of *MacGyver* and *Baywatch*.

Later in the week, Juan Carlos and I spent more time at his sister's house, and there the evidence of European culture insinuating itself deeply into the minds and habits of the Kawesqar was everywhere.

Maria Isabel is a few years older than her brother. She was sick as a child and was raised in Punta Arenas, on the Chilean mainland. She studied and lived in metropolitan Santiago. She never had a Kawesqar youth and can't speak the language.

"I am Kawesqar," she told me in Spanish, as if to acknowledge the inexplicable tug identity has on all of us. When I asked her if she intended to learn her mother's language, she insisted that she would. "I hope next year," she said, unconvincingly.

I spent a lot of time with Maria Isabel because her husband, Luis, was installing their first flushable toilet. When we weren't talking about Kawesqar, we were measuring holes, figuring out how to run a sewer pipe into the bay, and reading the toilet-assembly instructions (helpfully printed in five dominant languages). Eventually, the hole was properly centered, so we set down the beeswax ring, lifted the porcelain carefully, and pressed it into its permanent location.

Does anything say Western dominance quite like the flush of a private john?

Well, maybe one other thing. In our intimate chats and smokes, Juan Carlos told me about his own three children. He lives with them back on the mainland, in a house where two other adults speak some Kawesqar. One is Juan Carlos's brother, José, a professor of anthropology at the Universidad Arcis Magallanes in Punta Arenas. And the other is Oscar Aguilera, a linguist at the university. He's of Spanish descent, but he has devoted his life's work to the language of the Kawesqar.

Aguilera arrived in Puerto Eden from Santiago in 1975 with the simple intention of "describing" the language as a linguist. There he met a people nearly cut off from the outside world. Among the little contact they'd had, oddly, was with NASA. The space agency came to the village in 1959 to conduct experiments on the ability of humans to withstand extremely cold temperatures. An elderly villager told Aguilera that the NASA scientists asked one Kawesqar man to sit naked in a cold tent with his feet in a bucket of water. He fled in the middle of the night.

Aguilera befriended Gabriela's in-laws and knew Gabriela's husband well. He got to know her two young boys, and when they were teenagers, Aguilera took them to Santiago, where they finished school and went to college. Now they all live together in Punta Arenas with Juan Carlos's three young children, who use the affectionate term for "grandfather" with Aguilera.

When I visited the home for dinner one night, the three children ran up to greet me. They attend the local British school — and so were taught in Spanish and English. One little girl proudly read me last night's homework: "I played in the yard," and "I rode my bicycle." She beamed. It's cool speaking the dominant language.

Later, I asked Juan Carlos why they didn't speak Kawesqar at home. Wouldn't it make sense, since the children were at that magic language-acquisition stage of youth?

"We are going to teach them later," he said. Juan Carlos added that they needed the proper books. Of course, Aguilera is the man who compiled the grammar and teaching manual for Kawesqar and is working on a dictionary with José. But government funds for these projects are spotty, and Aguilera admits it will be years before they are completed.

Their answers revealed just how difficult language resurrection is. Learning a language, even your mother's, requires enormous motivation. Plus, Juan Carlos and José say they are "semispeakers" — in part because they were taken away from home so young to be educated in Spanish-dominated schools. Even the fluent Kawesqar speakers in Puerto Eden have occasionally asked Aguilera, the lexicographer, to remind them of a certain word.

"Some days," Aguilera told me when we were alone for a while, "I think that I might be the last speaker of Kawesqar."

Among linguists, the sorrowful story of the "last speaker" is practically a literary genre. The names ring out, like a Homeric catalog. Ned Maddrell, the last speaker of Manx, died in the village of Cregneash on the Isle of Man in 1974. Tevfik Esenc, the last speaker of Ubykh, died in Turkey in 1992. Red Thunder Cloud, the last speaker of Catawba, died in 1996. More are coming. Marie Smith-Jones in Alaska, the last speaker of Eyak, is eighty-three years old.

Farther south from the Kawesqar, I learned, lived the last speaker of Yaghan. Many people urged me to visit Puerto Williams and its native settlement, called Ukika, because of that intriguing notion — that all of Yaghan now dwells entirely in the mind of one elderly woman, Cristina Calderón.

Right away, though, I discovered that the "last speaker" of Yaghan is accustomed to charging passengers from the cruise ship that arrives each week for the privilege of taking her picture or hearing a few of the last words in her unusual-sounding language. From me she wanted impossible sums of money. When I tried to sneak in early one morning for a quick interview, word traveled in the village so fast that within minutes her granddaughter/booking agent was through the door and a screaming match broke out (not in Yaghan).

That night, Aguilera and I decided to pursue a rumor that there was in fact another Yaghan, a penultimate speaker named Emelinda, who hadn't mastered the cruise-ship racket. We managed to get inside Emelinda's house without attracting attention. She was a kind old woman whose Yaghan, according to Aguilera, was authentic. Our conversation was brief and brittle. When I asked Emelinda what could be done to keep Yaghan alive, she said she was already doing it, as if a formal program were under way.

"I talk to myself in Yaghan," Emelinda explained in Spanish. "When I hang up my clothes outside, I say the words in Yaghan. Inside the house, I talk in Yaghan all day long."

I asked her if she ever had a conversation with the only other person in the world who could easily understand her, Cristina Calderón, the official "last speaker" of Yaghan.

"No," Emelinda said impatiently, as if I'd brought up a sore topic. "The two of us don't talk."

After returning from Chile, I learned that the last-speaker hustle isn't new. Remember Red Thunder Cloud, the last Catawba speaker? Actually, he was Cromwell Ashbie Hawkins West, the son of an African-American druggist in Newport, Rhode Island. According to Ives Goddard of the Smithsonian, West was "a great mimic and fast learner." He quickly mastered the language, donned some turquoise jewelry, and, until his death in 1996, worked the last-speaker circuit. Usually, he could be found at county fairs, hawking Red Thunder Cloud's Accabonac Princess American Indian Tea — "fresh from the American forest to you."

There's a paradox in those last-speaker stories. After all, what is driving these languages off the cliff but sheer economics? It only makes a kind of poetic sense that in their death throes their speakers would resort to economic ploys. But this is also where the environmental metaphor of endangered languages falls apart. Getting down to a few in number is irreversibly the end of, say, a fern or a tiger. For humans, it's often the beginning of politics.

The very success of English as a global language is prompting a revival of ancestral tongues. Compared to the die-off now in progress, it's a drop in the bucket. Still, many Native American languages have reacted against these near-death experiences. The Miami in Oklahoma and the Mohawk straddling the Canadian border have full-scale programs for language revival. Native Hawaiian, also written off only a few decades ago, has eighteen schools teaching a new generation in the original language of the islands.

Partly with money from government lawsuits — the Catawba received $50 million in 1993 after suing over land claim disputes dating to 1760 — and partly with revenue from casinos, many of these tribes are rushing to get the programs up and running before the last of the speaking elders die. The Tuscarora tribe near Niagara Falls, New York, is down to Howdy Hill, the last speaker who grew up learning the language at home. But now a revival program claims as many as twenty-five new speakers.

Other languages are long past the last speaker, yet revival is still not out of the question. Stephanie Fielding is the great-great-niece of Fidelia Fielding, the last speaker of Mohegan, who died in 1908. Fielding is currently enrolled in MIT's linguistics program. She is fifty-eight and devoted to resurrecting her ancestors' language, largely from her aunt's diaries. The academic degree to which she aspires has not yet been accredited. A master's with a concentration in "language reclamation" will be available from MIT at the earliest by 2005 or 2006, according to Norvin Richards, an associate professor of linguistics.

"The number of people who contacted us in the last year is about twenty, which in linguistics is a bit largish," Richards said. MIT will have to compete with the University of Arizona and the University of Alaska Fairbanks, which already offer reclamation degrees.

Most of these language-revival movements model themselves on the national language of Israel. For more than two millenniums, Hebrew was found almost exclusively in Scripture and rabbinical writings. Its retreat was nearly complete — out of the public square, into the house, and finally into the scrolls of the Torah. But the early pioneers of what would become Israel faced a politically charged question: Which of their languages should dominate? Ashkenazi Yiddish? Russian? German? Sephardic Ladino? The commonly agreed-upon answer was supplied by Eliezer Ben-Yehuda, the Jewish linguist who used the stiff, formal language of the Bible to conjure into existence a modern version — now the main language of 3.6 million people. (Of course, Hebrew's comeback has helped drive Yiddish and Ladino into "endangered" status.)

Language revival as a means of identity politics may well be the way of the future. The big fight in linguistics over the past two decades has been about English First. But first is no longer the question. Now the question is, What will be your second language? In America, the drift in high school curriculums has always been toward a second dominant language — French, Spanish, German, maybe Chinese if you're a rebel. But what if the second language could be that of your ancestors?

That possibility is already proving to be quite popular with many people. As their initiatives succeed and become more visible, they will drive into the open a question for English-speaking Americans, the owner-operators of the dominant linguistic ecosystem. Do we want to dwell in a society that encourages linguistic revival and cultural diversity, knowing that with it may come a lot of self-righteous minority-pitying? Or, shall we just sit contentedly amid a huge cultural die-off, harrumphing like some drunk uncle at the family reunion angrily spilling his beer and growling, "Let 'em die"? Keep in mind that if the actuarial tables are correct, it means that once the languages start to die off in earnest, there will be a "death of the last speaker" article in the papers, on average, every twelve days.

The other paradox of this gathering twilight is that while the grown-ups are having their arguments about what we should and shouldn't do — and after the linguists have compiled their dictionaries and put together their grammars — the future of all these resurrections will depend on teenagers.

Will it become cool to speak and live and sing and groove in, say, Mohegan? It depends.

Twenty years ago, the distinct language of Welsh was in intensive care, destined to die. Now 21 percent of the people in Wales speak it regularly. Gaelic in Ireland has failed, by comparison. Maybe 3 percent of the people in Ireland speak Gaelic regularly today. Some argue that Wales needed something extra to distinguish itself from the English up the road, while the Irish live on an island. But other observers, like the author David Crystal, point to the influence of the kids. In his book *Language Death,* he cites a small scandal that broke out in 1998. The Welsh band Manic Street Preachers promoted a new album in Cardiff by hanging an enormous banner written in the old tongue. When he saw it, Peter Hughes Griffiths, a professor at Trinity College in Carmathen who teaches the language, condemned the banner for using slang.

"You would have thought the group would have made the effort to make sure the poster was grammatically correct," he fumed to an English newspaper. "Standards are not being kept up."

The professor was quickly hooted down by newspapers and by the Welsh Language Board. He had missed the point: Kids would propel the language, not him. Kids — with their mistakes, bastard-izations, slang, import words, and poor syntax — will be the ones who breathe new casual life into old formal syntax. That said, there always remains the other possibility — that the next generation will decide that the native tongue is preposterous, and poof.

On my last day in Puerto Eden, we didn't have the proper glue to connect the lengths of PVC pipe. So we improvised, building small fires beneath each end until the plastic softened enough to slip one pipe over the other. Problem solved, we went inside for a cele-bratory cup of tea. Luis and Maria Isabel have one child, a daugh-ter, Maria José, fifteen. She was visiting her parents from the main-land, where she's in school.

"I am Kawesqar," she said, just like her mom. But where Mom made solemn promises that one day she'll learn the language, Maria José swears to it while laughing. She had on a tight sweater and elephant bell-bottoms, and she had attached the bottom of each pant leg to the sole of her shoe, with tacks, to create a perfect flare on each leg. While we spoke, she watched the television set where a top-hits show blasted techno music beamed in from domi-nant-culture HQ some 10,000 miles away. She danced along. I lighted my last cigarette.

"Fire!" she shouted in perfect English, pointing to my match. She burst out laughing. "I speak Kawesqar!" Her mother laughed and leaned over to tell me that the Kawesqar word for "match" is precisely the English word "fire" — dating back to when the first British explorer handed a Kawesqar nomad a box of matches. Maybe it was Darwin himself; maybe that moment was the begin-ning of the end for this old language.

Or the beginning of a new Kawesqar. Maria José looked directly at the TV, carefully mimicking the latest moves, dancing and gig-gling out of control. "Fire! Fire! Fire!"

PAM HOUSTON

# The Vertigo Girls Do
# the East Tonto Trail

FROM *National Geographic Adventure*

FOR AT LEAST THE PAST 10,000 YEARS, the Grand Canyon
has been luring human beings into its depths. From the Desert
Archaics, who left behind their split-twig figurines, to the Anasazi,
who built villages of adobe; from John Wesley Powell's tumultuous
1869 river adventure to "Uncle Jimmy" Owens's turn-of-the-cen-
tury mountain lion hunts; from the 40,000 annual visitors (out of
four million total) who come to practice their survival skills below
the rim to the handful every decade who choose the canyon as the
place to end their lives: No one enters the Grand Canyon casually,
and no one, I would wager, leaves it without being variously and sufficiently awed.

My personal agenda on a recent backpacking trip was to make
up with the canyon after our last encounter: an eighteen-day river
journey in 2001 that was marked by near misses in the rapids, edgy
dynamics around the campfire, the discovery of a corpse, and a
takeout time of 9 A.M. on the morning of September 11. It is my belief that all natural places on Earth have their own distinct person-
alities, but few assert themselves as aggressively as does the Grand
Canyon, which has always seemed to me a little like a crotchety old
man, a trickster whose pranks are designed sometimes to thrill you,
sometimes to scare you to death. This time I wouldn't have the rapids to contend with, I would take with me only what I could carry
on my back, and I would travel with just one other person, my dear
friend Kelli. All I would have to do to make the trip a success was to

keep putting one foot in front of the other, find the next trail marker, and make sure we had enough water to drink.

Before setting out on our four-day hike, we talked to Kirstin, a ranger in the backcountry office who had just come off the eastern section of the Tonto Trail and told us that the conditions had been dry and "warm" (above 100°) and that she had taken five liters of water but had wished for at least one more. Until you've actually been on a trail like the Tonto, it is hard to imagine a situation where five liters of water would not be enough. But people have died on that trail, people who have started the day with what they thought was plenty of water.

Kirstin said there was a very nasty pothole in the west arm of Cremation drainage that we should use only in the event of an emergency and that there were some equally nasty pools in upper Lonetree Canyon that had a lot of "critters" living in them. She said the spring in Boulder drainage wouldn't get above ground until temperatures cooled significantly. That made our first reliable water source Grapevine Creek, where we hoped to make camp on the second night. She said her legs had got scratched up pretty bad in Cremation drainage and that it was too hot at night for a sleeping bag, but that the mosquitoes were so intense she decided to sweat. There were fires on the North Rim, and the smoke was causing some hikers respiratory problems. We talked a long time about a place in Grapevine drainage where the trail hugs the edge of a six-hundred-foot drop, gets narrow and broken off in places, and tilts toward the canyon for a couple of hundred yards. She called it "visually challenging" but not dangerous. People don't backpack the Tonto in the summer, because of the extreme heat and lack of water, she said, and there hadn't been enough people on the trail yet this fall to get it packed properly down.

Kelli and I awoke on October 3 to a cold, windy rain and thunder so loud and close it rattled the windows of our Grand Canyon Village hotel room. That's what I mean about Old Man Canyon. I had spent two weeks worried about heat and dehydration. Until that minute I hadn't given hypothermia a second thought. We decided to have a big sit-down breakfast and wait out the storm. We only had to get five miles down the South Kaibab Trail to the Tonto, then around the corner into Cremation drainage by dark.

"Please tell me you're kidding," Kelli said, when I told her our first night's camp would be at a place called Cremation.

I should probably mention, this was Kelli's first backpacking trip. Kelli's a former jazz singer who lives in Vegas. If she uses the word "hike" in a sentence, she most likely means "hike up," as in her skirt. This section of the Tonto Trail isn't the easiest trail in the canyon, nor is it by a long stretch the hardest. Kelli is of strong mind and body, an extremely good sport, and eight years my junior. I decided that if I could make the thirty-three miles in three nights, she could, too.

By 2 P.M. it was still thundering and pouring like crazy, but we'd run out of wait-time. At least, I thought, this should take care of the fires. We took the bus to the South Kaibab trailhead, donned the flimsy emergency ponchos we'd been sure we wouldn't use, and stepped out into the driving rain. The trail was a river of red mud, and small rocks were falling all around us. This was the first rain in months, and it had loosened and softened everything. The ponchos were worth exactly what we paid for them. They blew away from our bodies and up into our line of vision, and we were soaked in a matter of minutes, but I was stubbornly committed to the idea that if I resisted the urge to open my pack and dig out my real rain gear, the storm would end. Kelli's pack (an old and beloved one of mine but hardly state of the art) sat catawampous on her back, but neither of us wanted to stop moving long enough to fix it. It occurred to me, fleetingly, that we were fifteen minutes into our trip and already looked like one of those case studies in how not to behave when you are backpacking. I could just see the headlines detailing our untimely demise.

Then, about two thousand feet below the rim, the thunder quieted, the clouds parted, and a low sun emerged for thirty gorgeous minutes before setting behind the canyon wall. All of a sudden we were in paradise: the piñon, juniper, and cactuses, bright green and fragrant, refreshed by the rain; the red, orange, and vermilion of the canyon walls deepened by the low sun and the dark clouds that still filled the eastern sky.

What you can't begin to understand about the canyon until you get down off the rim is its size, what a vertical mile actually feels like when you are halfway down it and how that pretty wall on the North Rim that you thought you could reach out and touch from the South Rim is actually ten miles away. I felt like Jonah in the belly of the whale, Alice through the looking glass. While scores of day hikers were hurrying back up the trail before darkness fell, we were the only ones descending into the impossible beauty. The canyon stretched out before us, huge and imposing, grand indeed, nothing short of magnificent, and we seemed to have it all to ourselves.

When we finally reached the Tonto Platform, rounded the first corner, and threw our packs to the ground in what was left of the twilight, we discovered the following things in the following order: Kelli had lost one of her water bottles somewhere on the trail, my brand-new tent had a break in one of its shock-corded poles, and Old Man Canyon, that tireless comedian, was working up one more lightning storm and blowing it right toward us across the flat open plateau where we were trying to make camp.

I resisted the urge to run all the way back to the pit toilets at the South Kaibab junction to wait out the storm, regretted for the third time since leaving the Village my decision not to bring duct tape, rummaged the first-aid kit for something adhesive, located my headlamp, and went to work fashioning a splint for the tent pole. Within fifteen minutes, the wind had died, the lightning had moved off to the north, and the tent was crooked but standing. "Just kidding," the canyon laughed above me.

We used too little water to cook freeze-dried chicken and noodles with a packet of peas thrown in, tried to make up for it with hot sauce, ate quickly, and crawled into the tent, which was made mostly of mesh and was perfect for stargazing. The summer triangle had begun to set, a quarter moon close behind it. To the east Orion was on the rise, chasing the Pleiades across the sky, foretelling the approach of winter.

"Do you hear that?" I asked Kelli.

"What?" she asked.

"That guy," I said, "snoring."

"Don't lose it on me now," she said, and then we were both asleep.

A little before 6 A.M. we identified our snorer as he crested a little ridge about fifty yards in front of us: a desert bighorn ram in the rut in steady, if somewhat ambivalent, pursuit of a ewe who seemed more interested in her morning grazing than in him. He glanced at us indifferently and went on following her, making his snoring noises and occasionally butting her lightly in the rear.

We watched until they disappeared from view down-canyon; then we hoisted our packs and hit the trail. I had hoped that after the rain we would find potholes everywhere, but I didn't yet understand the nature of the Tonto Platform, which is made of dirt and shale and cactus and sandstone, nearly free of the outcroppings that make such good water catchers in other desert parks. Still, as we approached the very first Cremation subdrainage, we could see the silver glint of a thread of water.

"You've got to be kidding me," Kelli said as we stood over the little pool that was only two inches wide and two inches deep but at least a foot long.

"You'd be surprised," I said. "I bet we get two whole bottles out of that."

"What about the bugs?" Kelli asked.

"Yeah," I said, unwrapping our trusty Pur water filter. "That's why they call it survival of the fittest."

"I didn't mean we should worry about saving the bugs," she said. "I just wasn't sure about drinking them."

The pool yielded three full bottles, which still left a bit for the bugs. We hoisted our packs, feeling resourceful, hardy, and hydrated. Then we descended into the first real arm of Cremation and instantly got a sense of the scale of the map, how far we had come (almost no distance at all), and how far we would have to go that day to stay on schedule. Sitting between us and Grapevine, which was supposed to be our second camp, were two more arms of Cremation, as well as Lonetree Canyon, Boulder drainage, and several smaller subdrainages.

"Are they all going to be like this?" Kelli asked, as we struggled with the steep climb out of Cremation number one.

"We'll just take each drainage one at a time," I said. "If we don't make Grapevine, we don't make Grapevine."

Grapevine, I thought, the first reliable water source, and said a prayer of thanks to Old Man Canyon for the tiny puddles his rainstorm had left behind. We found more of them in Lonetree and refilled our bottles and soaked our shirts. The heat and exertion diminished our appetites, but I forced some food down both of us in the meager shade of a piñon. By the time we got to Boulder drainage, the sun was setting, and we made camp once again, only one canyon shy of our destination.

"You did great," I said to Kelli, and it was true. We had finally gotten her pack adjusted correctly that morning, and she had moved along steadily behind me for nearly ten miles. Now she had about 10,000 cactus needles in her shins and a look on her face that said I might no longer be one of her favorite people.

I tried not to look as happy as I felt. We had not seen or heard another human being all day, not an airplane (we were in the no-fly zone), not a car alarm, not the teenage boy who had announced at the top of his lungs upon emerging from one of the pit toilets back along the South Kaibab, "Well, that's five pounds less I'll have to carry out of the canyon."

Before we even started the long trek to the head of Grapevine drainage, I could see the bad spot that the ranger had talked about on the far wall. Not the trail as much as the lack of place for a trail. The canyon dropped nearly two thousand feet, sheer from the top of the Redwall limestone above us, through the shale and sandstone of the Tonto Platform where we stood, and down into the old granite of Grapevine drainage. The trail clung to the wall approximately halfway down. In the six miles it takes to circumvent Grapevine canyon, you spend about half of your time right on that edge. The issue is not the trail itself, which is always wide enough to walk on, but the lack of margin for error, and the tilt of the trail into the abyss. If you stumble or become unbalanced due to the weight of your pack or have a moment of dizziness from walking for so long on the cusp of that dark empty space just to your left and the blindingly bright desert off to your right, the trip to the bottom of Grapevine drainage is strictly one way.

When we reached the head of Grapevine, the sun was high in the sky and we encountered our first human, a woman from Kansas doing the same trip we were doing, in reverse, except she was taking seven days, in celebration of her fiftieth birthday. She was spending a rest day in Grapevine, had just washed her clothes in the first water source we had seen all morning, and was communing with the crow who lived there that was famous for being able to open pack zippers and steal food. She said that she hadn't been able to find a catch pool at Grapevine Spring — a few miles farther down the trail in a side drainage — and had therefore spent hours catching drips off the wall. Hours was one thing we didn't have, so I got on my belly to hang our water filter into her laundry pool while Kelli screamed at the crow whenever it neared my backpack. I had that sense of being in an instructional manual again, a picture of the Kansas woman's trip in the How To column, our trip filed under Don't Let This Happen to You.

The Kansan said the bad part of the trail (a ranger had warned her, too) had not been so bad after all, that she was in the middle of it before she noticed the extreme angle and realized, oh, this must be it. "I mean, I guess it could be bad," she said, "if you're afraid of heights."

"Well, isn't everybody afraid of heights," I asked, "if the heights get bad enough?"

With the onset of my fourth decade has come a nagging acrophobia that I have in the past been able to ignore or deny. It is not debilitating, but it makes my palms sweat and my knees shake, and I wanted neither sweaty palms nor shaky knees on the much touted bad part of Grapevine. By the time we got there, I had both, so Kelli crossed first and kept yelling back to me, "We've done harder!" And whether it was true or not, it got me across without incident.

We could sense the presence of water before we could see it, the smell of it, and the change it brought to the canyon bottom, the sudden profusion of medium-size cottonwood trees and more greenery than we had seen in days. The actual pool — where the water bubbled to the surface — wasn't big enough to fill a juice glass, but unlike all the other places where we had gotten water, this spring was running. We could see it trickling briefly down-canyon before it got sucked under again by the thirsty sand.

We could pump approximately a quarter liter out of the tiny pool, then we'd have to wait five minutes for the pool to refill. It would take us the better part of two hours and most of the remaining daylight to fill all eleven of our water bottles, plus the two full bottles each that we drank on the spot. The miracle was that it kept refilling; in this hot, dry, moody canyon, a trickle of clear, sweet water just kept bubbling and bubbling right up out of the ground. My original plan of making up with the canyon had been presumptuous. It couldn't care less about me; this time I had just put myself more in the path of its gifts than of its punishments.

What Kelli had been asking several times a day was, "Why would anybody want to do something like this?" It was a fair question, given the heat and her thirst and the needles in her legs and the blisters and the powdered food. A fair question from someone who would be much happier in her own kitchen or in an uptown restaurant or in a cool, dark bar.

"This is why we do it," I wanted to say to Kelli, for the feeling of unadulterated joy we have at the sight of this tiny spring. For the moment of realizing the man we heard snoring all night was a full-curl desert bighorn ram. For the pleasure of looking at the map and counting the canyons we have put behind us. For the thrill of waking up all alone in one of the seven natural wonders of the world. For the simple satisfaction of putting one foot in front of the other for hours and then days, with every single thing we need (and a few things it turns out we don't) piled on our backs. For all the times in the next year or two or five when, finding ourselves challenged or exhausted, we'll think, This is nothing compared to hiking thirty-three miles of the Grand Canyon in something well shy of four full days. For the color the sunset sky is turning above us and the way we are seeing it — not at all the way we see it through the windows of a house or a car or a plane.

The next morning we would climb nearly four thousand feet up and out and back to civilization. In the meantime we shared another liter of deliciously cool water and waited for the little pool to refill.

BEN RYDER HOWE

# An Impossible Place to Be

FROM *Outside*

IN YAVIZA, a town of *contrabandistas*, barefoot prostitutes, and drunken men fighting in the streets with machetes and broken bottles, I'm spotted by two Panamanian policemen and ordered to the *cuartel* (barracks). It's noon on a Saturday, and I've arrived in this forlorn 3,200-person trading outpost in the Darién Gap.

"*Pasaporte,*" demands the sour-faced officer at the *cuartel*. Taking it from my hands, he asks, "*Americano?*" Then he writes my name in his registry of visitors. "Have a seat," he says. "The *comandante* is coming."

Yaviza, thirty miles from the Colombian border, is famous for lawlessness — it's a magnet for fugitives, poachers, and bootleggers. Many of the restaurants openly sell sea turtle eggs (fried or scrambled), a prized but illegal delicacy. Put out the word that you want a blue-and-yellow macaw as a pet and eventually there will be a knock on your hotel-room door. Yaviza's whorehouses have long been favored by antigovernment guerrillas from Colombia — indeed, a high-ranking rebel is said to maintain a pied-à-terre here.

So there's irony in being grabbed by the police. But the humor vanishes when the balding *comandante*, dressed in fatigues, shows up and tells me the whole area has been shut down.

"Shut down?" I ask. "Including Darién National Park?"

The *comandante* nods. "For security reasons," he says.

The national park is what I have come to see. It's December 2003, and I've traveled 145 miles southeast from Panama City by a succession of rickety buses and farm vehicles. The 2,200-square-mile park, untamed and essentially roadless, sits like a lopsided U against the Colombian border. The rarely visited area, which makes for an impassible divide between North and South America, is a mystery zone within an extraordinary, much larger wilderness — the 10,000-square-mile Darién Gap. Stretching from the sandy shores of the Caribbean south to the rocky cliffs of the Pacific, the Gap begins just beyond the suburbs of Panama City and sprawls east, thickening as it goes, until it has erased all roads, all telephone lines, all signs of civilization, turning the landscape into one solid band of unruly vegetation filled with jaguars, deadly bushmasters, and other exotic wildlife.

The mere existence of such a throwback in the modern world suggests an inviolate timelessness. But as I learned in Panama City, the park is in trouble, jeopardized by its remoteness, the very quality that in the past has ensured its survival.

Indra Candanedo, a thirty-eight-year-old biologist in the Panama branch of the Nature Conservancy, introduced me to the possibility that the Gap might be eroding. As we sat in her office overlooking the capital's gleaming skyscrapers, she described a set of disturbing satellite images she had recently seen.

"It looks bad," she said, noting that huge swaths of the park appear to have been deforested.

Candanedo couldn't be certain about this, because satellite imaging usually doesn't give a complete picture in places like rainforests, with their heavy precipitation and cloud cover. So why not check things out on the ground?

That option isn't so easy. Neighboring Colombia, just across a porous border, is one of the bloodiest countries in the world, making the Gap an intensely dangerous place. In the mid-1990s, following a spate of kidnappings and massacres related to the endless Colombian civil war, conservation programs and scientific research were drastically scaled back — at a time when the Gap was coming under increasing strain from landless farmers making new homesteads, slashing and burning to clear agricultural plots inside the park. Even Panama's own security forces withdrew, leaving large sections of the park unmonitored.

Candanedo, who had been the park's director in the mid-1990s, knew exactly how vulnerable it was, and she had enough information to be troubled. "You should see it for yourself," she said. "If you can."

The next day, upon returning to the *cuartel* in Yaviza, I find that the police have inexplicably changed their minds. I will be allowed to continue toward Darién National Park, provided I receive permission from the police in El Real, another tiny town that serves as park headquarters.

Leaving the *cuartel,* I walk to the Yaviza waterfront. In the shadow of La India, a raucous cantina adorned by a mural of a naked blond, I make a deal with the owner of a dugout canoe and resume my journey, by river, into the heart of the Gap.

An "abyss and horror of mountains, rivers, and marshes," in the words of one sixteenth-century traveler, the Darién Gap is Panama's Bermuda Triangle: a place where things seem to go wrong more often than everywhere else. As an old saying goes, the Spanish conquistadores defeated the Andes, the deserts, and the Amazon but not the Gap, which foiled their advances.

The Gap is small compared with tropical wildernesses like the Amazon and the Congo. Yet it feels huge, with its slight population — roughly 100,000 people, half Afro-Caribbean and half native Panamanian — mainly concentrated in isolated bush villages like Yaviza. In Panama and Colombia, it is known as *El Tapón* ("The Plug"), because it blocks the flow of human exploration. The Spaniards discovered it in 1502, founded their first mainland colony there, and then set the tone for centuries to come with a staggering atrocity: the murders, over an eight-year period starting in 1513, of tens of thousands of natives, many of them killed by vicious war dogs that attacked their villages.

By the late eighteenth century, the Spaniards, repulsed by the Gap's inhospitable environment, had left the region to rot in peace. Nourished by one of the wettest climates on Earth — up to an inch of rain per day during the rainy season — Darién's jungle flourished unchecked, providing an ideal refuge for outlaws, pirates, runaway slaves, and fiercely territorial Kuna Indians. Over time the "myth of Darién" would arise from a series of spectacular tragedies, including the deaths, in 1699, of two thousand Scottish colonists (from shipwreck, malaria, and starvation) and, in 1856, of seven explorers who became hopelessly lost on a U.S. Navy survey expedition. Canals were planned for the Gap, which is approximately fifty miles wide at its narrowest sea-to-sea point, but none were executed.

Today, having resisted five centuries of encroachment, the Gap may finally be running out of time. As environmentalists have stood by, helpless to get involved on the ground, a multitude of unseen enemies — poachers, poor farmers, refugees, small-scale timber companies — have been whittling away at its forests.

The question is, How did the situation suddenly get so precarious? Hoping to find out, and ignoring a U.S. State Department advisory emphatically discouraging travel to eastern Panama, I first visited the Gap in the summer of 2003, spent three weeks unsuccessfully trying to get inside Darién National Park, and returned twice in subsequent months. On each occasion, I ran into the problem that has bedeviled outsiders from the start: access. Though not impenetrable, the Gap remains a formidable challenge to navigate. From Panama City there is only one road, the Pan-American Highway, which dead-ends in Yaviza. From there until Guapá, Colombia, some ninety miles away, there are nothing but mud tracks and footpaths.

The Gap is still a refuge for outlaws — only today, instead of pirates, there are the guerrillas and their ultrarightist enemies, the United Self-Defense Forces, who are generally known as the paramilitaries. The guerrillas belong to the Revolutionary Armed Forces of Colombia (FARC); they come to neighboring Panama not only for the nightlife in villages like Yaviza but also to buy and stockpile weapons. (According to a recent report by the RAND Corporation, a nonpartisan California think tank, Panama has become "the single largest trans-shipment point" for the majority of small arms flowing into Colombia, "mostly across the densely forested Darién Gap.") The paramilitaries, who are funded by Colombia's wealthiest landowners, come for the same reason, as well as to fight over a tremendously lucrative drug pipeline. The violent contest between these two groups constitutes the most urgent threat to the Gap today; the chaos they create prevents government and conservation watchdogs from doing their jobs.

Indirectly, their fight is also a threat to the United States. For decades the Gap has kept South American problems from spreading — not just illegal immigration but also contraband and diseases that, while not exclusively South American, don't exist in the north.

"We let the jungle protect our border," says Stanley Heckadon, sixty, a Panamanian anthropologist and former head of INRENADE, the precursor to ANAM, the national government's top environmental authority. Since the 1989 U.S. invasion to topple General Manuel Noriega, Panama has been without an army, and until recently its police forces have had an unspoken policy of not confronting the Colombian militants.

Letting the Gap serve as a natural barrier "requires very little investment," Heckadon adds. "And in the past, it has actually tended to work."

A week before my trip to Yaviza, on my first foray into the park, I visited Jaqué, a village of a few thousand people where the guerrillas buy groceries and get their cavities filled. Jaqué lies two hundred miles southeast of Panama City, just outside the national park, along a rocky section of Pacific coast marked by lengthy stretches of exquisite black cliffs. There are no roads nearby, and the government maps are covered with blank spots marked INSUFFICIENT DATA. As I flew in aboard the twice-weekly plane from the capital, I tried to keep track of our position, but all I saw was an endless span of green extending into the cloud-covered peaks of the local mountain range, Serranía de Jungurudó.

In the seat behind me was Julie Velásquez Runk, a thirty-five-year-old graduate student from the Yale School of Forestry. A native of Detroit, Runk has spent much of the past seven years studying historical ecology in the Gap and living with the Wounaan, an indigenous tribe that dwells along its rivers. I'd asked her to accompany me so I could see the Gap through her eyes. Our plan was to find a guide with a boat, then ascend twenty miles up the Río Jaqué to the heart of the national park.

Our base was the Tropic Star Lodge, a strange outpost five miles west of Jaqué that was built in 1961 by Ray Smith, a Texas oil baron. The Tropic Star sits on secluded Piña Bay, circled by mountainous jungle. It's a *Thunderball*-style palace that offers prime access to what many consider the greatest sportfishing in the world. After Smith's death, in 1968, the property was sold to a series of gringos who converted it into a $1,000-a-night resort, popular with U.S. senators, John Wayne, and Saudi sheiks.

After settling in, Runk, with help from a Tropic Star employee, found a *motorista* to take us upriver. We'd been under way for an hour when we arrived at a police station. There, a double-chinned *comandante* told us, "No one without a permit goes upriver."

So we turned around and found ourselves a poacher. Carlos,

an acquaintance of a Tropic Star employee, is a thirty-seven-year-old refugee who fled Colombia after, he said, "the paramilitaries started cutting off people's heads" in his village. He'd been living illegally in eastern Panama for nine years, supporting himself by hunting, also illegally, in the park. He wore a cobalt-blue tank top that read STALLION in big letters; at his waist hung a machete.

Carlos took us an hour west by speedboat to Punta Caracoles, a peninsula jutting out from the national park that teems with bush dogs, tapirs, and other tenacious wildlife. I'd been told that only the park's residents could hunt inside it, but Carlos, who lives in Jaqué, told me, "If I don't hunt here, someone else will." He grinned. "Besides, I only take a little."

Environmentalists consider poachers like Carlos, who are wiping out entire populations of peccaries, howler monkeys, and tapirs, a serious problem. "The greatest threat to the park is not some big entity like a multinational conglomerate or a development project," says Líder Sucre, the thirty-something executive director of the Asociación Nacional Para la Conservación de la Naturaleza (ANCON), Panama's largest nongovernmental conservation group. "It's the fact that the park is huge, its staff is small, and there are hundreds and hundreds of little guys whittling away at it."

After landing on a stretch of white beach, we plunged into the forest along a well-cleared path, which made me wonder how many hunters use this area. "It's not necessarily people who keep the paths clear," Runk said. "It could be white-lipped peccaries," a two-foot-tall species of wild boar weighing as much as sixty pounds.

I looked at Carlos, who was sniffing the air. "Do you hear them gnashing their tusks?" he asked. All I heard were the waves crashing on Punta Caracoles.

"It's quiet," I said.

"That's because the other *animalitos* are hiding," said Carlos.

"Watch out if the peccaries come our way," said Runk. "Climb a tree, do whatever you have to do. You don't want to be gored." As much as the peccaries scared her, Runk was hoping we'd see them, because, she explained, "a large herd of white-lipped peccaries is an excellent indicator of healthy forest."

"What's a 'large' herd?" I asked.

"Oh, two hundred animals. You'll definitely know they're coming."

Suddenly Carlos hissed for us to be quiet. We heard a grunt from the undergrowth, then a rustle of leaves, then something pawing impatiently at the ground. Carlos yelled, "Run!" Which he and Runk did, but my legs had turned to jelly. A streak of brown fur tore out of the bush and hit me squarely on the calf.

"What was it?" I yelled, looking down and expecting to see blood. But there was no wound. The animal, which must have weighed about ten pounds, wobbled dizzily back to the bush.

"I think it was a ñeque," said Runk.

"A what?"

"A ñeque. A little mammal. Sort of like a big rat."

I looked into the forest and saw the dazed ñeque, gearing up for another charge. Then I noticed Carlos, who was laughing so hard he'd almost fallen on his machete.

"I should have cut off his head," he said, gasping for air.

An hour later, we came across a poacher's campsite, an empty lean-to made of palm fronds, with the hunter's underwear hanging from the roof. Next to it, a campfire smoldered, and Carlos found two burlap sacks stuffed with smoked peccary meat. "This is too much," he frowned, taking out a fist-size chunk of the meat, which he tore into strips and passed out to us.

That afternoon, as we hiked eight miles farther into the park, we saw more signs of a healthy forest: the footprints of a jaguar, one of the five species of cat that lives in the Gap; an ancient palm called a cycad; and, back on the beach, a clutch of sea turtle eggs buried arm-deep in the sand. Runk decided that the forest in and around Caracoles was "doing more than OK."

"I've seen forest that's in worse shape," she said. "A lot worse."

War can be good for the environment — sometimes. In Poland during World War II, the wolf population increased substantially, and the Vietnam War gave the Vietnamese tiger an opportunity to rebound. One obvious benefit of armed conflict is that it scares people away from forest they might otherwise destroy.

Because of its proximity to the equator and its location between the continents, the Gap features an unusual mix of creatures, such as crab-eating foxes, brocket deer, and pumas, as well as an extraordinary level of biodiversity that includes at least 2,400 plant species and more than 900 species of mammals and birds. "There's nothing like it," says Líder Sucre, of ANCON. "No other rainforest in Central America is as well preserved."

The trade-off is that Panama lacks access to South America and has no control over its own eastern border. Thirty years ago, the U.S. government decided this was an unacceptable situation. It provided more than $100 million to build a section of the Pan-American Highway connecting Panama to Colombia. The rest of the highway was already complete, stretching from Alaska to the southern tip of Chile.

The physical obstacles were daunting, including swamps deep enough to sink a ten-story building. Nevertheless, it wasn't the terrain but a virus, foot-and-mouth disease (FMD), that kept the project from going forward.

FMD is the doomsday plague of the livestock industry, an illness whose outbreak can shake global stock markets. Most recently, an epidemic of FMD ravaged England in 2001, causing more than $7 billion in economic losses. No cases of the disease have been reported in Panama, and the last U.S. outbreak occurred in 1929. But in Colombia, FMD was endemic during the 1970s and remains present today.

"If FMD were to invade Central America, it could have very rapid access to the United States," says Harold Hofmann, sixty-one, associate regional director of the U.S. Animal and Plant Health Inspection Service (APHIS), an agency within the Department of Agriculture that's charged with protecting the U.S. food supply from pests and diseases. "Therefore, the government's plan is to keep it as far away as we can."

Because of concerns about FMD, in 1975 the highway plan was challenged in court by groups, including the Sierra Club. The project was eventually scrapped. Meanwhile, yielding to pressure from the United States, the Panamanian government established Darién National Park, in 1981, as a way to carve out a cattle-free zone in the jungle. Today, APHIS's $4.5 million regional budget covers the salaries of ninety Panamanian livestock inspectors who patrol the country looking for sick cattle. It also funds the battle against another potentially catastrophic South American scourge, the screwworm, whose larvae consume the flesh of live cattle, which can lead to fatal secondary infections. To control the insect, the agency drops a sterile male version of it from airplanes, in batches of 40 million, over the region every week.

"If screwworm got loose in the United States, the effect on producers would be about $800 million lost per year," says Hofmann.

"Foot-and-mouth would far exceed that. It's a very dangerous disease — something we all fear."

The good news is that Panama remains free of FMD and appears close to eliminating the screwworm; the bad news is that over the past fifteen years, the jungle on the Colombian side has shrunk.

"There's nothing left but cattle ranches," says ANCON's Sucre.

Meanwhile, the forest on Panama's side is dwindling, too, thanks to an influx of Panamanian farmers drawn by the opening of the Pan-American Highway from Panama City to Yaviza, in 1988. Since then, eastern Panama's population has doubled, and essentially every acre of forest not on a mountainside is in danger of being cut down or burned — which is what makes protecting the park so vital.

Twelve miles up the Chucunaque River from Yaviza, continuing my December 2003 journey from there by dugout, the owner of the boat drops me in El Real, a weirdly inert village where a smiling pig's head, bobbing in the river, greets me as I step on dry land. Eight miles west of the park boundary, El Real is the headquarters for fourteen dedicated but pathetically underequipped guards charged with patrolling an area the size of Puerto Rico.

At the ranger office — a wooden building with several basketball-size holes in the floor and a network of old PCs, none of them working — I meet Jorge Vásquez, thirty-eight, a Kuna Indian and senior park ranger. Vásquez is sinewy like a high school wrestler and endearingly oblivious to how odd it may seem that one's desk sits next to a hole in the floor. Initially he tries to be upbeat about the park's troubles. "We're doing great!" he tells me, though some of the rangers have gone months without paychecks, and their gasless speedboat sits on blocks outside the station.

Later, though, after a few beers at a cantina in El Real, Vásquez confesses his frustration. "We can't do our jobs," he says. "We don't have the resources or the security. You can't protect a park if you can't get around in it."

I tell him about the satellite images, and he says he has a pretty good idea where the deforestation is happening. Back at headquarters, he shows me a faded wall map. "See here?" he says, waving his hand over virtually the entire border. "This belongs to the guerrillas. It's too dangerous to patrol." He points at a different region. "This belongs to drug traffickers. We can't go here, either."

Sometimes war isn't so good for the environment. Before the guerrillas invaded the park, the rangers maintained three monitoring stations; now they have only one, a mountain retreat called Rancho Frío. The others, abandoned to poachers and *contrabandistas,* "haven't been visited in almost a decade," says Vásquez.

Meanwhile, refugees from Colombia have been pouring across the border. According to the Vicariato Apostólico del Darién, a local charitable affiliate of the Catholic Church, about five thousand Colombians have immigrated to Panama over the past seven years, more than three hundred of whom currently live inside or near Darién National Park. Those inside form clandestine communities that the church has tried to protect, because there's a high risk that they'll be killed if the Panamanian authorities send them back to Colombia. Manuel Acevedo, a human-rights activist at the *vicariato,* concedes that the refugees are among those burning forest and that during the dry season "the amount of smoke coming from the park is tremendous."

Vásquez and I decide to hike into the park; miraculously, the El Real police give us permission. "I'm going to show you what an amazing place this is," Vásquez promises.

We leave El Real on a dirt road that cuts through farmland and rows of spiny cedar, take a shortcut beneath some barbed wire enclosing a herd of cattle, and walk through several miles of scrubby undergrowth. Then we enter the park, and suddenly, dramatically, everything changes. The trees are bigger, of course: We see several specimens of roble, a prized hardwood, that might be a few centuries old. The atmosphere is dark, wet, even chilly; Vásquez points out the footprint of a puma. It's like walking into a dark room and realizing, when the lights come on, that you've stumbled into a cathedral. There's practically no need for trails, because the ground appears to have been swept clean. We are in one of the rarest of all jungle settings, a true triple-tiered canopy.

"What do you think?" Vásquez asks.

"It looks like God's greenhouse," I say.

An hour after sunset we finally reach Rancho Frío. We'll have to camp here, because the police at a local checkpoint have threatened to arrest us if we keep hiking.

"How much farther to where the deforestation shows up in the satellite images?" I ask Vásquez.

"A lot," he says. Vásquez is dour, and at first I think it's because of the station, which is dirty and abandoned. But, as I soon find out, he has something much worse on his mind. Last year, just a day's walk away from here, the paramilitaries invaded Púcuro, a hamlet on the park's boundary, where he grew up. During that raid they brutally killed his father, Gilberto Vásquez, fifty-eight, a village chief.

The incident began on January 26, 2003, during a coming-of-age ceremony in Paya, a Kuna village inside the park. The paramilitaries, disguised as guerrillas, entered the village and requested a meeting with the chiefs. At the meeting they turned their guns on the hosts and said they were going to punish the Kuna for helping the FARC. Two chiefs and an unarmed Kuna policeman were executed. Afterward, the paramilitaries stole the village's livestock, killed its dogs, and mined its paths so nobody could get in or out. Then they started marching toward Púcuro, forcing Gilberto Vásquez to serve as their guide. Someone had already alerted Púcuro, however, and the village was empty. So the paramilitaries shot Vásquez in the head inside his own house.

No Panamanian police officers were in Púcuro or Paya the weekend of the massacre. Since then, however, security has greatly improved — in Púcuro and Paya alone, the police have added one hundred officers — a development that Vásquez calls "the one good thing to come out of the killings."

Yet many find the changes disturbing. "Panama used to be neutral regarding Colombia," says Eric Jackson, the fifty-one-year-old publisher of a muckraking paper called the *Panama News,* in Panama City. "Now it seems it is starting to take sides with the paramilitaries." Villages thought to be guerrilla resting and staging areas have been ransacked and burned — not only by the paramilitaries but also by the Panamanian police.

"The government doesn't want people to know what's going on," says Manuel Acevedo. "And so no one does."

Vásquez and I leave Rancho Frío and return to El Real. Along the way, we pass through a few hamlets and chat with the remaining residents. "Most people got scared and left," says one resident. In one community, the only inhabitant is a toothless old woman tending chickens.

Soon, though, we come across an abandoned village that is starting to fill up again. "Who are these people?" I ask Vásquez. "Colombians," he says. "Refugees." One of the residents waves at us. He's wearing rubber boots and holding a Stihl chain saw. In his backyard, a little pile of brush is already burning.

Several months after my Yaviza visit, in March 2004, I return for another look. As soon as I arrive, I call the police and request permission to fly over the park to investigate the deforestation. Four days later I'm told that the national director of police, Carlos Bares, is personally "indisposed" to my request, because of the security situation along the border.

So I phone a tour operator, ANCON Expeditions. Loosely affiliated with the environmental group ANCON, the outfit flies ecotourists to an abandoned gold mine as far inside the Darién Gap as you can get, just five miles from the Colombian border. The mine, known as Cana, is halfway up a four-thousand-foot mountain and thirty miles from the nearest town. It's so isolated that the police consider it too much of a hike for the guerrillas and therefore safe for foreigners. The only way to get there is by plane.

A few days after my call, I squeeze aboard a charter carrying fourteen American birdwatchers to Cana. During the flight over the park, all I can see are clouds, mountains, and a lush lowland rainforest.

At the mine, a path leads into cloudforest, and along the way I can see over waves of razor-sharp ridges into South America. Nothing but a horizon-spanning canopy and layers of dark rain clouds fill the view. From here, crossing the Darién Gap looks as formidable as a trek across the Sahara.

During my first night at the Cana Field Station, a converted mining camp, I wake up at 1 A.M., having soaked the bed in sweat. The next day my temperature is all over the place, and a worker at the lodge discovers me shivering in bed.

"Uh-oh," he says. "Looks like malaria." I later find out it's hepatitis A combined with amoebic dysentery. The Darién Gap has started taking a toll on my body — I've lost ten pounds — so I'm extremely happy when a plane shows up the next day to take me back to Panama City.

I've been expecting its arrival: I chartered it before I left Panama City. Shortly before takeoff, I beg the pilots to let the ten-seat Islander "drift off course" by a few miles and fly at a lower altitude.

Once in the air, the Islander starts its usual route west before banking sharply to the north. Instead of climbing, it remains wafting above the treetops, buffeted by columns of warm air rising out of the jungle. A low ridge signals our entrance to the Tuira Valley, and suddenly below us lies the landscape that the police so determinedly tried to shield from our eyes — the area revealed by the satellite images as a minuscule yet potentially catastrophic fracture in the otherwise perfect seal of the Gap.

To be fair, it hasn't been turned into a wasteland. More than a few trees remain. Here and there, in fact, it appears that the ecosystem is already on its way to recovery. But one would never describe this landscape as "forested." On the contrary, it appears indiscriminately and brutally cut and in many places burned. Moreover, much of the destruction looks fresh — new fires burn below as we fly over.

Going back to at least the 1880s, when the U.S. Congress passed legislation calling for a hemispheric system of railroads, the end of the Darién Gap has been confidently and even gleefully predicted. But, like the oceans, the Gap's resilience seems endless — and yet, as with the oceans, we know it is not. Sometime during this decade or the next — without fanfare, almost certainly — a milestone will be reached. The last trees will go down and the first breach between North and South America will open.

"How far to the border?" I ask the pilots. One of them unfolds a map and measures the distance with his fingers.

"About twenty kilometers," he yells over the roar of the engines. Roughly thirteen miles. Thirteen miles of dwindling Gap dividing the hemisphere in two.

TOM IRELAND

# My Thai Girlfriends

FROM *The Missouri Review*

IN THE DREAM I'm served by a Thai woman wearing a white plaster mask. She and I are the only people in a large hotel dining room: antique table settings, six or eight to a table, and white linen tablecloths. The masked woman folds herself around me from behind, but along with the pleasure of being held comes the fear of impropriety. Foreigners are expected to practice restraint while visiting this country.

Upon waking I write, "At my age sex may be a thing of the past, but to live well, it's best not to rule it out entirely. The desire, not the act, is the important thing."

A year off from work requires complicated arrangements. Someone must be found to replace me at work, where for fifteen years I've been editing archaeological reports for New Mexico's Office of Cultural Affairs. I'm worried that my replacement will not do the job as well as I or that he will do it better. My house must be leased so I'll have enough money while I'm in Thailand. My medical insurance will be discontinued, putting me at the mercy of Asian diseases. I'll cancel my telephone, and the telephone company will give my old number to a stranger.

There's some explaining to do. It makes people nervous that I'm pulling up roots, leaving everything behind for a year. It causes them to question their own comfortable routines. They demand reasons. I say that I've always wanted to travel, which isn't true. The thought of going alone to an unknown country terrifies me. I say that I want to experience a foreign culture, knowing that it's no more possible to leave my own culture behind than it is to leave my own consciousness. Among coworkers, I don't say that my leaving has more to do with the disavowal of what I'm doing here than with anything I might find to do over there, which might remind them of their own dissatisfaction. Nor do I say that the real object of this adventure is not having to do anything at all.

One of the archaeologists at the office recommends Chiang Mai, a city in the cooler northern part of Thailand, as the best place to start. Chiang Mai has everything, he says — great food, friendly people, antiquities — and for Westerners, at least, it's incredibly cheap since the Asian economic collapse. He tells me how to use the red taxis, which only seem to be taking you miles out of your way. And he warns about the beauty of Thai women: "It's OK to sleep with them, but don't get serious. You'll end up having to support her whole family."

The Kingdom of Thailand issues me a visa that's valid from July 23, 2002, until July 22, 2002, that is, minus one day. I didn't want to go to Thailand all that much anyway, and now Thailand has complied with my basic reluctance to visit its country by granting me less than no time in the kingdom. The Thais are famous for politeness, and "Please come for minus one day" is probably their polite way of saying, "Don't bother to come at all." I call the Royal Thai Embassy in Washington, D.C., and talk to Mr. Pop. He apologizes and says there's been a mistake, which means I have to go after all.

As a going-away present, the Office of Cultural Affairs gives me a lifetime supply of condoms.

It might be Saturday. I'm alone in Chiang Mai, sitting on the wooden balcony that overlooks the courtyard of the Mountain View Guesthouse. Guests on the second floor are asked to walk lightly on the teak floors to keep from disturbing those in the rooms below. There's no view of the mountains, but Miss Daeng, the manager, says you can see them if you climb to the roof of the building after a rain.

This morning two real estate agents showed me an apartment in a high-rise condo called the Embassy, in the diplomatic district, across the river from the Old City. It was nice in a creepy way: the polished-stone lobby, the Winnie the Pooh sheets on the bed, the baby-blue carpet, an extra bedroom for the people from home who said they would visit. From up there I could see the mountains, the green valley, the red rooftops of the city, clouds and sky, the brown river down below with shapes of things floating in it. Chiang Mai looks much better from the tenth floor of the Embassy than it does from street level, but I'd rather be down here among the leaves at the Mountain View.

A woman named Jessica lives in the room next to mine. She's from Tucson, Arizona, and has a horse named Happy, a buckskin mare, whom she misses. She loves animals and thinks that Thai people do not treat them with enough kindness. Other times she was in Thailand, she didn't see some of the things she's seen this time around. Maybe because the country was so beautiful and the people so friendly, she didn't see the unpleasant things on her earlier visits.

Jessica calls me "Neighbor." I'm often sitting on the balcony over the courtyard when she comes and goes from her room. She's in Thailand to learn a therapeutic technique in which bundles of steaming herbs are applied to the body. She's buying the herbs in bulk and packing them in plastic bags to be sent back to Arizona. She's been talking to farmers in the region, trying to line up a reliable source of herbs for her business, but it's not easy to buy in sufficient quantities. Jessica has a large tattoo on her lower back, which I've come to think of as the *saddle* of her back, but I haven't been close enough to get a good look at it.

I ought to be seeing the sights of northern Thailand while I'm still a recent arrival here; otherwise I might become jaded and never see them at all: the orchid farm, the elephant camp, the snake farm, the water buffalo market, the umbrella village. One of the guidebooks says, "In order to experience the real Thailand one must leave the womb of the guesthouse," which I'm slowly preparing myself to do. For now I'm curled in the womb of the Mountain View Guesthouse with no view of the mountains, taking furtive looks at Jessica's tattoo and waiting to be born into the real Thailand. It must be here, within walking distance, and I'm convinced that it can be experienced by anyone with plenty of time to look, like me, or someone with less time but endearing personal qualities. I've been told that Americans are not yet hated here by the majority of the population — that if we are not exactly admired, at least we are looked upon with nothing more harmful than curiosity and envy. It's not the world outside that threatens as much as the task of being born into it.

Miss Daeng will know which of the sights in and around Chiang Mai are really worth seeing and which have been invented just for tourists. She and Jessica are in the lobby, a narrow space between the courtyard and the street decorated with sun-bleached posters of the orchid farm and all the rest. Miss Daeng is on the telephone long distance to India because Jessica needs to reach the teacher of some Indian martial art who might be willing to accept her as a student even though she is a Westerner and a woman. She wants to talk to him before traveling all that way for nothing, but Miss Daeng is having trouble getting through. Maybe the international telephone lines are tied up.

"Maybe India is closed today," I say.

She laughs at the joke. "Miss Daeng" (Miss Red) is her *cheulen* — a nickname. She knows a woman who has been called Miss Bank all her life because her mother worked as a bank teller before she was born and couldn't wait to get back to work after the baby was born. Miss Daeng is a short woman, even for a Thai, with disturbingly good posture. She's unmarried and has worked at her job as manager of the guesthouse seven days a week and all but two weeks out of the year for the past fifteen years, starting at six in the morning and finishing at nine or ten at night to support herself and her family, who live in Chiang Rai, another northern city.

"Maybe India is closed today," says Miss Daeng. "Ha ha!"

Eventually she gives up, and Jessica goes off to look for herbs.

"You're very kind to help your guests," I say. "You really ought to charge extra for your services."

"What do you mean?"

"In the United States people are paid for making arrangements for other people."

"How much are you going to pay me?" she says, sitting very straight in her chair. "One million?"

Jessica is buying a foot massage for Miss Daeng and Miss Nit, the guesthouse cook, to thank them for their help, and I've been asked along. The four of us walk through the wet nighttime streets making jokes about our umbrellas. Miss Nit, a sinewy woman with dragon eyes, has the biggest umbrella. It's blue, and if it were the only umbrella among us, it would be big enough to keep everyone dry. Miss Daeng has the next biggest and the most beautiful, with its garland of red and yellow flowers. The two Americans have the smallest umbrellas, which is funny because Americans are bigger than Thais. My sorry umbrella is crumpled from being turned inside out by the wind too many times. The women laugh at it as we walk along the wet streets where families are eating.

"You've got to raise your umbrella awareness in Thailand," says Jessica, "to keep from sticking it in people's faces."

The sidewalks are choked with parked motorbikes and eating stalls, the paraphernalia of family industry spilling out into the public space from lightless interiors. A man sits in a black cell full of blackened gasoline engines that take up all the room there is except for one oily spot of light, where he does his accounts. We walk past a floodlit, elephant-sized Buddha, past the Boys' School (girls are also allowed to attend), past ghostly temple courtyards closed for the night, and leave our shoes and umbrellas in the rain outside the massage parlor.

The masseurs, in their green-checked uniforms, are expecting us. The TV is on and stays on while we get our feet massaged. They smear our feet with Nivea and continually look over their shoulders to keep tabs on the action. Lots of shooting and fiery explosions. Jessica asks for the sound to be turned down. Miss Daeng translates from behind her newspaper. On the wall, a map of the human foot, its regions and municipalities, its major thoroughfares. When he's not watching TV, my masseur sometimes looks at me to see how I'm taking it. What I send back is my best imitation of a beatific smile even though his hands are very strong and just then when he dug his knuckles in I might have cried out in pain, but I didn't want to seem ungrateful or impolite.

The rain keeps coming down. My umbrella, left upside down, fills with water until it shifts and empties itself on the street. Next time I'll remember to leave it right side up, the way any intelligent person would.

Whenever I contemplate going somewhere else, getting on a bus or a train, I find reasons not to go. There's hardly enough time to travel out of town before my Thai language course begins. Anyway, what pleasure could there be in going alone and in being so uncomfortably conspicuous in one's aloneness, which is hard enough to accept when it goes unobserved? A man alone in Thailand, native or foreigner, is an object of curiosity, if not suspicion. You do not eat alone in a restaurant, or you do it well after dark, when the restaurant is full of other people and your solitude is not quite so loud.

Night justifies sleep. In sleep I can forget who and where I am and all the things I am not doing here: crossing borders, exploring the trackless jungle or lolling on the beaches, chasing women, meditating, finding my way in Thai society, volunteering in refugee camps. I'm not doing much of anything besides walking aimlessly through the city. At night I sleep and sleep in the womb of the guesthouse.

The best time is between deep sleep and morning's first dove, when dreams can be read in the language of the waking mind. Cigarette smoke finds its way into the room, which means that the koi are being fed in their pond beneath the balcony. As always, the man who feeds the koi is standing at the edge of the pool with a cigarette and a cup of coffee, looking into the water. Jessica asked him not to overfeed the koi. She used to work in a pet store and knows that overfeeding kills them. The man listened to her advice and promised not to overfeed, but now Jessica has left for India to study martial arts and the man feeds the koi the way he always has, generously. When a koi dies, he ladles it from the water with a board that he keeps hidden among the plants next to the pond.

A few days before she left, Jessica decided to overhaul the koi pond. She and Nit and I took a taxi to the koi market and bought hyacinth and lotus and a few small koi to replace the ones that had died. I carried the koi in a plastic bag through the market, where some boys were playing checkers with bottlecaps. Back at the guesthouse Jessica and I took off our shoes and waded into the pond and placed the pots of hyacinth and lotus where they looked best. Some of the pots would not stay put, and we had to weigh them down with rocks and bricks. Then I opened the plastic bag and released the young koi into the water.

"How is your class?" asks Miss Daeng.

"Boring. All the students are men except for one Korean girl who wants to be a missionary."

We are expected to wear long pants and refrain from asking questions, which takes time that could otherwise be used for practice. I don't mind wearing long pants, because it's cold in the classroom. Nobody is allowed to adjust the air conditioning except the teacher, Miss Patcharee. She warns against transgressions that we, her students, have hardly had a chance to commit: coming late to class, not reciting when the whole class is asked to recite en masse, not studying at least one hour at home for every hour at school.

The bright young men show their exasperation with the dull-witted sybaritic retirees: "*Khun! Khun!* Don't you remember yesterday? *Khun cheu arai, kraap?*" Miss Patcharee smiles that deadly smile of hers, the one that says, "I'll make you suffer for your ignorance and sloth." Some of us recognize instantly that *rongraam* means hotel. Others must employ tricky memory devices. (A man enters the wrong room in a hotel and surprises a couple in the act of love. "Sorry, wrong room," he says. "Wrong room" sounds a little like *rongraam*.) We are taught the names of fruits that few of us have ever seen, much less tasted. Durian. Rambutan. Mangosteen. Miss Patcharee wants the Thai to leap immediately to our lips without any mental translation process. English, we are told, doesn't have to enter into it at all. We will learn the language as a child learns it from his mother.

"Don't let me catch you saying *nung*," she says and makes a foolish face. "When you say *nueng*, I want to see your teeth." She shows us hers, which were prominent to begin with. That deadly, patient smile.

The class gives me a reason for being in Thailand. Now when someone asks what I'm doing here, I say, "Studying Thai," a far more respectable answer than "Sleeping and dreaming."

I experience a hunger for something sweet. Miss Daeng and Miss Nit are in the office at the end of their long work day, fighting off sleep. At this time of day their eyes are open but they can barely see.

Before going to bed, Miss Nit lights incense at the spirit house, a gaudy miniature castle by the door where the guesthouse spirits live. When people occupy a place, the spirits who lived there first need a new place to live. Like people, they need to be cared for, fed, satisfied.

Miss Nit looks sexy even when performing a religious ceremony.

George, an American with rheumatoid arthritis who's staying here, hired her to give him a massage even though she's the cook and doesn't know the first thing about massage. I would ask her for a massage, too, but it might be taken for an overture, and it might be one. What then? If desire is the important thing, then the act is not worth considering, and one had better stop considering it.

"Mr. Tom," says Miss Daeng, "what can I do for you?"

"I'd like two bananas, please."

"You have to ask me in Thai. If you want to learn Thai, you have to practice."

*"Gluay song by."*

Miss Daeng looks dully at me. She has fallen asleep sitting straight up in her chair. Either that, or I have forgotten to add the word at the end that makes it polite.

*"Gluay song by, kraap."*

"Aaah," says Miss Daeng. *"Hok baht, kaa."*

I give her the money. The bananas are small and starchy and sweet.

"Without question you cannot have conversation," says Miss Patcharee. She's right. I can't understand why this simple fact has escaped my attention for fifty-six years when I could have been having conversations with all sorts.

"You see pretty woman. You say, 'Hello, my name is John. I live in Chiang Mai. I come from America. I have motorbike. You are very beautiful.' No question. This is not conversation, *chay may?* So you must practice asking question every day in class. You must not be afraid to speak Thai. No one will laugh at you here."

I'm holding my own in the middle of the class, posing no challenge to David, the eager young American who teaches English to Thai children, or Sonjin, the Korean girl who intends to do missionary work, but managing to stay ahead of the dull-witted sybaritic retirees, such as Jeffrey, who's in his seventies and spends his evenings at the erotic massage parlor, and Howard, an Australian who's studying Thai so that he and his Burmese wife will have a common second language. The rest of us fall somewhere in the middle: Drew and Andrew, two young men who live in a Thai boxing camp where they work out seven hours a day, six days a week, and come to class beaten and exhausted; Peter, an ex-pat Irishman who spends his time between Montpelier and Chiang Mai, depending on the season; Min, a Burmese political dissident who fled his country thirteen years ago during the crisis; and Nigel, a spherical Brit who stays up until 4 A.M. every night drinking beer and carries a business card that says "Professional Yachtsman."

By the end of class every afternoon I have a headache from concentrating too hard. But it's worth taking note of small victories: ordering *khao sawy* in a soup kitchen without menus, a place where foreigners don't go.

Improvements are being made at the Mountain View Guesthouse. The owner, who is also a doctor of herbal cures and a landscape architect, supervises the workers as they come and go. They're building a new entrance from the parking lot, a formal gateway made of the same red clay brick that was used to build the walls of the Old City. There are plans for a waterfall that will empty into the koi pond. The stream will course through a tangle of make-believe dead trees made out of plastered chicken wire. Experts in the on-site manufacture of dead trees are doing the work.

Meanwhile, business as usual. The old hippie, Pondo (short for Ponderosa), who proudly claims not to have worn shoes of any kind since 1970, shows up for breakfast first thing every morning. He has respiratory problems. With the end of the rainy season the air is getting worse, and he'll soon have to move to the coast, where sea breezes blow the smog away.

Young Christians have retreated here to study the Bible and do charitable work among the hill tribes. Every morning after breakfast the students, mostly German, meet in the building on the other side of the courtyard and sing loudly and joyfully for thirty minutes before studying the Bible until eleven. I envy them each other, their energy and youth. They sing as if they really mean it. One of the German girls has smoky eyes, and I try not to look at her too rudely from my place on the balcony.

The maids, whose nicknames mean Miss Beautiful and Miss Good, come every morning to make the bed and sweep up the droppings of the pale house lizards called *jing-jok*. Miss Beautiful once studied English and would go back to school if she didn't have to work. Yesterday she asked me if I was married. Today she asks me if I would be interested in meeting a certain friend of hers, an educated woman who has a good job selling textiles.

"No thank you, I'm not looking for a woman right now, I'm studying Thai."

"Oh? You study Thai language? *Waanii wan aray?*" (What day is it today?)

We haven't studied the days of the week yet, so she has to give me the answer. Today is *waan aathiit,* Sunday.

An old man with a mottled face and skull, wearing what my father used to call "carpet slippers," does his laps in the lane that runs along one side of the courtyard, up and back five or six times, before allowing himself to go home and watch television. He takes extremely small steps. His feet slide along the wet pavement in the carpet slippers. He runs far more slowly than most people walk, but he's running nevertheless.

I meander across the campus of Chiang Mai University looking for the bookstore. Since leaving the Mountain View Guesthouse and all the way over here in the taxi, I have been rehearsing, *"Kaw thot, kraap. Raan nangseu yuu thii nay?"* (Literally, "I beg for punishment, sir. Where's the bookstore?") Everyone seems to understand what I'm saying. The following conversation, more or less, is repeated a number of times as I walk across the surprisingly large campus:

"I beg for punishment, sir. Where's the bookstore?"

"The bookstore?"

"Yes, the bookstore."

"The bookstore is over that way."

"Thank you, sir."

The bookstore is nowhere to be found. There is no bookstore, but nobody wants to be responsible for disappointing me, this foreigner who is trying so hard to speak Thai. What I find instead, by accident, is more like a stationery store, where they sell T-shirts and coffee mugs with the university insignia. I buy a pad of paper for homework assignments and a note card with a picture of an elephant for Aunt Nancy, who lives in Connecticut. She used to collect elephants of wood, stone, clay, and glass but eventually got sick of having them all over the house and donated them to the Salvation Army. Back in the guesthouse, I write an apology to my aunt for sending her a card with a picture of an elephant. Thailand is a land of elephants, I explain. It's almost impossible to avoid them.

*

A French woman, Nicole, is staying in the room that Jessica occupied before she went to India. Nicole leaves her room early each weekday with a cup of coffee in one hand, a satchel of massage equipment in the other, her wine-colored hair tied in a no-nonsense ponytail. One afternoon she and I happen to eat lunch together at the guesthouse, and she comments on the "pretty little bird" that is singing in the branches above the balcony.

"It's a red-whiskered bulbul," I tell her. "You can buy them in cages in the market."

"How terrible!" says Nicole. "The birds should not be in the cages."

"Well, you don't have to keep them. You can just give the people some money and they'll let the bird fly away. That way, everybody wins. The people earn some money, the bird is free, and you gain merit for your next lifetime."

"*Mais qu'il est barbare!* They should not be in the cages. They should be in the nature."

"Yes, I think so too. But this is Asia."

"I'm tired of it," says Nicole. "I'm tired of Chiang Mai. All the traffic! I cannot breathe here."

"Don't say anything bad about Chiang Mai to a Thai person. Chiang Mai is the Jewel of the North."

"Next week, after we finish the massage school, I want to travel."

"Where will you go?"

"I don't know," says Nicole. "To the mountains, where it's cool. Not too many tourists. I just want to be in the nature."

"Yes, I know what you mean. That's what I want, too, come to think of it."

"You should come with me."

Here's the company I've been wanting since I got here. She's sitting at my table and offering in no uncertain terms to go with me in search of the real Thailand. Someone to talk to, to negotiate with from one day to the next. Where to go? What to eat? To see the country through my eyes and insist on making me see it her way.

"I'd like that, Nicole. But I've got to finish school."

Miss Patcharee explains that Thai people are very curious and ask a lot of questions when they meet you. This is normal, she says: "In your country, it may be rude to ask somebody you don't know very well a lot of questions. 'How old are you? Are you married?

How much money do you make?' But in Thailand, everybody asks these questions. This is how we learn who you are and how to speak to you. So when a Thai person asks many embarrassing questions, do not be angry."

We practice asking embarrassing questions in class. When Sonjin, the Korean girl, asks me how many Thai women I have, I say four.

"What are their names?"

"Daeng, Nit, Suay, and Dii."

Nobody knows that I've given the names of women who work at the guesthouse. It's easier for them to believe that I have four Thai girlfriends than that I have none. Thais and foreigners alike assume that if you are a single man from the West, you have a Thai girlfriend or you are looking for one or you are gay. Anything is acceptable except not having a Thai girlfriend and not even looking for one. If you say you have one or more Thai girlfriends, they leave you alone, but if you say you don't have a Thai girlfriend, they say, "You don't? Why not?" and then you have to explain. You begin asking yourself, "What's wrong with me? Why don't I have a Thai girlfriend like everyone else?"

Miss Patcharee teaches us the words for the different times of day. She explains that these words come from another time when there were no clocks, only the movement of the sun and stars across the sky. Nothing could happen at 2:45, for example, in the time before there was time; it could happen only in the afternoon.

"Now," she says, "you ask me question with morning, late morning, noon, afternoon, evening."

"Miss Patcharee," I ask when my turn comes, "what are you like in the morning?"

A new woman has joined the Bible students, and I've angled my chair on the balcony in such a way that I can keep a surreptitious eye on her. She's older, although not as old as me. Asian, although perhaps not entirely Asian. Her hair is short and very black; it shines marvelously. She's wearing a gray business suit with padded shoulders. She stirs a straw in a pineapple shake and listens intently to the German man, one of the leaders of the retreat, who is talking about a worldwide mission, going global in scale. Finally he stops talking and goes away. She's alone. She takes a book out of a black leather handbag and reads. I'm attracted to women who read, because my notion of happiness includes lying in bed with someone reading. In this fantasy, we interrupt one another to speak only at long intervals, if at all. Our respect for one another extends to the other person's book. Right now while she's alone it would be possible to go downstairs and introduce myself. Everything would go well if I could remember to smile. If I smile too much, she might notice that I'm missing a front tooth and draw conclusions about me from that, but if she is the kind of woman who draws such conclusions, I wouldn't want to be with her after all. Anyway, she's too well dressed, too respectable, too Christian, and probably too married. The ring on her right hand. How would I appear to such a woman? A man with no apparent work or purpose in life other than studying a language that he will quickly forget when he leaves Thailand. A man who wears shorts and T-shirts and sandals, who rides songthaews or walks until the sweat breaks through his clothes. Just another of the aimless beer-sodden foreigners who spend all the hours after dark in tourist pubs looking hungrily at women. The only way I could distinguish myself in the eyes of such a woman would be to dress well and put on the guise of seriousness or ambition. The guidebook says that it's possible to reside in Buddhist temples in Thailand if one is a Buddhist or can "act like one." In the same way, couldn't one act like a Christian and win the admiration and maybe even the love of the woman with the shining black hair?

I pretend to be reading my book, which I got from the school library, to keep her from observing that she's being observed. Someone has left a scrap of paper in the book, probably for a bookmark, with a handwritten message on it: "Went to Soi 1 to investigate cushions."

Now and then, something turns loose in me, and I stop resisting the idea of being here. Then I'm yanked back into the resistance. The turning loose happens most reliably when I can make myself understood in Thai. I go to the airport to get my passport fixed. The woman in the immigration office smiles more than obligingly when I explain the situation in Thai, a smile of complete understanding.

"How well you speak Thai!" she says in English.

"*Khun paakwaan,*" I reply. You're just sweet-talking me.

"No, no! Really!" She fixes the passport stamp and says that I can stay in Thailand until September, a full year from the date of entry. After that I can apply for another year, and so on indefinitely because I have a retirement visa. I can stay forever if I want. I could get a job at the university, have students who idolize me, buy a big shiny motorcycle and travel around, get a house in the mountains and hire handmaidens to cook and clean. Why not? Sit out on my own balcony in a rattan chair like a colonial lord and have the handmaidens bring me iced drinks.

After dark the desire for something sweet overcomes me again. Something sweeter than bananas. In order to get to the sweets from the guesthouse, I have to cross Sriphum Road, wait for a break in the traffic, and make a dash for White Elephant Gate. There is no such thing as pedestrian right-of-way in Thailand. Just the other day an Englishwoman was hit by a motorbike trying to cross here and sat dazed on the curb, refusing my offer of a chair, until the ambulance arrived.

On the other side of White Elephant Gate, a moat separates the Old City from the world outside, and then comes Mani Nopharat, another four lanes of constant one-way traffic. I push the button that operates the traffic light, the only one of its kind in Chiang Mai, and when the traffic slows I make another run. It must be done in a way to make the drivers believe that you really mean to cross and will not stop for anything, and then you have to watch for those who will run the light, regardless.

On the other side I move through a carnival of eating stalls, clear-glass light bulbs strung treacherously head high, starving dogs with open sores, giggling schoolgirls in uniform with large bows at the neck, men selling shots of whiskey from a bottle on a wooden crate, a woman in tribal dress carrying a wok filled with rocks on her head, whole families, whole villages, all eating and talking, and not one person among them who knows me.

All at once I realize I'm in Asia. It's been here all along, no farther from the guesthouse than a mad dash through the gate, which isn't a gate at all but a gap in the ancient wall wide enough to admit a herd of elephants, an absence, incapable of keeping anyone out or in: invading armies or lone tourist in the throes of a midnight sugar fit. All it took to get here was the risk of my life.

With a bag of sesame candy I move through the pandemonium,

survive the return crossing, and reenter the guesthouse. Miss Daeng and Miss Nit have gone to bed. The night clerk is snoozing at his desk, and out on the wooden deck in the courtyard, where the half-formed shapes of ferro-cement trees lie fallen by the koi pond, the woman with the shining black hair is eating watermelon and reading a Bible smaller than the hand that holds it. She is so intent on her study that she does not look at me as I pass, nor does she offer me a slice of watermelon. On her perfect ankle, like volcanic islands in the process of being born, is a chain of infected mosquito bites.

I tell Miss Daeng that I'll be leaving the Mountain View when my Thai class ends.

"What's the matter?" she says. "Are you boring?"

"Yes, I think that's the problem."

The rain wakes up a gecko, or what I assume to be a gecko, having never heard one before, a clack like two pieces of wood being struck one against the other or water dripping into water in a cave, greatly amplified, or an old dog that has lost part of its voice. People here kill geckos because they're noisy, I'm told, but nobody would dream of complaining about the two small dogs at the end of the lane who throw demented fits of barking at all hours of the day and night.

The rain excuses sleep, and sleep puts off my need to make better sense of all this. It's not really necessary to make sense of it in the way that eating and sleeping are necessary, but I *think* it is, and the thinking creates its own kind of necessity. Making sense of things — for example, my compulsion to hear the word *gecko* in the mechanical grunts of a lizard — is human and forgivable. So I'll forgive myself for thinking, as I'll forgive myself for going back to bed on a rainy morning. I'll lie in bed listening to the "possible" gecko, as they say at the Office of Cultural Affairs. It may or may not be what I say it is. I'll listen to the rain on the guesthouse roof as sense departs.

After a night of heavy rain, the canal has flooded, and water is standing in four rooms on the ground floor. A nation of cockroaches emerges from flooded drains. Stunned by the light of day, displaced and having no other place to go, they collect on the walls, the branches of the manufactured trees, the tables and benches in the courtyard. They observe the guests and delicately taste the air with their long coppery antennae.

The staircase to the roof is opposite Miss Daeng's desk. It has been here every time I passed through the lobby to Sriphum Road over the past two months to walk along the canal or catch a songthaew, but this is the first time I've troubled to climb it. Three doors lead from each landing, rooms usually occupied by missionary students, all of whom have successfully avoided me for two months except in passing, and I them. They've all left for two weeks in the mountains to sleep on mats on the ground and eat the food that the villagers eat and talk about the Bible. Their final exam.

The staircase ends at a wooden deck where potted plants have been allowed to grow wild. Vines cling to the wire of a dovecote and meander between runs of pool-blue plumbing. The cook, Miss Nit, is there on break, smoking a cigarette. She leans against the parapet and watches the traffic on Mani Nopharat plow through the flooded street. Sometimes at night I've heard her screaming at her daughter, presumably for the same kind of reasons that parents scream at their teenagers in my country, and found it strangely comforting, a reminder of home in a land where it's considered rude if not disgraceful to show anger. Miss Nit's toughness shows in those dragon eyes at all times, even when she's enveloped in steam in the kitchen, and now, in the enticing way she leans over the parapet, pulls the smoke from her cigarette, and releases it into the air.

"So much water," she says in English. "Too much."

"Where I live, there's never enough."

"It's dry?"

"Very dry. It's so dry that the trees are dying."

"I cannot live in so dry country."

The mountains are slowly coming out of the clouds after the storm. Nests of fog have snagged in the trees of the lower slopes, and higher up, behind a veil of vapor, I can barely see the white ramparts of Wat Phra That Doi Suthep, the first place one is expected to visit as a tourist in Chiang Mai. I stand there on the roof with Miss Nit and watch the clouds dissolve.

"Have you ever been to the United States, Miss Nit?" ("Without question you cannot have conversation.")

"No. I want to go with my daughter. I would like to see your country. I would like to travel in different places and see different things. It must be wonderful to do that."

"Wonderful, yes."

"Where do you go now?"

"I don't know. I have to decide. Or maybe I won't decide. Maybe I'll just get on a bus and go."

"This is good way," says Miss Nit. "You visit Doi Suthep?"

The veil of cloud is lifting from the temple now. It stands newly washed and dazzling in the late afternoon sun.

"I've been too busy with my Thai class and everything. But I want to go soon, this week, before leaving Chiang Mai."

"When you go, please burn incense for me."

"Why don't you come with me? We can both burn incense."

"Thank you, but I have to work. You will burn incense for me on Doi Suthep?"

"Sure. Do I have to say anything?"

"No. Just light incense and think of me. Then give it to the Buddha."

*Dawnyen*. Evening. Soon the *jing-jok* will stake out their places on whitewashed walls all over the city and begin their remorseless hunt for insects.

MARK JENKINS

# Leap Year

FROM *Outside*

WE AT LAST ALIGHTED on the south coast of Spain. A family of four from America, traipsing through the Málaga airport with over-stuffed daypacks and four bulging duffels, four bulging bicycle boxes, and two sturdy computer cartons. Disheveled and greasy with the residua of transit, so exhausted that our two daughters' heads were bobbing, in any other country (especially our own) our huddled little mass would have been easy prey for customs officials with a taste for harassing tired refugees. Fortunately, this was *España*. The officers had trim Franco outfits but a languid indifference, and we barreled our laden carts straight out into a sweltering Iberian afternoon, no one even bothering to check our passports.

We had hoped to catch a bus, train, or taxi up the Mediterranean coast to our destination, the pueblo of Salobreña, but none would accommodate our small mountain of possessions. Instead, we rented an absurdly large moving van, loaded up our bags, squeezed into the cab, and set off just after dark along a winding contour line of asphalt. My wife and girls fell instantly into dreams while I navigated a causeway suspended between an indigo sky and the sable sea, two voluptuous bodies winking at each other like old lovers.

Creeping into Salobreña, I parked by moonlight and woke my family. The air was moist and perfumed with jasmine. It was not possible to drive to our new house. The road coming up from below was six feet wide, and the "street" dropping down steep steps from above was about the width of my shoulders — *"la calle más estrecha de Salobreña,"* the narrowest passageway in town. So we half-sleepwalked up the cobblestone lane to our oblong courtyard, gladly leaving our ponderous luggage in the van. Traveling light we were not, but then we weren't traveling — we were moving.

At noon the next day, eyelids heavy from jet lag and cascades of sunshine, we set about exploring. Our new casa was old white-washed stucco, and its big windows faced south, like all the other houses built into the hillside. We shared walls with our neighbors, who shared walls with theirs, and so on — a contiguous community called El Barrio de la Fuente, situated just below the ruins of a tenth-century Moorish castle. There were stone-tile floors and ceramic-tile walls, a porch lined with potted plants, and two terraces: a lower one, which looked out over a clanking welding shop and the town park, and another on the rooftop, affording a 270° panorama. To the west spread the hazy, azure Mediterranean, with Africa out there somewhere; straight ahead, to the south, the ancient alluvial sugarcane fields and the new condos inexorably consuming them; and to the east, the dusty brown foothills of the Alpujarras set against the cool whaleback of the Sierra Nevada.

It didn't feel like home, but that was the point.

Three months later, as I look out from the wide-open window of my office–cum–living room, the mercurial seascape is flat navy blue, as unmoving as an abstract painting. It is late morning, and my daughters, Addi, eleven, and Teal, nine, have caught the bus to their Spanish school, their backpacks stuffed with heavy textbooks. Sue, my wife, is taking a long run on the beach and then circling back to buy fresh shrimp for supper. Magdalena, our octogenarian neighbor, who is tinier than Teal, has taken her wee, blind, crippled, octogenarian dog — a beast whose bark sounds exactly like a baby crying (I've daydreamed of surreptitiously easing it into the afterlife) — for a walk, in her arms. Next door, infirm Antonia has flung a pail of mop water into the courtyard, and her grandson is feeding the bright, egg-size canaries in the rock cave beneath her house. Belinda, behind us, is bellowing from her terrace at little Manuelito, in the park two blocks away, to come home. *El panadero* has made his house-to-house deliveries with the large sack of baguettes; the propane-gas man has lugged an orange canister up to our front grate; *el cartero*, who buzzes around town on a yellow moped outfitted with yellow saddlebags, has delivered our day's mail from the States. And my father has sent an e-mail telling me not to worry — he fixed the toilet in our house, which churlishly broke after we left Wyoming.

So I guess we've settled in.

Sue and I talked for years about moving abroad, scheming and dreaming and putting money aside. It was part of my family history — when I was thirteen, my family moved to northern Holland for a year; my father, a mathematician, was on sabbatical. Although we spoke not a word of Dutch, all six of us kids were plunged directly into local schools. We floundered valiantly out of sheer desperation, quickly learned how to float with just a few words, began to kick a bit, then dog-paddled, and eventually swam (not gracefully but passably). Submerged in a new culture, that one year abroad altered us all. The world would forevermore be beckoning — vast beyond imagination, resplendent and revolting, perplexingly complex, contradictory, ceaselessly intriguing. Sue and I wanted our girls to have their own eye-widening opportunity.

Being a writer, I'm fortunate enough to have a transplantable job, so that wasn't an obstacle. And yet life got in the way and the years clicked by until one day we looked up, noticed that Addi and Teal were half grown, and realized that it was now or never. It was a simple decision, really: In six months we would leave on a yearlong sojourn. Thereafter, each piece more or less fit into an unfinished puzzle that we solved as we went along.

The high plains of Wyoming are rightfully famous for their brutal weather, and we all agreed that we wanted a change of climate. Sue is fluent in Spanish, hence a Spanish-speaking country seemed sensible. Beyond that, each of us had personal criteria. Sue wanted the girls to learn classic Castilian — the most widely used form of Spanish — versus Catalan, Galician, or Basque. I wanted to be no more than one hour from the mountains and, for my work, no more than two from an international airport. Addi and Teal, realizing we were presumptuously making decisions for them and convinced that they had thus far led deprived childhoods, living 1,200 miles from the nearest ocean, insisted that we be no more than an hour from the beach.

In this way, we chose Spain.

Unspoken but understood was that we wanted a community small enough to perambulate but that also had DSL. A community that was still Spanish — not an ex-pat colony of Brits, Swedes, or

Germans — but wasn't hidebound in medieval prejudices. A community that had paella *and* pizza. A tall order.

"Andalusia. That's where we'll go!" Sue announced one night at dinner.

In April, Sue and I flew over on a reconnaissance mission, rented a car, and found Salobreña on the first day. A town of 10,500 inhabitants, it could be traversed on foot in eight minutes. The beach was a five-minute walk away; eight-hundred-foot limestone climbing crags a ten-minute drive; the Sierra Nevada, Spain's highest mountain range, only an hour north. Before we left, we signed a lease on a furnished house, paid our first month's rent, and spoke with the principal of an elementary school for the girls.

In early August, after renting out our house in Laramie (fully furnished, plates to electronics), rearranging our banking to live off ATM cards, and loaning our two cars to kin, we pulled up stakes and fired ourselves, as if out of a cannon, over the big pond. In less than twenty-four hours, we had traded the dry, landlocked spread of Wyoming — where there are more deer and antelope than people, and nine months of winter — for the sticky, flesh-covered Costa Tropical, where some form of summer reigns year-round.

By day two, the bikes were reassembled and Addi and Teal were out exploring. In one week, we had obtained a *certificado de empadronamiento,* our census certificate. In two weeks, we had willingly converted from expensive microbrews to cheap microriojas. In three weeks, we had purchased a used VW Golf, the standard Euro family car, with 130,000 kilometers on the odometer. After a month, we had a high-speed Internet connection, supplementing our addiction to the BBC.

A little patience, *bastante dinero,* a lot of running around, and before I could properly pronounce *destornillador* (screwdriver), we were rookie members of the European community.

Living abroad, like isolationism and xenophobia, is a venerable American tradition. Benjamin Franklin lived in England for almost eighteen years and in Paris for more than seven. Mark Twain settled in Europe for a decade. Hemingway and Fitzgerald, Matthiessen and Plimpton, and many other Yanks temporarily sank peacetime roots into foreign soil.

According to a 1999 U.S. Bureau of Consular Affairs report, there are almost four million American civilians living abroad. A thousand in Tanzania; 38,000 in Taiwan; 450 in Mongolia; a hundred or so in Turkmenistan; about 95,000 in Spain. Among the millions are diplomats, Peace Corps volunteers, teachers, nurses, exchange students, and multinational corporate employees. All have chosen to forsake close friends and relatives, familiar neighborhoods, and routines to live overseas for a time.

Many go for the same reasons we travel: to experience the unfamiliar. To eat goat cheese from the green cave of Magaha, *queso de cabra* that is so acridly tart it makes your mouth water. To follow doglegging lanes in a mountain village until you're convinced you're lost, only to suddenly realize that you're right back where you started (the recursive metaphor of travel, again). To witness customs that we could hardly imagine: two oxen, say, garlanded with delicate violet blossoms, pulling a cart carrying a small statue of Santa Maria del Rosario, the patron saint of Salobreña.

Yet moving abroad is more profound than traveling. It goes beyond curiosity to commitment. If to travel is to be a stone skipping lightly over the water, to move abroad is to stop and allow yourself to sink into an alien world, gulping to breathe a different language. Moving abroad is full immersion in a strange country, being forced to make a new life there, using little more than whatever wit, wisdom, openheartedness, and evenhandedness you carry inside you.

Perhaps the principal difference is this: To travel is to expect much of the places you visit; to move to one of these places is to expect much of yourself. No longer just passing through, you must figure out how things actually work in your adopted nation.

Some of this is banal. When is garbage collected? (Midnight.) Where is the wine-bottle-recycling container? (By the bus stop.) What is the word for the female end of a telephone jack? (I still have no idea.) Which *ferretería* (hardware store) has *clavos pequeños* (little nails)?

And some of this is sublime. Discovering the back way to the girls' school, a paved path beneath limestone caves, past a goat pen, through tall sugarcane, around the last sugarcane factory in all of Europe, through the burnt-maple air to Colegio San Juan de Ávila. Sleeping on the rooftop on warm summer nights. Drinking a new red wine with a late dinner on the terrace and finding that

Sangre de Toro has the more poetic name but that nondescript Tarragona de Baturrica is more robust. Learning words that are so much more mellifluous than their English counterparts — *melocotónes meloso, ciruelas redondo, chorizo* (sweet peaches, round plums, sausage). It is through such words and such modest, quotidian undertakings that one begins, *poco a poco*, to learn a new language — the central challenge of living abroad.

At this moment, my daughters are at school. Addi is perhaps studying geography, learning the Spanish names for countries she never knew existed, or maybe she is working on division, which Spaniards write backward and which schoolchildren are taught to do entirely in their heads. Teal has a test spelling the ordinal numbers, *primero hasta tregísimo* (first through thirtieth), and later she'll be practicing the Spanish terms for the anatomy of the eye. All three of us will get another kitchen-table language lesson from Sue tonight. At the last tutorial, Sue informed me that it was time I stop speaking Spanish like a Latin Tarzan and get cracking on my conjugations.

It is not possible to know a country well without knowing its language. Language is the magic key that opens the imposing gates to another kingdom. Once inside, everything looks different, not the least of which is your mother country on the other side of the fence. What you actually see and feel and believe — that is, who you are — depends a great deal on where you're standing on the globe. Geography is destiny.

I've just returned from my noon bike ride. The loop begins with a cruise through the groves of cherimoyas — a sweetish fruit that you spoon out of its scalloped green skin — along the broad Guadalfeo River bottom. A gushing canal runs along the narrow strip of asphalt. Beyond the fruit trees, the road climbs into long-ago-terraced mountains, passing through several small villages where old men in berets sit in the shade of somnolent stone churches.

As the road curls deeper into the mountains, it becomes absurdly steep, which makes for a fabulous workout. It is a road steeper than anything ever allowed in the United States, but rules, wonderfully, are anathema to the Spanish. Speed-limit signs are as rare as traffic police, and people drive as fast as their little tin boxes will move. Drivers give cyclists a wide berth but, oddly, appear to aim for pedestrians. When a vehicle finally comes to a halt, it does so wherever the driver pleases, like a toddler falling asleep in the middle of the living-room floor. Double parking is de rigueur, triple parking fair play. Of course, the narrow cobblestone streets were originally designed to accommodate little more than a mule and a mule cart. Triple parking usually blocks the entire thoroughfare, giving all involved something to honk and yell and wave their hands about, which they seem to enjoy far more than actually getting where they're trying to go.

But this is to be expected — Americans always whine about how foreigners drive, from Madrid to Madras. Now that I'm the foreigner, I've quite happily learned how to park with half the car up on the sidewalk and take joy in using my horn. It's the consciousness of a culture that really matters, not so much its formal regulations. Fathoming this takes time and requires forbearance, a virtue that matures immensely when you choose to live abroad. Suddenly you are an uninformed minority — a healthy experience for an American. We are, after all, a nation of immigrants, yet within only one or two generations we so easily forget how difficult it can be to adapt to unfamiliar territory.

America's immense economic and military strength makes us believe we are a majority on this globe. Nothing could be more ludicrous. There are more Europeans than Americans, more Africans, more Indians, more Chinese, more South Americans. And yet living only in the United States, you could easily imagine that being number one in all things is a divine birthright. This has the potential to breed an ugly close-mindedness. Not surprisingly, then, one inevitable outcome of a move overseas is a renewed respect for the teeming diversity of humankind, a recognition that there are at least a dozen ways to skin a cat — and they're all right.

Of course, living abroad — even speaking the language and settling there for years — doesn't make you a true insider. You will always be a foreigner, but if you're lucky you may come away with a perspective on your new home that the locals don't have and find you've become a fledgling connoisseur of red wine and olive oil.

As I rolled back down into Salobreña, it was just after 2 P.M. From every household, the soul-nourishing aromas of home cooking wafted out the open windows and along the streets. Nose uplifted, I gloried like a bloodhound in the different smells: *cerdo* (pork) sautéing in garlic, *papas fritas* (fried potatoes), *sopa de albóndigas* (meatball soup).

We didn't move to Spain to recover some rustic, romantic, agrarian life. That's been gone for some time. Rather, we moved to live surrounded by whatever traditions are here now. As when, at the stroke of two, citizens one and all pull down the heavy metal grates of their work life, physically and metaphorically, and go home to their families for *la cena grande* — the big meal. Somehow, amid all the shove and shuffle of the modern commercial world, the Spanish have had the good sense to still organize work around life, instead of the other way around. Imagine stopping right in the middle of your fervid workday and taking a three-hour break. One hour to enjoy your meal with your family, one hour to converse extravagantly, using all body parts, and one hour for siesta. Can you think of anything more decadent or more civilized?

Pulling up beneath the kitchen window of my house, I could hear the girls, already out of school for the day, laughing, and I could smell Sue's shrimp paella cooking on the stove.

*Vivir la vida.*

MURAD KALAM

# If It Doesn't Kill You First

FROM *Outside*

I WANDER BAREFOOT out of the Grand Mosque through a cruel blanket of Saudi heat, floating in a sea of strangers from almost every country on Earth. It's my third day in the city of Mecca, where I've come to take part in the *hajj*, the annual five-day pilgrimage to some of Islam's holiest places. This trek is required once in the lifetime of every able-bodied Muslim, and I'm one of two million people, part of the largest mass movement of humans on the planet.

The birthplace of Muhammad, the prophet of Islam, born in the sixth century, Mecca sits at the base of the Hejaz Mountains in western Saudi Arabia, forty-six miles east of the Red Sea port of Jidda. To someone watching from atop the thousand-foot peaks that surround the city, we must look like countless insects as we spill out of the high, arching gates of the 3.8-million-square-foot Grand Mosque, the most important religious site in the Islamic world.

Mecca is home to 800,000 gracious people, any of whom will tell you not to worry about your well-being when you're here. "This is Mecca," they say. "No one will harm you." Maybe not, but the less devout might steal from you — I'm barefoot because somebody ran off with my sandals this morning when I removed them, as required, before entering the Grand Mosque to pray.

Meanwhile, it's a fact of hajj life that people die all around. Earlier, I watched the Saudi religious police — the *mutawaeen*, stoic, hard-faced men with henna-dyed beards — carry green-shrouded gurneys holding the bodies of five pilgrims who died today, setting them on the marble floor of the Grand Mosque for funeral prayers.

In one twenty-four-hour period during my pilgrimage, eighty-two hajjis will die. People perish in many ways, from natural causes like heart attacks to unnatural ones like dehydration and trampling.

Trampling is what I'm concerned about at the moment, and with each frantic step I become more worried about my safety. The problem is the hajj's sheer numbers. Despite many improvements, the hajj facilities and infrastructure — which are managed by the House of Saud, the ironfisted royal family that has ruled Saudi Arabia since 1932 — haven't expanded to meet the fourfold increase in attendance that has occurred over the past thirty-five years. The result is that people too often wind up in death traps.

In 1990, a stampede in the pedestrian tunnel leading from Mecca to Arafat, a rocky, arid plain twelve miles southeast of Mecca and one of the final way stations of the hajj, killed 1,426 pilgrims. Another 270 were trampled to death four years later at Jamarat, a site just east of Mecca where a ritual called the Stoning of the Devil takes place, and the most crowded of all hajj settings. In 1997, 343 pilgrims burned to death and another 1,500 were injured in a giant fire started by a gas cooker in the tent city of Mina, an encampment a few miles east of Mecca where all pilgrims gather near the end of the hajj.

It's a bizarre sensation, but I keep imagining my own demise, visualizing my shrouded body being carried into the Grand Mosque above the wheeling masses. Every Muslim knows that a believer who dies on this journey is guaranteed a place in paradise. Personally, though, I'd much rather live to tell about it.

Why take this risk? The answer starts with my spiritual beliefs. I've been a Sunni Muslim for nine years. (The Sunnis make up 90 percent of all Muslims but are the minority in Shiite-dominated nations like Iran and Iraq. Sunnis and Shiites differ on major theological matters — like who should have succeeded Muhammad after his death, in A.D. 632.) I was born in Seattle in 1973 to a Jamaican father and an American mother, grew up a lapsed Baptist turned agnostic in Phoenix, and started college in Boston, at Harvard, in 1994.

As an undergrad, I happened upon an English translation of the Koran, the written version of Muhammad's revelations from Allah. I was so floored by its persuasive power that I converted to Islam, stopped drinking, and adopted an Islamic name, Murad Kalam. Like many new converts, I was zealous and naive at first. I bought the fundamentalist line that the cause of all the Muslim world's problems — poverty, corruption, and repression — boiled down to a simple failure to apply the tenets of the religion, and nothing more.

Like every American Muslim, I've had a lot to think about in the past few years. When Al Qaeda launched its attack on September 11, 2001, I was a third-year law student at Harvard and an aspiring novelist. I had not yet traveled to Muslim countries, but I had made friends from Egypt, Saudi Arabia, and Jordan, and they'd schooled me in the complex realities of Muslim life. While Islam is dear to the majority of Muslims, they said, Koranic law should not be taken as the cure-all for everything. In many Muslim societies, religion was a smoke screen for old-fashioned greed, tyranny, and hypocrisy, as well as numerous distortions of Muhammad's ideas for twisted political goals.

Among the worst examples of that last problem, obviously, is Al Qaeda, which has been a scourge in the United States, Afghanistan, Kenya, Yemen, and, more recently, Turkey and Saudi Arabia itself. Though Saudi Arabia, birthplace of the exiled Osama bin Laden, has been relatively safe from terror in the past, that changed after my pilgrimage, which took place in February 2003. On May 12, 2003, Al Qaeda truck bombers hit a housing complex in the Saudi capital, Riyadh, killing twenty-six Saudis and foreigners working in the country, eight Americans among them. On November 8, terrorists, probably linked to Al Qaeda, killed seventeen Arabs in a similar strike.

In the aftermath, Saudi officials have cracked down on terrorism with a fervor that will likely translate into heightened security measures at the 2004 hajj, which runs from January 31 to February 4. The hajj itself has never been the target of a terror strike, but according to published reports, in a raid carried out not long after the November bombings in Riyadh, the Saudis uncovered a plot by Islamic militants to booby-trap copies of the Koran, allegedly in order to maim and kill pilgrims during the hajj.

The Saudi government has to be worried about terror occurring under its watch, since its role as keeper of the holy places is a major pillar of its legitimacy. The closest thing to such an attack occurred back in November 1979, when a radical cleric named Juhayman ibn Muhammad and hundreds of followers barricaded themselves in the Grand Mosque for two weeks to protest what they saw as political and religious corruption in the House of Saud. Before it was over, dozens of soldiers and more than a hundred of ibn Muhammad's partisans had died in gunfights.

Even though the hajj was not in progress, attacking the Grand Mosque was an incredible blasphemy, and the punishment was swift. After their capture, ibn Muhammad and his band were executed in cities and towns throughout Saudi Arabia — dispatched by means of public beheading.

Throughout the international turmoil following 9/11, I remained a devout Muslim, and I found myself torn between my beliefs and my country. I've worried that President George W. Bush has been too heavy-handed in his war against terror, both overseas and in the United States. At the same time, I've felt oddly insulated from any anti-Muslim backlash. Too pedigreed to lose a job, too American-looking to be assaulted, I felt alienated from my fellow Muslims in Boston, some of whom were attacked on the street by angry locals. I was drifting, missing prayers. I worried that I was failing Islam. So, in late 2001, I started thinking about trying the hajj.

To prepare for my trip, I read narratives of pilgrimages to Mecca, beginning with the hajj chapters in *The Autobiography of Malcolm X,* the 1964 book about the political and spiritual quest of the famous black Muslim activist. In older books I found tales of desert caravans, raids by Bedouin clans, near starvation, and hard-won spiritual enlightenment. For 1,500 years the hajj has been the ultimate Muslim adventure. It remains a soul-rousing journey that, I decided, could snap me into shape.

The hajj itself predates the prophet Muhammad. According to Muslim belief, Abraham established it and built the sacred Kaaba — a fifty-foot-tall windowless sanctuary made of black granite — but over time the rites in Mecca degenerated. Pagan Meccans set up 360 idols outside the Kaaba, and Mecca became a center for worshipping cult, tribal, and polytheistic gods.

Muhammad, born in A.D. 570, received his call at age forty and risked his life to establish Islamic monotheism in Mecca. Persecuted and facing imminent assassination for teaching that there is no god but Allah, he fled with his followers to Medina in A.D. 622. Later, after several battles between Muslims and nonbelievers, the Meccans converted to Islam, and the prophet returned to rule. During his final hajj, Muhammad stressed the equality of man, respect for property, and the importance of prayer, fasting, and charity.

The pilgrimage itself is a twenty-five-mile trip, made by bus and on foot, that starts and ends in Mecca, with shifting dates determined from year to year by the Islamic lunar calendar. Pilgrims begin arriving two or three weeks ahead of time in Mecca, where they spend several days performing rituals and prayers inside the Grand Mosque. At this point, many hajjis take a multiday side trip to Medina, the oasis city where Muhammad established his first community of followers.

In a transition that marks the official beginning of the hajj, all pilgrims start to converge on Mina, where they camp for the night. The next day they proceed five miles farther east to Arafat, to face the Mount of Mercy, a hill where they meditate on the day of judgment. The hajjis leave Arafat at sunset and walk three miles to the valley of Muzdalifa to camp under the stars. There they pray and collect pebbles, which they'll take to Jamarat the next morning. At Jamarat, two miles northwest of Muzdalifa, hajjis throw stones at three fifty-eight-foot-tall granite pillars, symbolically warding off Satan. After completing this, pilgrims shave their heads or cut off a lock of hair, to mark the end of the hajj. Then they return to Mecca to complete their final rituals inside the Grand Mosque.

Initially, I'd wanted to do all this in the most rigorous way possible. My hope was to take a boat across the Red Sea from Cairo — where I was living for four months while researching my second novel — and then ride horseback from Jidda to Mecca, camping out in the vastness of the Arabian Peninsula.

But after checking in with the Saudi embassy in Washington, D.C., I discovered that the days of romantic pilgrimages were over. The hajj is too dangerous to allow everyone to chart his own course, and under Saudi law, to get a visa, every pilgrim who has the financial resources must make airline and hotel reservations. The embassy passed me on to the well-oiled D.C.-based hajj machine, Grand Travel, where I was informed that not only was a package tour required but also that tours were segregated by nationality. I would be lumped in with ninety-eight other American Muslims.

Making one last stab, I asked the agent if he would book my flight and let me wing the rest. He laughed. "You want suffering, brother? You'll be suffering enough."

I set off for Saudi Arabia on January 28, 2003. Pilgrims prepare for the hajj by taking a ritual bath and putting on the symbolic robes of *ihram,* thereby entering a spiritual state in which differences of race, wealth, and nationality are erased. My robing took place in a hurry at the Cairo airport, where I followed a pimply faced Egyptian skycap into a dimly lit industrial closet.

"Get naked," he said. For ten Egyptian pounds (two bucks), the young man expertly dressed me in two white sheets, one placed horizontally around my waist, the other over my left shoulder.

Afterward, I jumped on an EgyptAir flight to Jidda. From there I traveled by bus forty-six miles to the Al Shohada Hotel, in Mecca, where I met my tour group. Once in Mecca, hajjis immediately proceed to the Grand Mosque, a massive coliseum that contains the Kaaba, the cube-shaped granite shrine toward which Muslims all over the world direct their daily prayers. Pilgrims are required to circle the Kaaba seven times, counterclockwise, praying as they go. This ritual is called *tawaf.* At the end of the hajj, when they return to Mecca, they must complete the *tawaf* again.

Two nights after I completed my initial *tawaf,* inside the airy, luxurious lobby of the Al Shohada, I got a first look at the American hajjis as we assembled to meet our tour leaders. Studying them, I felt a painful rush of our collective inadequacy. They were a collection of well-meaning people from all walks of life: taxi drivers, salesmen, mailmen, lawyers, doctors, and hotel workers. But they also seemed like a reflection of myself — slightly out of shape, self-conscious in pilgrim garb, clearly a little panicked.

We gathered in a hotel conference room, where Sheik Hussein Chowat, our spiritual adviser, paced before us, fielding questions. He's a squat, bearded, soft-spoken Arab in his forties who teaches Islam in northern Virginia. Here, it was his job to put the fear of Allah into us, stressing the need to do everything right. "You have to do the hajj carefully," he warned. "If you don't, Allah might not accept it."

Our group leader, Nabil Hamid, a grinning, Egypt-born chain

smoker from the Washington, D.C., area, also in his forties, sat by himself at a nearby table. He was the fixer, solver of the inevitable crises: lost hajjis, broken-down buses, sickness, emotional burnout. He fiddled with his prayer beads while Hussein responded to a question posed by a middle-aged woman, also from Washington, who had completed a hajj in 2002. (Like many pilgrims, this woman had returned to the hajj on behalf of another Muslim who couldn't make the journey.) She mentioned in passing that at the end of her first hajj, she had not completed a final *tawaf* around the Kaaba.

"Sister," Hussein interrupted, "your hajj was invalid."

The woman was stunned. The sheik, with iron certainty, seemed to be telling her she had gone through great expense and weeks of pain for nothing. I wanted to find out the woman's name, but it wouldn't have done any good. I couldn't approach her or talk to her: Personal contact between unrelated women and men is forbidden here.

Now, it's my third day. With a pair of new sandals, I wander down the rolling streets to enter the Grand Mosque and pray. After ten blocks of wading through crowds, I come to the mosque's towering granite minarets, entering alongside stone-faced Turks dressed in olive-green, African women in flowery headdresses, and a gaggle of tiny Indonesians dressed in white cloaks. The whispered prayer of millions sounds like rustling water along a riverbank. The Kaaba rises above the marble floor, and I move closer, meeting the stride of the floating multitudes and chanting along with them.

I exit onto Al Masjid Al Haram, Mecca's main street, which is thick with lame and disfigured beggars. Crying children from Africa kneel on the grimy road; when they don't cry loud enough, their mothers appear from street corners and beat them. One girl has wrapped a gauze bandage around her little brother's head and smudged it with lipstick to mimic a bloody wound.

Tired and starved for a glimpse of the world beyond Mecca, I retire to a café in the back of my hotel to watch CNN, hoping to get the latest on the still-pending war between the United States and Iraq. Inside, I run into somebody from my tour group, Aaron Craig, a handsome African-American engineering student from San Diego. Aaron is a recent convert in his late twenties, and he's dressed like a Saudi in a full *jallabeyah* robe — a flowing ankle-length gown worn by men. The robe isn't required for the hajj, but Aaron is signaling his burning desire to look 100 percent Muslim.

"You know," he tells me, sipping tea, "I've already seen lots of mistakes made by pilgrims. And the bumping and pushing and nationalism! And you wonder why we don't have Muslim unity."

This is Aaron's first visit to the Middle East. Like me when I converted, he seems convinced that pure application of Islam is the answer to everything.

"People are trying to change the religion, brother," he continues.

"What do you mean?"

"The sellout Muslims in America."

He's talking about moderates, people who live suburban lives, have non-Muslim friends, watch TV.

"Allah's religion is perfect. The sellouts want to say that jihad does not mean jihad. Meanwhile, Muslims are being attacked in Afghanistan, Chechnya, Palestine. You have to believe in it or you are a disbeliever."

This talk startles me. *Jihad* is a loaded word, referring to both armed resistance in defense of Islam and a private struggle to bolster one's faith. I wonder if he would think I'm a sellout. My jihad has always been intensely personal, concerning prayers, family, success, and finding the peace that lately has eluded me — peace that, so far, continues to elude me during this hajj.

In the evening, when the streets are empty, I call my wife, who's in the United States, from a nearby cabin with pay phones. It's staffed by smart-alecky young Saudis dressed in Western T-shirts and blue jeans. They look like they'd rather be listening to Tupac or dancing in a club — anything but herding us pilgrims around.

"Why didn't you tell me the streets are filled with crooks?" I jokingly ask them in Arabic. "My sandals were stolen from the Grand Mosque."

"All Meccans are good, all Muslims are good," one replies robotically. He offers me a Marlboro, one of the few naughty pleasures tolerated in Mecca.

"No," the other declares. "Some Meccans are good. Some are bad."

It's three days later, February 3, and I'm standing in the hallway of the Dallah Hotel with Aaron. We have left Mecca, boarded a bus for

Medina, and arrived at sundown, just in time to make the last prayers of the day. The ride here was soothing, with African pilgrims dressed in white walking the road beside us, chanting loudly, *"Labaik, Allah, labaik"* ("Here I am, Allah, here I am"). Medina is an oasis 210 miles north of Mecca. It's a smaller, more comfortable city, its streets cleaner and less congested.

The hotel is swarming with African-American converts and Kuwaitis. As we prepare to leave for the Prophet's Mosque, Aaron shares a big piece of news: His wife has been offered a position teaching English in Riyadh, and they're thinking of making the move.

"Murad," he says, "the Saudis — what are they like?"

There's a lot I could say about that. I spent a week in Saudi Arabia in 2002, and I was shocked by the restrictiveness of everyday life, where most pleasures, even innocent ones like G-rated movies, are banned. I've known too many American Muslims who studied in Saudi Arabia and found, alongside the unbearable dreariness, the same hypocrisies, vices, and bigotry that they thought they'd left behind.

In the end I say little to Aaron; I'm leery about interfering with his destiny. "The Saudis make loyal friends," I tell him. "But there is no social life here. I think you will miss the States."

Aaron sighs, then laughs. "I don't care," he says. "They've got Kentucky Fried Chicken and Burger King. That's all the culture I need. I just want to hear the call to prayer in the morning."

At twilight, Aaron and I wander down the windy street to the Prophet's Mosque. Set on flat land in the city center, its white granite walls are cast in beautiful greenish light. Six thirty-story minarets ascend from its corners, poking into the night sky. Inside, the shrine is huge, spanning 1.7 million square feet. At prayer time, each row of prostrate men extends nearly a mile.

Inspiring though it is, Medina does little to lift my sagging spirits during the six days we stay here. Aside from the physical discomfort — I'm suffering through my second case of flu, and my body aches from walking — something spiritual is missing. I cannot yet say that I'm feeling any different than before I arrived in Mecca, and I'm disappointed in the way the Saudis manage the whole thing, giving too little attention to safety and security. Not for the first time, I'm wondering if I'm crazy to be here.

*

After a week of Medina's prayer and quiet, our buses show up again on February 8, a Saturday, to take us about 210 miles to Mina, where all two million hajjis are heading to enact one of mankind's grandest mass rituals, starting tomorrow. Bounded by mountains on two sides, Mina is home to a permanent tent city that sits between the plain of Arafat and Mecca's eastern boundary. It's a small metropolis of 44,000 identical fifteen-foot-high, aluminum-framed tents, placed on a square-mile quadrant. The Jamarat overpass — a huge two-level walkway that leads pilgrims to the three granite pillars representing Satan — sits roughly a mile to the northwest, in the direction of Mecca. A string of mosques borders the tent city in every direction.

We float into Mina, across the dirt roads between the tents, which are sectioned off by region and country. The bus stops before the entrance to what's called the Egyptian section. Nabil Hamid, our group leader, has placed us in an area called 42/2.

"Remember that number," he says sternly, pointing to a sign. "It's the only way to get back. If you are lost here, you are lost." We find our tent space, a 10,000-square-foot enclosure for fifty men.

After nightfall, Nabil leads us out to the site of Jamarat to show us the mile-long path from the tent and back. Just before we leave, Sheik Ahmed Shirbini, a forty-something Egyptian-born Muslim from Denver who's on his third hajj, issues a warning about the dangers awaiting us at the Jamarat walkway.

"If you lose your sandals, if you drop your money, your sunglasses, do not go back!" he says. "I was here four years ago, and I saw with my own eyes a man who'd dropped his wallet on the overpass trampled to death by the crowds."

Nabil carries a twelve-foot sign that reads U.S.A. We wander across the dark dirt lanes, past patches of paved road where pilgrims sleep on the ground. We turn a corner, walking down a longer road, until we come to the infamous overpass, a mile-long, three-hundred-foot-wide structure. You can get to the three granite pillars from this bridge or an underpass below it. The structure is built to hold 100,000 people, but three times that number will crowd it in the thick of Jamarat. This overload caused a collapse in 1998 that killed 118 pilgrims.

One of our group, a young doctor from Pennsylvania named Shakeel Shareef, points to the street under the bridge. "That's where all the people were killed," he says.

Hearing this, Aaron swallows and his voice goes big. "Allah is all-knowing and all-powerful," he says. "If we are supposed to die at Jamarat, it is part of his will. What better place to die?"

But I can see the fear on his face. It's oddly comforting to know that he's as scared as I am.

It's eight o'clock on the morning of February 11, the day I'll perform the Stoning of the Devil ritual, and I'm lost. At the moment, I'm in Mina, walking on a street beneath the mountain valleys, surrounded by exultant pilgrims hustling toward Jamarat. On each side of me, the numberless tents sweep out beneath the mountains.

A lot has happened since this time yesterday. In the morning we left early as our bus raced toward the Mount of Mercy for the nighttime vigil. Hajjis in surgical masks streamed beside us in a fog of exhaust; young boys surfed the hoods of antiquated American school buses, their white robes flapping in the wind.

But this glorious motion didn't last long: We spent much of the day either stuck in traffic or walking around lost, and I got separated twice from my group. At sundown it looked like we might not make Muzdalifa by midnight. Sheik Hussein, our spiritual adviser, informed us that if we didn't get there by then, we would have to lay out cash for the sacrifice of a sheep in Mecca, to atone for this failure in the hajj.

When a pilgrim objected to this — shouldn't our group leader, Nabil, have to pay, since he is responsible for getting us around? — Sheik Hussein wagged his finger and said, "You do not understand worship! I don't care about the money! This is between you and Nabil! I am here to help you worship Allah!"

In the end we got there, but in these crowds, it's always easy to get lost again. Right now, pushing my way forward in the Mina morning, I have no idea where I am. I have a vague sense that my tent at the Egyptian camp is straight ahead, but Mina is so rambling, its hills so full of identical tents, that I can't be sure. I walk forward, pacing ahead of the crowds of half-sleeping pilgrims.

Two hours pass. When I finally get my bearings, around 10 A.M., I realize that I'm just one street removed from 42/2, but it's hard to get all the way there. Pushing through the crowds is like wading through waist-high water. I am caught on a street congested with pilgrims and tour buses, vans, and trucks on their way to Jamarat. Blocks away, pilgrims are flooding the street from both directions, coming back from Muzdalifa and racing toward Jamarat. Trapped in a hot, heaving crowd, I suffer the most terrifying claustrophobia of my life.

I force my way through the street until it is impossible to take a step forward. Suddenly there's an explosion of human pressure from all sides, and I find myself standing face to face with a small, neatly dressed Iranian hajj leader in wire-rim glasses. The Iranian's eyes go wide as pilgrims on each side of the road begin to rush toward us. Africans are shoving through. Saudi policemen stand on trucks and rooftops, doing nothing as they watch the street below them devolve into madness. Women shout "Stop!" in Farsi and wave their hands, but no one can stop the crowd from crushing in. I cannot move. I can only pray. The crowd erupts in frenzied screaming. A row of middle-aged Iranian women fall over like dominoes.

Nigerian pilgrims start pushing through violently. Feeble, veiled women shout the only Arabic words understood by every pilgrim: "Haram! Haram!" ("Shame on you!"). Women and small old men are getting trampled in the mud. I find an opening through the maelstrom and hurry to a parked truck. I climb into the truck, my sandals left behind in the street mud, my bare feet burning on the truck bed's hot, rusty metal floor.

Nigerians crawl onto the truck from all sides. I can do little more than watch as screaming Iranian and Nigerian women are crushed on the street beneath us, a sea of white burqas, angled shoulders, crying, pleading faces, the flashing of outstretched arms. I reach down and pull a young Nigerian woman into the truck. Like me, she is crying, her face racked with fear. An old Iranian woman in white clings to the Nigerian's waist as I pull her up, her body floating on a wave of white-cloaked women. In another language, she thanks me for saving her life.

And then, in what seems like just a moment, the street is somehow cleared behind us. Women lie moaning in the mud. The truck's engine chugs; it zips forward six or seven blocks down the now-empty street. I watch pilgrims in the distance climbing from the piled bodies to their feet on the muddy, empty road.

I jump off the truck and walk barefoot back to my camp through a cloud of diesel exhaust. The scene of the stampede is six blocks away, shockingly clear. When I return to it, the road has been swept of thirty or forty people who — I can only assume from what I saw — have been badly injured or killed. (I never find out, but the next day I read in the *Saudi Times* that fourteen people died a half-mile away in a different stampede at Jamarat.)

I am angry — angry at the Saudis for permitting such chaos. But beneath my anger, there is also exultation, something electric, happiness to have survived, the clarity that comes from facing death. Around noon, I finally reach 42/2, entering through an iron gate. Sheik Hussein is speaking with a veiled woman from the American group.

"I must talk to you," I tell him, sobbing.

He takes me by the wrist down a concrete path, and we stand in the shade of a fluttering tent. "I was almost killed, Sheik Hussein! There was a stampede in the street. I jumped into a truck. I pulled a woman up. I saved her life. I think people died there."

"It is OK," the sheik says. "It is OK if you touched the woman."

"No, no. I was not asking that. I wanted to tell you that I almost died today."

"Well, it is over now," he says, without emotion. Then he leaves me at the tent.

However deadly and frantic Jamarat is, it can't be worse than what I've just seen. Though I haven't slept in thirty-six hours, nothing matters now but completing this hajj. I step inside my tent and stare at my fellow pilgrims lying on a rug. Half of them have already gone to Jamarat and returned. They eat oranges or sleep blissfully on mats in the hot, cramped tent. The rest are waiting until evening, when Jamarat is safer.

I decide to go right now. I have lost all my fear. Along with Shakeel Shareef, the Pennsylvania doctor, and a few other pilgrims, I march to Jamarat in the midday heat, collecting pebbles along the way. The streets are congested, but we weave through the crowds. We watch a pilgrim coming back from Jamarat. He is bandaged and bleeding from the head, his *ihram* robes covered in blood.

We wander into a crowd of more than a million people. A couple hundred thousand pilgrims are striding on the overpass above. "Everyone is taking the overpass," says Shakeel, pointing. "The bottom level is safer."

We follow him, making our way through the rushing crowds to the smallest pillar to throw our seven stones, but we are too far away. Shakeel is not like so many other careless pilgrims. He will not throw at the first opportunity; he waits until he is certain he will not hit another person. I watch him, banged upon by rushing hajjis, measuring his throw, stopping, moving closer. I stand behind him, my hand on his shoulder, so that we stay together.

"We have to get closer," Shakeel shouts. "If we throw from here, we'll only be hitting pilgrims. Hurry."

We link arms and march into a wall of pilgrims. Hundreds of tiny pebbles pound against the sides of a granite pillar in little bursts of dust.

Right after Shakeel throws his last pebble, he is almost pushed down by a throng of Pakistanis. I grab him and pull him away from the scene. We run through the riotous crowd until we are outside again, safe, in the sun.

As we approach our camp, I turn and watch the arcing, sun-washed, overcrowded Jamarat overpass receding behind the tents. As I wander back, I realize I've made peace with the hajj and with this rough, beautiful, holy place. Everything I have suffered seems almost necessary, because I am overcome with an unutterable serenity. How is it that, by some miracle, so many people can exist in the same small place at once?

We reach our camp, shave our heads, shower, change out of our *ihram* robes into *jallabeyah* robes, roll out our mats, and sleep hard on the Mina dirt.

CHARLES MARTIN KEARNEY

# Maps and Dreaming

FROM *The Missouri Review*

## *Night in New Delhi*

SUZANNE AND I were nearing the end of a journey together that had taken us overland through Turkey, Iran, Afghanistan, Pakistan, and India. On the front steps of a hotel in New Delhi, I waited for a taxi among shirtless, mostly sleeping baggage men. My documents and belongings were packed. The hotel restaurant had air conditioning, and moneychangers — the grifters and hawkers who made Asia possible and impossible — had already grouped together close to its locked entrance, smoking cheroots, aloof, edgy, and as watchful and nervous as birds. An oxcart stacked with bundles of cotton scraps passed us in the street. Early morning cooking fires, tended by squatters, tribes of sick and poor, provided checkpoints of light close to ground. Overhead, slow blue clouds hid the moon.

It was about 3:30 A.M. and unseasonably warm even for late July. In the room upstairs I had showered, shaved, and dressed in European clothes. The manager of the hotel had brought me a copy of the *Herald Tribune* and a serving of coffee. I was awake enough but tired and thinking about Suzanne. We had met in Greece, when she was still undecided about her plans; she thought that she wanted a bodyguard for her trip through Central Asia, and I had gone with her, giving up for the summer my idea of crisscrossing the Near East, destined for Israel. We had gotten involved and for about three months had been close, starting in Athens, then Istanbul, Tehran, Lahore, and New Delhi. Now she was going on without me, riding the trains to Nepal, temporarily half blind.

Somehow she had scratched her cornea, and we didn't know how long it would take to heal. She thought it would be fine in a couple of days if she could keep it clean and not rub it. She didn't bother to see a doctor. Instead, she treated the scratch with tap water from the sink, a small amount of antibiotic cream, a gauze eye patch held in place by Scotch tape, and aspirin from a New Delhi pharmacy. This first aid left her with a hesitant walk because she had no depth of vision and had to lift her head a little, elevating her good eye. She didn't complain about having to wear the bandage or about the pain. But she did have to sit down to rest more often than was usual and at night drank more beer.

A few hours before, while I was still upstairs in the hotel with Suzanne, I'd made a last search of the room, checking for anything I might have forgotten to pack. Suzanne had finished taking care of her eye and turned her chair away from the mirror above the dresser. She'd showered first, ahead of me, and combed her wet blond hair off her forehead, straight down behind her ears, touching the nape of her neck. Her wraparound skirt showed one leg, ankle to thigh. While she was in the bathroom taking a shower, I had folded my khaki shirt into her shoulder bag — a long-sleeved, baggy shirt I had given her in Iran, where men had shoved and pinched her, spat, and jeered. Now her arms were once more immodestly bare in a blouse of her own.

When I crossed the room from the closet to the bed, Suzanne stood and helped me pull back the covers and lift the mattress. We talked mostly about train schedules and visas. We were absorbed in the simple details of getting ready for my departure. By three o'clock in the morning all of my gear was by the door, and I was asking myself if I could say anything to her that would make sense, however awkward and plain. I did try asking her about her money, whether I owed her any or she needed any, and about whether her eye hurt. I asked her if I should go with her to Nepal, and she said, "No" — an honest answer — and left the room in a hurry. I lay on the bed, dressed. It had not been love between us, though we had traveled as man and wife through Moslem countries, but it hadn't been much less, and neither of us was certain how we would feel after the separation.

Now my taxi, a late-1960s ivory Mercedes, slowed to a stop in sight of the hotel. A herd of cows and bulls and a line of herdsmen

— tall, shaved-headed boys slapping the flanks of their animals — blocked his approach, the herd moving toward the middle of the street, drawn by a scattering of vegetable cuttings spilled in the dirt. On a raised wooden platform near the taxi, a circle of women in saffron veils and white pajamas had begun to work a hand mill by the light of kerosene lamps.

"Sahib," the doorman of the hotel said to me and bowed slightly, fingertips touching fingertips, palms not quite pressed together, thumbs resting on his breastbone, asking me to step into and hire the horse-drawn tonga he had just hailed.

"Sahib."

I dismissed the offer by ignoring him and waved the tonga away. The doorman, who lived on tips from the tonga and trishaw drivers, stared at me angrily. The friends of the doorman, who lived on the steps of the hotel, asking baksheesh from the guests and stealing bags, were yelling back and forth to each other, mad because I had caused the doorman to lose money, a sum probably smaller than a few American pennies. I was nervous about what they were saying but didn't regret sending the doorman back down to the street. After months of traveling out of my depth, I had grown rude. So often, people had tagged after Suzanne and me, asking us to stay at their hotel, or called out to us, "English? Deutsche? Change money?" Or they fell in stride beside us to ask for alms — beggars of every imaginable sort. Such everyday occurrences had left me at my worst. For whatever reasons, I hadn't been able to learn anything in the East, not a thing, not renunciation from the Moslems, not acceptance from the Buddhists, not submission, not peace or generosity.

A week of high temperatures had not sweetened the air in the New Delhi streets. The buckets and pans of water that many Indians used to douse the ground in front of their shops (as if the heat were a carpet of fire underfoot) had only created rivulets in the dust and tiny puddles that muddied the dirt and then evaporated, the water cycling up, carrying with it the taste of gasoline and motor oil and animal fodder — straw, grass, husks — crushed by cart wheels. Families sat cross-legged on woven mats, eating peppered food. Such a heavy, laden atmosphere, like air inside a huge ark, made breathing harder, made thoughts appear and disappear lazily.

The lassitude and lightheadedness I was feeling had happened before. Suzanne and I had both had serious bouts of typhoid in Afghanistan, the result of eating bowls and bowls of unpasteurized vanilla ice cream in a tea shop, and for days afterward we had been dehydrated and delirious, then indolent and queasy, afraid to eat and afraid not to, living on Coca-Colas, Fantas, tea, coffee, boiled rice, bread, both of us losing weight, smoking cigarettes in bed rather than getting up and going into Kabul for food and medicine. As we traveled through Afghanistan, Pakistan, and India, my fever would return at night and keep me awake worrying about other ways of dying in Asia; the insomnia itself convinced me that I had diphtheria or malaria.

The taxi driver had seen me coming and had gotten out of his Mercedes. He was a husky, straight-backed Sikh with a turban and full beard. I complimented him on his taxi. It had a clean trunk and new tires and was washed and waxed. He touched my elbow courteously and said, "Please," leading me to the front of the Mercedes, where the hood ornament had been snapped off. He had lost and replaced the part five times. Thieves took the chromed metal circle, removed the star in the middle, and made a bracelet for themselves, he said. He was holding out his dark-skinned hand so I could see the bracelet on his own wrist.

The Sikhs are a minority faith in India, neither Hindu nor Moslem, who devoutly worship a God not unlike the Christian God. But they also believe in predestination and the transmigration of the human spirit; the first idea is Moslem, taken from the Koran, and the second is Hindu, taken from the Vedic texts. The sacred scriptures of the Sikhs, called the Granth, also teach a reverence for warfare and baptism by the sword. In observance of the laws of the Granth, a Sikh man will not cut his hair but fix it in place with a comb. Nor will he cut his beard. He will clothe his waist and hips with a single length of cloth, wear an iron bangle on his wrist, and carry a dagger. In India Sikhs often become policemen or officers in the army.

"We cannot prevent it," he said, referring to the thefts, his tone of voice very correct, very British, after the vanished civil servants of his country. "There is no fear in their mind."

*

The drive to the airport was a pleasure. I sat in the back seat, daydreaming, appreciating the anonymity of being a passenger with nothing to carry or guard. A joss stick of incense, broken in half by the driver, lay smoldering in the dashboard ashtray. I was thinking about the vastness of where I had been and wondering about how much of it I would remember. Coming into New Delhi by train from the north of India, the Punjab region, I'd seen water buffalos stranded belly-deep in flooded rice paddies, their black heads passive, their backs fat with light, and I'd wondered if their muscles were heat-bound and their eyes hypnotized by the glare. I recalled a woman from the hotel saying, "Traveling, you don't know what you'll remember. A friend of mine remembers trees."

I am not superstitious. I do not believe in charms and omens, fortunetellers and mystics, astrology and numerology. I don't believe in destiny or that one's life is masked in symbols that explain and interpret it all, like a parlor trick. I prefer to talk clearly about the tangible world. Yet that summer in India I was different, and even then I understood why. To survive and get anything done, to slip by, as I did every day, I had to compromise, loosen up. At times I gave up on logic altogether, gave it up for mood and atmosphere: pilgrims bathing in the rivers, monks in orange robes, prayer wheels and monkey gods, carved devils, the red snake painted on the bride's hand for luck. In return for my trust, India seemed to unclench, especially in the evening, and allowed me safe passage till sunrise, the start of business. For me, these truces were as real as the dark road out of New Delhi, and the reason why I had left at night.

The doors of the airport terminal were a short distance away, in sight, when the driver stopped the taxi — he had no other choice — and flashed his headlights, the high beams, at the acres of Indians sleeping in the grass and in the road and on the wide sidewalks. A handful of Indians did move, sat up, respectful of the others beside them. "This is fine," I said. There was no traffic. "I'll get out here." After the taxi left, I stood alone for a minute in the night air and let the badge of sweat on the back of my shirt dry.

The bright moon was still visible, and the Indians, dressed in cheap white cotton shirts, seemed to sleep under its soft protection as deeply as sunbathers at a beach. Miles back, a man sitting on the shoulder of the road, his legs crossed and his arms folded, had closed his eyes to the lights of the taxi, lost on the periphery of my last night in India. Not until much later did I remember him as he had been: fragile, destitute, and luminous.

## Border Station at Islamquala

Like da Vinci, who wrote backward in his notebooks, to keep the entries in them a secret, Suzanne could fill a page of her journal with sentences that I could not read unless I held the handwriting up to a mirror. "I was sick in bed," she told me at Islamquala, the border station in western Afghanistan, "and I wrote sixty — no, more than sixty — lines of *Paradise Lost*, backward, in less than a minute." The record in the *Guinness Book of World Records* was fifty, she said. "Left-handed, I can do about fifty." I gave her a minute, and she wrote a long, unintelligible paragraph. On the opposite page of the journal, in green ink, she had columned together sums of money and listed the serial numbers of her spent travelers' checks. I was staring at the abstract shapes and lines she had doodled in the margins when she said, "I've got it figured down to the penny. I'll arrive home broke."

It was past noon, and we had been waiting for hours, reading paperbacks in the shade of a tree, drinking Coca-Colas, and talking. On the shoulder of the road behind us, Afghani soldiers and Afghani customs officers searched the bus for expensive cameras and watches, European editions of *Playboy*, cassette tape recorders, and lightweight kitchen appliances from Iran. Out of view, in the lobby of the blockhouse where our passports and visas had been stamped, a second team of Afghanis was opening boxes, cutting twine off packages, asking questions of the owners, holding back taxable goods, marking luggage — pieces that had already gone through — with different-colored nubs of chalk, and then throwing them onto the bare floor, making waist-high piles — archipelagoes of scuffed leather, backpacks, dented aluminum trunks. The thoroughness on the part of the customs officers was their way of stalling, to encourage bribes from the groups of Afghanis who returned home from good jobs in Iran. These Afghanis brought hard currencies into the country, dollars and pounds and deutsche marks, which had to be declared. For practical gifts for their families, such as toasters and radios, each one had to bargain at the bor-

der, negotiating how much baksheesh to pay and making sure that
it went to the correct person. Because of these prolonged hag-
glings, Suzanne and I soon fell out of line to rest.

A furious American student walked over to the open-fronted stall
that sold glasses of tea and bottles of Coca-Cola and began to argue
with the Afghani man standing there. Until the moment when the
American's voice lifted us from the calm of the shade tree, only two
things had divided the monotonous desert: sunlight and steady
heat, and the sounds of bell straps dangling from the necks of
heavily laden, tethered camels. "He's mad about the wait," I said to
Suzanne. She looked at me, ready to smile yet not willing to do it.
She had been watching the American and the Afghani, listening to
it all, as if trying to make up her mind about whether to be amused
or embarrassed. Like Suzanne, I was divided. In the recent past,
we'd had to maintain restraint but were both tired of it.

On a long journey, the only secrets that are kept are the ones
that people forget to tell. When you're living in close quarters without many physical comforts, no amount of card playing and small
talk can allay the homesickness and loneliness. Some people, of
course, do remain laconic and reticent. But the demands and disappointments of a remote place, the actual facts of it, press you to
talk.

Suzanne was an artist, a young American painter, who had left
the East Coast of the United States to travel around the world on a
$6,000 grant from the Museum School of Fine Arts in Boston, Mas-
sachusetts. Before I met her, she had sublet her Cambridge studio,
embarked from the States on a cruise ship, docked in London during a Christmas snowstorm, stayed in Cornwall by the sea to paint,
left for France and Spain after a Saint Patrick's Day pub crawl with
her English friends, punched a Spaniard in the face while riding
on a train out of Madrid — he had refused to keep his notions
about blonds to himself — and lived for three months in Greece,
painting the islands of Mykonos and Naxos. I met her in Athens.

I was reading a borrowed *Herald Tribune* in the small community
room of the Athens Student Hostel. A series of front-page articles,
originally written by American journalists for Stateside newspapers,
reported on the recent election of Menachem Begin in Israel, the
ascendancy of the Likud Party in the Knesset, and the possibility
of war in the Middle East. The newspaper belonged to a sandy-

haired, blue-eyed, scruffy nineteen-year-old South African boy named John. To escape mandatory service in the army, he had left his home in Cape Town and gone to Bombay, on the west coast of India. When he started to run short of money, he signed on with a merchant ship that took him across the Arabian Sea, into the Gulf of Aden and the Red Sea, and through the Suez Canal to Haifa, where he disembarked and found work on an Israeli kibbutz. Laboring in the irrigated desert fields, he had cut bunches of bananas from their stems with a machete. "Little bananas," he told me. "No bigger than my finger." He also told me his opinions about the next big war in the Middle East, which he said would probably start in the upcoming winter months; he used a worn Israeli tourist bureau map to plot it out for me.

I still had John's newspaper when Suzanne came over to my table. I had seen her sitting with friends, discussing novels, and I had mistaken her for a teenager, a high school student. She asked me if she could have the newspaper when I was finished with it. She wanted the crossword puzzle on the back page. "It's not mine," I said. I told her that John had left the hostel to have dinner in the Plaka. I did offer to tear the puzzle out for her. She said she could wait for John and asked me if I had been out to the Greek islands yet. "Santorini and Ios," I said, turning around in my chair to look at her. I had spent the day in the rain and drizzle, hitchhiking into Athens from the port city of Piraeus, and I was cold, hungry, thinking about going into town for a drink, and preoccupied again about Israel. In a month I would be there, and for a month I had been second-guessing the wisdom of arriving in summer, when the kibbutzim would be overrun with volunteers and tourists.

That night in the community room, I was able to hear the other side of Suzanne's friendliness and get the message that her charm had a purpose. From Greece she was going to Turkey, to start across Asia, she said. In her shoulder bag, she had a book about Afghanistan that friends of hers, teachers, had loaned her, along with a sizable bottle of malaria pills. She could get herself and a horse to India with her supply of pills, she said, handing me the prescription quinine. Then she opened her travel book to the color photographs of minarets in Herat, the first city she would reach in Afghanistan. I told her that a friend of mine had been to Afghanistan. He had liked it. It was part of his winding down after his tour in

Vietnam. I mentioned that he had gotten sick in Asia, nearly gone blind, and every joint in his body had swollen with fever. "He made it home, though," I said. Suzanne asked me about Vietnam. Had I been there? I said that my sister had talked me into going to college instead of enlisting in the Marine Corps, and so I had a student deferment. Then in my freshman year at school, I fell in love with a girl from New Jersey; the next year it was a girl from New Hampshire. Semester by semester I sort of forgot about the marines, I said.

The talk came around to Israel, the Arabs, my living on a kibbutz. I told Suzanne that I was decided about settling in Israel, war or no war, and that I was not worried about getting shot. It would have been truer to say that I was headstrong and still young enough not to be ambivalent about dying. "My mother and sister think it's dangerous over here," Suzanne said. Her cigarette was in the ashtray. The filter had teeth marks on it. "I wish I'd hear from them," she said. It had been months since their last bundle of letters. "They usually write," she said.

A short Greek man, bringing rolls of toilet paper to the stalls on each floor, announced that he was turning off the lights for curfew and asked everybody to retire to their rooms and dormitories. Suzanne had a private room down the hall from the community room, and I had a cot in the men's dormitory upstairs. I walked her to the open doors of the hallway. I was telling her that I would like to hear what she had to say about getting the right vaccinations and visas for crossing Asia. I asked her if we could talk again tomorrow. "We could have breakfast," she said. There was a restaurant in downtown Athens that sold American food: scrambled eggs, toast, sausage, coffee. The Greek man was studying us from the far end of the hall. To acknowledge that I saw him standing there and that I was not trying to sneak into Suzanne's room, I raised my hand in the air, like a police officer directing traffic. It was the wrong signal, and it brought him running straight at me. "Your mother, your sister," he said. "Your mother, your sister, your father, your brother." His face was gray. Suzanne was hugging her shoulders. His screaming continued. Speaking pidgin Greek to him, Suzanne said, "Friend, my friend." His right arm was cocked, the heel of his palm aimed upward. I was taller than the Greek and I outweighed him, and I thought that he would see that I had the advantage and leave.

He did, and afterward I asked Suzanne, "What was that all about?" In the Mediterranean and Asia, certain words, like *taxi,* and certain gestures, like opening your palm at a man, were universal in meaning, she said. I had insulted him and cursed his family. "You should have seen yourself," she said.

During the night, a man threw a fit in the large, blacked-out communal dorm where I was sleeping. The pain in his voice woke me. He was thrashing about in the dark and yelling. I heard his steps near my cot, and I heard the door leading into the hall slam shut.

Someone switched on the chandelier that hung from the center of the ceiling. Naked men and men in their underwear sat up in their cots to gauge the trouble. In the dark, there had been an urge to act. In the sudden light, the curiosity and adrenaline changed to discomfort. I told Suzanne about it the next morning, on our walk back from the restaurant to the hostel. She told me that if I was tired and needed to sleep, I could use her room while she went to the American Express office at Syntagma Square to collect her *poste restante* mail. She said that if there was no mail for her, she would stay downtown and use the transatlantic telephone lines to call her mother in California.

Suzanne's room did not have windows or a sink. Nor did it have clear paths from corner to corner — because the springs in the bed were bad, she had laid its mattress on the floor. The wall was the headboard. Her winter clothes and her paintings had been packed in cardboard boxes that were also on the floor, flaps open, the shipments addressed to her mother in Los Angeles. The largest box had her sleeping bag and a pair of boots in it. The two boxes beside it were filled with rolled-up canvases and drawing paper, the pieces of art fitted neatly inside, each box as orderly as a honeycomb. She told me she was sending her work to the States rather than carry it with her. She would just take one pack, she said, the essentials, the necessities. I thought she had overdone it. Tracts of land that are arid in the daylight can fall below zero at night, and she might regret not having the sleeping bag. Her calf-length, rubber-soled boots would help in the rain. She would need a hat and a water bottle, too, for the sun. I did notice that she had a Swiss Army knife and American cigarettes, but otherwise it seemed that she had purged herself of simple comforts. Her unloading of extra weight and luxuries may have been one of the lessons of Europe, where heavy luggage can slow the day to a standstill. Or it may have been the result of reading her book on Afghanistan, seeing its stark photographs of the land, Central Asia's severest — the geography of religious denial. Or it may have been in her temperament to collect and discard on a whim, the choosings done haphazardly, her methods instinctive, the trivial and the not so trivial exchanged for whatever she thought was important to her.

The rain had moved inland overnight, and the change in the barometer had left Athens cooler and made it possible to sleep in the afternoon. I was under a sheet, using my arm for a pillow, and dreaming about being asleep. Then I was awake. Suzanne was pacing, rummaging through the room, her black-and-white Arab *kaffiyeh* settled on her shoulders like a scarf, its ends tied in a big knot, inches below her neck. She was crying. I stood, asking her what had happened. She said there had been a letter from her mother at the American Express office. After reading it, Suzanne had telephoned Los Angeles. In the aftermath of the letter and the talk with her mother, Suzanne had started trembling, as if wind had entered her. I read the letter. It was long, written in a beautiful hand, and it closed with the definitions of five words that Suzanne had asked her mother to look up in a dictionary: *Carrefour:* Where four roads meet. A crossroads or intersection. A public square or plaza. *Diadem:* A crown. An ornamental cloth headband worn as a crown. Royal power, authority, or dignity. *Diapason:* The entire range of a musical instrument or voice. A swelling burst of harmony. A tuning fork. *Sibyline:* Of or like the sibyls or their prophecies. Prophetic. Oracular. Mysterious. *Mellifluous:* Sounding sweet and smooth. Honeyed.

I read the letter and the answers to the crossword puzzle again. The person in the writing, Suzanne's mother, had a voice that did not withhold or insist, and the sentiments in her letter had a grace and directness that could not be misunderstood. "She doesn't want you traveling alone," I said.

It was midafternoon, and the sun was behind us, in Iran. The Afghani man from the stall had spread his prayer rug on the ground and had knelt down on it. He recited his prayers quietly, holding a closed book in his hands. Suzanne was looking at him. Her pens and journal lay in the lap of her long skirt. Immaculate dry air burnished her blond hair and fair skin. Dust, as fine as silt from a river bed, covered her sandals and feet. The smell of straw, bundled and lashed to the saddles of the camels, and the smell of burning charcoal from a brazier reached us like the raked-over remains of a burnt stable, the aftertastes of a fire. We had been at Islamquala for ten, maybe twelve hours. If we had boarded the bus right then, we could have reached Herat by sunset. Either way, if we left, if we did not leave, I was reconciled to it. If we stayed — and we did in fact stay — I would see the Afghani man praying again, bowing down in the sand, his arms and legs tucked in close to his body, the cool black, pinpoint heaven of the desert night set over him like a shell, the delays and extortions of Islamquala, its dull corruptions, purified.

## Sultan Ahmet District of Istanbul

In Istanbul, a tall, sinewy Turkish man in his thirties fell in love with Suzanne. His name was Cetin, and from the day we met him in the Old City and asked him for directions until the day we changed hotels so that he would not be able to find us, he tried doggedly to befriend me, lower my guard, and impress Suzanne. She was, he would say to me in a whisper, "Very beautiful, very beautiful," or he would say that she was like a movie star, like Kim Novak, as she walked ahead of us in the street, the Turks in the doorways looking at her, and then at us as we caught up with her. I nodded in agreement — the tolerant, bemused husband of an attractive wife — and Cetin touched his mustache, stroked it absently, as if wondering what I would allow from him. Then, acting like a guide with bored tourists, he regained his enthusiasm and told us about growing up in the Sultan Ahmet district of Istanbul, where his mother took him and his brothers to the Turkish baths, and his father took him to the cinema to learn English, the language of those who had money and businesses. His English had gotten him a job with the Germans, and once a week he would board a train for Munich, lay over for the night, then drive back to Turkey in a new car and deliver it to a dealership. He was saving for a car of his own. "Thunderbird," he said. "A Ford car."

It was all lighthearted at first, his talk and his courtesies, his chivalry — he carried Suzanne's bag, opened doors for her — his anecdotes about Istanbul, all of it meant to please Suzanne, his way of endearing himself to her. To me, the flirting was understandable and innocent, the infatuation that any man could feel for a younger woman from a foreign country. I thought that it was to be expected of a man who had been raised as a Moslem and forbidden women until he married but who had seen Europe's broad avenues and fashions, its cafés and rathskellers, the barmaids in their twenties.

But I was foolish to believe that I could handle Cetin, make him our translator, let him lead us through the bazaars and recommend museums. He did sometimes give advice. "Police very strong Fascist," he told me. "Very careful. Very bad here." There had been demonstrations every day, he said, people shot every day. To emphasize the shootings, Cetin made a fist, as if he had a gun in hand, and pulled the trigger. In a different conversation, by the fountain in the courtyard of the Blue Mosque, he advised us to wash our hands, remove our shoes at the door, not to touch anything near the pulpit, and, wherever we were in the assembly hall, not to step in front of the men praying. Their prayers went to Mecca and then to God, who would not hear them if you stood in the way.

Across the street from the Blue Mosque, at the Lale Restaurant, where Suzanne and I ate rice pudding in the morning and where Cetin would appear like a messenger, searching for us, there was a public bulletin board. It was crowded with notes to friends, offers of sleeping bags and cameras for sale, tour schedules, passport photos left as a compliment to the Lale's thoughtful employees, and notices of rewards for information about missing people: Americans. Swiss. Australians. Last seen in Baghdad. Last seen in Beirut. Last seen in Calcutta. The notices, which included names, home addresses, telephone numbers, descriptions of height, weight, eye color, hair color, were usually written in English, French, or German or all three. Most of the people had been missing for over a year, and it was hard to be optimistic about them.

Flushed and upset, Cetin was striding, gaze forward, hurrying Suzanne and me along. "Many people are in prison," he said. "Communist people. For politics." We had to be careful, he said. I looked around us. As far as I could see, the street was quiet. No cars. No carts. But I knew what Cetin meant. Nearby, in the back streets of the Old City, we had come upon a long column of Turkish men, the majority of them standing idly on the cobblestones, a few of the demonstrators holding red flags, loudspeakers, signs, and white political banners. I would have stayed in the area and watched, for a while anyway, if Cetin had not panicked. I might even have trailed the Turks to their rally and stood off to the side of it, guessing at what the Turkish speakers were demanding of Prime Minister Sulyma Demirel. He was the right-wing strongman, whose government had made the Turkish currency worthless. His troops were the troops we saw in the streets, the enlisted men outfitted in coarse, green wool uniforms, with cumbersome bolt-action rifles. These soldiers had been conscripted from the provinces — uneducated boys, farmers, day laborers whose faces were a fair sampling of the Mongols, Tartars, and Kurds who had created the Ottoman Empire. Fed bad food, paid little, housed like chickens in wooden barracks, beaten, these troops would not quarrel with a chance to fight a mob of students and workers. Their only other enemies were boredom and fatigue. The only other relief, sex. It was commonplace in Istanbul to see teenaged riflemen gently touching hands.

When Cetin led us past the Lale Restaurant, I asked him to stop, but he refused. He was agitated, skittish. I told him I wanted to stop for chai. He tried to pull me aside and lecture me, but I peeled his fingers back from my wrist. He hesitated, the bully in him figuring, but I was obviously not going to be manhandled. "Every day," he said, "the pudding shop." We should go to a place for Turks, he said. There were many places for Turks. He would show us. He would pay. While he spoke, he rolled up the sleeves of his shirt, its creases already damp with sweat. I told him that I would carry Suzanne's bag if he was tired. No, he said, Turkish men were very strong.

Cetin placed a sugar cube in his mouth and sipped Turkish coffee from a tiny porcelain cup. Suzanne and I drank tea poured into glasses, brought to us on saucers. Our spoons lay on the grainy, scalded wood of the table. Cetin and I were joylessly smoking his pack of cigarettes. The smoke drifted, gathering in the cobwebbed corners of the ceiling. There were not many customers in the hot room, but there were flies. "I'm going," Suzanne said to me and Cetin, who was sitting across from us. Her statement overcame the stalemate of downcast eyes. Reproachfully, Cetin asked why. I pretended not to hear it, and yet I took a cold look at Cetin — his appalling swagger, his explosive pride. Leaning toward me, he asked, "What do you want? You want drugs?" With no caution about being noticed, he waved a packet of white powder at us. "You want drugs?" he said, loudly. "I have drugs." He palpated a vein in his arm. "You want injection?" Suzanne was standing. Her daylong look of bereavement had changed to healthy fury. I stood up. Cetin did the smart thing and stayed in his chair.

We made what midcourse changes we could make. We changed hotels. We avoided the Lale Restaurant. We studied the ferryboat schedules, crossed the Bosphorus, and landed at Uskudar on the Asiatic side of Istanbul. By taxi, we drove to Haydarpasa Station and looked into booking passage on a train out of Istanbul — a deluxe compartment with berths, we hoped — but the locomotive had been shunted off the main tracks onto a spur line, its diesel engine in disrepair; it was not expected to be serviceable anytime soon. Irritated, haggard, sooty from the depot, we backtracked to the European side of Istanbul, eating dry cheese pastries on the ferryboat, sipping dark, boiled tea, both of us sullen. A blind man shuffled back and forth in the aisles between the wood benches, coughing from tuberculosis, ringing a hand bell as the ferry shuttled him from Uskudar to Kabatas, the top of Asia, the bottom of Europe.

In the Old City we bought tickets for a three-day bus trip across Turkey — Istanbul to Tehran, nonstop except to eat and drink. The eastbound bus would not leave town for another four days, the ticket salesman said, counting our money. I asked him if it was possible to arrange to leave tomorrow. "No," he said, "the driver has to sleep."

After the break with Cetin, we moved into a hotel that was not a regular tourist hotel. Its staff, the maids and the desk clerks, did not speak English, and the hotel itself was hidden back in the quieter outskirts of the Sultan Ahmet district. At night the streets around it were deserted. The discolored blocks of apartments were dark. The intersecting alleys were full of cats. There were cul-de-sacs but no courtyards, no gardens, no sidewalks, and no streetlights. As a place to walk, it was somber and bare of distractions, private. I walked through it thinking about Cetin, who might have been a drug dealer and police informant. There were a lot of Turks who sold local heroin and hashish to Europeans and then sold their names to Istanbul's plainclothes detectives. There were also Turks smuggling drugs into Europe, and Cetin's job delivering cars from Munich, coming and going from Turkey to Germany with visa and work permit in order, could have made him valuable as a courier for narcotics. It was my fault, I said to Suzanne, I had gotten us involved with him. Suzanne, generous and civil about it, said that she had worried from the outset about getting too close to him. It had been the same for her in Greece: You could make friends with people, but you eventually had to draw the line.

I often took wrong turns when heading back to the hotel, and one night, lost in a fine mist of rain, I stopped on a brick street to get my bearings. Not too far ahead I saw a Turkish man screaming up at a lamplit window, slashing at it with a knife, threatening it with his fist, his shirt yanked out of his pants. The shutters of the window hung open, and I could not see anyone standing in the room. The Turk, who looked exhausted and sounded drunk, waited beneath the window, flatfooted, doing his best to attack it or draw someone out into the street. His voice was choked and desperate. There had to be a woman in the room, I thought, to have made him so crazy. Walking the slick cobblestones of the side streets, I thought of Suzanne, warm and maybe asleep in our room. I recalled her shiny Swiss Army knife, with its corkscrew and bottle opener, nail file, and screwdriver, and how peeved she had been a few days before when the maids at the hotel had fooled with it.

In the tourist hotels in Greece, we could leave everything we owned, including money and passports, on the bed, the chairs, the windowsills, and not have to worry about anything being stolen by the Greeks who came in to change the sheets and clean. Suzanne had once left a pair of nylon stockings in her room as a tip for the maid and then checked out of the hotel. The Greeks at the hotel searched for Suzanne, found out where she was staying on the island, and sent the stockings back to her, thinking she had mistakenly left them. On the mainland of Greece, in Thessaloniki, I left a belt pouch on the bureau in our room, and it was brought down to us by a maid while Suzanne and I were still paying our bill. I had to ask her to keep it. "Please," I said, "for you." Otherwise I would have to throw it away, I told her. I unbuttoned my shirt to show her the soft leather money pouch that hung around my neck. Suzanne had given it to me to use in Turkey, against pickpockets, and in return I had given her my passport-wallet case, which she carried in the waist of her skirt, in a pocket she had sewn in the lining.

But in Turkey, at the hotel in Istanbul where the Turks did not speak English, we made an effort to have everything of importance with us whenever we left the room: travelers' checks, cash, visas, passports, health cards, and door keys. Books and journals, and our clothes, we zippered into the backpacks and shelved in the closets. When we left the hotel for the first time to go to the railway station for tickets, I told the front desk clerk that we did not want the maids to make the beds. "OK?" I said, and pointed at the number on the key to our room. "No clean," I said, fleshing out my pidgin English with elaborate pantomime. "The room OK. OK?" The clerk gave a quick tilt of his head. "OK," he said. That evening, after Suzanne and I had returned to the hotel from Haydarpasa Station without any tickets, both of us drained and jumpy from hours of hiking in the sun and the disappointments of the day, we found the beds made, curtains open, bathroom scrubbed, and floors swept.

Swearing under my breath, I pawed through the backpacks, stacking shirts and jeans on the rug, counting socks, first-aid supplies, and packs of cigarettes. I gathered the loose change, much of it Greek money, from the side pockets of my pack and scattered it on the bedspread. Suzanne, defiantly silent, stalked about the room hunting for her Swiss Army knife. It had been on the nightstand, she said, but the nightstand had been dusted, and the knife was not in any of the drawers. Nor was it in her shoulder bag, which she had rummaged. "It's not here," she said. Lips tight, eyes wide and moist, she was eager for a fight. We were both overwrought and resentful. "I'll go down," I said. "I'll talk to them."

The lobby of the hotel was dimly lit. Men in robes and others in threadbare suits lounged in overstuffed chairs, having coffee. An electric fan at the front desk rattled as it rotated to the left, to the right, the air in the room musty, mildewed. The night manager was reading a Turkish newspaper. "My friend," I said. He smiled. "My friend," I said. "I have a problem." I told him about the Swiss Army knife. He answered in Turkish. I patted my chest with the palm of my hand. "My wife," I said. "Upstairs." I pointed at the ceiling. "My wife is very angry." I rolled my eyes. I sighed. Suzanne had bought a gold wedding band for herself in Athens as a prop for our quasi-marriage, but I did not have any kind of ring, so I pointed at the

Turk's wedding band. "My wife, upstairs," I said. I turned to the five Turks sitting in the chairs behind me. "English?" I asked them. The men shrugged. I turned back to the night manager. "My friend," I said, "look." I reached past his newspaper and picked up his closed fruit knife. "Knife," I said. I opened it. He rose from his stool. "Knife," I said. He went rigid. I turned — to explain to the Turks behind me. Abruptly, like assassins, the men drew their knives from the sheaths of their pockets. A short, unshaven man spoke to the others in Turkish. It sounded bad. Doing everything very slowly, I put the knife down and said, "OK. It's OK. Forget it."

Sometime later, inside the Amir Kabir Hotel in Tehran, I had lunch with Bob, an intelligent, easygoing American from New Orleans. He had ridden with Suzanne and me on the bus from Istanbul. Before Turkey and before Tehran, he had spent a year in Sweden, working on the assembly line of a Volvo plant. He was traveling overland through Asia for the summer, just to see it, have the experience, before he returned to Boston to study law. Harvard had accepted his application, mailed from Scandinavia, and his coursework would begin in the spring.

Relaxing, drinking fruit juice in the air-conditioned lobby furnished with ottomans and large pillows, we talked about women, and we talked about living overseas. Bob had not liked most Swedish women — too cool, too domineering — but he did love his fiancée, a Swede, and he had liked Europe. Grudgingly, he said that he liked and did not like Asia. "The drivers are maniacs," he said, referring to inner-city Tehran, a city that was overbuilt, ugly, its low skyline hazy with exhaust fumes. We had both witnessed taxis using sidewalks as traffic lanes, and we had both sat in taxis that could not move forward or backward or to either side of the lane, the drivers howling at everyone, their taxi radios playing sonorous, melancholy, tinny Middle Eastern music.

I told him that Suzanne and I were thinking of going north to the Caspian Sea to escape Tehran, have fun, see water that had pooled down from the inland shores of Russia, go swimming, eat sturgeon and caviar. Bob listened, nodding. Like us, he was ready to abandon the group that had boarded the bus in Istanbul. It had been a claustrophobic, desolate trip, with flashes of temper and privations. A Swiss couple was journeying into Asia for cheap heroin. The wife was plump and slovenly, with black hair and doughy skin. The husband was frail and gaunt. Both of them were addicts and had gone into withdrawal on the bus. At the Iranian border crossing, the husband bought a fifth of Scotch as paregoric for his tremors and drank it like spring water, gulping it as he walked, oblivious to shouts from us as he lurched into a big drainage ditch. The couple would meet another addict at the Amir Kabir, a young European boy, and he would take the husband into Tehran immediately, to quell his withdrawal and to buy a quarter kilo for the long ride to India. The European boy lived in a single room at the Amir Kabir, reading and rereading old issues of *Readers' Digest*, eating candy, dying. I had seen him, or his ghost, sitting on the edge of his cot, the door to the room ajar, the blinds of the windows reflecting the Persian sun.

I told Bob about Suzanne and me hitchhiking from Athens to the Turkish border without a map, strolling the coastal roads of Thessaloniki, coaxing cars to stop for us. About Suzanne discovering a lime-green tree frog in the bowl of a toilet, hanging on to the enamel above the waterline, Suzanne taking me in to see it, the frog's splayed fingers clinging like roots. At dusk, a big lorry, driven by a Greek man, had stopped for us. That night, in the middle of the night, he stopped again, for coffee, to keep himself awake on the high curves of the roads that followed the shoreline. When he shut off the lorry's engine, Suzanne and I could hear a chorale of faint, muffled chirping. Suzanne asked him what he was hauling in his truck. We stepped out of the driver's cab, and walked to the rear of the trailer. The Greek, beaming at us, encouraging us to enjoy the surprise, lifted back the canvas flap. Inside were thousands of baby chicks in stacks of wire cages.

After our talk, Bob went to the Tehran Hospital to ask the doctors there about getting the shots required for Afghanistan and India. I had begged off, telling him I would go tomorrow. As the afternoon passed, things disappeared into me: peanuts, beer, sandwiches, white wine. Suzanne, fresh and rested, clean from a hot-water shower, came into the Kabir's lobby and sat down with me. I told her that Bob and the long-haired guy from Britain and his cranky but voluptuous girlfriend were interested in our Caspian Sea idea. The Brits had not been with us on the bus from Turkey, but I remembered them, unhappily, from a *pension* on the island of Ios.

Their small bedroom and my small bedroom had shared a common wall, and their prolonged, mournful lovemaking sounds had gone on all night.

Hours passed. I slept and Suzanne shopped for bread and cookies. I showered and Suzanne washed clothes. I wrote aerograms in the room while she mingled in the restaurant. After three days of sitting elbow to elbow, sleeping shoulder to shoulder, eating bland rice, washing with lemon water from a bottle, drinking Coca-Cola for the sugar, and drinking halazone-treated water until Suzanne's legs and ankles swelled, we had a dispirited telepathy and could sense when the other needed indulging. It was like love in some ways, yet kinder, since neither of us was in love. Like a family in exile, we rationed what reserves of sympathy we had, saving it for each other.

These kinds of favors, which could fall into play at any time, about anything, had started in the Sultan Ahmet district of Istanbul, with Cetin, and at the hotel, with the Swiss Army knife. Suzanne, justifiably, could have been obstinate and not overlooked my blunders with Cetin, who never did find us at the hotel or report us falsely to the police, and I could have been angry as well, after she told me that she had recovered the Swiss Army knife — the maids had tucked it into her cosmetics bag. Instead, because there had been no guile between us, and no meanness, such mistakes were let go.

THOMAS KENEALLY

# Romancing the Abyss

FROM *Condé Nast Traveler*

THE WHITE SHIP I approached on the pier at Acapulco one monsoonal afternoon in September had a name that took up a great part of its bow: *Akademik Mstislav Keldysh*. It was named for a respected Russian scientist of the Soviet era, and it was muscular Russian crewmen, rather than white-gloved youths uniformed à la Cunard, who lugged our baggage aboard. The *Keldysh* was already a legendary ship to me — a mother ship of deep-sea exploration. I had read much about the scientific work conducted on it and had also seen film footage, shot from two fabled submersibles launched from the *Keldysh*'s decks, of various maritime depths and of the remains of the *Titanic* and the *Bismarck*.

The two submersibles — *Mir I* and *Mir II* — were the reason the scatter of passengers I stood among were joining the ship. We expected to see them glittering high as a billboard on the ship's superstructure, their plump shells encasing a titanium-steel orb large enough to hold a pilot and two passengers. One of them, I knew, would carry me not to a famed wreck but on a remarkable voyage nonetheless — 8,600 feet to the bottom of the sea and practically to the start of life itself. But more on that shortly . . . For now, there was no sign of the *Mir*s. They were garaged away somewhere near the ship's stern.

The twenty-three-year-old *Keldysh* is a scientific vessel weighing a little over six thousand tons, measuring four hundred feet in length, and resembling more than anything a well-kept interisland steamer. It was carrying forty-seven Russian marine biologists, geologists, seismologists, and other scientists. The white castle of living quarters and laboratories amidships offered enough room for a cabin for each of our group of eighteen paying customers, of whom eight were to make dives.

The Soviet Union once absorbed the expense of operating the *Keldysh*, but with the collapse of the USSR, the ship and its *Mirs* faced an uncertain future. An Australian named Mike McDowell, who had earlier founded and run trips to the Poles, entered into a symbiotic relationship with the P. P. Shirshov Institute of Oceanology, which operated in the Russian Baltic port of Kaliningrad and owned the *Keldysh*. If the scientists of the *Keldysh* could stand it, he would find passengers to pay to go on diving expeditions and hence preserve the vessel from being broken up for scrap or left to corrode at its mooring. The filmmaker James Cameron became a good customer of the resultant company, Deep Ocean Expeditions, using the *Mirs* regularly for deep-sea filming of previously unvisited ocean beds and famous wrecks, including the *Titanic* (some of this footage appeared in his feature film).

One of McDowell's partners, New Zealander Belinda Sawyer, had told me about DOE's upcoming summer schedule for the *Mirs*, which included dives to the wreckage of the *Titanic*. But it was the last trip on the itinerary that truly engaged my imagination: a dive, the first for the *Keldysh* team, to an until recently unknown series of hydrothermal vents brimming with curious sea life. The vents were located along a fault line at the bottom of the Pacific Ocean, between the Cocos and Pacific plates, some 570 miles southwest of Acapulco. At Nine North, as this area is called (for its location: latitude 9° north), the ocean is in touch with the earth's core — cold, deep water rushes down the fractures, or vents, in the seabed and is spat back out, superheated and laced with minerals such as hydrogen sulfide, cyanide, copper, zinc, gold, and platinum. Down there, far too deep for the sun to penetrate and cause photosynthesis, we were to meet creatures that operated by chemosynthesis. With the help of bacteria spewed forth from the vents, they live by converting heat and many chemicals toxic to "normal" organisms, including us, into their life force. Extremophiles, as they are called by biologists, are complicated creatures that flourish in defiance of all the rules, making easy work of the tremendous pressure, toxic water, and intense heat — up to 750° — emerging from the various vents and smoking outcrops.

Nine North is a window on the sea as it was at the volatile start of life on Earth, Belinda said. To visit it is to contemplate prehuman times, when the organisms from which we ultimately evolved existed in an unstable chemical broth. Nine North represents the earth before our coming, the sea before we knew a sea. That concept sticks in the brain. Who, if he could possibly see such a place, would pass up the chance?

Having agreed to the idea in theory but being more neurotic than most, I wanted to become acquainted with these *Mirs*, to see how sturdy they look and — above all — how well maintained. The first evening at sea, under a bath-warm rain before sunset, I prowled the *Keldysh* and found them, in two hangars on the starboard side of Deck 4. Mine was a layman's reconnaissance, but they certainly seemed sturdy and well kept. Built in 1987, each was about twenty-six feet long, glistening white with bright orange tops and two orange tail fins for maneuvering. There were propellers aft and on each side, but what was most fascinating was the cutaway bows. Beneath a brow of steel, each of the *Mirs* housed all that was needed to work on the seafloor, arranged into a sort of mechanical face: six 1,200-watt halogen lights, articulated steel armatures with claws folded like those of a resting crab, trays on which the samples that the armatures picked up could be stored, and a box containing collection tools (including brass dustpans and minishovels), a slurp gun for catching sediment, and bottles for taking samples of gases. The *Mirs* were tested to descend to 20,000 feet if necessary (still over 15,000 feet short of the deepest point on Earth, in the Mariana Trench, reached by a manned submersible in 1960), and they certainly conveyed a comforting impression of uncrushability.

The creation of deep-ocean submersibles has become possible only with the development and casting of titanium-reinforced nickel-and-steel alloys. Among the first was a vessel named *Alvin*, designed in the 1960s by the U.S. Navy and now the workhorse of the Woods Hole Oceanographic Institution. Astonishingly, there are now only four other such vessels in existence: one Japanese, one French, and the two *Mirs*. The man who designed the *Mirs*, a Russian engineer named Anatoly Sagelevitch, runs the diving program aboard the *Keldysh* and is the *Mirs*' chief pilot. He was onboard, and I wondered how he felt about his beautiful Finnish-built submersibles, designed for scientific oceanography, being reduced to carrying fee-paying tourists.

At dusk that first evening, as I contemplated the *Mirs*' three small windows, each two and a half inches thick, I found it unimaginable that I might soon be aboard, at a depth of 8,600 feet, looking at the ocean floor and its beasts. The *Mirs* would take us to an active seabed, where new lava sometimes flows and chemicals brought up to the vents by boiling water precipitate out to make silty chimneys that disgorge minerals and chemical smoke — black from some, white from others — as energetically as any factory flue.

In getting us there, two passengers at a time, the *Mirs* would be piloted on a rotation basis by Sagelevitch and the *Keldysh*'s two other submersible pilots, Genya Cherniaev and Victor Nischeta. All three were willing, at any time, to expound on the idea that as a species we are woefully underresourced to explore such hydrothermal fields as Nine North, more and more of which are being discovered. Nine vents have recently been identified, for instance, on a midocean ridge running north of Greenland to Siberia. Starting in 1988, the *Mirs* themselves have found new vents and identified new species; in fact, a hitherto unknown shrimp discovered in one vent area in the early nineties by a *Keldysh* scientist was named *Mirocaris Keldishi*. In 1990, shortly before *Alvin* found Nine North, the *Keldysh* identified a hydrothermal vent area in the Bering Sea and others off the Big Island of Hawaii. Wherever there are pressure ridges between tectonic plates in midocean, similar vents are likely to be found. "It will take many more submersibles than we have before they can be fully studied," Sagelevitch would tell us.

I had met my shipmates at a hotel in Acapulco the day before leaving. There were forty-seven Russian scientists, fifty-three *Keldysh* crew, and twenty-four submersible crew and technicians permanently aboard. The eighteen itinerants included Thomas Bachmann, our doctor; he had dived before and was willing to give up his Munich practice for two weeks just to be on the *Keldysh* again. Fred McLaren, a formidably cultivated retired nuclear submarine captain and ex-president of the Explorers Club, was on hand to introduce us to the biology of the sea floor with such passion that those who had previously dived were full of renewed urgency to do so, and those who were there purely to observe promised never to find themselves here again without diving. He too was a *Keldysh* devotee and had made a number of *Mir* dives but would not be diving this time. Two charming biologists from the University of Alabama at Huntsville would also be lecturing. One of them, Owen Garriott, an astronaut twice over who had worked on the International Space Station, would raise two fascinating and related ideas. One, if there could be life at the bottom of the ocean at Nine North, then life could — and indeed would — be found on planets where similarly extreme conditions prevailed. Two, the bacteria vented into the sea at Nine North bore a resemblance to fossil bacteria found on Mars and suspected to still exist in its crust, thus raising the possibility that the bacteria got to Earth by way of asteroids. Like McLaren, Garriott and his colleague, Joe Ng, were nondiving passengers, as were a young British marine biologist and a Danish journalist, and all of them would be kept busy visiting the labs and conferring with the Russian scientists.

The reason for the disparity between the number of passengers and those who were diving was the price differential of some $19,000 between a delightful cruise (four days out to Nine North, four or more engrossing days on-site, and four days' return) and the dive itself. Anyone who wished to descend in the submersibles also needed medical clearance: One had to confess one's lesser disorders and list any pharmaceuticals regularly taken. But triathlete-level health was far from required. The main disqualifying issues seemed to be cardiac problems, extreme obesity, and urinary and bowel ailments, as well as a tendency to anxiety fits or acute claustrophobia. I had already been assured that we would be given a pithily named urinary device, a Travel John, for the twelve-hour journey to the vent.

Any fantasy I might have had about my own adventurousness was at once undermined by the presence among the divers of three eloquent widows in their seventies who already had eight *Keldysh*-launched dives among them, chiefly to the wreck of the *Titanic* and to the Rainbow vents off the Azores. None of the three seemed prodigiously wealthy — it was more that they were prodigious enthusiasts, and this was the supreme journey for them. One had brought her daughter along for the ride. The remaining divers were an American lawyer, Mike Lyon, who had been involved in brokering the voyage of American multimillionaire Dennis Tito into space; Avi Klapfer, an Israeli engineer; and two Australians, including myself.

Here's to small (air-conditioned) ships, I say, for all their informality and companionability! Each passenger had a cabin to himself, a shower, a desk, a bunk, and, as is so often the case on smaller ships, superbly adequate portholes. I found that people interested in the deep are engaging and loquacious company, with a range of engrossing interests. We had our own dining room, which would prove a fine setting for the raconteurs in our midst, and the expectation of a diet of borscht was put to rest by chefs who prepared meals of an extraordinarily high order — haute cuisine rather than canteen. Doctor Bachmann proved a generous and persistent dispenser of wine, although the divers would need to go easy on that as we approached the dive site. At night, we sat in the bar/conference room talking or else, in the pleasant after-heat of the day, on the aft deck above the garaged *Mirs*. A great deal of chat arose from the morning and afternoon lectures, and all conversation, wherever it went, returned to the topic of the abyss. One of the women told me that she was willing to pay a high price for descending to Nine North, because it was akin to an interplanetary flight. Mars was no more hostile than where we were going, she told me, and no more beautiful.

This closer planetary space — the sea floor — had been directly explored only in the most patchy way, especially when it came to its biological quirks or areas of volatile terrain. In his lecture, Sagelevitch told us that when planning the *Mirs*, he had wanted to design vessels that would make 98 percent of the seabed accessible to human investigation (the remaining 2 percent being beyond their range). The lately discovered vents at Nine North confirmed, he said, that though we might know the seabed's contours, we are far from knowing its secrets.

As we neared the site, latitude 9° 45′ north and longitude 104° 16′ west, the aft hangars were opened and the *Mirs* hoisted to an upper deck, so that we could board and become familiar with them. We entered our assigned *Mir* via the hatch on top and descended a ladder to find the pilot sitting and sweating at the joystick-operated controls in the seven-foot-diameter orb of a cockpit. "Two-inch nickel steel," Sagelevitch declared, punching the metal between the ports. On either side of the pilot were two benches, one for each of the scientists — or passengers — who'd be going down with him.

The air pressure in the cockpit would be kept the same as at sea level, Sagelevitch told me, but the pressure on the *Mir* and on the glass in its three portholes would be four thousand pounds per square inch — sufficient, we had already been merrily informed, for instant and painless death should the integrity of the cockpit be compromised. With a patience I found quite touching, Sagelevitch demonstrated the main systems of hydraulics and mechanics for descent, bottom travel, and ascent. Our living area included three control systems for returning to the top, one of them for emergencies, concealed by a flap, which would allow us to ascend by dropping almost eight hundred pounds of nickel shot and jettisoning the armatures and thrusters, an eventuality I didn't worry about because I was too engrossed by other things. Once we were down, we would operate on twenty hours of battery power, and the tail propeller and side thrusters would take us through that dense, chemical-thickened, high-pressure sea at five knots (almost six miles an hour). Our twelve external sensors would begin transmitting pressure, temperature, and saline readings. We would each be looking out our own small porthole — the pilot's some eight inches in diameter, the passengers' five inches. Inside the cockpit, the pilot and passengers could live off high-pressure oxygen for some eighty hours, aided by the merciful operation of cylindrical carbon dioxide scrubbers at the rear of the cockpit, which extracted the gas from the air we were breathing.

In calm water, we ran out sea anchors atop the Nine North vent area. On the first morning at the site, a telephone relay device was lowered into the sea, and four transponders were sunk to the bottom to guide *Mir I* and *Mir II* around the vents. The next morning, two Russian scientists were to dive on one *Mir,* Mike McDowell and another Russian scientist on the other. Very early on dive day one, Sagelevitch convened a meeting in the *Keldysh's Mir* communications center on Deck 4 of the two dozen crew members whose jobs involved launching and retrieving the submersibles and briefed them with an admirable precision. The hatches atop the *Mirs* were raised, and a launch, the *Koresh* ("friend" in Russian), was lowered into the sea, followed by a rubber dinghy manned by three sturdy-looking frogmen. At last, after the passengers and pilots in their blue dive suits had climbed the ladders to the *Mirs* and dropped down into the cockpit, the hatches were sealed. The ship's crane lifted the *Mir I* from its starboard pad and, with a strange mechanical delicacy, lowered it into the tranquil, intensely blue sea. One frogman climbed atop the submarine to disconnect the crane's fragile-looking connection. Then the *Koresh* dragged the submersible away from the ship's side to where the dive was to begin. Here, the *Koresh*'s cable was disconnected, the frogman returned to his dinghy, and the *Mir* began its part glide, part free fall to the bottom. The process was immediately repeated with the *Mir II*.

While waiting for the first divers to come back, we attended further lectures on the vents and their life forms, and Fred McLaren told us of his historic charting of the Siberian continental shelf, unbeknownst to the Soviets, at the height of the Cold War. We swam in *Keldysh*'s blood-warm pool, while the crew and some of the younger passengers played volleyball. Finally, we spotted the lights of the *Koresh* through the porthole — a sign that the first of the *Mir*s was returning.

The Nine North region was in exceptional condition, McDowell reported. There had been no recent seismic activity or lava flow to interfere with the vent area's prolific life. In the baskets at the front of the *Mir*s lay mineral and biological samples collected with the pincered arms of the submersibles, operated by the pilot at the scientists' instruction. I saw a yellow-brown fragment of one of the smoker stacks, a snow-white crab about a foot across, and giant tube worms, riftia, which had lost their hemoglobin-red vividness now that they were no longer subject to the extreme pressure at which they lived. I also got a good look at the shell of a robust clam, a foot in diameter, that siphoned up poisoned and superheated water for nutriment. Why, I wondered, did these creatures not explode up here on the surface? A busy passing scientist took the time to explain that precisely because they lived under such pressure, these animals of the deep lacked the bladderlike, explosive spaces we have: lungs, for example. As the biologists and geologists came forward to collect their samples from the *Mir*s, the excitement was palpable. So much previously inaccessible material had been garnered in one day.

The next day, the women divers scrambled down through the *Mir*s' hatches and, twelve hours later, returned ecstatic, struggling to capture the wonders they had seen in the poor net of language.

Above all, they stressed the vivid colors of the organisms down there and the drama of the smokers, the chimneys that lay along the vents and gushed chemical-rich steam with ferocious energy.

Before the final dives — mine included — there would be a day's delay to let the pilots rest, and we spent it visiting the sundry labs where scientists were at work on samples from both Nine North and the previously visited Rainbow vents. Among the issues that arose were the pharmaceutical possibilities raised by the creatures at Nine North, so identifiably of this earth yet so surprising — so downright unearthly — in their capacities. The plentiful red six-foot-long riftia have no digestive system — the bacteria from the vents seem to do their digesting and feeding for them, converting hydrogen sulphides into energy. The lobsters and crabs are able to detoxify sulphides with their gills — but how? Might humans develop the ability to live on toxic planets with the help of artificial means developed from studying the white crabs of Nine North?

For the forty-eight hours before our dive, we were to avoid alcohol because of its likely effect on our urinary system and bodily functions and to eschew rich food for the same reasons. Trevor Montgomery, my fellow Australian, a farmer from the wine country northeast of Melbourne, accompanied me to a fitting for our flame-resistant diving overalls. As we prepared ourselves, other passengers — particularly Captain McLaren, who would have loved another dive himself — kept half-jokingly offering us plates of beans, in the hope that loose bowels might disqualify one of us. I slept soundly that night and awoke ready. Perhaps a person should lead his life as if the next day he were going to the bottom of the sea.

Montgomery and I donned our dive suits and accompanied Sagelevitch to the *Mir* communications center, from which our dive would be monitored, for a final meeting. The cranemen, the frogmen, and the *Koresh* crew were all there. Sagelevitch was satisfied with his crew, he said, as if Montgomery and I were professionals. Then he and the crew clapped their hands, and we were out on deck, briskly descending gangways like pros, climbing the ladder positioned against the *Mir I*'s side.

By arrangement, I took the starboard padded ledge — Montgomery and I, like two overexcited kids on a train, had devised a plan to switch sides halfway through the day (we never would). The hatch closed, the crane lifted us deftly into the sea, the work of the frogman on the roof was soon over, and with a slight lean forward we tilted into a sea of bubbles, waving like schoolchildren on an excursion to an underwater photographer from the *Keldysh* who came with us a short way.

And then, very swiftly, total blackness.

I passed the dark descent by taking note of the outside temperature and depth readings, which Montgomery could not see from his bench. At 745 feet down, the sea temperature had dropped from 80° to 53° but after that decreased only gradually, eventually falling to 36°. At a depth of more than 1,600 feet, Sagelevitch turned on some of the *Mir*'s external lights to enable us to see fields of shining plankton.

Another 5,000 feet down and we were at the bottom — about 8,600 feet below the surface of the sea. All of the *Mir*'s external lights were switched on, and what we saw at first was a desert of pillow lava, molten rock that had been spewed up through the vents as recently as the early 1990s and had cooled to make these glistening bulbous shapes — obsidianlike, reflecting our lights, easily broken to form grottoes and cavities. Using the *Mir I*'s ballast system, Sagelevitch kept us perhaps thirty feet above the pillow lava. We saw the occasional thin-limbed giant starfish, and the rocks were suddenly rendered matte by masses of bacterial life and sported beautiful orange anemones with long fronds. Sagelevitch moved us cautiously closer to the dark edges of fractured rock and into an area where pillow lava had broken up to create a rough plain. In its midst we saw, with superb visibility, an astonishing proliferation of smokers — many fifty feet high — and living creatures.

This wasn't simply a matter of minute, struggling life forms. Rocks slanting in all directions were populated by multicolored microorganisms, by yellow or red giant anemones, by white crabs of a similar size to the edible ones we know from lesser depths, and by albino lobsters. Everywhere, propelling itself casually among the anemones and the crabs and the banks of colored growth, were specimens of a well-proportioned creature resembling at the same time an eel and a conventional fish, an honest journeyman named bathysaurus. Nothing here possessed the nightmarish features seen in the deep-sea encyclopedias of our childhood. I surmised that those monsters lived at midlevels of the sea, where light was still an issue, and the creatures' hunger to trap it encouraged giantism and (in our terms) ugliness.

We were following these tumbles of populated rocks in a south-easterly direction, along a line very close to where the Pacific Plate and the Cocos Plate meet. Soon we came within a few feet of one smoker. It was white and gushed white smoke and boiling water. Even though at this depth water does not boil until it reaches 730°, the water beyond our portholes shimmered and bubbled. The chemicals in the smoke and hot water add further mass to the chimney, which will eventually cause it to fall.

On the smoker's flanks, near holes from which more steam and hot water emerged, were the riftia worms, their big white cases thick as a piece of cane and shiny as alabaster, and their bodies, emerging from the cases, a rich red. We got extremely close — within a few feet — and could see them flourishing in the shimmering water amid banks of large clams.

At a second white smoker, Sagelevitch tried to take a sample from a spur with one of the *Mir*'s armatures, but it proved to be very soft, the material crumbling away even as the metal claws tried to grasp it, and he regretted not having collection nets on this dive. Next, black smokers — resembling satanic mills and, if anything, richer still in species — loomed ahead of us. "Less pure steam, more chemicals," Sagelevitch explained. We heard the sound of impact as we scraped against something — an overhead spur of the caldera, or of a grotto or a smoker. Minor damage to the *Mir*'s flank would be visible when we got back to the surface, but Montgomery and I were so engrossed in the spectacle all around that the incident produced not even a shiver of fright.

The *Mir II* was down by now and had joined up with us. The two sets of lights brought greater intensity to yet another black smoker. And then the most wonderful thing happened: We sighted a rare and extraordinary octopus named — too cutely but very accurately — Dumbo by the crew of the *Alvin*, who first saw it. Legend has it that a giant, sub-crushing octopod lives at the bottom of the sea. The truth is that perhaps a most beautiful one does. Here, at four thousand pounds per square inch of pressure, was a figure of ineffable grace. Its eight legs were connected by translucent webbing, so that when it bravely displayed itself to the *Mir*s, it looked like a star. It had two elephant ear–like protrusions on either side of its large head, which it used to propel itself with extraordinary fluidity. How wonderful to go to the bottom of the sea and find an animal so identifiably a being of our planet, a fellow pilgrim.

Lyon and Klapfer, the passengers in the other *Mir,* and Montgomery on the port side of ours, got the best views of Dumbo, but in limited space Sagelevitch edged the *Mir I* around to give me a better look at this rarest of beings.

Dumbo departed, and while Sagelevitch took smoke samples from the gaseous coronas of both black and white smokers, a small light-brown lobster swam past my porthole. Nowhere near as big as the hardy-looking white ones that populated the rocks below, it was perhaps five inches long and looked, to a layman, like a freshwater crayfish. This small angel of chemosynthesis, separated from me by a thick, polished pane, remained in place on the window casing for forty minutes, as we drifted close to riftia and past banks of crabs and lobsters.

We had been told that the twelve hours of our dive would pass in one dense instant of astonishment. And so they did. Sagelevitch gently announced when our time was done. Rising from the bottom after 5 P.M., we at last remembered to eat the lunch that the chefs had packed — and to congratulate ourselves on not having had to use the Travel Johns.

After twelve hours of darkness, I was surprised to see from my porthole the *Keldysh*'s white flank glittering in the last rays of the setting sun. Back on deck, uttering superlatives, we did our clumsy best to say what we had seen and to give it all the weight that it deserved.

The next night, at a party featuring vodka, wine, and a suckling pig, Sagelevitch celebrated his sixty-fifth birthday. There's a lot of piloting left in him yet, and he sees a long future ahead for his *Mir*s. He says that exploration of the massive and undervisited abyss has barely begun. Though the world at large is not possessed by any urgency to complete this task, Sagelevitch and his crew of scientists are. As for me, my understanding of what life means, my sense of connection to other life forms, my awareness of the earth and its place in the universe — all have been enlarged in a way that haunts me months later. You don't get that from your average vacation.

# Adrift

FROM *Esquire*

VERY CAREFULLY, and very professionally, that's the way to abandon ship, but even though I have all day, fair weather, a crew to help me, and a ship that doesn't really require abandoning, as soon as we begin to launch the raft, things rapidly spiral out of control, as in a real disaster. First there's some debate about whether the raft stays in its blue canvas bag. There are pictograms on the bag, the sort of universal language you'd send out on a space probe, but nothing per se on the in-the-bag-or-out issue. Good thing we take it out or it probably would've sunk — or exploded! Then Scott Harrington, captain of the fifty-three-foot *Fish Hunter*, and I heave the heavy, compressed block of canvas over the transom. Young Marcello, the cocaptain, is keen to yank the inflation cord; there's a *Pffftt!* sound as the $CO_2$ canister pops, a puff of mist, and then the raft does this dramatically animated Transformer thing — "Fucking cool!" Marcello says — and it is suddenly there, upside down, on the bounding main, a pentagonal slab of black plastic fabric stretched between pontoons and quivering against the seas like the jelly between luncheon sausages.

Immediately I'm awash with the bad sort of adrenaline, the fight-or-flight type, pulse rate escalating. It's nothing like the raft I had in mind when I thought "raft." It's not Huck and Jim on the Miss'sip, kicked back on something stable and commodious, smoking pipes and watching the world drift by. It's more like an inflatable kiddie pool. It's hard to believe I'm about to take it for a spin on one of the world's fastest ocean currents, the Gulf Stream. By doing so, I hope to explore the authentically gigantic through the lens of the suddenly truly sorry.

Marcello, who is skinny and agile, leaps onto the raft to right it (as pictured on bag). As the raft comes over, dunking Marcello, two smaller upright pontoons catch the wind, unfurling a light canvas half dome like on a baby carriage. Captain Scott hauls to on the inflator rope and Marcello springs out. "You going to be sick in there, man!" he says.

That's what everybody has been saying the past two days while I've hung out in Miami, waiting for the wind to lay down. I mean specifically the guys at Sea Tow Services International, proprietors of the *Fish Hunter* and experts in marine salvage and every other seagoing bummer. "Even the guys who never get sick get sick in those rafts," they all said with theatrically raised eyebrows and disbelieving laughter at the idea of *voluntarily* submitting to that world of hurl.

As for *mal de mer,* I chose denial, pretty effective right up to the present moment. I'm on hands and knees on the lurching deck of the real boat, leaning out to tear open a sturdy plastic sack laced to the aft pontoon, the raft's guts. It's full of survival stuff — French survival stuff, to go by the labels — including the sea anchor, a parachutelike stabilizer tied to a hundred feet of rubber-band-bound strapping, which, immediately upon release, floats under the *Fish Hunter* and entangles the props — Hey, Marcello! — and all of a sudden it's getting kind of late and the weather doesn't look all that great, either.

On second thought . . . upon closer examination of the facts . . . Gentlemen, my bad! My real identity is Jacques Lapine, an escaped lunatic from France with a harmless compulsion to hire boats . . . But I have already clambered down onto the trampolinelike surface of the raft floor, and captain and mate are passing me my considerable supplies: emergency communications and rescue devices, changes of clothes, water for a week, food for the rest of my life. Led by the rioting water jugs, everything topples, rolls, slides in a jumbled pile to the depression in the middle of the floor around my sunken feet. Ropes, rings, strings, packets — Jesus! — there has to be a bail in here somewhere. The *Fish Hunter* rises on a swell, the raft drops down into the trough; down dips the *Fish Hunter,* up bobs the raft. And so, in that seesaw fashion, politely bowing to each other, the two crafts begin to drift apart. I'm waving, bailing with a sponge, when I see the raft's instruction manual floating among the debris of hasty departure.

*"Gardez votre sang-froid,"* it reads. *"Et votre bonne humeur."*

*Mais oui!* I am fifty miles out to sea off the southern tip of Florida, on the far eastern edge of the Gulf Stream, in a rising wind, in a violently tossing raft. I find a couple of dangling electrodes and connect them, which turns on the little red strobe atop the dome. We're open for business, ye bogeys of the sea. Already it's deepening dusk, the sharking hour. In a very little while, it will be dark.

Off my starboard bow, to westward, where the horizon still glows eerily with the lights of the south-Florida megalopolis (even at fifty miles!), there's a cruise ship lit up like Christmas. Harmlessly distant but a reminder I'm smack in the middle of major shipping lanes with a couple of bath-toy paddles that would at most propel me in a tight, frantic circle. In my pretrip jitters, I imagined being rudely awakened by the prow of a container ship — Ahoy! — then blindly throttled, crushed with unspeakable force, and finally chopped up by the props. Raw superstition crept in, too, fear of monsters and of discovering holes in the fabric of my soul. Of Bermuda Triangle types of doorways to other dimensions, like death. The Atlantic Ocean at night, in a raft, man. Fortunately, reality is proving less frightening, being more reliably real.

The reality is this: The raft rides a little rough in these two- to four-foot seas. It slips no blows. It meets every wave head-on and scrunches like an accordion. Bulges up at the midriff. Stretches out lengthwise as if to ingest the wave and then passes it out under the shuddering aft pontoon like a four-foot fart. For sheer variety of motion, it's the worst ride at the fair. I've given up bailing for the time being and so far have organized my gear mainly by repeatedly kicking it as far to the front of the raft as its varying properties allow.

On the plus side, the raft points reliably into the wind, thanks to the sea anchor, I think. And I've had an ace up my sleeve all along. I'm not in the raft; I'm on it — perched sidesaddle on the leeward rail, left hand tightly twisted in the rope that rings the raft, right arm outstretched for balance like a bronco rider's. Yee-haw! And I'm doing all right. Not a bit sick yet, thank you. Of course, I'm on "the patch" — transdermal Scopolamine — and it's fucking me up like a horse tranquilizer. Sort of centers consciousness about a millimeter off to the side, so that you're looking at yourself from outside yourself and thinking, You'd like to puke, but you don't strictly speaking have to puke, so what's your problem? Still, every time I crash through one of the bigger waves, my spirits rise. Riding out the rough seas is a sport, at least, like white-water rafting a river without end.

Wind's getting a little too frisky, though. Snapping in the tent canvas. Freshening, as they say. This despite a spectacularly clear night, the sky a plasma of stars, glowing planets, blinking satellites, a few wayfaring planes. A poem or a pop song in every one of them. And me in a spotlight of glowing green, as every cresting whitecap ignites a world of bioluminescence, little green buggers that come up to the surface to fuck the stars. For them the weather is perfect.

Better not to look down at those glimmering universes. I had a fever dream once, barely out of toddlerhood, back when my brain remembered being a blastomere. It was about the sizes of things. Terribly tiny things. Like atoms, only smaller. Things god-awfully huge. Like container ships. Only bigger. A lot bigger! Then I forgot about the maddeningly minuscule and the astoundingly huge; I rounded things off to the nearest whole integer. Sought the middle way. As Frost says of the beachcombers' watch, neither out far nor in deep.

But today at sea, I've seen things: seen Miami's tallest skyscrapers shrunk to a delicate gray fuzz on the horizon, till the whole thing would fit in a thimble ten times over — a world in a grain of sand, or vice versa. As soon as the cityscape faded entirely, about fourteen miles out, it sprang up again — by persistence of vision, apparently — in a ring all around us, encircling us with an imaginary New Jerusalem, the city beyond the waves. By then we were in the Stream, which we knew from the blueberry hue and its heat, the *Fish Hunter*'s digital water-temp gauge ticking upward: 76,77.3, all the way up to 80°. We had hit the main vein of the Western World, the artery to its brain, you might even say, since the northeastern United States and northern Europe are what they are, and where they are, because of this ocean current and the heat it carries. Suited up in neoprene to be injected like one of the microbe-sized explorers in *Fantastic Voyage*, I'm having a look at things too big to see.

Wham! The raft takes one right on the snout. A real canopy crumpler. Never saw it coming. Slam! Jesus Christ!

This is space travel. Things abstracting, going blank. Yeah, sure, the sea, now and now and now, but with a Moe's repertoire of *nyuk-*

*nyuk-nyuks.* Fucking ocean! The stars yo-yoing with the raft's rise and fall. I'm in a new zone of disengagement. No longer alert. So long as we're not going to capsize, then, OK: waves, wind, spray. Not a panic situation. Just hold on. Ten past ten by the glow of my watch. Five hours on the raft and a chill in the air now. Time to layer up: life jacket off, wet-bag clinched between knees, sweatshirt out, sweatshirt on, fleece out, fleece on, life jacket back on, wet-bag booted forward. Better now.

"Brandy, you're a fine girl . . . !" I sing.

A million thumps later — midnight! Made it. Come on, twelve-o-one! The real night watch now. Everything done that can be done, which is very nearly nothing about anything. Sea, raft, stars. All is one. None. One. Nodding off for moments at a time on the rail. How idiots are separated from rafts. I watch the horizon. I watch the sky. Until the *stars throw down their spears.* They really do. The last thing I see is a pair of vast figures hurrying toward me from the stars. "The Celestial Couple" I call them, slack-jawed, awed. They're as tall as cathedrals but gauzy like wraiths of light. Kindly somehow. Kind of corny. Mama? Daddy? Or was I already sleeping?

Time to assume the position — fetal, that is — on the flooded raft floor. Damn the container ships, and let the waves crash where they may.

I wake up astonished to have slept but oriented at once by a be-mused narrative voice: Dude, you're in a raft! I'm shivering. Cold, but not *cold* cold. I mean, the water I'm lying in feels warm; I'm kind of warm myself. But shaking convulsively. Gentle convulsions. A pleasant sort of hypothermia. Best of all, it's no longer night, if not yet exactly dawn, and the wind has slackened appreciatively, too. Seas still chuck the raft under its chin, hiss, and seethe, but it seems the ocean wants to make nice after last night's squall.

When it's indisputably morning, I climb back up onto the lee pontoon and look out onto a subsiding field of silver seas — two to three feet and confused. The seas, I mean. Guzzle some water from the nearest gallon jug. Munch a few saltines. I don't have much appetite. More alarmingly, I have no saliva — severe cottonmouth another side effect of the behind-the-ear seasickness patch. This is a blow. The loss of eating as a pleasurable activity opens a huge hole in my day.

Better organize my shit. Rescue gear aft: a flare pistol and six shells to send arching across the sky. Half a dozen French hand rockets that look like giant firecrackers. (I'd love to fire one off, though at the risk of my hands.) An aerosol bullhorn. Whistles. A sat phone. Handheld GPS. VHP radio. Coast Guard EPIRB in a James Bond–esque case. Great stuff that would have the normal shipwrecked person off a raft in no time. The paradox is that I'm not in trouble, so I can't be rescued. Or am I in such deep trouble that these things have sought me out, as this situation has done, to make that point?

"*M'aidez! M'aidez!* Have capsized and am entangled in rescue gear!" When I asked the guys at Sea Tow if there was one thing I should absolutely not forget to bring on the raft, the old salt Captain Joe said — no hesitation — "Yeah, a blond!" Guy knows his shit or what.

The MRE carton got soaked and fell apart in the night, spilling plastic bladders of plastic wrappers of foil packets of carrion in carrion gravy. My tins of sardines? In my dreams. A sack of oranges — *Arrrgg!* matey — for the scurvy. All of you water jugs to the starboard rail. It's the rope for you. But nah! I can tell it's the sort of task I just ain't got the Bligh in me for. Besides, how much better off will I be when they're bound? You see? And now for the bailing. That's what I've really been wanting to do, to be done and be dry.

It's like this, as I learned last night when I didn't have the means to study the problem. The bottom of the raft being malleable, it collects water wherever it is weighted. When I kneel, I corral a couple of gallons of it — along with two hundred feet of yellow plastic rope, a flashlight, the raft's blunt-bladed knife, and half a dozen MREs — but I can't get the water that's right under me. The problem is Archimedean. And then no matter how much I sop up and squeeze out over the rails, the volume of the water in the raft never seems to change. Though that's hard to verify. Except by pressing down hard with my feet and collecting a new puddle, which I mop up with renewed, but not infinitely renewable, enthusiasm, going so far as to poke down on the depression with one finger so as to mop directly under my feet. At last I conclude that somewhere between the pontoons and the floor, there's a leak below sea level, so in effect *I'm trying to sponge up the whole fucking ocean!*

A small matter. A very small matter. The raft won't sink. (If only it would!) But it means I can't change out of my neoprene into dry clothes. And since the zipper in this farmer-John-type wet suit only goes down to my navel, peeing into my pee bucket (you can't lean out to piss because there's nothing to hold on to) means a regular Bowflex workout of stretching rubber. Gotta kneel to do it, and in a damn puddle. Important to stay hydrated, though. The wind and the sun and the salt will wick the moisture right out of you — along with the *bonne humeur,* if you're not careful. So I'm gulping my way through the jugs and flinging repeated contributions over the rail.

Everything I see around me, and miles more that I can't, is the Gulf Stream, and what powers the current is literally everything in my present physical circumstances — those things that I can feel and those things I never can. The Trades. The heat of the sun. The tilt of the earth's axis. The Coriolis effect of the planet's eastward spin, driving water hardest on the western margins of all the ocean basins. The desire of water for its own level. The Gulf Stream plows northward for the Arctic in part because the Arctic water sinks, being cold, dense, and very salty. Thermohaline circulation, it's called. It's a subtle process, but it moves two massive entities — the water that is here and the water that is there — that are none-theless balanced on a razor's edge.

As annual temperatures have risen in the North Atlantic and the Greenland ice cap has melted, the cold end of the Stream has freshened considerably, gaining heat while losing salt (the "haline" in the term). The Arctic Sea is slowly (for now) beginning to lose the wherewithal to sink to the abyssal bottom and begin its slow creep to Antarctica. It's not getting out of the Gulf Stream's way, gunking up a vital cog in the ocean conveyor. The gyre stills turns, but the falcon can't hear the falconer. Things fall apart. Ironically, though the culprit is global warming, the result will be a new ice age, triggered by the sudden failure of the Gulf Stream.

That's the worst-case scenario, anyway. An October 2003 Depart-ment of Defense report titled "An Abrupt Climate Change Sce-nario and Its Implications for United States National Security" cites climatological studies of Arctic ice-core samples that reveal that similar warming trends in the past have shut down the ocean con-veyor, triggering centuries-long ice ages. The worse news is that when it starts to go, it can go fast.

The consequences for six billion human beings, even in sober DOD-speak, sound biblical in wrath and scope. Siberian cold in northern Europe. Storms of furious magnitude. Drought and dust bowls and wildfires in formerly fertile croplands. Wholesale famine. The Haves bunker down, and the Have-Nots sharpen sticks. "Every time there is a choice between starving and raiding, humans raid," the DOD report intones in a *Dr. Strangelove*-ian passage.

Sounds promising in terms of employment for young untrained males with machine guns and pickup trucks. Welcome to the Global Smackdown. In the doomsday scenario, the Gulf Stream may still flow as far north as Florida, but it might be heavily mined. I'm seeing it while it's safe.

Can I feel the Gulf Stream hurtling me north at almost four knots an hour? Facing into an east-southeast breeze, plopping and dropping, bending and heaving, can I feel a lurching, ratcheting progress to leeward? Maybe, maybe not. The Stream may be fifty miles wide here, as much as a half mile deep. And no fixed objects anywhere. Just a few toots of cirrus drifting across the sky. Lovely view, though. A whole fucking lot of blue water. So much that you have to serve it to yourself in great glittering slices, splicing together a circle of endless planes in order to take in the whole pie chart, of which you are the infinitesimal nub. For lunch, Fig Newtons. An indomitable cookie, the Fig Newton. Not without its chewy goodness though the world were ending. After lunch I'm thinking about moving to the other side of the raft.

Godzilla walks and civilization crumbles! The water jugs topple and roll. The lid is somehow off the lone grape Gatorade bottle, dumping purple into the puddle. By the time I climb over the medical kit and the MREs and my dry-bags and settle onto the hot starboard pontoon, the raft is a shambles. Now my back is turned slightly more to the wind and the waves. And oh, man, it's much worse over here. How could I have thought it would be better? That's a mistake I won't make twice. It's better for fishing over here, though, maybe. Six casts of a spoon, and who do I think I'm fooling? Six thousand casts and I might get a strike. Because of the risk of mayhem, a rafter should never land a fish longer than the span from his elbow to his fingertips. These things you can learn from experts. If I caught a fish, I would eat its eyes, because that is what rafters should do.

At last, midafternoon, I spot a container ship on the eastern horizon. Bring it on, big guy! This after hours of uninterrupted vigilance, back on the lee side, seeing no other ships, no whales, no sharks. Just a fireball sun, the myriad glinting chevrons of its reflection, and the roving, crisscrossing scalpels of light with which it probes into the blue. Of sea life, just three little frilly brown Sargasso fish (they're like toadfish) and a squid — the looker in that quartet. These are the first creatures to colonize the shade of my floppy hull. Survivors of real life-raft disasters, like Steven Callahan, author of the brilliant nonfiction book *Adrift*, report that the undersides of their rafts become veritable oases of sea life, being a precious something in the midst of so much nothing. First come the bait fish, then come the game fish and the sharks, and if you're really in it for the long haul, barnacles and coral. Callahan owed his survival over a nearly three-month ordeal to the practically amorous attraction to his raft of dolphinfish (mahimahi), which he was occasionally able to spear. I haven't yet felt any thumps on the bottom of the raft, which would signal the arrival of dolphin or cobia.

But my life as a floating ecosystem is forgotten with the arrival of the container ship. In the brilliant afternoon light, it gleams wondrously white, like an iceberg with telephone poles on it. In all this ocean, it's making straight for me. What were the odds? Excellent, I always thought. But the big ship bears north ever so slightly and misses me by a quarter mile. There's not even going to be any wake-surfing. It's very disappointing.

It's going on twenty-four hours in the raft now, probably seventy miles of drifting. The day has begun to subside. I still don't have my sea legs, which means I still have to steady my brains on the horizon line or I may puke. And I'm afraid once I start puking, I won't be able to stop. Attention to that duty has become a burden, like consciously monitoring my heartbeat. Do it now. Do it now. Do it now. It's times like these when heroes of isolation write novels in their heads, arrange and rearrange an imaginary collection of CDs, or conjure up a pair of all-time NBA teams and play out a seven-game series in their minds. Such feats lie on the far side of boredom, and I'm just dipping in on the near side of the Stream, listening to a horrible dial tone coming from its depths. I've taken on the demeanor of a dullard, slumped on the rail. I could easily drool.

It's then that somebody calls my name. From maybe ten feet behind me. In a perfectly normal, conversational tone of voice.

"Bucky!"

Yeah, what? What?

Now I'm straining to hear the voice again, hearing only the wind. The gentle pishing and pshawing of seas. *Plickle-plunk, tiddledee tiddledee.* Captain Scott warned me about going to the edge: "You might fall through." He talked about finding an empty raft.

"Hey, Bucky!"

Fuck off! This is intolerable. It's like meditation at gunpoint. Only sun-point. Help! Help! My thoughts have twisted in an ever-tightening spiral until they've reached a single conclusion: The only thing to do on a raft is plot your way off of it. Paddle like crazy. Fire off a flare. Pick up the radio. Given the choice between raft and rescue, human beings have always reached for the radio. But not just yet.

It's night again at last. Done it again, I'm thinking. Reached my goal. That was sixty seconds of sixty minutes of twelve hours of daylight, and hardly a moment squandered on distractions. The sea is jealous of its wonders — its mythological-looking sunfish, its singing mermaids. Beginners cut their teeth on monotony. I did have my Star King and Queen, though. Seems ages since I saw them. I was a mere pup in life-raft years, and now I'm nostalgic for the man I was yesterday. More the fool, but with *bonne humeur* to spare. At least I've learned a lesson better than I ever thought I'd know it: that time may wait for no man, but it brakes for rafters.

Time for me to layer up again: life jacket off, et cetera. Strobe light on. Open for business. Some awful long time later, brooding in the dark, sulky as Queequeg, I see something. There, on the south horizon — the White Whale! I snatch up the VHP. We've got a container-ship-in-the-night situation. Punching in Channel 16, I overhear Captain Scott on the case already.

"Captain of the northbound container ship, do you read me? Captain of the northbound ship, do you read? Son of a bitch isn't even listening to his radio! This is the *Fish Hunter,* do you read? Better turn on your flashlight!" This last is directed to me.

I'm waving my flashlight, thinking about sending up a French hand rocket. But then the poor devil might think he has to stop his barge and rescue somebody.

"Okay, fisherman, what do you want?" It's the container-ship captain, who sounds tired and bored. But Captain Scott apparently can't hear him. He keeps at the radio: "Do you read me? Do you read me?" This is bad. This is a breakdown of basic rafting.

The giant misses me anyway, sliding by like a city block on casters. Whew! A close call. But not that close. Still, it was somehow unnerving. But was it unnerving enough? Am I in fact unnerved? No. Nope. Not really. I can't even properly dread the future now that I'm cramping up in the back from riding the pontoon for most of thirty hours. I really need to lie down in the bottom of the raft and sleep, but then I'd be soaked. And then I'd get cold. But I could get warm again. Or could I? Am I in extremis, or would I not know extremis if it bit me on the butt? I only know that there are two kinds of trouble: the kind you are going to be in and the kind you're in now, and the one must get out of the way of the other so that life may fucking go on.

Reach for that radio, pal, and you'll regret it for the rest of your life. Who said that? My better self, that hard-ass nutcase. I'll just check in, I tell my not-so-good self. To Captain Scott on the radio I say, "I'm having my doubts."

"I'm sure you are," he says. "Look, you don't have to prove anything to anybody. It's not like you're trying out for the Navy SEALs."

But I'm always proving something to somebody, and that's exactly what I'm always trying out for. Tough enough to last on a raft? At least one more night? But then it will be day again. I've seen a day on a raft at sea. See two? In the end, it's human sympathy that rescues me, lifts me out of the time warp of confined isolation under stress. A friendly voice.

"All right," I say. "I'm done."

And then — *boom! whammo! alacazam!* — the very next moment, not counting a nanosecond dragging the raft onto the stern of the *Fish Hunter,* a brief chat on the flying bridge, a warm shower and a change of clothes, prone time unconscious on the sofa in the cabin — almost instantaneously I'm standing on a swank dock in Fort Lauderdale with my stuff back in boxes, waiting, with what felicitous ease, amidst all the riches of dry land, for a cab.

# Tight-Assed River

FROM *The New Yorker*

## *Pekin*

THE "PEKIN WIGGLES" are halfway up the Illinois River, between the Mississippi River and Chicago. On the radio, other tows tell us how they are doing in the Pekin wiggles. During the forward watch, on this tow, the captain mentioned them when they were still three hours upstream. They would not be his to negotiate. Two in the afternoon and the pilot, Mel Adams, of the back watch, the after watch, is addressing them at the moment. He has made a sharp turn to the left followed by a bend to the right and is now going into an even sharper turn to the left that will line him up with the Pekin railroad bridge, of the Union Pacific. There is not much horizontal clearance under the Pekin bridge.

Mel is tall and lanky, fed in the middle but lithe in the legs. He has a sincere mustache, a trig goatee, and a slow, clear, frank, and friendly Ozark voice. He lives in southern Missouri, on Table Rock Lake, which has seven hundred miles of shoreline. The eight other people in the crew of this vessel all call him "Male." They are from Kentucky, Tennessee, Oklahoma, southern Missouri, and southernmost Illinois. They work twenty-eight days per stint. When they report for work, they show up in Paducah and are driven in a van from Kentucky up into Illinois or anywhere else this towboat happens to be. Its name is *Billy Joe Boling*.

Over all, the Illinois is a fairly straight river, only 10 percent longer than its beeline, the fact notwithstanding that the bends at Pekin corkscrew like fishing line that has come untied. Mel understands monofilament. He is wearing shorts, sandals, a cap with the word FISHING sewed into it, and a T-shirt covered with fish. Each morning, before he goes off watch at five-thirty, he cell-phones his wife, Aurora, and gently awakens her. When he is at home, he routinely gets up at four-thirty, goes fishing, is off the lake by nine, and by nine-thirty has cleaned his fish and put them in the freezer. He says his personal best is a twenty-eight-pound flathead catfish. In his Bayliner Trophy 1703 with center console, he penetrates the bays and skims the shoals of that seven-hundred-mile shoreline, his touch grooved with experience.

A lot of good that will do him here. This vessel is no Bayliner with center console, and the Illinois River is not a big lake in the Ozarks. The mate Carl Dalton has gone up ahead with his walkie-talkie to serve as a pair of eyes for Mel in the pilothouse, near the stern. Carl is a tall guy who played Kentucky high school basketball, but when he was halfway up the tow, near the break coupling, he was already a tiny figure, and now, all the way up at the head, he is an ant. This vessel is a good deal longer than the *Titanic*. It is thirteen feet longer than Cunard's *Queen Mary 2*, the longest ocean liner ever built. It is 44 feet longer than any existing aircraft carrier. It is 105 feet wide. And with Carl calling off numbers — "12 wide on the port . . . 200 below . . . 12 wide, 150 below . . . 8 wide on the port, 125 below . . . 7 wide on the port . . . 6 wide on the port" — Mel is driving it into the crossing currents of the 150-foot gap between one pier and the other of the bridge's channel span. It helps that the railroad tracks have been raised. In their normal position, they are three feet lower than the *Billy Joe Boling*.

The Illinois River is in most places a little more accommodating. With exceptions here and there, the demarcated channel is three hundred feet wide. But you are not going to do a doughnut with this vessel. You are not going to do a Williamson turn. Both maneuvers describe closed 360° circuits. This vessel is nearly four times longer than the channel is wide. The entire river in most places is about a thousand feet from bank to bank. Our bow wave quickly spreads to both shores. We could not turn about if we had all of the river to do it in. If we were 90° to the direction of the channel, we would block the river solid and spill over both sides into the trees.

Among American rivers, only the Mississippi and the Ohio float more ton-miles of freight than the Illinois, a fact that does not seem to have done much to raise its national profile. People say, "The Illinois River? What's that? Never heard of it. Where does it go?" Actually, there are three Illinois Rivers in America, each, evidently, as well known as the others. One is in southwestern Oregon. One rises in western Arkansas, describes a vast curve through eastern Oklahoma, and goes back into Arkansas as a tributary of the Arkansas River. The autochthonous Illinois River begins not far from Chicago, at the confluence of the Des Plaines and the Kankakee. From river town to river town, it draws a bar sinister across the state of Illinois — Marseilles, Ottawa, Starved Rock, Hennepin, Lacon, Rome, Peoria, Pekin, Havana, Bath, Browning, Beardstown, Meredosia, Florence, Hardin — descending 273 river miles to Grafton, Illinois, on the Mississippi River forty miles up from St. Louis.

In the thousand feet in front of Mel are fifteen barges wired together in three five-barge strings. Variously, the barges contain pig iron, structural iron, steel coils, furnace coke, and fertilizer. Each barge is two hundred feet long. Those with the pig iron seem empty, because the minimum river channel is nine feet deep and the iron is so heavy it can use no more than 10 percent of the volume of a barge. The barges are lashed in seventy-six places in various configurations with hundreds of feet of steel cable an inch thick — scissor wires, jockey wires, fore-and-afts, double-ups, three-part backing breasts, three-part towing breasts. The *Billy Joe Boling*, at the stern, is no less tightly wired to the barges than the barges are to one another, so that the vessel is an essentially rigid unit with the plan view of a rat-tail file. In the upside-down and inside-out terminology of this trade, the *Billy Joe Boling* is a towboat. Its bow is blunt and as wide as its beam. It looks like a ship cut in half. Snug up against the rear barge in the center string, it is also wired tight to the rear barges in the port and starboard strings. It pushes the entire enterprise, reaching forward a fifth of a mile, its wake of white water thundering astern.

Carl Dalton, on the head of the tow, now says, "Six wide on the port, fifty below."

Mel, in the pilothouse, is grinning. He has come up to this railroad bridge many times before and evidently it amuses him. "This place is so narrow you have to put guys out on the head to tell you where you are," he says, and laughs.

Where is he? Fifty feet from the bridge, and his head corner on the port side is lined up so that it should miss the nearest pier by six feet. He is steering the *Queen Mary* up an undersized river, and he is luxuriating in six feet of clearance. Meanwhile — back here a fifth of a mile — the dry riverbank is ten feet behind the stern rail. The stern is so close to the bank you could almost jump off without getting your feet wet. Mel is not standing at a wheel. On this vessel, a wheel is a propeller. There is no wheel in the pilothouse. He is handling instead a pair of horizontal sticks — beautiful brass fittings with pearl handles, one for the steering rudder, one for the flanking rudder. He also has two throttles, one for each engine. Each throttle has a forward and a reverse position. If he goes forward on one and back on the other, he can walk the whole tow sideways.

Years ago, our captain — who is off duty and in his room sleeping — was a deckhand on a tow that hit this bridge and scattered all fifteen barges.

"Five wide," Carl says. Carl is five feet from the pier and has drawn even with it.

"That's perfect," Mel tells him. "That's all. I got 'er."

"Getting set" is vernacular for being moved sideways by current. When Mel is steering through less complicated reaches of the river, he will choose an object under a mile in front of him (an island, say) and another object (say, a church steeple) directly behind the first one and much farther away. If the steeple moves to the left with respect to the island, the tow is being set to the left. If the steeple moves off to the right of the island, the tow is being set to the right. He doesn't need any church steeples here. There is nothing subtle about the current under this bridge. We are about a third of the way through now, and the current has begun to shove the head from the west side of the channel toward the east, skidding the whole big vessel from one pier toward the other. We started sixty inches off the west pier and — after moving forward 1,145 feet — we end up sixty inches off the east pier as the stern slides by it.

Mel aims the tow into a mile and a half of dead-straight river. Skyscraping grain elevators line the eastern bank. Beyond them, and behind a high levee, are the invisible streets of Pekin. "When we was going through the bridge, we had to favor the leg on the left side 'cause the current will push us over to the pier on the right side, so we had to favor the pier on the left side real close," he says. "You could feel the current catching the head, pushing it over toward the right. So we pushed it through about another two hundred feet, then let it run on straight rudder for a while. By the time we got through the bridge, we only had about five feet of clearance on the starboard side. That's how you take it through that bridge, especially when we got some current running, like we do now."

After lighting a cigarette, he adds, "There are seven different ways to run a river — high water, low water, upriver with the current on your head, downriver, daytime, nighttime, and running it by radar. Once you learn those seven ways, you can run any river. We made the Pekin wiggles in one try."

## Open Sleeve

In this sort of journey, there is no real departure or precise destination. Its structure is something like a sleeve open at both ends. Several days go by, a couple of hundred miles, and then a machine in the pilothouse suddenly springs to life as if it were the tenth member of the crew. Staccato and syllabic, its voice blurts out, "You . . . have . . . ree . . . ceived . . . new . . . orr . . . derrs . . . Please . . . ree . . . view . . . them . . . as . . . soon . . . as . . . poss . . . ibb . . . bull." A printout comes forth like a tongue. Upriver in a day or so, we will be turned by the *Ashley Lay*. On the Mississippi River, a tow might consist of forty-nine barges in seven strings — a vessel more than 1,500 feet long and nearly 250 feet wide. The diesels pushing it will develop as much as 10,500 horsepower. To enter the Illinois River and not plug it up forever, the numbers have to go down to fifteen barges and, say, 3,600 horsepower, like the *Billy Joe Boling*. Nearing Chicago, the waterway becomes tighter and flatter (less current), and you don't need the *Billy Joe Boling* anymore. You want the *Ashley Lay*, 2,800. Even closer to Chicago, where concrete walls close in on the waterway and bridges don't draw, "jackoff" boats take over. For dipping under bridges, their pilothouses go up and down hydraulically. They move six or eight barges at a time. On a boat with the power of the *Billy Joe Boling*, you go up the river until another crew turns you. You pick up their barges and go back down to the Mississippi, where, say, you turn the *Edwin A. Lewis* and the *Edwin A. Lewis* turns you. Then you go back up the Illinois.

Ours are Memco Barge Line barges. Memco moves upward of two thousand barges on Middle American rivers and is third in a very large field. When I called Memco not long after sending the company a formal request for a ride, Don Huffman, in St. Louis, said, "What day would you like to go?" It was as if I were talking to Southwest Airlines. Tows are moving about the country all the time. When and where would I like to get on one? I flew to St. Louis and went up to Grafton, where the *Billy Joe Boling* came along after a while and picked me off the riverbank with a powered skiff. Some five hundred miles later, the skiff would put me ashore in the same place. In an equal number of days last year (and by daylight only), I rode six times as far in a tractor-trailer. Faster, certainly, but barge companies are committed to pointing out that a fifteen-barge tow like this one can carry what 870 tractor-trailers would be carrying on highways. This comparison is not without precedent. In 1805, barges on the Middlesex Canal, in Massachusetts, transported more than nine thousand tons of freight, and it was said that if the same freight had traveled on dry land, 56,000 oxen would have been needed to move it.

Six A.M. of the forward watch and Tom Armstrong — the captain himself — is at the sticks. The voice in the machine has been sounding off, and I am wondering about the changing of orders and the turning of tows. "How long do you usually know what's going to happen?" I ask him.

"Usually there's no usually in towboats," he answers.

He lights a Marlboro. He is thirty-nine — the fifth oldest in the crew of nine. His jeans are patched in the seat and he wears an aquamarine T-shirt lettered GECKO HAWAII PRO SURF TEAM. Of medium height and strongly built, he has a precise, navigational mustache. He is left-handed, his hair is brush cut, his vision is 20/13. His eyes, remarkably bright, seem to project forward as horizontal periscopes. He has a constant, knowledgeable smile. "Towboating — it grows on you like a wart," he says. "See what I'm sayin'?"

Fond of that question, he repeats it many dozens of times per day. Phonetically, it emerges as "See what I'm sane?"

The sun appears above the trees, and Tom says, "Every day is a holiday, every meal a banquet. Got it made. Just don't know it." Another mantra. Another Marlboro. Sixteen years ago, he was a green deckhand on the lower Mississippi. He has held the rank of captain eleven years, working all rivers, mainly this one. His competence seems as absolute as his youthfulness seems indelible. Holding the sticks, he sits on his seat with his legs curled up under him, like anybody's grandson.

Captains all "come up through the deck," as the expression goes — the towboaters' equivalent of the merchant mariners' "coming up the hawsepipe." After working as a deckhand for two years, you can get a steering license. After you steer under a captain for eighteen months, you are eligible for a pilot license. You pass the physical, the radar training, and the simulator class in Paducah. A new, framed certificate appears on a bulkhead in a pilothouse somewhere: "William Thomas Armstrong . . . is licensed to serve as operator of uninspected towing vessels upon western rivers."

Tom is not hesitant to call the work stressful: "It takes good nerves to come down on a bridge sideways — I'm not sure I want to be out here driving a boat at sixty-five." He tells a story about a doctor who rode a towboat on the lower Mississippi to do stress tests on the captain. In the middle of the testing, the doctor was so stressed he asked to be taken off the boat. "One captain dropped out of medical school because his father died, and he came out here and was still here thirty years later," Tom goes on, in free association. I ask him how many skippers are women. "Two women worked their way up to the pilothouse," he says. "One of them is still out here, the other hit a bridge."

We are surrounded by glass in the pilothouse, large windows on all four sides. Our eyes are thirty-six feet above the water. The pilothouse smells like a bar under the old Third Avenue El. It is not a beer smell. Alcohol is forbidden and there is no evidence of it in sniff or behavior on the *Billy Joe Boling*. The pilothouse, which is swept and scrubbed clean every day, so reeks of tobacco smoke that the smell seems painted on the air. This is because Tom is a chain smoker and Mel just smokes a lot. Between them, they are in the pilothouse twenty-four hours a day. Others in the crew are also present here for varying lengths of time. Seven of the nine are smokers. Gene Diebold, the chief engineer, comes up to the pilothouse in the evenings to sit and look at the river. The chief, as everyone calls him, is a round and pleasant man, about sixty, a onetime automobile mechanic who has developed hearing loss in his eight years on the rivers. A Missourian, he grew up in Benton, south of Cape Girardeau. He says he has "no high-pitched hearing left; if several people are talking, I can't understand a thing." Yet he generally ignores the large-cup ear protectors that hang on pegs outside his engine room, preferring inserted plugs. You see him in there with a blue-and-white towel wrapped around his head as if he were out here to hide from Homeland Security. The chief, as it happens, is allergic to tobacco smoke. But that does not alter his affection for the pilothouse and his evening contemplation of the river. By 9 P.M., Tom is past the second pack of his day. Tom says, "It's hard to find people who don't smoke these days. They tried to set up a boat that would be a nonsmoking boat, but they couldn't find the crew members, see what I'm sane? Cigarettes aren't bad for your health, just ask the tobacco companies."

Mel and Tom, in the course of their watches, both dip snuff. They dip mint-flavored Skoal. They dip wintergreen long-cut Timber Wolf. Tom offers me some and supplies instructions. I haven't smoked a cigarette in forty years, let alone dipped wintergreen Timber Wolf. I put it inside my lip and soon feel as if I've had a five-shot latte. Tom confides, "I dip snuff to try to cut down on cigarettes."

Six hours a watch is a long time for him and Mel to be up here, their hands on or close to the sticks. They can't leave and go below when they need to urinate. So a toilet is a part of the furniture in the pilothouse — open, unscreened. It's just there, in one corner, like the radar. At first I felt I shouldn't use it. For the skipper to pee in my presence somehow seemed politically correct but not vice versa. I got over that in the first thirty-six hours and have been peeing up here in the pilothouse as if the toilet were a bush on a fishing trip.

"There are two places in the world — home and everywhere else, and everywhere else is the same," Tom says, looking out at the levees, the miles of river, the willows, the cottonwoods, the silver maples, the roofs of small, concealed communities. Tom is from Cadiz, in western Kentucky. "Kay-diz," he says, his accent on the "Kay." "It's a two-stoplight town" less than twenty miles from Tennessee, on Lake Barkley of the Cumberland River. He went into the army without finishing Trigg County High School (class of 1983), and out of the army into towboats, on which he now makes sixty-some thousand dollars for working half the year. "I make pretty good money," he says. "Out here is a pretty good job. The money

and the time off attract all of us. If we're not out here, we're not going to be no professor in a college, we're going to be in a factory
five, six days a week. A factory worker, if his job is to put this screw
in that gun, that's what he does all day every day for twenty years.
Imagine how old that would get." Entrepreneurial, conscious of
world money markets, schooled in the biographies of historic cap-
italists, Tom owns and rents out "a couple of dozen units" (rooms,
houses, agricultural acreage) and additionally owns a hundred-
acre farm with twenty beef cattle on it. While he is away on the *Billy
Joe Boling*, his wife, Debbie, manages the property. Also a library
clerk, Debbie is Tom's third wife. Separately and together, they
have had no children. When Tom is at home and is not making
rounds on his motorcycle from one unit to the next, he is probably
out on the Cumberland River piloting his ski boat.

## Hennepin

We are two hundred miles up the river and approaching Hennepin, ninety minutes — seven more miles — upstream. This tow has
about as much contact with the towns it passes as a tractor-trailer
does on I-55. To the Hennepin Boat Market we have faxed ahead
for food. We don't stop for much but navigation locks. Almost everything is brought to us by service boats as we drive on. However,
we need to dock at Hennepin today to take on water.

The deckhands of the forward watch are straining at their
cheater bars, revolving the ratchets that tighten the cruciate, inter-
barge wires, which are strung horizontally among timberheads and
cavels, and in most places are only a couple of inches above the
decks and gunwales of the barges. The deckhands are tuning the
tow like a piano, and the work is beyond heavy. Closing pelican
hooks, putting keepers in place, cranking ratchets, they make the
wires so taut that if they stand on them the wires don't touch the
deck. As we look down on the deckhands from the pilothouse, Tom
takes a drag on a Marlboro, emits a gray cloud, and says to me, "If
you didn't go to school and get a good education, you'd be out
there working your ass off tightening them wires."

Rick Walker and Jason Beuke are the deckhands of the forward
watch. Jason, of Paducah, is a two-tripper, this being his second trip
ever on a tow. A wrestler when he was in high school, he weighs

three hundred pounds. He carries it easily. Rick lives near Golconda, Illinois, close to the Ohio River. If you did not know him, you might say he has a demeanor that is vaguely sinister. If you do know him, you would probably say that he likes to give that impression. Thirty-four years old, fatless and wiry with dark bright eyes, he may not yet have met his first barber. An almost unceasing worker twelve hours each day, he is the *Billy Joe Boling*'s second mate. Tom Armstrong refers to him as "the black-haired dude."

Rick is paired with Tom and Jason manning this immense vessel from five-thirty to eleven-thirty in the morning and five-thirty to eleven-thirty in the evening, the punctually observed hours of the six-to-twelve watch. If Rick is not out checking barges, tightening wires, or straightening up the captain's room, he is generally up here in the pilothouse polishing the windows inside and out, shining the metal surfaces, thickening the smoke. He takes note of my routines with unconcealed contempt, in part because I don't have any. I get up about when he does, a little before 5 A.M., awakened by knocks on my door by a deckhand on the twelve-to-six watch. After a fast breakfast in the galley, I climb to the pilothouse, arriving usually as Mel turns the sticks over to Tom. Since there is nowhere to go — no long, Emersonian walks among the fifteen barges — I sit or stand in the pilothouse sixteen hours a day, staring at the river with an open notebook. Rick Walker makes clear that he looks upon this as idling in the *n*th dimension. One morning, he said, "Why don't you pick up a broom and do something useful?" At the end of my sixteen hours, when I stir to go below, he will say with incredulity, "Don't tell me you're going off to bed," accenting the "bed" as if it were a synonym for cowardice. Rick and Tom are not out of synch. When I mentioned that I have a fishing shack up a river somewhere, Tom said, "It's probably 10,000 square feet."

Meals are the bright punctuation of the day out here, never mind that dinner is at eleven in the morning, supper at five in the afternoon, and breakfast in the creeping dawn. The after watch eats at those hours and goes to work. The forward watch eats some minutes later and goes to bed — everybody sleeping and everybody working twice a day. Everybody but Bryan Velazquez, who is called upon when needed — mainly in navigation locks — and has to be available twenty-four hours a day. After a dinner of round steak, brown gravy, okra, hominy, green beans, and mashed potatoes, Tom remarked, "They feed us slaves like kings. Fish Friday, steak Saturday, chicken Sunday — towboat tradition." A sled dog would understand how long it takes us to finish. The galley is behind the engine room at the rear of the main deck, and to get there you walk a narrow route along guard chains beside the river. You fill your plate and sit at a counter, all diners facing in the same direction. When I first sat down there, the cook, Donna Hobbs, told me to take my hat off when I eat.

Donna is highly regarded for smoking only behind the counter and not over the stove. Eighteen years on various rivers, she is from Paducah now, but she went to Jefferson High School in Rockford, Illinois. She wears flip-flops or thick-soled white running shoes, sweatpants, T-shirts, an embroidered square-neck short-sleeved cream blouse. Her hair is blond and she keeps it in a ponytail. If she is making cinnamon buns, her day begins at 2:45 A.M. No cinnamon buns, she gets up at 3:00. On Sunday mornings at breakfast time, she is not in the galley. On Sunday mornings, she is allowed "to sleep in," and she gets up at 7 A.M. to prepare dinner. "I sleep in shifts," she remarked one evening at six when I lingered in the galley to talk to her. Finished for the day, she said she was going to take a shower and watch *The African Queen*. The story is appealing on a towboat and she has watched the movie innumerable times. We talked about Bogart and the leeches, Bogart at the end in the reeds. She said it was amazing how fast he fixed that prop when he dinged it in the rapids. Donna is a quarter Cherokee. "You can see it in my high cheekbones," she said, turning sideways in her Kentucky Wildcats T-shirt, a gold cross hanging from her neck. She has a tattoo on her right arm — a dream catcher on a bear's claw around a bear's head. It filters out bad dreams. She was divorced in 1987, after which she lived with a man nine years. She told him to do what he wanted when she was on the boat but not to run around when she was at home. He didn't.

Two buzzards circle the tow. Tom, steering, looking up at them, says, "They know who the cook is on this boat. They're waiting for one of us to die." This is outrageously unfair to Donna, and he knows it. "Some cooks are young," Tom goes on. "The company, they prefer the Fifty-five Club — fifty-five years old and fifty-five pounds overweight, see what I'm sane?" He mentions a regular cook on the rivers who is in her upper seventies. He also mentions

Granny, whose real name is Mary. "There are fewer young ones than men cooks," he continues. "They call them in for an interview, see that they're young and beautiful, and she isn't hired. The company, it isn't their first rodeo, see what I'm sane? If she's young and beautiful, she has to be smarter than the average bear to survive. Good-looking woman, the men are like buzzards on a fence. If there's a young cook, the buzzards are sane, 'These are the best hot dogs I've ever eaten.' An old woman, she could serve them a six-course meal and they'd bitch."

Along the riverbank just below Hennepin, we pass two dozen covered barges, loaded with grain at the Hennepin elevator and now moored in fleets waiting to be picked up. Some are tied to trees, some to massive chunks of concrete set in the bank. Old propane tanks serve as mooring floats. Wires from the moorings are tied to three bunched auto tires whose collective elasticity is neither too great nor too modest to control the wayward lurchings of two thousand tons of loaded barge. Chains large enough to anchor oceangoing ships in turn connect the tires to the concrete chunks in the bank or are looped around cottonwoods and maples. We tie up the tow, detach the *Billy Joe,* and run in to the Hennepin dock. Backed into a berth beside the dock is the *Robert J.,* a condensed general store that is a small boat in itself and ordinarily would come out on the river and attach itself to the running tow. Spectacularly varied, crowded with goods, it is stocked with everything a towboater might need or find attractive — a video, for example, called *Oral Orgasms* and subtitled *Carpet Munching Extravaganza.* Close by *Oral Orgasms* are *Scientific American* and a twenty-gauge shotgun up for raffle. Mark Judd, big and friendly, runs the *Robert J.* When towboaters telephone or fax ahead for something he doesn't have, he will go and get it — sometimes driving considerable distances — and he charges nothing for the service. He collects their prescriptions, goes off, and fills them. If your tooth is aching, he will take you to the dentist. Heart? Liver? Duodenum? He will take you to a doctor. He went to a Wal-Mart once to buy Mel Adams a pair of glasses. He gives the towing companies a long rope. A towing company once owed him $300,000. Donna Hobbs, shopping in Mark's store, runs an eye over the porn shelves but does not bat it.

The Hennepin Boat Market, up the levee and into the town, is also owned by Mark Judd. It is the only bulk grocer serving the river's vessels in three hundred miles. The check-off shopping lists we get from them by fax say that Hennepin Boat Market "provides a 25-hour, 8 days a week, 53 weeks a year midstream grocery delivery." With Tom's permission, while he is taking on water and supplies, I walk a loop through the streets of Hennepin — a spread-out town of open spaces, with contiguous lawns, few sidewalks, and almost no fences, as if the houses were married quarters on a naval base somewhere, the dead silence of nine in the morning broken only by birds in the oaks and maples. Seven hundred people live in Hennepin, which is named for a priest who accompanied the Sieur de La Salle portaging out of Lake Michigan and into the Illinois River system in 1679. Father Hennepin, chronicler of the expedition, is described in James Gray's *The Illinois* (Farrar & Rinehart, 1940) as "a vain, pretentious priest who claimed the achievements of his betters" and "made love to himself on paper." I am late returning to the *Billy Joe Boling*, which has taken on its water, stowed its provisions, and for fifteen minutes has been ready to go. Tom, in the pilothouse, 9:30 A.M., supposes aloud that I have been to a bar. Add that to my 10,000-square-foot fishing shack, and I have suddenly become a rich alcoholic. Tom has had his wife, in Kentucky, check me out on the Internet. Now he says on the phone to her, "He's got a couple of daughters. Check them out, too. See if they robbed a bank or a liquor store."

## Calling Traffic

When I told my friend Andy Chase that I was coming out here, he said, "The way they handle those boats — gad! They go outrageous places with them. The ship handling is phenomenal." Andy is a licensed master of ships of any gross tons upon oceans, and he is also a professor at Maine Maritime Academy. His credentials notwithstanding, he said he would envy me being here. This tow is not altogether like an oceangoing ship. We are a lot longer than the *Titanic*, yes, but we are a good deal lighter. We weigh only 30,000 tons. Yet that is surely enough to make our slow motion massive, momentous, tectonic. Fighting the current with full left rudder and full left flanking rudder in the 80° turn at Creve Coeur Landing, Kickapoo Bend, Tom Armstrong says, "I'm trying to get it pointed up before it puts me on the bank. There's no room for maneuvering. You can't win for losing. You just don't turn that fast. You just don't stop that fast. Sometimes we don't make our turns. We have to back up. The Illinois River's such a tight-assed river."

We are anything but alone. In addition to pleasure craft, other long tows are before us and behind us on the river, like a string of airliners on final in a long line to Newark — the *Austin Golding*, the *Frank Stegbauer*, the *Martha Mac*, the *Tamera Pickett*, the *Starfire*. With this difference: Another succession of thousand-foot tows is always coming toward us in the opposite direction, sharing the same channel in the same small river. Tows moving downcurrent have the right of way. If you are headed upstream, you have to pull into a hold-up spot and wait for them to go by. Hold-up spots, in some parts of the river, are far between. Both Tom and Mel have their own copies of the *Illinois Waterway Navigation Charts,* a publication of the U.S. Army Corps of Engineers. They have identified hold-up spots that will work under present conditions and have marked them in pencil — places ample enough for putting the nose into the bank without blocking the river. When you are waiting for another vessel to pass, you literally stick your head into the mud at the edge of the river and hold there obliquely ( / ). Places are rare that are wide enough for two to pass while both are moving.

Trains run under centralized systems. These people are self-organized, talking back and forth on VHF, planning hold-ups and advances, and signing off with the names of their vessels: "*Billy Joe Boling* southbound, heading into Anderson Lake country. *Billy Joe Boling,* southbound."

This is known as "calling traffic."

"*Billy Joe Boling* heading down toward the Marquette Bar. *Billy Joe Boling* heading toward the Marquette Bar. *Billy Joe Boling.*"

A deep-voiced acknowledgment comes into the pilothouse: "*Billy Joe, Jon J. Strong.*" The captain of the *Jon J. Strong* has got the message.

"*Billy Joe Boling* heading southbound into Abe Lincoln. *Billy Joe Boling.*"

For anyone within VHF range, this means that the *Billy Joe Boling* is soon to pass under Interstate 39's Abraham Lincoln Memorial Bridge. It means "I'm coming down, get out of my way." At Abe Lincoln, the river bends 90° and soon goes under a second bridge.

Tom calls to another captain, "You'd better give them a shout down there before you get committed." In other words, before you

proceed you need to know that the river is open to — and including — your next manageable hold-up spot. St. Louis to Chicago,
Chicago to St. Louis, this is like jumping from lily pad to lily pad. It
is also reminiscent of the way that airplane pilots in flight constantly study their charts, picking out airports where, if need be,
they can make an emergency landing. "We don't try to plug up a
hole and then try to get in the hole," Tom Armstrong says. "It don't
make for a good day. We have to move from hold-up spot to hold-
up spot and not think we're going to get in one when someone else
is in it. On-the-job training is the only way to learn this."

On the job calling traffic — and in the interest of making time at
the expense of others — some captains learn to deceive. As Mel
Adams puts it, "They sometimes lie. They lie in both directions."

No one is going to be lying when two moving tows, in adequate
water, are passing. The captains say to each other, "See you on the
1," or "See you on the 2." Passing on the 1 always means that both
boats would turn to starboard to avoid collision. Two boats, meeting and passing on the 1, will go by each other port to port. Therefore, passing on the 1 in opposite directions is different from passing on the 1 when overtaking. Passing on the 1 when overtaking is
to go by the other boat's starboard side. The stand-on vessel, nearly
always the vessel heading upstream, maintains everything as is. The
action vessel maneuvers. If you are learning this on the job, you
may by now be up a street in Peoria. If you are still on the water, you
may be feeling the hydraulic effect of the other tow sucking you toward it. One of my notes says, "The *Mark Shurden* with three barges
carrying black oil passes us and sucks our stern, swinging our head
toward the red buoys." The riverbank is variously wicked and benign. It can pull you in or fend you off. Mel says, "There's a real
fine line between bank cushion and bank suction. An extra five feet
and it sucks you right over to it. You've got to stop and break the
suction," while the *Billy Joe* shudders with cavitation.

Approaching a ferry, Mel on the VHF volunteers to drift while
the ferry crosses the river. The ferryman says, "Keep her coming. I
don't want to slow down the economy." The economy goes past the
ferry doing four miles an hour. Tom says the tow moves more
gracefully when it is going downstream: "It slides more, and is more
dangerous, going down — at bridges, for example, with the current on your stern — but it's more graceful, and you have the right
of way. Going upstream, it's easier to stop if you have to." Flanking

is a downstream move. You slow your engines at a bend and let the current push the tow around. "Every bend is a challenge, though. You're pushing it to the max every day — pushing the drafts, toting the heaviest barges you can, going as fast as you can." Going deep is "steering as close to the outside of a bend as you can and still make the turn." It is what you would do in a canoe in a small stream, and this canoe is longer than the river is wide. "So shallow and so small, this river is more difficult to navigate than the Lower and the Ohio," Tom says. The Lower runs past Memphis, Vicksburg, and New Orleans.

They use the searchlight all night, a thousand watts, its beam a bright cylinder through the saturated air. It picks out green can buoys and red nun buoys — reds on the right going north. Not all the buoys are always in place. Picking his way in the dark across the seventeen broad miles of Peoria Lake, Tom describes what he is doing as "an Easter-egg hunt." The white beam is galactic with bugs — enough mayflies, it seems, to feed all the trout in the Rockies. Elsewhere on the river, missing buoys have been dragged away by tows. "This is like driving a car with your damned eyes closed," Tom says. "If you run aground, try to be going slow enough so you can back off." The Coast Guard buoy tender *Sangamon* passes us, pushing a small barge. On the deck, lined up like naval ordnance, are row upon row of new green and red buoys.

The swing indicator in the pilothouse measures the degrees to port or starboard that the tow is turning. Also close around the person at the sticks are the fax, the cell phone, the computer, the radar, the AM-FM radio, the tape player, the Qualcomm, two depth finders, two VHF marine radios (in order to monitor two channels), the GPS, the searchlight controls, and the general-alarm switch. There is no need for a compass, heaven knows, and — given the swing indicator — no need for a gyroscope. Knotted rubber cords hold back the books on the shelves under the fax. This vessel will wait a long time to ride its first swell, but when the *Billy Joe Boling* goes around a bend and its stern gets close to the bank and the wheel wash strikes the rudder, the vibration could sift a silo.

Coming up in the evening for his look around, the chief engineer says we are burning about 2,400 gallons of diesel fuel a day. Not bad. We are getting nearly two hundred feet to the gallon. As a rule of thumb, a towboat burns one gallon per horsepower per day, but — at 3,600 horsepower — that's not our thumb. The *Billy Joe*

*Boling* has a tank capacity of 62,000 gallons. We do not need any-thing like that amount of fuel, but we fill her up anyway because we prefer not to "burn light." Tom says, "The lighter the boat gets, the sloppier it steers." It is best that the tanks not be less than half full. Putting that another way, diesel fuel is in use as ballast! As the barge industry is always ready to point out, in fuel consumed per ton-mile, a tow is about two and a half times more efficient than a freight train, nearly nine times more efficient than a truck.

There are five dams on the Illinois River, none very high. Some are weirs, really, consisting largely of steel-and-timber wickets that can be lowered in high water so that tows can ride right over them, ignoring the navigation locks off to the side. In its 273 miles, the river drops about ninety feet, indicating that the state of Illinois is almost as flat as it looks, its state-crossing river dropping down to the Mississippi six inches per mile.

At the higher dams, the navigation locks lift us or lower us about ten feet. "Locking through," the term that has described the proc-ess since the sixteenth century, is not, on this river, a simple matter of drain valves and filling valves. The locks consist of a "short wall," aligned with the current and standing in the river, and a "long wall" (or "guide wall") running along the bank. The short wall is rounded off at each end, a configuration known as the bull nose. The barges, three abreast, have five feet of clearance between the short wall and the long wall. The lock is six hundred feet long. Our vessel is nearly twice that. What to do?

Gingerly, you inch your 30,000 tons up there past the bull nose. If you are heading downstream and you come in at too much of an angle, your head can become wedged between the short wall and the long wall while your stern is swung around by the current, with the result that your vessel becomes a lever prying at the navigation lock until masonry breaks, wires snap, loose barges are draped all over the dam, and your *Billy Joe Boling,* whatever it may be called, is hanging on the brink and listing.

You inch your tow up the long wall until nine barges are in the lock, and then you cut your vessel in half. You undo the wires at the break coupling. With the aft six barges, you back out. A door closes, sealing off the lock chamber. The drain valves are opened. The nine barges are lowered. Another door opens, and a mule — a wire on an electric winch — hauls the nine barges down the long wall to timberheads, where they are moored. The lock is refilled to receive the rear half of the tow. When it rejoins the front half, deck-hands start leaning into their cheater bars at the limits of their strength, in all seasons and weathers, turning the ratchets that tighten the wires and restore the vessel to its complete integrity. You don't do this in ten minutes. We spend hours in the locks and more hours near the locks waiting our turn. For smaller tows, there are rearrangements like the knockout single and the set-over single that pack all components into the lock at one time, but we are vastly too large for that. The term for what we do is "double lockage."

Of Peoria Lock, Mel Adams says, "This is a tough lock to get into southbound when it's running some water. You get your head in there and it wants to suck you over toward the dam, bad. If they're running more than three feet of water through the dam, get a tug. The tug puts the head end up against the wall, pins it on the wall, lets you get your head inside the bull nose, and you can get your stern in with your engines. If you don't have the tug, you can get wedged in, and the current takes the stern around and the barges break up and go into the wickets."

Below the lock at La Grange, and close to it, the rush of heavy water through the wide-open tainter gates of the adjacent dam is creating an eddy, which Mel — northbound here — calls a whirlpool. It turns clockwise, swinging around from the foot of the dam and running into the bull nose. Mel is inching up there, pushing his port head toward the long wall, his starboard head toward the bull nose. He could get over on the long wall, catch a line on the port lead barge, and rub this footprint aircraft carrier up the long wall, but that does not seem to be his default mode of ship handling. Maybe he can just go in there in one shot, and if he gets lucky he won't have to catch a line. The mate, Carl Dalton, will not have to humiliate him by throwing an assistive rope around a timberhead.

Carl is on the port head as the tow moves upriver. Mel says to him on the walkie-talkie, "They're all out at the dam. It won't be lookin' purty when I get up there."

Carl calls off distances, long and short. Distance from the long wall. Distance from the lock gate. Distance from the bull nose. "Two hundred and fifty to the bull nose."

"I have to have the head on the wall to get it inside the bull nose," Mel mutters to himself. "You don't want to wedge in there. You could tear up barges, tear up the gates on the lock." But nobody needs to catch any lines as the huge vessel slides by the thundering rapids, absorbs the shock of the eddy, and aims for its five feet of clearance between the two walls.

"One hundred to the bull nose."

"Fifty to the bull nose."

"Even with the bull nose."

The tow, having smothered the whirlpool, now moves up between the walls and into the lock chamber.

When it stops there, Carl says, "The head never got more than a foot off the wall."

Mel says, "Sometimes you just get lucky."

Off Mayo Island, Ottawa, in pitch darkness, the *Ashley Lay* turns us and we turn the *Ashley Lay*. If we were in the Hudson River and had started at the mouth, we would be in the Adirondacks. The six strings of barges lie abreast, and the *Billy Joe Boling* keeps them in place, its light beam aimed at the bank and holding steady on the trunk of a tree. Mayflies — fewer here — go through the beam like comets. A heron goes through like a stork. In a curious ritual, the *Ashley Lay* picks up our head gear — running lights, flagpole, heavy nylon lock lines — and carries it to the head of our new tow. We hand over their groceries. They give us a wad of cash. We take their head gear with us to the upstream end of the strings, where we drop it off, then wire up to the new tow, facing downstream toward the Mississippi.

In the thousand feet of barges we now have before us are grains for export, corn for Baton Rouge, and coke for Kentucky. We brought 12,000 tons of coke up the Illinois River, and now we are pushing 14,000 tons of coke down the Illinois River. Tom Armstrong, coming on watch at 5:30 A.M., takes this in and says, "One day, they'll figure it out and put us out of a job."

## Empty Pockets II

Mel Adams at the sticks in a long straight stretch of the river. A white cabin boat is in midchannel directly in front of us, about three thousand feet away. It is not moving. We cannot see people aboard. For Mel, there is no possibility of maneuver, no possibility of stopping. Surely the cabin boat will move. Referring to our blunt head end, three barges wide, Mel says, "When they see a 105 feet of steel coming at them ten feet high, they'll get out of the way."

They do not. Mel, with binoculars, thinks he may have glimpsed a swimmer's head in the water, but that could have been a trick of the eye. As we bear down to 2,000 and then 1,500 feet, the cabin boat stays where it is, dead in the water, less than two minutes from destruction. Mel gives it five short blasts, the universal statement of immediate danger. At just about the point where the cabin boat would go into our blind spot — the thousand feet of water that we in the pilothouse can't see — people appear on the cabin boat's deck, the boat starts up, and in a manner that seems both haughty and defiant moves slowly and slightly aside. We grind on downriver as the boat moves up to pass us port to port, making its way up the thousand feet of barges to draw even with the pilothouse. Two men and two women are in the cabin boat. The nearest woman — seated left rear in the open part of the cockpit — is wearing a black-and-gold two-piece bathing suit. She has the sort of body you go to see in marble. She has golden hair. Quickly, deftly, she reaches with both hands behind her back and unclasps her top. Setting it on her lap, she swivels 90° to face the towboat square. Shoulders back, cheeks high, she holds her pose without retreat. In her ample presentation there is defiance of gravity. There is no angle of repose. She is a siren and these are her songs. She is Henry Moore's *Oval with Points*. Moore said, "Rounded forms convey an idea of fruitfulness, maturity, probably because the earth, women's breasts and most fruits are rounded, and these shapes are important because they have this background in our habits of perception. I think the humanist organic element will always be for me of fundamental importance in sculpture." She has not moved — this half-naked maja outnakeding the whole one. Her nipples are a pair of eyes staring the towboat down. For my part, I want to leap off the tow, swim to her, and ask if there is anything I can do to help. We can now read the name on the transom behind her: *Empty Pockets II*.

This is happening between Brushy Lake and the Six Mile Slough, if you see what I'm sane. Pleasure craft are anywhere, everywhere up and down the river. We traverse a reach in Peoria through the Cedar Street Bridge and the Bob Michel Bridge and the Murray Baker Bridge among at least two dozen pleasure craft spread over the river and framed between the arches. Pontoon boats, jet boats, powerboats — they go into the locks behind us, ahead of us. At the 89 bridge, Mile 218, a marina is on one side, a boat launch on the other, and twelve pleasure craft are visible, eight coming toward us, and who knows how many we can't see. Pleasure craft are like the bugs in the searchlight beam. On Peoria Lake, some of them are under sail. Southbound, a three-deck cruiser called *Bewitched* comes down on the Marquette Bar. "See you on the 2 whistle," says *Bewitched,* as if he were a thousand feet long. Above the Marquette Bar, forty-some pleasure boats are beached along a sand strip like white walruses. A boat crosses in front of us dragging two small kids on a tube. When pleasure-craft numbers get really high, a deckhand is sent to the head of the tow as lookout.

The wheel wash of the *Billy Joe Boling* goes out astern like a No. 10 rapid in the Grand Canyon, which "cannot be run without risk of life." The class of the rapid counts down, of course, with distance from the stern, and jet boats and jet skiers, playing in the wake, flirt their way forward through the rising levels of risk. If some macho jet skier were to cut in close to the stern, he would fast become soggy toast. Pleasure craft constantly cross in front of us, too, and when that happens Tom Armstrong will say, "He has a lot of faith in his engine, doesn't he."

Slow as tows are, they sometimes hit pleasure craft, although it is usually the other way around. A skier or boat that comes in from the side to jump the wake can be sucked into and through the propellers. If a water-skier falls a thousand feet in front of the tow, the skier has sixty seconds to get out of the way or the skier can go under the entire tow and into the propellers. As a pleasure boat passed us one day dragging a small boy on a tube, Mel said, "If the line broke, that little boy would be sucked right into the wheel wash." While Mel was crossing Peoria Lake a few years ago, a boat with a water-skier disappeared under his head and reappeared without the water-skier. Then the boat turned around, disappeared again, and reappeared dragging the skier out of the way. A day or so ago, we came down on a fisherman in a flatboat with an outboard motor, fishing in the middle of the channel. Mel, with binoculars, saw him tugging and tugging at his starting rope. Another fishing boat threw him a line and saved him. "People dropping skiers right in front of us, people falling off their jet skis right in front of us — it's enough to make a nervous wreck out of me," Mel has said. "Pleasure boats sometimes raft together, drinking beer, paying no attention, drifting down the channel. Get too close to 'em, you put a suction on 'em and pull 'em right to you. I get so dang worried that I'm going to run one of them over, kill someone. I couldn't live with myself."

If the head end is running a notch or a spike, a pleasure boat coming up behind us with intent to go around us can be lethally surprised. A notch is one missing barge. A spike is a barge at the head of the center string with notches on either side. Tom tells of an accident in which an intoxicated man was letting his kid drive their boat and the kid raced up the starboard side of a tow that appeared to him to be four barges long. Sharply rounding the fourth barge, swinging to his left to cut in front of the tow, the kid suddenly, and — too late — saw a fifth barge, a spike, at the head of the center string. After crashing into its side, father, son, and boat were plowed under the starboard string. Of the operators of pleasure boats of all sizes, Mel says, "They are ignorant, ignorant, ignorant."

The crew of the *Billy Joe Boling* is always mindful of pleasure craft, in no small measure because they are forever hoping for "tit shots." This, I think, was the first towboater term I learned after coming aboard. It bounced off the windows of the pilothouse from dawn until dark every day. But nothing happened. From each of many hundreds of pleasure craft, there was nothing even suggesting a tit shot. I thought the captain and the crew were fantasizing, on their way to hallucinating, and probably should be committed. Now, though, *Empty Pockets II*, which slowed up as she drew abreast of us, puts on a burst of speed and curls around our stern and through our wake. Coming back to us on the starboard side, she picks up even more speed and races down before us on wings of white spray.

I say to Mel, "I thought that was just a myth — that it didn't happen."

Mel says, "It happens all the time."

## Call Me Tom

Another clear, warm day, and Carl Dalton is painting the tow knees with Doug Gable. The tow knees are two flat columns of steel —

taller than Carl or Doug — that stand on the towboat's squared-off bow and butt up against the barges it is pushing. Mel Adams, steering, looks down from the pilothouse, thirty feet above, and communicates with Carl by walkie-talkie. He is telling him, inning by inning, how the Cubs are doing against the White Sox and how much cork the Cubs are using today. Carl, the first mate, is in equal measure strong, responsible, funny, and upbeat, always greeting with evident pleasure the grueling physical day that begins at midnight and includes two six-hour watches. Doug, from Granite, Oklahoma, his face a ten-o'clock shadow, his teeth not altogether present or accounted for, his longish hair flowering behind his red baseball cap, suggests the legacy of the Western mountain trapper. Fourteen days off, twenty-eight days on, he used to take a Greyhound from Oklahoma to Kentucky to report for work, but for this trip he bought himself a car. He dropped out after two years at Western Oklahoma State and worked as a driller and blaster in rock quarries before becoming a deckhand on towboats. The phone rings in the pilothouse.

The crew dispatcher in Paducah asks to speak to Carl Dalton. Mel relays the word to Carl, who leaves the main deck and climbs the interior stairs to the pilothouse. Mel turns off the baseball game. Carl says hello to the crew dispatcher and listens as the dispatcher asks him in some detail about a guy he hopes to sign up as a deckhand. After listening for at least three minutes, Carl says, "He's over thirty years old and he sleeps with a night-light." There is an extended silence in the pilothouse as the dispatcher continues to speak to Carl. Then Carl says, "He's not much on the working thing." An even longer silence follows as Carl patiently listens to Paducah. Then Carl says, "I don't want him on here."

The crew dispatcher works for B&H Towing, which leases its boats from Memco, which then charters the boats; and that, in the words of our captain, "is how they busted up the unions out here." The hunt for willing-and-able deckhands is a difficult one for the dispatcher, as Carl — third-ranking person on the *Billy Joe Boling* and invaluable himself — is much aware. When guys are riding to Paducah for their fourteen days off, the company will call them in the van to see if they want to go at once to another boat. Carl lives in Wickliffe, about thirty miles from Paducah. He played his basketball at Ballard Memorial High School, where he dropped out in

1980, he says, "like a fool." He knows everybody. At breakfast one day, he told me, "There's not that many blacks in Wickliffe, but we're all kin."

The work is hard on deck anytime, he said, but especially in winter. The tows punch and punch again at the ice to break a trail. Sometimes at dusk they can look back and see where they started at dawn, while the deckhands tighten wires in snow or freezing rain. "You go out there to jerk up a ratchet, you fall, slip, the deck is so slick." The ice on the river may be eighteen inches thick. Sometimes a trail is broken with one barge while the fourteen other barges — each tied to the next — follow the towboat "like a train on a track." Danger may be highest in winter, but it is always present. "Duckpond" is the towboaters' term for any open space among the barges where a member of the crew could fall in. The ends of some barges are squared and vertical, the ends of others beveled, trapezoidal, raked. The rakes are for streamlining at the head and stern ends of the tow, but they may be anywhere in the assemblage, and if rakes abut in the middle of a tow, they form a duckpond. Some "oddball barges" are not quite as long as the others — a cause of additional duckponds. On the subject of hazards to deckhands, Tom Armstrong says, "Lines break, slice 'em in half like a damned banana. Or a nineteen-year-old kid falls off a head barge, goes under, and dies." The *Billy Joe Boling* has not had a lost-time accident in two years. What happened? "A guy was homesick. He really wasn't injured. He said he had a sprung back. Once he got off, he sprung back to healthy."

Of most deckhands, Tom says, "Even if they're sick, they get up there and do it." For their twelve-hour days, deckhands start at $80 a day. ($6.66 an hour). They work their way up to $119. Resourceful, hardworking, in a class by themselves, they remind me of people I knew in Alaska, with the difference that many of the towboaters are more than a little apologetic about themselves, variously confessing their small towns and calling themselves hillbillies. The Alaskans I'm thinking of saw themselves as a class apart, meant for a different geography, without much interest in the place they called the Outside. "We may not all have come over on the same boat, but we're on the same boat now," Tom Armstrong says. And Rick Walker remarks, "There's a lot of kids out here right out of McDonald's, and they'd be better off if they'd stayed at McDonald's. But if you can handle this work, you can make fifty to eighty thousand a year without a college education or even a high school diploma."

Tom, owner of beef cattle and rental properties, spends a part of each day meditating upon incomes higher than a captain's — how large a part of each day only he would know. The part he shares is on the cassettes he plays in the pilothouse, listening to a narrator who says, "In just a few moments, I'm going to give you the formula for getting rich," and goes on to ask, "Whose drum are you marching to, even assuming you're marching to anyone's?" Repeated reference is made to "the gold mine between your ears" and to "M.S.I." — "the great key" — multiple sources of income. "Five ideas a day is twenty-five a week — that is, if you don't think on weekends." The tapes refer to "America's results coach," and they quote Oriah Mountain Dreamer in praise of people who "refuse to die with their music still in them." That is, they cause it to pour forth before it is too late. He listens to Dan Millman quoting Ashley Montagu on Bertrand Russell and the pursuit of happiness. Among Tom's favorite books — present on a shelf in the pilothouse — is *Think and Grow Rich*, by Napoleon Hill, the book that resulted after Andrew Carnegie prodded Hill to study five hundred successful people. Impulsively, Tom will start up the tapes at any moment of the day or night between six and twelve. Steering the *Billy Joe Boling* from light to light in the dark, he listens to *Discover the Value of Lifelong Learning* and *Twenty Minutes That Can Change Your Life*. On the VHF, he advises the captain of another towboat to put cattle on land that the other captain owns near Pekin. "Then it's a farm and a tax write-off," Tom explains. "That's the way to go, brother. Money ain't in the cows, it's in the tax deduction."

Doug Gable and Mel Adams are the only crew members who went to college, and Mel — with a degree in computer science and marine biology — is the only graduate. In the pilothouse, he listens to National Public Radio. When he is holding up — tow head near the bank, waiting for another tow to pass — I have more than once found him standing over the chart-book-and-radar cabinet, slowly turning pages, taking notes. He is in deep study and appears to be plotting some sort of course, but he is actually compiling an order from a Bass Pro Shops catalog. The threadfin shad and the brook silverside are forage fish in Table Rock Lake — that is, the white bass eat them. Mel reads to me from an article he has saved on lure colors: "In clear water, use blue-and-chrome, black-and-chrome, black-and-gold, and anything that looks like a threadfin shad. In stained water, chartreuse." His selections include the Bandit Deep Diver, the Excalibur Fat Free Shad, and some Norman Deep Little N crankbaits in gel-coat colors: sun-green shiner, sun smoky shad. Mel grew up frog gigging, crappie fishing, and noodling — catching catfish by hand from nests in the bank ("It was risky. What if a big cat bit you or the nest included water moccasins?").

Mel has a tattoo on his right arm: a skull and wings. He says, "Actually, that's a six-pack of Mickey's barrel-mouth." In the navy, aged twenty-two or so, in San Francisco, he drank the Mickey's barrel-mouth and went in for the skull and wings. On his other arm is an island sunset, pricked on Guam. He regrets both tattoos. "It's all the go now — that and body piercin'. Back then, if you had a tattoo you were a biker or a sailor." Mel was a chief petty officer. He sailed on ships of many kinds — guided-missile cruiser, fast combat supply ship, aircraft carrier. He was six years on Guam, six in Hawaii. Aurora, his wife, is Filipina. She grew up near Olongapo, a Death March site on the Bataan Peninsula, where her parents had a fish farm. Her father was a shipwright at Subic Bay. Mel and Aurora have three teen-aged kids, one on her way to becoming a registered nurse, another a performing musician hoping for Juilliard.

Mel once piloted a tow from Corpus Christi to suburban Chicago carrying 11,000 tons of black oil. He went 1,600 miles up the Gulf-coastal waterways, the Atchafalaya River, the Lower, the Upper, and the Illinois River to Lemont. And now, after one more night on the Illinois, dawn appears. He calls Aurora and awakens her. Two miles out of Peoria Lock, he is southbound, approaching *Clark Dock*, on the right bank, four miles up from the Pekin wiggles. The *Billy Waxier*, with two barges, is tied to the *Clark Dock*, so Mel, in his words, is "favorin' them red buoys" along the left side of the channel to give himself plenty of clearance as he passes the other tow. Having come up to the pilothouse before breakfast, I have been here since we left the lock a few minutes after five, in ample time for the next event.

This is the next event. At 5:25 A.M., the *Billy Joe Boling* and the fifteen barges instantly lose 100 percent of their momentum and come to a sickening, shuddering, completely unexpected, and convulsive stop. This 1,145-foot vessel has not just been sliding in mud; it has run aground hard. The port wing wire has snapped, and, as we will learn soon enough, seven other wires have snapped, too. The port wing wire runs from the last barge in the port string to the *Billy Joe Boling* itself. Now, ghastly, that barge and the one in front of it begin to drift slowly away. Grain and corn excluded, half a million dollars' worth of barges are taking off on their own for New Orleans. Tom Armstrong appears in the pilothouse like a genie. It is, after all, five-thirty in the morning and time for him to relieve Mel and take over the hapless sticks. Simultaneously, Tom and Mel reach for the general alarm. Tom raises its red plastic cap. Mel throws the switch.

Every crewman is on the deck anyway, at the changing of the watch. The gap between the grounded vessel and the two loose barges widens. Fifteen feet. Twenty feet. There may be a chance to catch a line. Doug Gable, who has disappeared from the main deck, reappears with a bright-white brand-new line, a large eye at one end. Coils in one hand, eye in the other, he heaves the line, attempting to lasso a steel, sausage-shaped cavel on the barge. He has time only for the one throw. The line falls into the water. The barges drift farther away.

Mel, inspired, reverses the throttle of the port-side engine and gives it full power. The reversed wheel wash drives a No. 10 rapid upstream at the side of the *Billy Joe* and into the escaping barges. Slowly, magically, the runaway barges forget New Orleans, go back upstream, and return exactly to their original positions in the port string. Mel says, "Those barges, when they hit, looked rared up — you know, pushed up in the water. Anybody says they never ran aground on the Illinois River it's because they never ran the Illinois River."

In the space of a few minutes, Rick Walker, second mate, lays twenty feet of frayed and broken wing wire across a wire cutter and trims it back with a sledgehammer. He picks up the intact new end, curls four feet of it into a new eye, splices it, and leaves a foot of protruding tail. He lays the new eye over a cavel on the stern port-string barge. The additional wire has come off a winch like fishing line off a reel. Rick with steel cable can make loops like an angler. The winch tightens the new wing wire. Up the tow, Rick and others replace the three fore-and-aft wires and four breast wires that also broke. The port lead barge remains stucker than a postage stamp. Knocking keepers off pelican hooks with sledgehammers, deckhands detach the port lead barge so that Tom will be able to back up the rest of the tow and, with a lock line, yank the port lead barge free.

"There's one aground every day up here," Tom says. "It's not a deep river. If you can't back it off, you have to take the barges apart and dig it off. All it costs is time."

Mel, turning at the head of the stairs, has a parting word for me. He says, "When you write all this down, my name is Tom Armstrong."

ROBERT YOUNG PELTON

# Into the Land of bin Laden

FROM *National Geographic Adventure*

SOMEWHERE ON THE BORDER between Afghanistan and Pakistan, a thunderous *whup, whup, whup* is the soundtrack to a graceful, intertwining aerial ballet above my head on a cold December morning. Two Huey helicopters are circling a hilltop five hundred yards to the east. They zoom in close enough to my perch that I can smell their turbine exhaust and clearly make out a bug-helmeted door gunner gripping his minigun.

The flat, deep sound echoes off the mountains as one Huey prepares to land, feeling for the ground as if hesitant to touch down in this hostile place. The other helicopter dives and swoops behind the hills like an angry hawk, looking for attackers. On each hilltop surrounding the base is a sentry post hastily built of Hescos — four-by-four-by-five-foot-high gray cardboard-and-wire-mesh containers filled with gravel. On top of these are sloppily stacked sandbags and a clutter of ammunition tins; silver loops of concertina wire add a touch of paranoid sparkle. At a distance these makeshift citadels have the look of Crusader castles.

From my own redoubt atop a steep cliff, I overlook a wide valley across the barrel of a battered antiaircraft gun aimed toward Pakistan. Below sits an unnamed armed outpost, a mud fort manned by Special Forces and Afghan troops and unmarked on any official map. Its loaded weapons are pointed at an ally nation; its vehicles and gear are left packed for a hasty departure.

"Your Americans!" says the smiling Afghan soldier who's manning the post alongside me, pointing to the arriving choppers. Outfitted in U.S. Army–style fatigues and blue-tinted fly sunglasses, he is one of about forty hired guns — "campaigns" — at this base, each of whom makes a healthy $150 a month. The tiny base beneath us watches over a well-known mountain pass between the Pakistani city of Miram Shah and its Afghan neighbor, Khost. Between them lies the Durand Line, the official boundary between the two countries that was established by the British in the nineteenth century and has been ignored ever since.

There are four of these quickly thrown-together bases along this border, the front line of the war on al Qaeda. Miram Shah was a famous supply and R&R base for *mujahidin* rebels who fought against the Soviet occupation in the 1980s and remains a major smuggling center. The mountainous Pashtun tribal areas between Khost and the northern Pakistani city of Peshawar are also where the U.S. military, the Pakistan government, and others believe Osama bin Laden is hiding. This is the region where bin Laden worked and fought with the *muj* in the eighties. This is where he helped build the massive cave system at Tora Bora. This is where coordinated attacks against Afghan and American forces continue at their highest rates. Bin Laden is even believed to have used the area around Khost as the backdrop in his videos sent out to threaten the Western world.

For all the secrecy and danger at the front, however, the base was not hard to locate or to reach. Informants in Khost, easy to spot with their $800 Thuraya satellite phones and eager American slang, gave us directions. The bearded Afghan commander of this firebase seemed unsurprised to see an unarmed American show up at his front gate in a battered yellow taxi.

I am back in Afghanistan almost two years to the day after the start of the war in late 2001. Back then, my host was Northern Alliance general Abdul Rashid Dostum. I had traveled alongside a covert American Special Forces team who, it could be said, turned the tide of the war. I was at Qala Jangi when the famous Taliban prisoner uprising occurred, when John Walker Lindh was captured, and when the first American combat casualty of the war turned out to be a CIA paramilitary, Johnny "Mike" Spann. At the time of my five-week visit this winter, the U.S. military had just kicked off Operation Avalanche, which will send some two thousand troops and hundreds of helicopter sorties into the border area around Khost. Their goal is to eliminate both the resurgent remnants of the Taliban (the indigenous radical group that took over the country in the mid-1990s) and the loose network of foreign, mostly Arab, extremists known collectively as al Qaeda. In 2001 Dostum and the Regulators, as my companions in the Special Forces unit dubbed themselves, were practically brothers-in-arms by the end of their campaign. But two years is a long time, especially in this part of the world, and I was anxious to see how Afghanistan's hosts were getting along with their American guests.

What I quickly learned was that in the borderland, the enemy has returned in force and the Americans and Afghans are attacked and ambushed on a regular basis. The United States has already abandoned two of its four border outposts, those in nearby Lwarra and Shinkai. The others, soldiers here tell me, come under increasingly frequent attack and occasionally change hands between the Afghans, the Taliban, al Qaeda, and the Americans.

The attacks come from the Pakistan side and almost always happen at night. The Afghan regulars say that the fiercest begin with rockets, followed by rocket-propelled grenades, and finally three-wave assaults: one waiting to advance, one lying down to fire, and one advancing to repeat the process. Often, the mystery attackers take the base from the Afghans for a few hours, only to be chased out by arriving American air support or daylight. The nearby border-patrol base at Shinkai came under fierce attack in August. When the sun came up, the rudimentary base was surrounded by more than twenty dead bodies, their identities a mystery. One Afghan fighter insisted that the attackers couldn't possibly have been Islamic fundamentalists. "The bodies were already rotting the next day," he told me. "We could smell alcohol. They had been drinking cheap wine."

As I scan the area through my binoculars from my clifftop aerie, to the right I can see rolling foothills, steep valleys, and widely spaced scrub pine trees. Off to the left, in the foreground, is a mountain from which my Afghan hosts say the frequent rocket attacks have been coming. Far below us on the dusty road, colorful and overloaded *jinga* trucks clank and groan as they bring goods from Pakistan into Afghanistan. Or to be more accurate, toward Afghanistan. One reason that bin Laden and former Taliban leader Mullah Mohammad Omar are still at large is that things can get fuzzy in the Pashtun borderlands. The U.S. military denies that any of these bases along the Durand Line, armed by Afghans and utilized by American forces, are situated outside of Afghan territory. Maybe my GPS is acting up, though. It indicates that I'm standing eight kilometers inside Pakistan.

At the landing area, the two Hueys depart, leaving a group of silver-haired officers, each wearing a bulletproof vest and a pistol. Driving toward the base are two armored tan Humvees, a beige camouflage pickup with an orange marker panel on top, and a brown-and-green-camo Land Rover to transport the VIPs, all followed by a convoy of Toyota pickup trucks overflowing with Afghan troops who wave and show off their heavy weapons and their new sand goggles, shooting gloves, and sunglasses.

I walk over from my perch and casually begin talking to the assembled American soldiers guarding the landing area. This looks like part of Task Force 121, an elite group drawn from U.S. Army Special Forces, Delta Force, Navy SEALs, and CIA paramilitaries and ordered to hunt for "high-value targets." (The group's existence — and ability to operate inside of countries, like Pakistan, where conventional U.S. forces are not stationed — was a closely held secret until the *New York Times* reported its existence in November.) The group here comprises a sergeant from the U.S. Army's 20th Special Forces Group, a unit of army reservists shipped in from Alabama, a young Air Force Combat Controller, and an unshaven American in civilian clothes: khakis, photographer's vest, hiking boots. He wears Oakley shades and keeps a finger-forward grip on a battered AK-47 — an unusual weapon for an American, even in this neck of the woods, and the mark of a contractor rather than a soldier. He quickly leaves after the convoy disappears.

I strike up a conversation with a young sergeant. He has a wispy beard, and his M4 rifle has been spray-painted brown and tan. He seems a little rattled by the recent attacks in the area. "We got hit pretty bad a few weeks ago," he tells me, adjusting his dirty Jack Daniels cap. "Six guys in our unit got Purple Hearts. [Our air support] can't chase them all the way back into Pakistan. So we just wait up here to get hit again."

He points to a spot a little more than a mile away. "They fire rockets right from that hill on the Pak side. The joke is we meet with the Pak officials every month right on the border. They smile, we smile, they B.S. us, and we B.S. them. Then they watch us get attacked without lifting a finger."

I ask him if the men who attacked him were Taliban, Pakistanis, or Arabs. He looks up at me and squints in the sun and spits.

"I have no idea who we are fighting."

In the chaos of the ground war in 2001, having a go-between like General Dostum had been invaluable. He kept me informed and, on more than one occasion, kept me alive. On this visit, I knew that if I was going to understand the situation in the Taliban-friendly borderlands, I needed the support of a local potentate. The word in Kabul was that 120 members of the Pashtun leadership were holding a meeting in a compound outside of Gardez, a few hours south of the capital. The meeting had been called to discuss the new national constitution and why most of them had been left out of the ratification process.

It is there, during a break between the endless discussions, that I was introduced to a man everyone calls Hajji, who had been railing at the group about the need for the king (how they describe the nation's ruler) to be a Muslim and married to an Afghan and for Pashtu to be the official language of the new nation. In Pashtun greetings, the palms-out, half-lean-forward air kiss is for strangers, and the big bear hug and double buss is reserved for good friends. Hajji gives me the air kiss and holds my hand while he talks to me. The fifty-something elder from the Khost area, with his big white beard, large turban, and ready smile, does not stand out from the others, but he seems to command a special respect from them. Hajji is well known from his days as a *mujahidin* commander fighting the Russians and, before that, as a cross-border trucking czar and drug smuggler. He was also a supporter of the Taliban back when they were better known for crushing warlords than for hosting al Qaeda. He's now retired but remains a man who can be called upon to resolve critical problems and defend the weak. Without hesitation he invites me to stay at his home for a week, on the condition that I not reveal its exact location or his full name.

I am surprised that we drive to his home in a beat-up Toyota hatchback with Dubai plates. His son is behind the wheel. "Only NGOs and the Americans drive big cars around here," Hajji says. "I keep my Land Cruiser in the garage." Hajji sits in the front seat, carefully telling his son which routes to take and which to avoid. "Mines," he explains. When we pass the shrine of *shaheeds* (Taliban martyrs), Hajji holds his palms up in prayer. Martyrdom is a powerful force here; the Taliban and the Arabs who have died in this war and the war against the Russians are revered even by their enemies.

Afghan society is structured along ethnic lines and divided into tribes. These tribes are led by elders, whose power comes from consensus among the members of the tribe. It is democracy at its simplest, with a dash of feudalism. The elders do not lead solely by dictate but rather by suggestion. They are called upon to meet and make decisions on legal, family, property, and other disputes. To disagree or ignore the advice or decision of an elder is to risk confrontation and ostracism. Even Afghanistan's interim president, Hamid Karzai, cannot order or demand something from an elder, for if his request is refused, he has no recourse and thus loses face. In the Pashtun regions, the elders typically accommodated the Taliban. Recent rumors from the area suggest that bin Laden still travels between Gardez and Khost, the historical center of Taliban and foreign *jihadi* strength.

A measure of Hajji's importance is that he lives in one of the largest compounds in the Gardez area. Each of the four walls is more than nine hundred feet long and thirty feet high. (He is known as Hajji in honor of his having made the pilgrimage to Mecca. Ironically, "Hajji" is also an all-purpose derogatory term used by American soldiers to refer to local Afghans.) The compound sits on a barren plain just outside of town under the dramatic backdrop of the Taliban-infested mountains around the U.S. firebase at Gardez. In the mountains to the south is the deadly Shahikot valley, the location of March 2002's Operation Anaconda in which eight American servicemen died trying to dislodge al Qaeda holdouts. Beyond that is the mountain redoubt of Zawar Kili, another massive cave system built by bin Laden in the 1980s to defend against the Russians. To the north and east are poppy fields.

Inside the compound is a guest house and beyond that two more walled areas, one for Hajji's family and the other for his crops. His home is designed for maximum defensibility. Even the outside toilet, a long walk up a rickety ladder, has three gun ports. Each corner of the compound has a large square tower for defense, and every section is fully stocked with weapons and ammunition. The towers used to have antiaircraft guns, Hajji tells me, but he removed them out of fear of being bombed by the Americans.

Hajji and I immediately fell into a thrice-daily pattern of a long meal served on the floor, followed by endless cups of green tea and hours of conversation through a translator. The first night we engaged in small talk. His stance was neutral. Yes, he supported the Americans, he said, even though he still seemed to harbor resentment over something that happened in 2001; he wouldn't specify what it was. Yes, he thought the Taliban were finished. The second night we discussed more detailed concerns: There is violence here, no government, only one school but no teachers. By the third night, as the remains of dinner were picked up and tea was poured, Hajji was more forthcoming. I asked him if the reports of the Taliban's return to the area were true.

"Yes, they come here. Usually at night. They ask for food or shelter. They do not stay long, and we do not ask them where they are going. In some cases they intimidate people, and in other cases they pay. But they seem to know who to talk to. In every group of twenty or so Taliban, there are about four or five Arabs. They need to be with the Afghans because they do not know the way and they do not speak the language."

Hajji has enough stature to speak his mind about the Taliban, but even he sees the need to be cautious when discussing the Arabs. "People do not like the Arabs here, because they are arrogant and act superior to the Afghans." He laughs. "We like to say they are more interested in taking videos than in fighting."

It is clear that al Qaeda is still here and still intimidates. Back at the tribal meeting before Hajji invited me to stay with him, I asked to stay with another prominent elder from the border region, and the long-bearded man replied, "You are welcome to stay, but the Arabs will leave a letter at my door that unless you leave the next day, they will kill me and my family." I thanked him for his offer and accepted Hajji's invitation.

"During the *jihad* against the Russians, there were people in every village who would cook food and help us," Hajji says. "No one ever worried about being betrayed or discovered. No one even posted sentries. Now these same people are scared when they see the Talibs or the Arabs. The Arabs have to use sat phones to communicate and sneak into villages at 3 A.M., usually leaving before light the next day."

Hajji says he first met bin Laden in the 1980s, when the wealthy young Saudi was helping the *mujahidin* from the Pakistani town of Peshawar. Pakistan's secret service (Inter-Services Intelligence, or ISI) had given Hajji three truckloads of rockets but no way to transport them back to Afghanistan. "What was I going to do with three truckloads of rockets? The ISI told us that Osama had an office near the University of Peshawar and to go and ask him for help.

"The odd thing about Osama was that he used to work only on Fridays. We went to his office and filled out an application so that he would pay for the camels and mules. They wanted to know things like how much the rockets weighed. I didn't know how much the rockets weighed." Since Hajji wasn't with one of the Saudi-backed *mujahidin* commanders, bin Laden said he couldn't help them and sent them on their way.

What does he think of bin Laden now?

He pauses as he sips his tea. "I never thought that bin Laden would turn into something like this. I just thought he was someone helping the *mujahidin*."

Is bin Laden winning in Afghanistan?

"I don't think Osama will succeed. The Afghans are tired of migrating and fighting."

Where does he think bin Laden is?

"Chitral would be the most likely place." Chitral is a valley town on the Pakistani side of the border. "That is where people traditionally hide from those who seek them. There is little movement there in the winter. The airplanes don't work well that high up, and you will know when people are coming. Bin Laden knows the tribal areas very well, and the tribes know him very well." His answer makes sense but doesn't quite ring true somehow. Bin Laden's Pakistani biographer recently told CNN that he believes bin Laden is roaming southeast Afghanistan and that his latest videotape was shot near Gardez. My guess is that Hajji probably has a pretty good idea where bin Laden is but knows that it would be dangerous for an Afghan to be known to possess such information. A close friend of his was sent to Guantanamo Bay for knowing the same people that Hajji knows.

What about Mullah Omar?

"Mullah Omar was in Miram Shah during Ramadan and has now moved to Quetta [a Pakistani border city] for the winter." This time his tone is matter-of-fact. He doesn't say how he knows this, but his guess coincides with Karzai's statements that Omar and other senior Taliban have been spotted at prayers in Quetta, long a bastion of Taliban support.

Despite having worked with the Taliban, Hajji has little good to say about their reign in Afghanistan.

"I met many times with Mullah Omar and all the other Taliban commanders. They were not educated men. They were not even good Muslims. The Taliban took all the prostitutes to Kandahar, and the Arabs were all screwing around. In time, they considered themselves separate from the people. To them a foot soldier was more trustworthy than a tribal elder."

What does he think of the Taliban now?

"There are two categories of Taliban: the *jihadis,* who want martyrdom, and the people who fight for money."

Hajji places himself in neither category.

"The Taliban are not Pashtun. We have dancing, we sing, we make decisions in *jirgas* [traditional voting councils]." The Taliban, Hajji says, are entranced by Wahabis, the Saudi-backed religious extremists. "Afghans do not like Wahabis. The Taliban relied on other people and lost touch with the Afghan people. That is why, in the end, the Taliban could never be governors, only occupiers."

What about the Americans?

"I can guarantee you the Americans will not succeed. They rely on people they pay money to. Now they are surrounded by people who want money. They have turned away from the tribal elders and made bad friends."

I ask him which ruler he would choose if he had to: the corrupt Taliban or the American-backed Karzai.

"I try not to involve myself with these things," he says with disgust. It is clear neither has his full support, perhaps because both seem to view the role of tribal elders as increasingly irrelevant under the new system.

From the early morning until late into the night, the sky above the compound is filled with Apaches, Blackhawks, Chinooks, B-1B bombers, and jet fighters. At night, after our talks, I leave the warm, damp guest house and climb up the rough-hewn ladder to the walls. Above me, stars are sprayed across the sky. I listen to muffled booms and automatic gunfire. I watch the blue-gas triangles of afterburners and listen to the sound of blacked-out helicopters ferrying troops. In the crisp, frosty mornings, the sky is etched with contrails from bombers; low-flying helicopters return from missions, and, later in the day, unmanned Predators whistle through the sky.

One day while driving around on a tour of Gardez, Hajji tells me that he is in the midst of mediating a dispute. A widow was found in her room with a man. The man was shot dead by members of her family, and the woman sought shelter in a house of a neighbor. The widow's family wants her returned so that she can be stoned to death and has informed the family giving her refuge that they have forty days to turn her over. How this will be resolved is unclear, but he is certain she will pay with her life. Hajji shows me the spot already chosen for her stoning.

In an attempt to explain bin Laden's ability to hide in this region, much has been written about the Pashtun code of hospitality, sanctuary, and revenge. *Melmastia* is automatic hospitality shown to visitors without expectation of reward; *nanawatey* is the obligation to provide sanctuary to those who seek it, even at the risk of one's own life; and *badal* is the righting of wrongs, regardless of how much time has passed. Hajji insists on the necessity of a system in which the entire family and tribe takes responsibility for the act of one person, even if that requires stoning one's own widowed daughter for promiscuity. The goal is to resolve disputes with finality and allow the tribes or families to coexist peacefully once the sentence has been carried out or reparations paid. Penalties, he says, can be as simple as fines or as drastic as death, but justice must be done.

Later, at the compound, lit by the yellow glow of a propane light, Hajji explains to me how one tribe or group can sometimes take over or resolve another group's blood feud. When an injustice is done and a tribe is weak, he says, another tribe or elder may take up their feud. The weaker tribe is then indebted to the stronger one. This is a natural way to build power. Hajji says this explains not only how the Taliban are indebted to bin Laden but also why they insist on revenge at all costs.

In the Pashtun worldview, a wrong that has been done to one

person has been committed against an entire tribe. Hajji cites as an example an American bombing raid that happened nearby a few days ago, in which nine children were killed.

"When will this wrong be righted?" he asks.

I grow to like Hajji, and he treats me like a son. He insists that I sit on his right-hand side. He urges me to eat the best part of the sheep and won't clear the vinyl eating mat until I have eaten to his satisfaction. He makes sure I sit on the warmest part of the floor. He pesters me to grow my beard out and tugs at it every day as if that will speed the process.

That night, Hajji tells me a story that he had been reluctant to share. In December 2001, as it became obvious that al Qaeda and the Taliban were truly beaten, Hajji and eighty other tribal elders headed off toward Kabul to meet with Karzai, who had returned to Afghanistan as interim prime minister. En route they were stopped by the warlord Pacha Khan Zadran, who refused to let them pass. "Khan is a simple man, a former truck driver who was working with the Americans then. He told us that we could not go to Kabul, because Karzai is not the legitimate king of Afghanistan. We knew we couldn't get by him, so we turned around and chose another route, one we knew from the *mujahidin* days," he says. "We called the U.S. embassy in Islamabad [Pakistan's capital] and the UN and told them that we were driving on this road and not to bomb us.

"That night we could not get over a mountain pass, so we turned around. Then I heard jets. They hit the trucks behind me first, and I ran as fast as I could."

The bombing began at around 9 P.M. and continued until four the next morning. Eleven elders were killed and twenty others wounded. Some forty Afghans in surrounding villages were also killed. Hajji, however, seems most concerned about having lost a pickup truck in the bombing.

"The Americans continue to search our women, bomb our houses, and kill our children. Even Karzai said they were wrong and promised to replace my pickup. But nothing has been done." Hajji does not seem to be angry, just stating fact.

"There is a saying the Pashtuns have that if you take your revenge in a hundred years, you are rushing things."

Hajji looks upward in an exaggerated supplication to heaven, then lowers his gaze straight at me. "Now God has sent an American to me so that I can trade him for a new pickup truck." He laughs with a goofy, rasping laugh, but I check his face carefully to make sure it was a joke.

The next morning, Hajji picks a driver to take me to the "secret" base by sending his oldest son to the taxi stand. He tells his son to make sure the driver is a member of their own Ahmadzai tribe. Out in the countryside, that is more important than a truckful of armed guards, for if someone harms him or his passengers, they will have to deal with Hajji and anyone else he brings into the blood feud. His instructions to the young driver are to "go where he goes and never leave." He also sends for a local doctor, someone educated who speaks English, to act as my interpreter and guide. A few hours later, our tiny crew sets off in a battered yellow taxi. The stereo blared Hindi pop songs, and the road dust swirled around our heads as we drove into Taliban territory. The first thing my driver tells me is how he made a lot of money driving Arabs escaping from Gardez to Khost after the war. He drove the highway with his tiny Toyota Corolla wagon loaded with the Arabs and their families, weaving around burning Hilux pickup trucks, ripped corpses, and craters. The Americans would attack trucks and Land Cruisers but let taxis go through. It is no coincidence that when Afghan eyewitnesses saw bin Laden leave Jalalabad in a convoy of fighters in December 2001, he was riding in a small white Corolla hatchback.

As we begin to climb toward the Shahikot mountains, I'm told that we are officially in Taliban territory. "The fighters will watch from the mountains, and if they see a suspicious vehicle, they will stop it or attack it," my driver tells me. This is the same area the Taliban stopped a *Christian Science Monitor* reporter's car and beat the off-duty driver when they discovered there was no journalist inside to be kidnapped. Thankfully, our well-worn taxi is just as invisible to the Taliban as it was to the Americans.

After cooling my heels for a couple of hours at the American outpost's landing area, waiting for the officers to depart, I once again bump into the American with the AK-47 — the Contractor, as I'll call him. He starts off not with a greeting but with a warning. "They're not gonna let you cross into Pakistan."

I ask him who "they" are.

"T.F." is his curt reply. Task Force.

Apparently, some quick videotaping I did earlier has not gone over well. "You've filmed their base and vehicles. If the bad guys catch you across the border, they will use it to hit this place."

He asks how I got here without getting attacked. "Did you see those antennas on all four corners of that pickup truck?" he says, pointing to one of his vehicles. "Those are jammers. People around here bury antitank mines and then detonate them with cell phones or car-alarm triggers. They hire kids to sit at the side of the road and wait for Americans. They tried to kill Musharraf yesterday, and his jamming system was the only thing that saved him.

"Delta can't figure how you got here in one piece. I am sure they are looking you up right now." He smiles, then walks off.

I head down to the main firebase. The once friendly Afghan commander quickly approaches. "You came here to take pictures," he says. "You have enough pictures, now please go." His orders are to get me off this hill and going in the opposite direction of Pakistan. Then, in a typical Afghan gesture, he asks me to join him for lunch before leaving.

The Contractor reappears as I am packing to leave and inquires about my destination. I tell him I've been staying in Gardez with Hajji and invite him to join me. The opportunity to go through Taliban-friendly territory obviously intrigues him. He tosses his battered mountaineering backpack into the ancient taxi. We start to head back toward Khost, but first I insist we stop at a small market a few miles from the base. Sixty dollars turns my new American friend into a rough facsimile of a bearded farmer, complete with wool hat, waistcoat, and light blue *salwar kameez* tunic. Satisfied we both look like idiots — but Afghan-looking idiots — we take off.

As we head into the series of switchbacks that mark the start of the mountains, the Contractor starts to loosen up. Despite his initial bluster, he is not used to being so exposed, so out in the open. As we come up on various Taliban checkpoints, he drills me on how to evacuate the car from the same side, how to keep a pistol under my leg, and how the windshield will deflect rounds. We have a long time to talk on the ride, bouncing and rattling down the potholed dirt roads. He agrees to answer some questions about his work but makes clear that he won't talk about anything that might harm his mission and asks that neither he nor his home base be identified. I agree.

"These days the Agency has plenty of money, so it's easier just to hire us than train new people," he says. He is one of about a hundred paramilitaries operating along the border. "There are the soldier-of-fortune, beer-bellied, raucous, ring-wearing types you see in town. Then there's us, the guys who are into fitness, in their late twenties to late forties." Most of the operators are "sheep dipped," he says, serving in some official capacity to provide a plausible military or civilian cover but actually working "black ops," top-secret operations that are never revealed in their military CV.

"Working in Afghanistan is pretty easy," he says. "I was contracted at about $150K a year. You sign up, train up, and fly in. Most of the operators go into Tashkent [in neighboring Uzbekistan] via commercial and then to Kabul on a military flight. You land there, and they pick you up in a truck and check you in at the hotel. Nobody asks any questions. You don't show ID except for the helo ride to the base.

"They divide you into teams. 'Victory' are the security guys; 'Eagle' are the hunter-killers; 'Wolf' do escorts and surveillance; and 'Viper' is the rapid-response team for case officers who get into trouble. You check in, get a couple days in town, and then talk to the chief of base. You get your walking papers and fly out to Khost, Ghazni, Kandahar, or wherever you're going." The going wage for most contractors, he says, is $1,000 to $1,250 a day, slightly better than in Iraq. Three months is the usual tour of duty. "People get freaky if you leave them out here more than ninety days."

Our driver and interpreter, whom I've dubbed "Doc," stare straight ahead, looking for freshly disturbed potholes, where the Taliban like to hide remote-detonated mines. I've told them that the Contractor is my cameraman, and he is enjoying his undercover role as sidekick. He uses his GPS to mark checkpoints and track the road as we travel up into higher altitudes. The checkpoints, manned by Taliban and warlords' foot soldiers, are simply speed bumps followed by armed men who stare into the front of the taxi. My driver boldly waves them off and keeps going. I try to look as Pashtun as a blue-eyed *feringhi*, or foreigner, can. I tuck my glasses in my pocket, pulling my dirty brown blanket tightly around my face and staring impassively out the front window. With his heavy beard, the Contractor looks more like an Afghan than I ever will. We somehow easily pass through four more checkpoints where both trucks and passenger vehicles are being stopped and emptied.

The first base the Contractor was assigned to, he tells me, was set up in the most remote area that could be resupplied by helicopter. "They flew us in dark on a nighttime resupply mission on a CIA Russian helo — a bird that wouldn't say 'Here come the Americans.'" A four-truck convoy came out to meet them. The new crew hopped off, the old crew hopped on, and the helicopter was gone.

"When I first saw the terrain through the NVGs [night-vision goggles], all I could think of was the surface of the moon. There was nothing but stars, rocks, and a medieval mud fort in the distance. Inside there is this big bearded guy with a Western hat, warming himself over a diesel fire in a fifty-gallon drum. He sees us, laughs this crazy laugh, with his face lit by the fire, and yells out, 'Gentlemen, welcome to the edge of the empire!' Man, I got the crazies when I heard that."

Some of the men in Task Force, the Contractor says, are recent ex-military brought in through the trusted old-boy networks, but most are Special Forces, Delta, and members of the elite SEAL Team Six, recruited in advance of discharge. "The line between traditional military and covert work is blurring. People make fun of the Agency, but all the Special Forces guys are trying to work there. You get whatever you need, you don't get messed with, you have your own chain of command, and you don't answer to the local military commander. You travel on your own passport using a tourist visa."

The hunt for bin Laden, he says, is not like the hunt for Saddam, with thousands of troops looking under every carpet and behind every tree. Even the Pakistanis can't operate in the tribal areas without serious backlash.

"Our job is to shake the apple tree," the Contractor says. "We aren't hunting bin Laden from the top. Our strategy is to focus on the little guys. Just like how they do drug busts in the States. Put the heat on the runners and little guys until they get nervous and start contacting higher. Then we intercept their calls and the hunt begins. We are just hired killers. Guns with legs."

The Taliban, he says, aren't a priority. "Mullah Omar is not an issue for the U.S. government. We are looking for al Qaeda, or whatever you want to call al Qaeda. These days that's pretty much shorthand for a foreign national — an Arab, Pakistani, or whatever. We are looking for people connected to bin Laden.

"We ask simple questions like, Where do they sleep at night? Once we can find where they sleep, we can monitor them. When we find the house, we can pick up any electronic communications and send them directly to Langley, [British intelligence in] Cheltenham, or Washington.

"Once you find their base, you don't want to hit 'em; you let 'em talk and use that intel to roll up the lower-level people. We can do voiceprint on them and even know who they are talking to if that person is in the database. If they set up a meeting or give us a GPS location, somebody might get hit the next day. If they still don't contact higher-ups, then you snatch another guy or make him disappear. You do that a couple of times and they will get nervous."

The Contractor adjusts his rust-colored wool hat and admires his Afghan look in the mirror. Doc, I notice, has been listening intently.

"The trouble is that we are doing this inside Pakistan," he says. "That's why you need a contractor. Our government can say that 'we' are not going into Pakistan. But you can be damn sure that white boys are going into Pakistan and shooting bad guys."

He shifts his AK, then smiles. "These days the Agency is looking for Mormons and Born Agains. People with a lot of patriotism and the need to do good. At least we start that way." Most of the contractors at his base spend their downtime working out, running sprints between the helicopter pad and back, and doing triceps presses with big rocks.

"We like to stay in shape. When you're in combat, you want to make sure you're using everything you got. You want to make sure you take a few guys with you even if you have only your bare hands. Most of us are into steroids big-time. D-balls [Dianabol] to bulk you up and Sustanon to help you maintain what you gained. The doctors turn a blind eye to it. We get the stuff across the border in Pakistan. When you see guys bulked up, you know what they are on. We keep control of it, though.

"I don't drink, smoke, or eat crap," he says, smiling. "My only weaknesses? Pepsi and women."

*

Hajji welcomes me with the bear hug and double buss of a prodigal son. He quickly senses that my friend is much more than a cameraman — in addition to carrying an AK and Oakleys, the Contractor has a habit of pacing twenty yards back and forth as if doing a security sweep, and he scans every room he enters for hostile elements. But since the Contractor is my friend, he is welcomed without question.

At dinner, Hajji wants to know all about my trip. He pushes food directly in front of the Contractor: choice cuts of greasy mutton with fresh bread and a dish — specially prepared by Hajji's wife for the guests — of what seems to be curdled milk with oil poured into it. The new guest keeps his arms folded and declines, mumbling, "Gotta get to 10 percent body fat." Hajji makes several attempts before giving up, stares hard at the Contractor, then looks at me. "Just pretend to eat something and compliment the food," I mutter. He doesn't take the advice. The Contractor frequently stands up in the middle of the hours-long meal, making excuses about having to shoot some video. When he leaves the room for good, Hajji turns to me and asks, through the interpreter, "What's wrong with your friend?"

The scene is repeated at each breakfast, lunch, and dinner for three days. The Contractor mostly stays silent. He appears genuinely interested in the conversation but doesn't seem to know how to interact with Afghans who aren't informers. We are usually joined by two of Hajji's sons and an ever changing parade of locals who've come to ask favors from the elder. Hajji's brother visits with his three-year-old grandson and occasionally asks me to come by and try to fix his satellite phone. The Contractor refuses to eat even a grain of rice, and I come to dread Hajji's stonefaced looks in my direction. Hajji even tries shopping for us himself, apologizing for not having eggs at one breakfast because it is too cold for the chickens to lay. The Contractor, meanwhile, gets by on Atkins Bars and sips of bottled water, pulled from his pack at daybreak and before bedtime.

Hajji adamantly wants his opinion of the recent bombings to reach someone of authority inside the American forts. Finally, on the third day, he breaks out of Pashtun protocol and tells the Contractor the jist of what he has already told me about the increasing frustration that the tribal elders have with the Americans. He has received word that a family of eight has been found dead in an abandoned house in the nearby town of Seyyed Karam. How he knows the details of their deaths so soon is a mystery to me.

"A local thug lived there for eighteen years and has been threatening to rocket the meeting in Kabul," Hajji tells us. "An informer called the Americans, but by the time the air attack took place, the man was long gone. Instead another man and his family were hiding out in the house because the man had killed someone in a property dispute. He, his wife, and his six children were found buried under a wall."

Hajji explains that the people in town are upset. Not about the fugitive, since this was perceived as an odd form of justice, but for the man's innocent wife and children, who had no quarrel with the Americans or townspeople.

"This man could have been arrested with a minimum of violence, but the Americans chose to attack the house with aircraft and weapons designed to destroy tanks."

What's going on is clear to Hajji. "The informers are making money from both sides." The Contractor says he understands, and the meal ends in silence.

After breakfast I thank Hajji for his hospitality. He talks to me like a clucking mother hen, pushing me to get a move on and to stop messing around with my camera. He is in a hurry to have us go in case we are spotted outside of his compound. Across the horizon, the rotors of Blackhawks slice through the crisp morning air. As we pack up, I don't bother to relay Hajji's repeated joke about keeping one American to exchange for his lost pickup truck. I don't think the Contractor would find it funny.

On our way back toward the border, the Contractor wants to stop in at another base and talk to someone from OGA, or "other government agencies," a euphemistic term used to describe high-level clandestine operators from the CIA, FBI, and other groups that don't fit into the traditional military structure. He seems eager to pass along Hajji's complaints about the Americans' use of excessive force and reliance on double-dealing snitches. I stay outside.

He emerges shaking his head. "Seems the OGA guy wouldn't even get off his cot to say hi. He just sent his local peon to say he already had the intel."

The Contractor holds up a stack of dirty Pakistani rupees. "The puke said thanks and here are some rupees for the cab ride." He shakes his head. "Company policy is to always give something to someone bringing intel."

Looking at the pile of grubby notes, he shakes his head. "That's f——d, man."

To be fair, the idea that an armed American civilian would just stroll into a firebase with relevant information about the Taliban might give any official pause; also, I assume OGAs prefer to work only with established intelligence sources. But it is clear that being on the other end of a wad of dirty rupees ticks off the Contractor.

"A while back, Rumsfeld said we might be creating more enemies than we are killing," he says, getting back into the car. "Well, duh. Before last summer, we had Yale graduates hiding in hotels, using the phone to meet informants inside bazaars. Their idea of intelligence work was posing as a cell phone engineer, setting up meetings, and handing informants five hundred bucks every time they handed over information. Good or bad."

The lack of good relations with the local population compounded the security problems, he says. "When you do a *madrasah* hit" — that is, a raid on an Islamic secondary school — "the locals get pissed. You don't always find bad guys, but everyone gets slammed to the ground, zip-tied, bagged, and tagged. You forget to give them a hundred bucks at the door and they'll swear to get you. They will, too. The next time the Americans are on patrol in their Dumbvees, they are set up."

But he insists things are improving. "Now we want to get inside the heads of the people we are dealing with. We want a softer, more personal relationship, instead of basing the transaction on money. Just like when you meet with people. People trust you because they like you, not because you pay them."

At the end of January 2004, the American general in charge of operations in Afghanistan declared that bin Laden would be captured this year. Newspapers published an outline for a major spring offensive that would include sending U.S. troops into the mountainous borderlands of Afghanistan and Pakistan. President Musharraf immediately responded by saying that U.S. troops were not welcome in Pakistan.

"For some reason Pakistan is still like the Catholic Church, where you have sanctuary," the Contractor tells me. "The bad guys are inside Pakistan using Pakistani protection to attack Americans inside Afghanistan and then running back knowing they won't be chased. Hopefully, things will change."

For now, though, covert operations continue and Task Force looks for excuses to cross the border, the Contractor says. An American civilian operating inside Pakistan could need help, which gives the U.S. military a reason to cross the border in support, hot pursuit, or just to call in mortar and air fire on nebulous "bad guys."

This new war depends on men, like the Contractor, willing to work and fight in a shadowland largely beyond the reach of U.S. power. I ask him if there's an extraction plan if a mission in Pakistan gets messy. "The extraction plan is that once you are across the border, you are on your own. There is no uplift. You are screwed if things go wrong." But that vulnerability is essential to the role of a contractor. "You are not in the federal system or in the military system," he says. "You are deniable, disposable, and deletable."

That independence — and the secrecy that goes with it — is part of the Contractor's code. And, as far as he is concerned, it should remain inviolate even in death. "We have lost two guys set up and ambushed," he says. "We lost a case officer in a training accident. That, along with Spann getting killed in the middle of an interrogation, adds up to four CIA operators killed in this war." Traditionally, the CIA does not disclose an operative's connection to the Agency, even if he is killed. But in those four cases, the Agency released the men's identities to the public, an action the Contractor sees as a breach of faith even if it means the men are honored as heroes.

"This is a war where terrorists have global reach," he says. When the identities of operatives are disclosed, "it exposes the tradecraft and leaves the wives and families exposed." While willing to live and even die according to the harsh code of his tribe, the Contractor now finds himself embittered at seeing that code compromised.

The Contractor asks me to leave him off a short distance from his base. He doesn't want to have to explain what he was doing driving around in Taliban territory in a taxicab. I say goodbye to him near his little mud fort at the edge of the empire and carry on in my little yellow taxi.

DAVID QUAMMEN

# West Highland Peace Trek

FROM *National Geographic Adventure*

SCOTLAND IS A PUZZLING PLACE, a sort of geographic and political oxymoron: severe but welcoming, blood-soaked but peaceable, independent yet British, hard and soft at the same time, like
the heather-cloaked shoulders of its sternest, most angular mountains. Think of the national emblem, a blossoming thistle, and you
have a hint of its prickly charm.

From the soggy ground protrude rocks, ancient rocks that can
punish a person's feet like police truncheons. If you were to hike a
long stretch of Scottish countryside — let's say, a trail called the
West Highland Way, spanning ninety-five miles across moors and
mountains — you would want to carry duct tape and iodine for re-
pairing your blistered, banged toes. You'd also be wise to pack rain
gear, sunscreen, extra socks, a fleece pullover, trail snacks, a good
map, a clean shirt, a compass, and not much else, except a judi-
cious selection of history books to explain narrative paradoxes the
map doesn't address. Other necessities and felicities, such as shelter, real food, and single-malt Scotch, you would find abundantly
available along the way.

So I've been told, anyway. It sounds luxuriously robust: backpacking for grownups, with no need to lug a tent or a sleeping bag
or freeze-dried pilaf or instant oatmeal, because a village hotel or
a roadside inn awaits at the end of each day's march. I've booked
my stopovers in advance, spaced at reasonable one-day intervals.
I've equipped myself with an authoritative field guide to the single malts, from Speyside to the western coast, from Glenlivet to
Lagavulin. And now, on a mild morning in early September, I

stride forth from the south terminus of the West Highland Way, marked by a stone obelisk amid a pedestrian mall on the outskirts of Glasgow. My destination is a similar obelisk in Fort William, just over a hundred miles (counting detours into villages) and seven days away. Life can seem blessedly simple, tra-la-lee, at the outset of an old-fashioned walking tour. Then again, Scotland has never been simple.

At its indecorous beginning, the West Highland Way follows a concrete bridge across a garbage-fouled creek, past construction scaffolding and parking lots, before dipping away from traffic into a mossy oak forest known as Mugdock Wood, like something out of *Winnie-the-Pooh*. The route is sponsored by an agency called Scottish Natural Heritage; wherever necessary at ambiguous junctions, it's blazed discreetly with posts bearing the totemic image of a thistle and an arrow pointing onward. Farther along it will climb across mountain passes and over blustery moorlands, following old military roads and drovers trails, but for now the terrain is flat and easy, a suburban stroll.

Within a mile Mugdock Wood opens onto a small loch, upon the still surface of which a fisherman stands in a boat, casting a fly. The trail, sun-exposed here, is lined with bracken fern, wild rose, blackberry bramble, purple loosestrife, and other cheery weeds. The blackberries are fat and tart, abundant enough to make a lunch. Reddish-brown butterflies work among the thistle, though it's late in the season for nectar. Already the city of Glasgow seems distant, as if I've walked through some secret portal into a different milieu of space, culture, and time. The rhythmic swish of the fisherman's strokes, hauling his line back, looping it forward, punctuates the quiet morning with whispers of reassurance that this is a gentle land, except when it isn't.

My traveling companion is an English photographer named Steve Pyke, a lean, urban guy with a distinguished portfolio of portraiture — he's done Keith Richards, Noam Chomsky, the Dalai Lama, Bill Gates — and a new pair of hiking boots for this jaunt. His fifteen-year-old son expressed mystification, Steve says, that any sane adult would choose to walk a hundred miles. Steve himself finds it a roaring good idea, but he'll walk only portions of the route, dodging ahead in a gear-filled car to choose his moments of light and vista, while I slog along. His job is to make pictures, not miles.

My own boots are past their prime, and seldom used lately, so my feet have forgotten the calluses that should compensate for the boots' pinches and cracks — as I'll be reminded, discomfortingly, within a couple days. I've neglected to bring bug juice for Scotland's famously nasty midges or binoculars for its birds, but I've gone heavy on books. My portable library includes a volume titled *The Massacre of Glencoe,* by the famous Scottish novelist and statesman John Buchan, better known for his thriller *The Thirty-Nine Steps,* which I'm carrying, too. Glencoe, a remote valley lying adjacent to the route on day six, is my goal as much as Fort William is. Tucked between high mountain walls, draining to Loch Leven, it's the site of a notorious slaughter — an act of genocide, in fact, the Wounded Knee of Scottish history — perpetrated by Scottish soldiers in service to an alien king in London against one recalcitrant branch of a Highland clan. Thirty-eight MacDonalds, including at least one woman and some children, were murdered with ugly efficiency on the snowy morning of February 13, 1692. An indeterminate number of others escaped through the snow or died of exposure on surrounding hillsides. The best way to approach Glencoe, I figure, is the same way those soldiers did three centuries ago: on foot. During the intervening days, maybe I'll learn something about how the wet Scottish climate and the good Scottish whiskies have rinsed away — or not? — the sense of tribal outrage at that event.

Approaching a hamlet called Blanefield, the Way winds through tranquil farmland, with shaggy brown cattle and black-face sheep pastured in deep grass behind stone walls, and here and there a cottage. On the brow of one hill, Steve and I inspect a cluster of weathered megaliths, known as the Dumgoyach Standing Stones, which date probably to the Bronze Age, according to my map, and were carefully arranged for some arcane ceremonial purpose but now lie fallen and mute. From that patch of high ground we catch a glimpse of Duntreath Castle, in the valley far below. It's a large edifice, looking well kept after just five or six centuries, with gardened grounds and a flag flying from its turret. Not far beyond, we divert through a field to the Glengoyne Distillery, a tidy enterprise with its visitors shop facing the highway, where tour buses can stop, and its warehouses backed to the West Highland Way. Employees wear T-shirts bearing the company motto, "Air Dried," meaning that's how the malted barley is processed. Like some other venerable single-malt distilleries, Glengoyne is now a boutique operation owned by a larger company, which sees fit to let the volume stay low and the quality high. We've timed our stop wrong for taking the tour, but no matter — I've already gotten my share of distillery-hopping this year (on an earlier Scotland visit, a honeymoon, with my wine-preferring but saintly, accommodating bride), seen the copper stills and the spent mash, fingered the raw barley, scooped the yeasty air to my nose from a fermenting vat. After sampling a dram of ten-year-old Glengoyne, I buy a small bottle and a whisky cake, purely for emergency sustenance, then hike on. Steve catches a ride back to Glasgow, from where he'll converge with me later.

By noon on day two, I've passed through a shady conifer plantation called Garadhban Forest, crossed a small stream, and come out upon a grand view: open moorland for almost a mile, beyond which a shapely little mountain called Conic Hill rises, like a big dune, above the south end of Loch Lomond. Conic Hill is only 1,184 feet high, but it commands the scene. Purplish-gray patches of blossoming heather, the first heather I've seen so far, show amid the varied greens of grasses and ferns. No blackberries here. The landscape is changing. Dark shadows from blimpy clouds move across the ground, deepening the heather tones to a glum purplish black. But the shadows pass, one by one, and otherwise it's a dazzling afternoon. Within an hour I've crested the windswept north shoulder of the hill, from where I can gaze down at Loch Lomond, Scotland's largest lake, stretching linear and blue for miles northward. Overhead, a dozen crows circle on thermals, looking for mischief. I write in my notebook: "Now we are definitely in the Highlands."

It's a geological fact, not just a moody sense of place. The Highland Boundary Fault, a fracture line marking the slow-motion smash between two great slabs of crustal rock, runs right through here, on a diagonal from the southwestern coast to a point in the northeast near Aberdeen. That collision occurred about 450 million years ago, during an active period of tectonic rearrangement. Old continents had broken apart, plates were sliding, an ocean gap grew narrower until, finally, the Scottish landmass slammed into the English one. Rock meeting rock with such cataclysmic force yielded a mountain-building set of events known as the Caledonian Orogeny. The Highlands became high. It wasn't the only time Scotland and England have collided, of course, but it was the one that defined the topography. Here at the southern end of Loch Lomond, including Conic Hill and some small islands dappling the loch, is where the boundary fault shows itself most clearly, at least to a geologist's knowing eye for fractured and metamorphosed strata.

Ever since then, the Highlands have been different not just from England but from southern Scotland — loftier, chillier, wetter, more harsh and demanding. Within the past three million years, glaciations have modified those ragged old mountains by the grinding power and weight of ice and then by erosion whenever the ice melted, shaping deep lochs, high-sided glens, little tarns on the moors, and fjordlike firths opening wide-mouthed to the sea. Eventually there were people on this landscape, but never many, and the weird, proud, sequestered culture they developed fit well enough with the severity of their environment. Clinging together in small tribes and family groups within remote glens, piling stones to make cottages, doing a little farming but never quite losing the wild twitch of the pastoral nomad, keeping cattle or stealing some from a neighbor, fighting over matters of property or gallantry, fighting for the sheer bloody joy of it, they became clannish. Over centuries, they took clannishness to its apogee.

"The Highlands were the home of a clan system which was half autocratic and half communal," wrote John Buchan in *The Massacre of Glencoe*. At the head of each clan was a chief, combining the roles of warlord, feudal landholder, and patriarch. "The life was barbarous and brutal," or anyway so it appeared to Lowlanders, who valued virtues such as "order, sobriety, prudence, industry" and had little patience for the feckless romanticism of the Highland clans. It wasn't just that the Highlanders feuded violently and rustled one another's cattle; sometimes they came south, armed and dangerous, to support some factional leader as loyalists or mercenaries or simply to prowl in small bands, robbing, extorting, bragging about their sense of honor. "If Scotland was ever to become a civilized land," Buchan added, characterizing the opinion of an archetypal

Lowlander of the late seventeenth century, Sir John Dalrymple, "it must get rid of this lumber of the Middle Ages." Dalrymple himself, serving the court in London as secretary of state for Scotland, came to feel that not just the lumber, not just the trappings and spirit of Highland clannishness, had to go. He decided to exterminate an entire branch of Clan Donald — a small and unpopular one, the Glencoe bunch — as a dire example to all the rest.

Coming down off Conic Hill, I find myself favoring my left foot, on which the little toe seems to be getting mooshed. This leads to thigh cramps from the uneven downhill braking, and I hobble the last mile to a village pub, on the loch shore, like a man with cheap aluminum knees. The view from the hilltop was magnificent, Steve and I agree, but we'll have to make better time this afternoon or be late into our night's stop at Rowardennan. Refreshed by a lamb casserole and a pint of Scottish lager, I find the walking easier again on a level trail along the east side of the loch.

In late afternoon we pause for a chin-wag with four young men, loitering at a picnic beach, who offer us beers as we trudge past. For some ungodly reason, in this land of hearty brews and noble whiskies, they're drinking longnecks of Miller Genuine Draft. The alpha guy among them is a former paratrooper, a Lowland Scot who found his niche in the British Army. Served half a dozen years, he tells us, and came out as a corporal. Burly and solid, he wears a T-shirt, a New York Yankees cap, and a dark smudge of beard under his lower lip. His three pals are younger and scruffier, with baby fat and missing teeth. The paratrooper in his day made more than seven hundred jumps, including one freefall from 27,000 feet down to very damn near the ground. Plunging through clouds, you get soaking wet, then you pop out into daylight and in seconds the air-rush dries you. "It's better than sex," he says. Steve sips his Miller companionably, but I can't resist marring the bonhomie with a sublimely irrelevant question: Ever been tempted to walk the West Highland Way? Not hardly, says the paratrooper. No, he got his fill of forced marches in the army.

By early evening we're ensconced at another pub, the Clansman in Rowardennan, where the dinner menu offers "haggis, neeps, and tatties," a cultural dare I can't resist. On the television over the bar, England's soccer team is playing Macedonia in a qualifier match for the European cup. We treat ourselves to a couple tots of

Aberlour, spicy and rich in the subtle Speyside way, and watch the game. When England scores two quick goals — one on a penalty kick by Beckham himself — Steve lets out the whoop of a patriot. Then we both notice, more quietly, that no one else in this bar full of Scotsmen and -women shares his enthusiasm. As far as they're concerned, it might be Macedonia losing to Paraguay.

Fiona MacMillan, a small woman of youngish middle age, with graying hair and a wry smile, runs a cozy bed-and-breakfast in the woods just outside Rowardennan. The rooms are modern; the carpet pattern is tartan. On the morning of day three, Steve and I tuck away immoderate portions of her eggs, bacon, sausage, beans, and tea while Fiona chats, at my coaxing, about the MacMillans (her husband's clan) and her own family origins on the island of Islay (renowned for its peaty soil and its bold, seaweedy whiskies). Family facts and the clan subject lead us somehow to public dramas of Scottish history, such as the persecution of the MacGregors.

Clan Gregor fell afoul of the king in 1603, after a battle against one of his client clans, at which point the very name MacGregor was banned by law. Those who answered to it were forbidden to gather in a group, or to carry a weapon, under penalty of death. Within a year, thirty-six MacGregors had been tried and executed, six others hanged without trial. One source reports that any outlaw, wanted for other offenses, "could earn a pardon by coming before the justices with the severed head of an obstinate MacGregor." Upright citizens were also invited to kill a MacGregor "like a beast of the wayside," claiming the victim's land and possessions. The surviving MacGregors, at least some of them, fled their home territory to live as bandits and resisters on Rannoch Moor, a majestically desolate sweep of open ground that happens to lie just east of Glencoe. In the context of this lighthearted breakfast discussion, I raise a question that's been puzzling me. Why is Scotland so peaceful?

More explicitly, I ask Fiona: Given its bloody past, given its long history of feuds, civil wars, political murders, atrocities, clan pogroms, and blood grievances, why is Scotland nowadays such a pacific country, free of car-bombings and tit-for-tat assassinations, whereas many places marked by similar experiences — Israel, Northern Ireland, Kosovo, among others — are not?

"That's a very good question," she says, and makes no attempt to answer. I can't tell whether she's shy about speculating on deep sociopolitical conundrums or just humoring my fancy for a riddle that doesn't engage her. She suggests I might ask one of her Rowardennan neighbors, a professional historian.

But it's time to get hoofing, since today for me will be a twenty-one-mile push, my longest day of the route. Steve and I set out together again, on a sinuous trail through oak forest along the east side of Loch Lomond. The trail, cobbled with oak roots and rocks where it traces the shoreline, loops higher in some sections to climb over a headland amid alder and bracken, then back down. Occasionally I linger to admire an especially venerable oak, hundreds of years old, its roots clenching the stony hillside like an arthritic hand. Several miles along, I divert from the path and clamber down across boulders to a sheltered crevice above the loch that, by tradition, and possibly from historical fact, is known as Rob Roy's Cave.

Rob Roy was a MacGregor, born in 1671. By that time the interdiction against his clan had been lifted; his own eventual status as an infamous outlaw was achieved through a lifetime of personal effort. As a young man he fought for the Stuart king James II, who was Catholic by religion and Scottish by extraction, against William of Orange, the Dutchman invited over by English Protestants to accept the crown. Most of the bitter conflicts in Scottish history are complicated by the overlap of such political and religious dichotomies: not just Protestant versus Catholic and Scot versus English but also Presbyterian versus Anglican, Highlander versus Lowlander, MacDonald versus Campbell, government versus Mac-Gregor, royalist versus Whig, and Stuart royalist (also called Jacobite, from James) versus any supporter of an alternative claimant to the British crown. Never mind the details. All you need to know is that when people got angry and fought, they fought under these labels.

Rob MacGregor was a Jacobite but also a bit of a freelancer. He was an aggressive businessman, a formidable swordsman, a dashingly handsome fellow, with fierce red hair from which came the Gaelic nickname "Ruadh," red, and from that the anglicized "Roy." Later in life, after a soured business deal with a powerful marquis, he went on the lam. Still later, he led his clan in another uprising on behalf of the Stuarts, again unsuccessful, and found himself charged with treason but escaped. Escaping variously from tight spots and incarcerations, plus his talent for cattle hustling and rustling, made him a folk hero in the Highlands. The cave along Loch Lomond was putatively one of his hideouts. Authentic or not, it has been a focus of Rob Roy tourism since the early nineteenth century, not long after Sir Walter Scott turned his life into romance as a novel, *Rob Roy*. By the time I arrive, the only evidence to distinguish this crevice from any other is a large graffito in white paint on a boulder nearby: CAVE. Evidently that's useful to tour boats.

I walk, and keep walking. The east side of Loch Lomond is the tranquil side, away from traffic, shaded by steep cliffs, overgrown with hawthorn, silver birch, and old oak. Around half past four I pause briefly at a trail juncture that diverges to Inverarnan, a village just north of the loch, toward which other hikers seem to be headed at the end of their day. Steve turns that way, too. For me, because of how I've measured my stages and booked my hotels, there's another seven miles to the village of Crianlarich. I eat some raisins and peanuts, then hike on.

The trail traces a slot through Glen Falloch, with the River Falloch tumbling among reddish-black boulders below. Power lines sully the vista, and I can hear traffic swooshing along a highway, but at one point I catch sight of a twenty-foot waterfall in the gorge — which seems, at this end of a long day, like a private vision of majesty vouchsafed to keep my legs moving. Farther, a prim white-stuccoed cottage sits vacant beside the river, its windows blank with plywood, only a door plaque reading DERRYDAROCH to testify that this once was a homestead with human presence and identity. From there the trail crosses over the river, then beneath the highway, to join an old military road, stony and lonesome, on a high traverse along the west slope of the glen. A late afternoon drizzle becomes an evening rain.

Hours later I straggle up to the hotel, drenched and footsore but otherwise feeling good. Steve, preoccupied with a cell phone call, waves a welcome. Inside, I peel off my bloody left sock and order a Macallan, smoothest and most soothing of any malt I know.

On the morning of day four, in my room, I work with duct tape, gauze, and scissors, carefully fortifying my beat-up feet. Then, frustrated by this ridiculous fragility, I hobble back out onto the West Highland Way. The sky is blue, freshened by last night's rain, with one puffy dark cloud obscuring the summit of Ben More, the big mountain to the east, like a slouch hat on an angry God. The trail rises through conifer forest, then descends again into an open valley drained by the River Fillan, beside which sits an ecclesiastical ruin known as St. Fillan's Chapel, after an eighth-century Irish monk who came as missionary to the Scots.

There's a rich agglomeration of stories and legends surrounding this holy Irishman, St. Fillan. According to one, he played his greatest role in Scottish history posthumously, by way of a fancy relic — his arm bone, encased in silver — that gave miraculous inspiration to Robert the Bruce, going into battle against an English army in 1314. Wait, you say, who was Robert the Bruce? Another bighearted but murderous Scottish hero. He stabbed his main rival (during a truce meeting, in a church), had himself crowned king of Scotland, and eventually drove the English invaders back south of the border. Why do we call him the Bruce? Because he was the eighth Robert in his family since the Norman Conquest but the most notable, because the original name in its Norman form was "de Brus," and because it sounds cool and imperious, like Trump, the Donald. Just ahead is another spot associated with Robert the Bruce, a battlefield called Dalrigh, where according to legend he was defeated, captured, and disarmed by the MacDougalls, who had been allies of his murdered rival. He managed to kill them and escape, with or without help from the magic of St. Fillan.

This valley is known as Strath Fillan. Near its end, the West Highland Way transects Auchtertyre Farm, where a modest sign advertises along the roadway: LAMB, BEEF, LOCAL VENISON, WILD BOAR. I haven't noticed Scottish boar offered on any menus, but if it's as good as the wild boar served in Romania, another lovably peculiar country, on the other side of Europe, then I'd seize any chance for simmered boar shank or boar stew, the sort of earthy meal that might properly be washed down with a searing dram or two of Talisker. Apart from the trade in domestic and wild meats, Auchtertyre Farm sells tourist accommodation, under the aegis Strathfillan Wigwams. I know from guidebooks that a wigwam, as the Scots have adopted that word, is an inexpensive bunkhouse. Amid these wigwams, there's also a food shop. This is where you stop if you're a penniless young student eager to meet other hikers. I keep walking.

Not far beyond, where the trail rises again into a narrow gulch

between forested hillsides, I encounter an elderly English couple
out for a stroll. Dignified but doughty, they both wear parkas and
hiking boots. She is tall and straight as an egret, hardly seeming to
need the high-tech walking stick she carries. Her eyes, beneath a
tweed cap, are pearly blue. He is short and stooped, with rheumy
red eyes that twinkle wetly. In lieu of a walking stick, he totes a
canelike folding stool. They live in Edinburgh, I learn, but their
son owns a hotel hereabouts, and they come out for weekend ram-
bles. After a bit of chitchat, I pose them the same question I asked
Fiona MacMillan: Why is Scotland, despite its bloody history, so
peaceful?

Well, says the man, they've got a very fine army regiment that
keeps order. That would be the Black Watch? I hazard. This celebrated military unit — I've seen it reverently saluted on Scottish
monuments to the dead from two world wars — was originally recruited, in the eighteenth century, from Whig clansmen who opposed a Stuart restoration and chose to help the British army pacify
the Highlands. Yes, the Black Watch, that's it, says the man.

The woman has a different slant. "There is still a lot of anti-Eng-
lish sentiment." It crops up in the schools, she says, and in sports
matches, even in commercial offices — she saw it herself when she
worked in the insurance business. Pressing no further, I try to picture this sweet matron and her husband as icons of English hege-
mony, targets of Scottish loathing. I suspect that, kindly folks, having adopted Edinburgh as their home, they have a low threshold of
hurt.

Through the afternoon, I follow an old roadbed along one
shoulder of another broad valley, passing through sheep farms and
beneath domed mountains. I'm on a tributary of the River Orchy
now, headed toward a village called Bridge of Orchy and lodging at
the Bridge of Orchy Hotel. The landscape is sparse out here; nam-
ing is uncomplicated. Sustained by raisins, an apple, a Mars bar,
and ibuprofen, I toddle onward, the raw spots on my feet jamming
forward into my boots whenever I descend a slight hill. Going up-
hill is better. Around five o'clock, I notice a large flock of sheep on
a distant slope — tiny white shapes moving fast, like a swarm of ter-
mites — as they race homeward for the night. That's how I feel:
Let's get to the barn.

But when I reach the hotel, my day isn't over. Showered and

changed, I backtrack with Steve in his rental car to a roadhouse on the highway near Inverarnan. He discovered it yesterday, when he took the cutoff through there. You've got to see this place, he tells me.

It's called the Drovers Inn, a two-story stone building with rooms above, pub below, and a foyer where visitors are greeted by bedraggled items of taxidermy: a bear with a missing snout, a couple of ptarmigans, an owl, a one-eyed deer whose vacant socket is plugged with cotton, and the dried head of a cow. The inn itself has existed for 298 years — so I'm told by a bartender — and looks as though it has never been redecorated. At the back of the pub is a large stone fireplace, burning coal. Above it hangs a yard-long salmon. The other walls are ornamented with old paintings, mementos, and weaponry, including a two-handed broadsword, a shield and mace, a still life elegantly depicting the severed head of a black-face sheep, and a ragged, dusty tartan of red-and-blue plaid. Whose tartan? I ask the bartender, a tall fellow in a black T-shirt and a kilt, with a knife scar on his right cheek. He knows what I mean by "whose": which clan? "Stuart," he says. Been there a long time, has it? I inquire stupidly. "If they take it down," he says, "the wall will fall." Perched on the bar is a stuffed eagle. A few locals sit hunched on stools, not quite so stuffed as the eagle but getting pickled, and several tables are occupied by people who seem to be, like Steve and me, tourists. There's a second bartender, also tall, also laconic, also wearing a black T-shirt and a kilt, whose role is to stoke the coal fire and occasionally give the other fellow a break. Together they look like a pair of dangerous skinhead bikers, apart from the kilts. The second bartender, I swear to you, has a knife scar on his left cheek. Say, who does the hiring around here?

Steve and I lurk quietly at our table, sipping drinks, chafing with curiosity, wondering how to break the cultural ice and get something human out of these two fabulous, dour guys. They don't encourage small talk. I make a few tries but receive only terse answers and scowls. Two hours pass. I can't recall just what I've sampled tonight — Oban, Dalwhinnie, Glenmorangie? Finally I plop onto a stool beside the second bartender and manage, with difficulty, to pry open a conversation. We talk about haggis, we talk about blood pudding, we talk about whiskies . . . and then, bingo, we talk about clans.

Do either of you belong to one of those famous old families? I ask. Just a lucky stab. Yes, says the second bartender, I'm a Buchan. You're a Buchan, no kidding? What's your first name? *John* Buchan, he tells me. With a smile of shy pride he admits that he's the great-great-grandson of the writer.

I greet this coincidence with such an outburst of astonished appreciation — what, John Buchan? I'm carrying two of his books in my damn pack! — that Bartender John, letting the smile stretch, confides something further: He himself owns the manuscript of *The Thirty-Nine Steps,* bequeathed to him by his grandmother because he's the namesake. No! say I. Yes! says he. Keeps it in a vault. He also has a signed first edition, presently on loan to the British Museum. Within a short while, and not many more drams of whisky, we are great barstool pals. John mentions having trained as a gourmet chef — when he's not shoveling coal or pulling lager here at Drovers, he cooks elsewhere — and describes the episode, some years earlier, in which he acquired the facial scar. It was five guys, outside a pub. They went to prison, where mates of his got to them (he confides, with a dark smile) and settled accounts. At this slightly illogical moment, I pop out the question that I've come to think of as The Question: Why is Scotland so peaceful? Apart from occasional bar fights, that is.

"We've learned our lessons from the past," says John Buchan the Younger. "There's no point in feuding anymore." He adds: "Violence causes more violence."

Yes, but — I think, still unsatisfied. Yes, but that's exactly the baffling part: Violence does cause more violence, except when it doesn't.

Beside the River Coe is a place called Carnoch, marked nowadays by a stone monument. Just over three centuries ago, it was the home site of MacIain MacDonald, the elderly chief of the Glencoe MacDonalds. The monument shows a coat of arms, a memorial inscription in English, and a Latin motto: *"Nec tempore nec fato."* Neither passing time nor cruel fate will obliterate this family.

MacIain MacDonald stood six-foot-six, give or take an inch, broad-shouldered as well as tall. He was variously considered a man of "integrity, honour, good nature and courage" (by those who liked him) and "the worst thief and robber in the Highlands" (by some who didn't). As he neared seventy, age had bleached his red hair but hadn't made him soft, weak, or humble. "He had the dark wild eyes of Clan Donald," according to John Buchan, not the bartender but the writer, "and a fierce nose like the beak of a galley. His white hair fell almost to his shoulders, and two great mustachios like buck's horns gave him the air of a Norse sea-king." In early 1692, MacIain got himself crossways with the powers in London for neglecting to swear an oath of allegiance to Britain's new king, William. He did swear the oath, in fact, but not before the required date of January 1. By missing that deadline, MacIain gave William's perfidious henchman for Scottish affairs, John Dalrymple, a pretext for doing what he wanted to do anyway — that is, to squash MacIain and his family as an object lesson for all Highlanders. Within a month Dalrymple had ordered soldiers to march on Glencoe, billet themselves on the MacDonalds as though for an amicable visit, and then "maul them in the cold long nights." He specified that, when the moment came, "let it be secret and sudden."

On February 12, a certain Major Duncanson passed instructions to a captain on the scene: "You are hereby ordered to fall upon the rabelle, the Macdonalds of Glencoe, and to putt all to the sword under seventy." It began at five the next morning, amid darkness and wind-driven snow. A lieutenant accompanied by several soldiers came to MacIain's house and asked to see him, with the lie that they were leaving Glencoe and wanted to say thanks. Roused, shuffling into his clothes, calling to his household for some liquid hospitality, old MacIain was shot from behind — once in the body, once in the head. He fell across his bed, face ripped open at the exit wound. The soldiers stripped his wife and, according to Buchan, "tore the rings from her fingers with their teeth." Farther up the glen, other troops shot and bayoneted members of other MacDonald households. An eighty-year-old man was killed, a boy of thirteen, another child no older than five, a woman, and every able-bodied MacDonald man who didn't escape through the blizzard. Some of the bodies were thrown on a trash heap and covered with dung. A child's severed hand lay on the snow. The soldiers turned livestock out of pens, set fire to cottages and huts. By the time another military contingent arrived around midday, the blizzard had ended and the glen was filling with smoke.

These other troops, four hundred of them, had marched down from Fort William, which in those days was a real fort. Arriving late for the massacre, they burned what cottages they found still standing. They killed an old man who, emerging from ruins, made a break for the river. They saw fresh bodies on a midden but, other than the old man, no living MacDonalds. When the two sets of soldiers met, their officers conferred about who was dead and who was just gone.

Major Duncanson's order had stressed the need to close off escape routes so that "the old fox and his sones doe not escape your hands." Despite that, MacIain's two sons did escape. They and quite a few others, helped by the blizzard and their familiarity with the terrain, managed to scramble off amid the gruesome confusion. These surviving MacDonalds hid among the side valleys or lit out for refuge in neighboring glens. "Glencoe was left to the peace of death," as Buchan wrote, "and soon the snow shrouded the charred roof-trees and the bloody hearthstones."

MacIain's sons, John and Alasdair, reached a truce with the government in a surprisingly short time, by May of the same year, after which the officer who brokered it reported complacently: "The Glencoe men are abundantly civil." That was temporary. One of MacIain's grandsons led a force of his clansmen in the last uprising for the Stuarts, in 1745, until its grim end at the Battle of Culloden. From there, the trail of Glencoe MacDonalds becomes more diffuse. The old clan culture itself began to break down after Culloden, under pressure of new economic factors and arrangements, including private instead of communal land ownership, tenant farming, evictions and clearances, and large-scale husbandry of sheep. Many displaced Highlanders went off to the cities, looking for wage work, or reinvented themselves as fishermen along the coasts. Some went into the army, some to America. If you read Faulkner carefully, you'll hear of their offspring turning up in Mississippi. Descendants of Glencoe MacDonalds could no doubt be found today among the law-abiding and peaceable Scottish populace. But where? And how would they respond to The Question?

Just east of Glencoe, a switchback trail called Devil's Staircase ascends a high saddle across which that second contingent of troops marched to the massacre. On this amber afternoon, day six of my walk, I'm headed the opposite way. At the crest, I pause to stare back toward Glencoe and be pecked at infernally by midges. Then I hike on, following a shoulder traverse around handsome peaks with difficult Gaelic names, their lower slopes decorated with soggy sphagnum, ferns, glacial boulders, and purple heather. Soon I come to a vista overlooking the forested valley of the River Leven and, where that meets Loch Leven, a town. It's Kinlochleven, the last stop before Fort William. With relief and regret, I realize that from this vantage point I can almost see to the end of the West Highland Way. My feet are now feeling better each day, not worse. I'm running out of distance and time, and, despite having asked many people, I still don't have an answer to The Question.

Next morning I climb out of the Leven valley, through alder and birch woods, to another traverse on the north side. The little zigzag trail converges there with an old military road that ascends gradually up a wide glacial valley known as Lairigmor. The name means "the great pass," though its high point is only 1,082 feet. After a hard morning rain, the sky has remained overcast, and Lairigmor is windswept, blustery, chilly. I'm savoring this raw Highland weather and the last handful of miles. But I'm frustrated by my failure to elicit a persuasive explanation of how Scotland has transcended its legacy of violence.

Just beyond Lairigmor, according to my map, lies a gentle slope downward, then a big bend, another wooded valley, and finally Fort William, where Steve Pyke may already be booking us a table for a fine end-of-trip dinner. Meanwhile, there's this little pass. All I've got to do now is what the Scottish people, in their mysterious stolidity, in their native wisdom, have somehow managed to do: get over it. The moment is so subtle that when it happens I don't even notice.

# The Vision Seekers

FROM *The Sophisticated Traveler*

HERE'S THE TRUTH: I have traveled more than four thousand miles to the middle of the Peruvian Amazon to be "cured" by shamans. It's nighttime. The riverboat I'm on plies dark waters, the jungle thick on either side, emitting loud reptilian sounds that drone on like police sirens. I see no lights, no villages anywhere. My companions are Kevin, a pan-flute maker from Canada; Wendy, an acupuncturist and energetic healer from Massachusetts, and her husband, Joe, a burly carpenter who wants nothing to do with us or shamanism, who has said upward of five words so far and who busily reads *Chomsky on MisEducation* as the jungle slides by.

Hamilton Souther, our shamanic guide, sits with long, burnished legs on the guardrail of the boat. "Our greatest fear is the fear of death," he's telling us. "During the *ayahuasca* ceremony, you'll be taken to the edge of that fear, taught to surrender to it, release it." He has the classic good looks of a *Baywatch* actor. Hamilton is twenty-six years old, a native of California who has practiced shamanism for several years. His company, Blue Morpho Tours, features a "shamanic healing center" in a remote area of the Amazon. Listening to him is like listening to the newest Castaneda. He talks constantly about spirit friends and alternative realms of reality.

I discovered Blue Morpho Tours while investigating the huge variety of New Age trips offered on the Web, many stressing shamanism in various cultures as a means of reaching spiritual "transformation." Skeptical but curious, I wondered what that meant and how it worked. Not quite sure what to expect, I signed up for the trip.

Our boat ride will take fourteen hours from the Peruvian town of Iquitos, followed by another river journey to reach our destination. On the deck below, passengers' hammocks crowd together like rows of cocoons, bodies swinging and bumping into one another, frenetic guitar music rupturing the mosquito-filled night.

It's midday. We're all in a dugout, heading up a narrow river into the depth of the jungle. Giant butterflies with wings of blue satin fly sluggishly over the water. Nests of parakeets let off raucous squawks, rivaling the boat's motor. The sun and its sticky heat burrows into my skin, exhausting me.

In our boat are two local shamans we picked up this morning from the tiny river town of Genaro Herrerra. Don Julio, eighty-six, is widely considered by locals to be one the greatest living shamans in the Amazon; his only baggage consists of a small woven pouch full of *mapacho* (sacred tobacco) cigars, which Peruvian shamans smoke to secure the favor of spirits. The second shaman, Don Alberto, forty-six, Hamilton's current shamanic mentor, rests on the gunwale and winces at the sun-dappled waters.

The sun vies with the clouds; large flies land painlessly on me, swelled with blood before I notice them. Joe has stuck the Chomsky book, now dogeared and smudged, in the back of his jeans. His wife, Wendy, on this trip in part to try to improve her energetic healing abilities, has her camcorder out, recording our journey up the river. Kevin, who said he chose to go on this tour to "hopefully release issues," sits silently beside me. He is middle-aged, shy, unmarried. I tell Hamilton about the inexplicable daily migraines that started in just the past year and how they leave me temporarily blind in one eye.

The motor is killed. We pass through a swamplike area of low branches into a small lagoon. High on a nearby slope sits Hamilton's healing center: a large hut made of rainforest planks and palm-leaf thatch, with the jungle imposing on all sides. A single family acts as caretakers. Hamilton introduces us to their youngest girl, Carlita, only five, a budding shaman who already knows the sacred *icaros,* or shamanic power songs. Carrying a Barbie purse around her arm, she gives us all a deep, penetrating stare that unhinges me.

Shamans don't cut down medicinal plants in the jungle without first asking the spirits' permission and giving thanks. Victor, our jungle guide, teaches us about this as he takes our group on an afternoon trek, stopping abruptly before a fresh skeleton on the ground.

"Bushmaster," Victor says, beaming like a proud father.

The bushmaster is the largest venomous snake in the New World. Victor has also introduced us to a large wasp whose venom kills tarantulas and incapacitates humans. And now, overhead, he taps his machete against a vine that, if severed, he says, will leak a fluid that easily burns through human flesh.

These are only a few of the dry-ground threats, which don't include the fare of the waterways: piranhas, electric eels, alligators. It's a shaman's paradise, shot full of formidable creatures and the spirits that command them.

I return to the hut with another of my migraines. Kevin and I decide to attend Hamilton's energetic healing class, Hamilton taking us on a guided visualization. The idea, he explains, is to feel connected to the earth's center and the universe. "See yourself heading to the stars," he says. "Tell me when you see the planet Mercury."

It's hard to concentrate. Joe has been lecturing Victor on the uncanny similarities between George W. Bush and Genghis Khan.

"Thank the emerald light for taking you to the golden arc of the sun and the eternal flame," Hamilton is saying.

I'm starting to hope that I'm not stranded in the middle of the Amazon with a bunch of lunatics. Little Carlita sits nearby, staring at us from the crook of a rocking chair. She takes slow puffs from a shaman's cigar, her eyes narrow, face expressionless.

Last night, Kevin, Wendy, and I met in the hut to participate in the first of our three shamanic ceremonies. We drank the "sacred visionary medicine" called ayahuasca, which had been prepared by Don Alberto earlier that day. Perhaps because it had been burned accidentally, we felt nothing.

Today, a new batch is being prepared, and tonight's ceremony promises to give us a real shamanic experience — whatever that will entail. Anxiety settles in my gut. "Ayahuasca" itself is the name of a jungle vine, but the word is used as shorthand for a concoction of boiled plant essences that, when drunk, allow for — as Hamilton puts it — "journeys into the realm of spirit."

Our group joins Don Alberto in collecting and preparing the fixings for the special brew. Any would-be Peruvian shaman must master an extensive knowledge of Amazonian plant species, each of which, the shamans believe, has a spirit that contributes protection or guidance to the ceremony. Don Alberto puts several different ingredients into a large cooking pot to be repeatedly boiled for the next several hours: pieces of tree bark, crushed ayahuasca, and fresh, green chacruna leaves.

"Once you take ayahausca, you can meet any spirit you'd like — deceased loved ones, guardian angels, power animals," Hamilton tells us seriously. "Just call upon them, and they'll come."

"I've always wanted to meet Walt Whitman," I muse out loud.

The hour arrives — 9 P.M. Having fasted for seven hours, Kevin, Wendy, and I take our seats in the middle of the hut. We each get a plastic bucket and a roll of toilet paper for wiping our faces. Shamans believe that the inevitable vomiting — "purging" — caused by the ayahuasca mixture is a physical manifestation of negative energy being dispelled from the body. The more disgorged, the better.

Hamilton, Don Alberto, and the ancient Don Julio sit before us, lighting their cigars. When they yawn, which is frequently, they make undulating sounds like horses neighing. Don Alberto blows tobacco smoke into the bottle of thick, brown ayahuasca, then whistles under his breath. Spirits, Hamilton says, are now filling the hut. All manner of wholesome, positive spirits. Don Alberto begins pouring out cups of ayahuasca, blessing our serving before we drink; the ayahuasca has the taste and consistency of Bailey's Irish Cream. The shamans are last to drink.

I wait. Ten minutes. Twenty. It looks as if the rafters of the hut are swaying. Someone extinguishes the kerosene lamp and there's complete darkness. The shamans start shaking their *shacapas,* leaf rattles, and singing loudly. I lie down, eyes closed, a pleasant vibration coursing through my body to the beat of the shamans' songs.

A piercing scream tears through the hut. I hear violent gurgling and retching. "Hamilton!" Wendy yells. "Get this out of my head! Make it stop!"

Hamilton stops singing for a moment. "Wendy," he says soothingly, "that's just your fear speaking. Ask God to take your fear away."

Now Kevin lets out a loud wail. "Oh, God! Help me! No! *No!*" He throws up, and I hear the loud, mysterious plop of something large landing in the bucket.

The shamans get up to perform healing songs over Kevin and Wendy, who are vomiting now. "Don't resist," Hamilton tells them. "Surrender to your fear. Surrender. Let it all out." He comes over to me. "The spirits tell me that your migraines are caused by worry energy trapped in your head. I'm going to take that energy out for you now." He puts his lips to my temple, sucking hard several times and spitting the unsavory energy over his shoulder.

I start to see geometric patterns. Colorful realms. Shapes and forms coalesce into an endless stream of beauty and perfection. An old man in a white robe walks toward me, smiling. He greets me with a long hug, kissing the top of my head. Walt Whitman!

Wendy and Kevin's desperate bellows retreat into distant space. The visions end. I feel an awful, painful ball of nausea in my gut and vomit prodigiously into the bucket.

Kevin has stopped screaming and sobs now. "I see angels," he chimes. "It's so beautiful."

The shamans fall silent. Don Julio announces that he's called back the spirits and ended the ceremony early because the forces were too strong for Wendy and Kevin. A light goes on. I open my eyes to see Hamilton holding Kevin in his arms like a small child. "You're back," he's cooing to him. "Welcome back."

Kevin looks around him in wonder, smiling. "I've never been so happy," he says.

We all received a day of downtime after the ceremony. Wendy had met me outside the hut, crying and distraught, and I didn't know what to do for her. Hamilton assured us that she'd soon feel better, that she was still "resisting the experience." Luckily, Victor had taken her and Joe to see some pink dolphins, which seemed to calm her. Ignoring her protestations, Kevin and I went ahead with our final scheduled ayahuasca ceremony on the last night; we both had little vomiting and our visions were pleasant ones.

It's almost the end of the trip. Wendy sits before Don Julio and Don Alberto, reading their palms. Joe passes me a bumper sticker: "Bush Lies — Who Dies?" I catch Kevin smiling. He initiates a conversation with me for the first time and takes out his pan flute to serenade us.

"How are you feeling today?" he asks me.

I try to be scientific about it. My migraines are completely gone, I tell him. I'm enjoying a bizarre, inexplicable feeling of happiness and peace that actually transcends my usual writer's angst.

The others leave. A few days later, on my own overnight journey back to Iquitos, I lie beside Hamilton on the roof of the riverboat and discuss what has happened. "OK," I say, "so how do I know if any of this was real?"

He chuckles knowingly, putting his hands behind his head and staring up at stars so bright that they burn afterimages on my retinas. "It doesn't matter if you think it's real or not," he says, "just as long as it works."

SETH STEVENSON

# Trying Really Hard to Like India

FROM *Slate.com*

*Subject: Learning to Like India: A Five-Step Approach*

It's OK to hate a place.

Travel writers can be so afraid to make judgments. You end up with these gauzy tributes to the "magic" of some far-off spot. But honestly, not every spot is magical for everyone. Sometimes you get somewhere, look around, and think, "Hey, this place is a squalid rat hole. I'd really rather be in the Netherlands." And that's OK.

For example, the last time I went to India I just haaaaaaated it. Delhi was a reddish haze of 105° dust. And while, of course, the Taj Mahal was great . . . the streets outside it were a miasma of defecating children. I could not wait to go home. (Disclosure: I was there on a previous assignment for *Slate*. And actually, I loved Ladakh, which is in northern India — up in the Himalayas. But I don't really count Ladakh, because it's more like Tibet than like India. Anyway . . .)

Now — mostly because my girlfriend wants to come back — I'm back. I'm giving this dreadful place a second chance. And this time I vow I will try really hard to like India.

I'm convinced it's a reachable goal. My plan involves sticking to South India, far away from Delhi, staying exclusively at beach resorts and luxury hotels, and stocking up on prescription-strength sedatives. But there are other important steps as well, which I will be outlining over the course of this week.

*Step 1: Making Peace with Poverty and with Parasitic Worms*

After flying into Bangalore and acclimating for a couple of days, we visit a town called Mysore (rhymes with "eyesore"). There's a famous temple here and an opulent palace — big tourist attractions both. But to me, the most interesting thing to see (in *any* place I visit) is the daily life of the people who live and work there.

For instance, from our hotel window in Mysore, we look down on a pile of garbage. Every night, this pile becomes dispersed as it is picked at and chewed on by rats, then crows, then stray dogs, then cows, and then homeless people. Every morning a woman dressed in a brightly colored sari sweeps this masticated garbage-porridge back into a pile. It is the worst job I can imagine. (Previously, the worst job I could imagine was navigator for a rally-car driver, because I get nauseous when I read in cars. But this woman's job is much worse than that. And really, with this added perspective, rally-car navigator doesn't seem so bad anymore.)

When we leave the hotel and walk down the (urine-soaked) street, we get assaulted by auto-rickshaw drivers, by hawkers, by tour guides . . . and by tiny children pointing to their own mouths. This last one is rough — at least the first few dozen times. Sometimes these kids are part of a scam. They're forced to beg by adults who run panhandling teams. (We've read stories about teams that cut out kids' tongues, to make them seem more pitiable.) But sometimes these kids are just honestly looking for food. Because they're starving. They might eat out of that big garbage pile tonight. Once the dogs are done.

On the train ride back to Bangalore, monsoon rains slap at the window. I gaze out on wet, destitute slums. Wherever one can build a shanty, someone has. Wherever one could be pissing, someone is. The poverty's on a mind-blowing, overwhelming scale, and you feel so helpless. The money in your pocket right now, handed to any one person out there beyond the window, would be life-changing. But you can't save a billion people and turn the fortunes of this massive country. (You're not Gandhi, you know.) And after all, back in Bangalore we hung out with highly paid IT guys who worked for Infosys. There's a lot of wealth in India, too.

The thing is, if you go to India as a tourist, you'll have to make some sort of peace with all this. Because it's one thing to see poverty on television or to get direct mail that asks for your charity. It's different when there are tiny, starving children grabbing your wrists and asking for money wherever you go.

For my part, I've resolved to send a check to some worthy Indian charity when I get home. (Suggestions are invited.) It's the best solution I can come up with. Because I'm not going to get through this trip until I've reached an understanding with myself . . . and until I take some Pepto-Bismol, because my stomach is just killing me. Which brings me to the other thing you'll have to be prepared for.

You *will* get "Delhi belly" soon after touching down in India. And you won't enjoy your trip until it's gone. My illness takes hold on the train ride back to Bangalore, as my intestines suddenly spasm into a clenched fist full of acid. The restroom — should this come into play — is a hole in the floor of the train. (A sign on the door requests that we not use the hole while the train's in a station — for obvious reasons.)

For the next day or two, I find myself playing a game I call "Could I Vomit in This?" The idea is to pick a nearby object and then decide if, in the event of an emergency, it could be puked into. For example, potted plant: Certainly. Water bottle: Sure. Magazine: Iffy but worth a try.

The good news is that it won't take long before your stomach adjusts to these new microbial nasties and you're back to feeling fine. Unless, of course, like my friend who was here a few years ago, you've got a parasitic worm and you lose forty pounds and need medical attention.

## *Step 2: Escaping Backpackers, Traveling in Style, and Once Again Coming to Terms with Rampant Poverty*

I have a problem with backpackers. The problem is that wherever they are, I don't want to be.

Partly, it's that I don't go somewhere like India so I can hang out with a bunch of nineteen-year-old German dudes (though I'm sure they're lovely people). Also, it's that I look at all these backpackers . . . and I see myself. And frankly, I don't like what I see.

For one, I'm not properly bathed. And for another, I've got this massive, geeky pack on my back, which dwarfs my torso and bends me near double under its weight. (Because of this, I have, I'll admit somewhat irrationally, refused to use a backpack on this trip. Instead I've brought a wheeled carry-on suitcase, which has worked quite nicely. Just try to call me a backpacker now! No backpack here, Heinrich!)

But above all, I hate the ambience that forms around a backpacker enclave. The ticky-tacky souvenir shops. The sketchy tour guides. The rabbit warren hostels. And the way the locals start to eye me like I'm nothing but an ambulatory wallet.

There are two ways to escape the backpackers. The first is to get off the beaten path, wander around, and discover a private Eden not yet ruined by backpacking hordes. This takes more time than my vacation will allow. So I've opted for the second (much quicker) method: money.

Yes, the simplest way to find solitude is to buy it. Thus we've arrived here at the Casino Group Marari Beach Resort.

This idyllic spot is on the west coast of India in the state of Kerala (the setting for *The God of Small Things*). The resort's lovely bungalows are tucked between groves of palm trees. The beach is wide, empty, silent. Each evening, the sun melts down into the Arabian Sea. By day we lounge around a heated pool, eating big plates of samosas. Nearby, in the recreation area, an older Italian woman is playing badminton in a bikini.

Wait, you say, why bother to go to India for this? If a beach resort's all you want, there are plenty back home, right? I assure you this is different for several reasons, such as . . .

*The food:* Each night, we enjoy delicious Indian specialties, prepared by actual Indian chefs, in India. (Pause to lick tandoori chicken from fingers.) You just can't get that at home.

*The cost:* We're paying about $70 a night for our bungalow. Pretty much anywhere in the States — for a luxury resort with a private beach — you'd pay at least quadruple that. Consider the fact that Sir Paul McCartney once stayed here. When I can afford a hotel Paul McCartney stays at, you can be certain it's a bargain.

*The sheer solitude:* You'll rarely find a beach this nice that's also this utterly empty. There's nothing here (as my pictures attest). Several hundred yards away are a few wooden fishing boats, which haul up their catch on the beach each afternoon. Also — and I swear this is somehow charming (remember, it's hundreds of yards away) — you'll see a few village folk squatting amid the tides. This is because they don't have indoor plumbing.

*The world beyond the hotel gates:* Walk outside your beach resort in Florida . . . and you're still in Florida. Walk outside your beach resort in India and . . . oh, man, you are unmistakably in India. Lots of heartbreaking rural poverty. Lots of sad-yet-edifying tableaux (which is no doubt what you came here for, correct?). It's sort of the best of both worlds for the tourist who fancies himself culturally aware: Live right next to the picturesque misery — but not in it.

Before you condemn me to hell, please see again Step 1: Making Peace With Poverty. Again, unless you're Gandhi — and you're not — you can't come here without diving headfirst into a salty sea of unpleasant contradictions.

For yet another lesson on this theme, take our last night at Marari Beach. We somehow end up drinking in the bar with a thirty-something American woman — let's call her "Debbie" — who is six stiff drinks ahead of us. Between sips of some tropical concoction, she delivers a slurry monologue explaining that she has come to India on business. Her business: designing doormats. No joke.

One of Kerala's big industries is *coir* — a textile made from coconut husks. On a bike ride we took around the village (yes, "the world beyond the hotel gates"), we could see into huts that had looms and people weaving coir into simple mats. These mats get trimmed and finished (by some big export factory) to Debbie's design specs. Then they get shipped to North America and end up in some middlebrow home-furnishings catalog where you can buy them for $26.99.

Debbie is drinking heavily because her job here is wicked depressing. She buys in bulk from the big exporter, who pays a shady middleman, who (barely) pays the villagers here. The villagers can make about three mats per week — all of excellent quality — and for this they get paid a few cents per mat. The middleman of course takes all the profit.

Debbie, goodhearted human that she is, is on the verge of drunken tears as she describes all this. She knows the whole thing is grossly unfair. And that she perpetuates it. But if she wants to keep her job with the American firm she works for and still make deals with Indian exporters, there's not a damn thing she can do about it.

And unless you have carefully avoided buying any products made by Third World labor — and chances are you have not — you're really no better than Debbie. Let's drink to that. Believe me, Debbie already has.

## *Step 3: Getting Spiritual and Getting Medicated*

You often hear tourists call India a "spiritual" place. It seems as though half the Westerners here either (a) come with the intent to live on an ashram or (b) somehow end up at one anyway.

I appreciate the drive to find deeper meaning. I honestly do. And I'm a huge fan of pantheism. Why limit yourself to one god when instead you could pick and choose from a sampler of gods? It spices things up. The Brahma-Creator/Vishnu-Preserver/Shiva-Destroyer thing is a badass metaphor, too, even if I don't fully understand it.

But the truth is, I'm not quite wired to surrender my will to a higher power. And, getting back to my main point, I certainly don't see why India should corner the market on spirituality. Why do we get all mystical and fuzzy-headed the moment we hit the subcontinent?

Look at *The Razor's Edge* — the W. Somerset Maugham classic I've been reading over here. Protagonist Larry Darrell begins as a run-of-the-mill Midwesterner. Then he goes to India. By the time he gets back, he's received illumination and communed with the Absolute. Also, he has telekinetic powers.

I'm not sure I believe in the Absolute. But I do think I would enjoy having telekinesis. Mostly so I could alter the outcome of sporting events. (Oh, wide right! Too bad!)

To this end, I've decided to get me some spirituality here. It seems there exists a sort of Hindu metaphysics known as Ayurveda, which aims to heal both body and spirit (and, most important, has been championed by Deepak Chopra). I figure this will do the trick. And since they happen to have an Ayurvedic spa at our beach resort, I also figure: Why not seek deeper meaning on a massage table?

I arrive at the Ayurveda center and ask for an appointment. Maybe thirty seconds later I'm buck-naked in a small room with a smiling Indian man. His name is Sajan. He hands me a loincloth and helps me tie it. Then he guides me to the table, lays me down, pours a healthy dollop of oil on my chest, and begins to rub his hands all over my body.

Understand that I get slightly uncomfortable when I'm made to hug a person I've just met. I've got a thing about strangers touching me. And when it comes to strangers rubbing oil on my upper thighs, well, I get even more ill at ease. (Perhaps if the stranger were French actress Julie Delpy? But does she count as a stranger? I feel I know her so well from her films.)

Still, I've had professional massages before, and I've mostly enjoyed them (once I'm past the initial squeamishness). The key in the past has been the kneading of my knotted muscles — thus dispersing any stored-up tension. But as best I can tell, there is no kneading in Ayurveda. Just rubbing — and gallons of oil. While I hesitate to use the term "molestation" (and there was nothing sexual about it), I will say that Sajan's hands were not at all shy. I will also say that my loincloth seemed unnecessarily small and loosely fastened.

At one point — while my eyes were closed — a second pair of hands came out of nowhere and jumped in the mix. This alarmed me, insofar as it was sudden and unexpected. Like an ambush. Also, soon after this, the soothing tabla music that had been playing came to a stop and left us in silence . . . save for the sound of four well-oiled palms briskly sliding over my torso.

In the end, my spirit remained undaunted, but in no way was it illuminated or healed. This was the first massage I've had where I felt *less* relaxed walking out than I'd felt walking in.

Anyway, if I want to relax here, I've found a much better method: prescription-strength sedatives. I'd like to thank Lord Brahma for creating benzodiazepines. And also Lord Vishnu for preserving a loosely regulated Indian pharmaceutical system. I can walk into the "Medicines" shop in pretty much any town over here, plunk down fifty rupees (a little more than a dollar), and walk out with a great big bottle of 2 mg Ativan tablets.

This becomes especially key on the overnight train ride from Kerala to Goa. There are cockroaches perched on the wall above my head, across the aisle a man is coughing up phlegm (in a manner that suggests a highly communicable and highly fatal tropical disease), and I'm still trying to shake my traumatic memories of the massage. All of which is making it hard for me to sleep.

I suppose I could call on Lord Shiva to destroy all the roaches. Or the phlegm. But instead I just call on Lord Ativan, destroyer of consciousness. Cockroaches could scurry up onto my face, oil their many legs, and administer an Ayurvedic massage to my eyelids. I'd sleep right through it, given sufficient dosage.

## Step 4: Acceding to Chaos

Our first day out in Mumbai (formerly Bombay), we were approached by a man who — I'm fairly certain of this — planned to kidnap us. He gave us this carefully polished spiel about needing to cast a few extras for a Bollywood movie and how we'd be perfect for this scene he was shooting, so if we would just hop into his car with him . . . Tempting, but no dice. (It sort of cooled our jets when, in the middle of the pitch, this other Indian guy ran over and shouted, "Be careful with this man! This is a dangerous man!")

I'll admit, this Bollywood scam was brilliant. It played on my vanity and my long-held desire to appear in a Bollywood movie (preferably in a dance scene). I salute you, my would-be abductor.

But other pitches were not as well crafted. For instance, there was this guy who smiled weakly and asked us, with a halfhearted shrug, "Monkey dance?" Our eyes followed the leash in his hand, which led to the neck of a monkey. The most jaded, world-weary monkey I've ever seen. The Lou Reed of monkeys. He looked like he was about to sit down, pull out his works, and shoot a big syringe full of heroin into his paw. Needless to say, we declined the monkey dance — which I'm guessing would have been some sort of sad, simian death-jig.

The upshot of all this: Mumbai is not the place to go for a carefree, relaxing vacation. Just stepping out on the streets can be a difficult ordeal. The air smells like twice-baked urine, marinated in more urine. The sidewalks are a slalom of legless beggars and feral dogs. Hundreds of times each day you walk right past something so unfathomably sad, so incomprehensibly surreal, so horribly unfair . . .

The only way to cope is to stop resisting. Embrace the chaos. If you see a woman rolling around in the gutter clutching at the massive, bulbous wart on the side of her face and moaning loudly . . .

well, that's part of the scenery. No one else here (certainly no native Mumbaian) will pay her any attention. So why should you? Just say to yourself: Wow, that's crazy stuff and marvelously edifying. Doo-dee-doo, keep on walking.

That's harsh and simplistic. The truth is, the chaos can be wonderful sometimes, too. There's a goofy sense of freedom that comes with it. A sense of unknowing.

Back home in the States, it can feel like we've got life figured out, regulated, under control, under wraps. But here in India, nothing seems even close to figured out. Nothing seems remotely under control. You're never quite sure what will happen next, and you're working without a net.

Terrifying? Yes. But also invigorating. On the train ride up from Goa, I perused a women's magazine (sort of an Indian *Cosmo*) that we'd bought at a newsstand. The cover story was about women who'd lived abroad — mostly in the United States and Britain — but moved back because they liked India better. All these former NRIs (Non-Resident Indians) had gotten homesick . . . *for the chaos!* Yes, the West was clean and orderly. But that was sort of boring. They missed the hubbub, the craziness, the randomness of India. I see what they're saying. But in honesty, I prefer to see it from several stories up, in the air-conditioned cocktail lounge of the Oberoi Hotel. Ahhhh. Soft music. Lovely view. No legless beggars.

From up here, sure, all that chaos is beautiful. It's amazing to ponder (while calmly sipping a stiff rum and Coke) how one billion people manage to coexist in a single, sprawling democracy. It truly is impressive that this country keeps chugging along — massive, bulbous face warts and all.

In fact, I've come not just to like but to love India — in a way — from afar. It's the underdog. It's dirty and hectic and insane . . . and I find myself rooting for it.

## Step 5: Actually Liking Stuff

In the mid-1970s, famed author V. S. Naipaul (of Indian descent but raised in Trinidad) came to India to survey the land and record his impressions. The result is a hilariously grouchy book titled *India: A Wounded Civilization*. Really, he should have just titled it *India: Allow Me to Bitch at You for 161 Pages*. I hear you, V. S. — this place has its problems. As you point out, many of them result from the ravages of colonialism . . . and some are just India's own damn fault. Still, I've found a lot to love about this place. For instance:

1. I love cricket. The passion for cricket is infectious. When I first got here, the sport was an utter mystery to me, but now I've hopped on the cricket bandwagon, big time. I've got the rules down, I've become a discerning spectator, and I've settled on a favorite player (spin bowler Harbhajan Singh, known as "The Turbanator" — because he wears a turban). I've even eaten twice at Tendulkar's, a Mumbai restaurant owned by legendary cricketer Sachin Tendulkar. Fun fact: Sachin Tendulkar's nicknames include "The Master Blaster" (honoring his prowess as a batsman), "The Maestro of Mumbai" (he's a native), and "The Little Champion" (he's wicked short). His restaurant here looks exactly like a reverse-engineered Michael Jordan's Steak House. Instead of a glass case with autographed Air Jordans, there is a glass case with an autographed cricket bat.

And in what could turn out to be a dangerous habit, I've begun going to Mumbai sports bars to watch all-day cricket matches. These last like seven hours. That is a frightening amount of beer and chicken wings.

2. I love the Indian head waggle. It's a fantastic bit of body language, and I'm trying to add it to my repertoire. The head waggle says, in a uniquely unenthusiastic way, "OK, that's fine." In terms of Western gestures, its meaning is somewhere between the nod (though less affirmative) and the shrug (though not quite as neutral).

To perform the head waggle, keep your shoulders perfectly still, hold your face completely expressionless, and tilt your head side-to-side, metronome style. Make it smooth — like you're a bobble-head doll. It's not easy. Believe me, I've been practicing.

3. I love how Indians are unflappable. Nothing — I mean *nothing* — seems to faze them in the least. If you live here, I suppose you've seen your fair share of crazy/horrid/ miraculous/incomprehensible/mind-blowing stuff, and it's impractical to get too worked up over anything, good or bad.

(This is a trait I admire in the Dutch as well. They don't blink when some college kid tripping on mushrooms decides to leap naked into an Amsterdam canal. Likewise, were there a dead, limbless child in the canal . . . an Indian person might not blink. Though he might offer a head waggle.)

4. I love how they dote on children here. (I'm not talking about dead, limbless children anymore, I'm being serious now.) At our beach resort in Goa, there were all these bourgeois Indian folks down from Mumbai on vacation. These parents spoiled their children rotten in a manner that was quite charming to see. In no other country have I seen kids so obviously cherished, indulged, and loved. It's fantastic. Perhaps my favorite thing on television (other than cricket matches) has been a quiz show called *India's Smartest Child,* because I can tell the entire country derives great joy from putting these terrifyingly erudite children on display.

5. I love that this is a *billion*-person democracy. That is insane. Somehow the Tibetan Buddhists of Ladakh, the IT workers of Bangalore, the downtrodden poor of Bihar, and the Bollywood stars of Mumbai all fit together under this single, ramshackle umbrella. It's astonishing and commendable that anyone would even *attempt* to pull this off.

6. I love the chaos (when I don't hate it). Mumbai is a city of eighteen million people — all of whom appear to be on the same block of sidewalk as you. If you enjoy the stimulation overload of a Manhattan or a Tokyo but prefer much less wealth and infrastructure . . . this is your spot. (Our friend Rishi, whom we've been traveling with, has a related but slightly different take: "It's like New York, if everyone in New York was Indian! How great is that!") And whatever else you may feel, Mumbai will force you to consider your tiny place within humanity and the universe. That's healthy.

There's more good stuff I'm forgetting, but enough love for now. Let's not go overboard. As they say in really lame travel writing: India is a land of contradictions. A lot of things to like and a lot of things (perhaps two to three times as many things) to hate.

It's the spinach of travel destinations — you may not always (or ever) enjoy it, but it's probably good for you. In the final reckoning, am I glad that I came here? Oh, absolutely. It's been humbling. It's been edifying. It's been, on several occasions, quite wondrous. It's even been fun, when it hasn't been miserable.

That said, am I ready to leave? Sweet mercy, yes.

WILLIAM T. VOLLMANN

# They Came Out Like Ants!

FROM *Harper's Magazine*

IT WAS ON GOOD FRIDAY NIGHT, at the threshold of that
church on Avenida Reforma, in Mexicali, Mexico, with the Virgin
of Guadalupe's image invisible overhead and the border wall
faintly discernible, like a phosphorescent log in a dark forest, that
I first met the sisters Hernández. When the loudspeaker sighed
*María, la Madre de Jesús,* I thought they looked sincerely distressed,
Susana in particular. The Crucifixion had just occurred again.
When they mentioned Jesus, Mary, and Judas, they were speaking
of people they knew intimately. Later our talk turned to Mexicali,
and they began to tell me about the time of the great fire when all
the Chinese who lived secretly and illegally under the ground came
out "like ants," to escape the burning, and everybody was shocked
at how many of them there were. Susana and Rebeca had not yet
been born when that happened, but it remained as real to them as
the betrayal of Christ. I couldn't decide whether to believe them.
When was this great fire? They weren't sure. But they knew that
Chinese — *many, many* Chinese, as they kept saying — used to hide
in tunnels in Mexicali.

Chinese tunnels. Well, why shouldn't there be Chinese tunnels
in Mexicali? I'd seen the Valley of the Queens in Egypt (dirt and
gravel hills, sharp-edged rock shards, then caves); I'd convinced
myself of the existence of Pompeii's Anfiteatro, which is mainly a
collar of grass now, with a few concentric ribs of stone beneath.
Havre, Montana, still maintains its underground quarter as a
source of tourist revenue: Here's the bordello; there's the purple-
glassed skylight; and don't forget to see the old black leather den-

tist drill, a foot drill, actually, which was operated by the patient! Why shouldn't there be more than sand beneath Mexicali?

José Lopez, a freelance tour guide with two blackened front teeth, told me that a year or two ago a friend of his had delivered a truckload of fresh fish from San Felipe up to a certain Chinese produce market in Mexicali. What was the address of this market? José couldn't say. It was surely somewhere in the Chinesca, the Chinatown. The merchant opened a door, and José's friend glimpsed a long dark tunnel walled with earth. What's that? he asked. You don't need to know, came the answer. José's understanding was that even now the Chinese didn't trust banks. They kept their money under the ground.

The owner of the Golden China Restaurant believed that there were four or five thousand Chinese in Mexicali. A certain Mr. Auyón, said to be a world-famous painter of horses, informed me that there were currently eight thousand Chinese, thirty-two thousand half-Chinese, and a hundred Chinese restaurants.

Most of the Chinese were legal now, but in the old days they'd come illegally from San Felipe, and then their relatives or Tong associates had concealed them in those tunnels, which, it was widely believed, still extended under "all downtown," and there was even supposed to be a passageway to Calexico, California, though none of the storytellers had seen it, and some allowed that it might have been discovered and sealed off decades ago by the Border Patrol. I've read that during Prohibition *in the Chinese district of Mexicali, tunnels led to opium dens and brothels, and for the convenience of bootleggers, one of them burrowed under the international line to Calexico,* which might have been that tunnel, or a precursor, under the cantina around the corner from the Hotel Malibu. Mexicans bought me drinks there and insisted that the tunnel still existed.

A tunnel under the Hotel Del Norte was discovered and closed in the 1980s; the Chinese didn't have anything to do with that one, I'm told. In the autumn of 2003, people with guns and uniforms found another tunnel that began in a mechanic's shop east of the Chinesca and came up in Calexico — in a fireplace, I was told — but it wasn't a Chinese tunnel. A whore in the Hotel Altamirano said she knew for a fact that the Chinese had been behind that tunnel, because *they always work in secret.* Frank Waters recalls in his memoir of the days when the Colorado River still flowed to the sea that in 1925 Chinese were smuggled across the border *in crates of melons, disguised as old Mexican señoras, and even carried by plane from Laguna Salada.* Perhaps they traveled by tunnel as well. From the Chinatown in Mexicali to the one in Los Angeles, both of which have since burned. *They came out like ants!*

My own mental image of the tunnels grew strangely similar to those long aboveground arcades on both sides of the border; on certain very hot summer nights when I have been under a fever's sway, with sweat bursting out on the back of my neck and running down my sides, the archways have seemed endless; their sidewalks pulse red like some science fiction nightmare about plunging into the sun, and as I walk home out of Mexico, the drunken woman and the empty throne of the shoeshine man are but artifacts, lonely and sparse, within those immense corridors of night. I wander down below the street and up again for the border formalities, which pass like a dream, and suddenly I find myself in the continuation of those same arcades, which are quieter and cooler than their Mexican equivalents. Bereft of the sulphur-sweet stink of the feculent New River, which loops northwest as soon as it enters the United States, they extend block after block in the same late-night dream.

It seemed that everyone knew about these tunnels — everybody in Mexicali, that is. But when I crossed the border to inquire at the Pioneers Museum, two old white men who'd lived in Imperial County all their lives stared at me, not amused at all, and replied they'd never heard anything about any tunnels. Up in Brawley, Stella Mendoza, wife, mother, ex-director and continuing representative of her Imperial Irrigation District, passionate defender and lifelong resident of Mexican America, who spoke Spanish, traced back her ancestry to Sonora, and went to Mexicali "all the time," said that the tunnels were likewise news to her. But why should we Americans know anything about Chinese tunnels in Mexico?

## Vampires and Cigarettes

The clandestine nature of the tunnels lent itself to supernatural evocations. About thirty years ago a rumor had settled on Mexicali that the Chinese were harboring a vampire down there. Later it came out that the creature was human but a "mutant," very hairy, two of whose lower teeth had grown like fangs right through the skin above his upper lip. He "escaped," said the woman who'd seen him, but the Chinese recaptured him, and that was the end of the story. I asked José Lopez whether he believed this tale, and he said, "Look. You have to keep an open mind. In the 1960s the Devil himself came to Mexicali. He actually killed a woman! Everybody knew it was the Devil. If you keep a closed mind, you can't believe it. But why not believe it?"

*They live like cigarettes,* said a Mexican journalist on a Sunday, cramming all his upright fingers together as if he'd shoved them into a box. He advised me to search for people who looked *like this* (pulling his eye corners upward), because only they could tell me everything. Although he'd never seen one, his sources inclined him to believe that there might be a tunnel under Condominios Montealbán, those ill-famed grimy concrete apartments beside the Río Nuevo, where tired women, some Chinese-looking, some not, complained about the illnesses of their children, and teenagers sat day after day in the shade of an old stone lion. It had been at Condominios Montealbán that a Mexican mother had compared her country and my country thus: "Here we're free. Over there they live like robots." We live like robots; Chinese lived like cigarettes. And they protected a vampire, and they *came out like ants.*

The people I met on the street didn't like the Chinese; nor, it seemed, did many of the intelligentsia, the journalists, or the archivists. A young boy I met, who had worked in a Chinese restaurant for five years, told me: "They come from far away from here, so their character is different from ours, and it's bad. They don't share." I asked him if he'd ever heard anything about tunnels? "Never," he said, "because these kinda people, they don't wanna talk to no one about their life." A white-haired, pleasant, round-faced lady named Lupita, who had once worked in the office of a semi company, had graduated to being a security guard in a prostitute discotheque, and now held afternoon duty as the moneytaker for a parking lot beside a shut-down supermarket, allowed that her favorite aspect of Mexicali was her friends, and her second favorite was the Chinese food. Would she consider marrying a Chinese? I inquired. "No! I'm not a racist, but no Chinese, no nigger!"

## *"Them Damned Nagurs"*

Imperial, by which I mean not only the Imperial Valley but also that valley's continuation south of the border, is a boarded-up billiard arcade, white and tan; Imperial is Calexico's rows of palms, flat tan sand, oleanders, and squarish buildings, namely the Golden China Restaurant, Yum Yum Chinese Food, McDonald's, Mexican insurance; Imperial contains a photograph of a charred building and a heap of dirt: *Planta Despepitadora de Algodón "Chino-Mexicana."* Imperial is a map of the way to wealth, but the map has been sunbleached back to blankness. Leave an opened newspaper outside for a month and step on it; the way it crumbles, that's Imperial. Imperial is a Mexicali wall at twilight: tan, crudely smoothed, and hot to the touch. Imperial is a siltscape so featureless that every little dip made by last century's flood gets a christening, even if the name is only X Wash. In spite of its wide, flat streets and buildings, Imperial is actually a mountain, Gold Mountain to be precise.

By 1849, word of the California gold rush had reached China. Mr. Chung Ming got rich right away. Hearing the news, his friend Cheong Yum rushed to California and achieved equal success. In 1852, 20,000 Chinese, mostly Cantonese,* made the journey to try their luck. A little more than a decade later, there were 12,000 of them digging, blasting, mortaring, and shoveling on the transcontinental railroad. *Wherever we put them we found them good,* reported a white magnate who happily paid them less than he did his Irishmen. The Irishmen noticed. One of them lamented: *Begad if it wasn't for them damned nagurs we would get $50 and not do half the work.*

"Chinamen" and Indians received preference for employment in the vineyards around Los Angeles, and in 1860 a contingent of white laborers gave up and departed for Texas. In 1876 a chronicle of Los Angeles reports this news: *City still rapidly improving. During June anti-Chinese meetings were the order of the day.* Those words were written a mere five years after the infamous Chinese Massacre.† In

---

* According to the owner of the Golden China Restaurant, in 2003 this was still the case, although a number of Mexicali's Chinese also came from Shanghai.

† The way one county history tells it, two rival Chinese mobs fighting over a woman "on either side of Negro alley" began shooting at each other on 23 October 1871. On the following day, a policeman and two citizens who were doing what they could to bring peace got wounded in the crossfire; one citizen died. "The news of his

spite of the anti-Asian movement's best efforts, *An Illustrated History of Los Angeles County,* published in 1889, estimates that between two and three thousand Chinese walked the streets: *The Chinese are a prominent factor in the population of Los Angeles . . . The Chinaman, as a rule, with occasional exceptions, is not desirable help in the household. On the ranch . . . he can be tolerated, when white men are not obtainable.*

Meanwhile, in 1898, the Britannica Company contracted with Mr. Ma You Yong to bring a thousand Chinese to Mexico for railroad work. A tunnel cave-in killed seventy-seven. And they kept right on, from Oaxaca all the way to Salinas Cruz and Jesús Carranza. Onlookers no doubt remarked that they live together like cigarettes. In the sixth year of their labors, Jack London published a bitterly logical little essay entitled "The Scab." *When a striker kills with a brick the man who has taken his place, he has no sense of wrongdoing . . . Behind every brick thrown by the striker is the selfish will "to live" of himself, and the slightly altruistic will "to live" of his family.*

Under capitalism, continues London, we are all scabs, and we all hate scabs. But not everyone takes his reasoning that far. The Chinese coolie, whom London mentions in the same breath as the Caucasian professor who scabs by being meeker than his predecessor, was to haters of *damned nagurs* a dangerously particular case. You see, in California the Chinese do more than we, in exchange for less. In that case, we'd better make it hot for the Chinese. Hence anti-Chinese riots; hence the Chinese Exclusion Act of 1882 and its many descendants.

"The Scab" saw print the same year as Mexicali's founding. The Chinese were already there.

## They Came for the Work

A soft-spoken old Chinese shoe-store owner at Altamirano and Juárez (who became less open with me once I started badgering him about tunnels) told me that his grandfather came in 1906 to pick cotton. He worked for an American company, but he couldn't remember the name. I suspect it was the Colorado River Land

death spread like wild-fire, and brought together a large crowd, composed principally of the lower class of Mexicans and the scum of the foreigners." The predictable result: lynchings, shootings, arson, pillaging. Nineteen Chinese were murdered. (Another source gives the casualty figure of a probably inflated seventy-two.)

Company, which had already hired Mariano Ma. In later years he'd be seen at the racetrack with the governor of Baja California, but in 1903 he spent his days with Chang Peio and the other *braceros*, leveling roads, digging canals, all for a wage of fifty centavos (twenty-five additional for food); whether this was paid daily or weekly is not recorded. Señor Ma remarks: *In that place there were a lot of mosquitoes. Many people died on account of the various sicknesses caused by insect bites, rattlesnakes, and the intense heat. Some people were buried underground by quicksand and whirlwinds.*

The old Chinese-Mexican mestiza Carmen Jaham told it this way: *Mexicali began with about a hundred or a hundred and fifty Chinese.* And between 1902 and 1921, 40,000 or 50,000 Chinese came to Mexico. In 1913 there were a thousand in Mexicali alone. And they kept coming.

Steve Leung, the owner of a shop on Calle Altamirano, a middle-aged third-generation Chinese, told me that most of the Chinese workers who came here had been farmers. They saw the desert wasteland standing fallow and they cultivated it. Later, when the Mexicans started moving in, the Chinese ran grocery stores and laundries. They were successful with the groceries, but then the Mexicans started taking over that business, so the Chinese pulled back to restaurants. "Mexican people have not been able to take that over, since Chinese work longer hours," Mr. Leung said. "They don't fight with the local people; they let them come in; they just pull back."

And in my mind's eye, as Mr. Leung said this, I could see them pulling back into the tunnels. Whether or not his version of events correctly explains the facts, it certainly fits in with them, for the photo albums in the Archivo Histórico del Municipio de Mexicali do show an awful lot of Chinese grocery stores.

## *"A High-Pitched Voice Was Screaming Chinese Orders"*

The historian Hubert H. Bancroft, whose many-volumed work on California is a monument nearly as eminent as the border wall, expresses his epoch when he tells us: *These people were truly, in every sense, aliens. The color of their skins, the repulsiveness of their features, their under-size of figure, their incomprehensible language, strange customs, and heathen religion . . . conspired to set them apart.*

In around 1905 we find Mr. Hutchins, the Chinese inspector, carrying out his task at Jacumba, *which is to allow no unentitled Mongolian to cross from Mexico into the United States.* When he catches them, they're jailed and tried.

In one of Zane Grey's novels, published in 1913, a rancher on the Arizona side of Sonora explains to a cowboy that *of course, my job is to keep tab on Chinese and Japs trying to get into the U.S. from Magdalena Bay.* (That same year, the Colorado River Land Company imports another five hundred Chinese into Mexico from Hong Kong.)

In 2003 the man in the *casa de cambio* on First Street assured me in a gleeful murmur that of course there were tunnels *everywhere* in Calexico because if they started over *there* in Mexico then it stood to reason that they'd come up over *here.* He was Chinese. His building had three tunnel entrances, he said, but unfortunately he couldn't show them to me because they were closed. But he knew for a fact that the old building that now housed the Sam Ellis store had a tunnel. The kindly old proprietor of the latter establishment showed me photographs of the way the border used to be; he advised me to go to the chamber of commerce for an interpreter; as for the tunnels, every time I asked if I could just take a peek in his basement he didn't seem to hear me, but he did say: *You're never gonna find any of those tunnels.*

In 1925, Dashiell Hammett's crime story "Dead Yellow Women" envisions Chinese tunnels in San Francisco, all the while keeping faithful to the expectations of his public: *The passageway was solid and alive with stinking bodies. Hands and teeth began to take my clothes away from me . . . A high-pitched voice was screaming Chinese orders . . .* That was one passageway to alienness. In another, which the protagonist reached through a trap door, *the queen of something stood there! . . . A butterfly-shaped headdress decked with the loot of a dozen jewelry stores exaggerated her height.*

When Fu Manchu movies went out of fashion, new authentications of menacing alienness became available. Zulema Rashid, born in Calexico in 1945, remembers being scared every time she had to buy something in the Chinese store on Imperial Avenue *because the Chinese were Communists who tortured people.*

A fighting-cock breeder from near San Luis Río de Colorado, told me during a match in Islas Agrarias that *of course the Chinese are all into slavery.* That was why one never saw any Chinese beggars. He got even more animated in the course of telling me that seven years ago the authorities had rounded up many illegal Chinese in Mexicali and sequestered them in a stadium under heavy guard, but some had mysteriously escaped, an occurrence that he considered both uncanny and hateful; he turned bitter when he mentioned it. He supposed that they had disappeared into one of their tunnels.

## *"A* Raw *Smell"*

*They came out of the ground like ants.* So why shouldn't there be tunnels? They exist, asserted Beatriz Limón, who was a reporter for *La Crónica.* She, however, had never seen one. One of her colleagues had entered a tunnel with Chinese guides, but the smell had been too terrible for her — a *raw* smell, said Beatriz with distaste, a smell like sewage.

Oscar Sanchez from the Archivo Histórico looked up at me from behind his desk and said: "They are there. But I can tell you nothing concrete. Originally they were there for shelter from the heat, but then they started to install the casinos. Oh, but it is difficult. These people are very closed!"

Men said that there once had been tunnels beneath the dance hall Thirteen Negro, which was whitewashed over its ancientness and cracked through its whitewash, doing business on and on at the center of the brick-fringed archways of arcades, lord of not quite closed sidewalk gratings, with blackness beneath. Why wouldn't there be tunnels under the Thirteen Negro? And if they *were* there, why wouldn't they still be there? But the waiter denied it. What did his denial mean? I asked him how often he got Chinese customers and he said every night. I asked him if he could introduce me to a Chinese regular; maybe I could buy the man a drink. But the waiter said he didn't want any trouble.

## *The Tale of the Air Ducts*

My next tactic was to bang on Mexicali's nearest prominently ideogrammed metal gate, and that is how, ushered down a tree-shaded walkway and into a courtyard, I had the inestimable pleasure of meeting Professor Eduardo Auyón Gerardo of the Chinese Association Chung Shan.

This *world-renowned painter, known especially for his paintings of horses and nude women,* had a Chinese mother and a Mexican father. In 1960, when he was thirteen years old, his father brought him to Mexicali to join his grandmother.

Mr. Auyón was not especially pleased to see me. He told me that I really should have made an appointment. In fact I'd banged on the gate two days ago and made an appointment through his nephew. This did not mollify the *world-renowned painter,* who sat unsmiling amidst his *sumi* paintings and brass lions. Well, to business: First he tried to sell me a gold-plated commemorative medallion, which he had designed. It was pretty but expensive. Then he offered me a dusty copy of his book, *El Dragón en el Desierto: Los Pioneros Chinos en Mexicali,* for the special price of thirty dollars. Comprehending that if I didn't buy something from him my interview would be terminated, I paid for *El Dragón en el Desierto,* after which he brightened slightly and began to relate snippets of Chinese-Mexican history.

I asked him if I could please meet a Chinese family.

It's very difficult, he explained, because my countrymen are not very communicative. But *El Dragón en el Desierto* does have ten chapters. You can read all about the Chinese in there. That was perfect. My research was now at an end. We agreed that if and only if I read his book thoroughly and maybe memorized it, then came back in a month, it was possible that he might have found a Chinese family to tell me something innocuous.

That point having been settled, I asked him about the Chinese tunnels. They don't exist, the world-renowned painter of horses assured me. The people couldn't survive in them if they did. They could not sleep. It would be too hot down there.

Just in case there were tunnels after all, Mr. Auyón, where do you think they might be?

That heat, the body cannot withstand it, he replied. In the nighttime one has to sleep. One has to live down there — that's why the snakes live underground — but in the summer it's too hot.

So there are no tunnels?

Every locality has tunnels like a house has a cellar. There are businesses that have two or three branches. They have cellars and connections. On Juárez at Reforma, one man has seven businesses. Underneath, it looks like another city.

Could I see one of those cellars? He didn't think that that was possible. Then, looking into my face, and this was the one moment when I felt that he was actually being genuine with me, he said: Do you want to know the history of Mexicali? *Every ten acres, one Chinese died.*

I'm sorry, I said. He looked at his watch. The world-renowned medallionist had an important appointment.

I asked him if he could show me one of the cellars that he'd mentioned. He took me into the Hotel Chinesca next door and past the fancy lobby into the open-air courtyard giving onto tiny double-bedded rooms, and from a chambermaid he got the key to the cellar, which looked and smelled like a cellar. There he pointed to a "communication" passage in the corner of the wall. It was small and square and had a screen over it; it was, he said, an air duct. Inside it I could see light and stoneworked walls. A small child could have hidden there. Triumphantly, Mr. Auyón declared: This is what they call a tunnel.

## Under the Volleyball Court

So it went. I could tell you about my interview with the taxi driver who knew for a fact that a tunnel had once led from the Chinesca right across the border, but they closed it; or the tale of Leonardo, the "tour guide" from Tijuana who was down on his luck, so he followed me down the street at around midnight, trying to interest me in young girls. Did I want fifteen-year-olds? I did not. Well, then, he could get me twelve-year-olds. He could deliver them right to me if I went to the Hotel Mexico. He had a hatchet-shaped, smooth little face, and he was little and vicious. Since he could do anything (he'd already told me the story of how he'd obtained excellent false papers for *pollos* in T. J.), I told him to take me into the Chinese tunnels, about which he'd never heard. So he did research. It took him a day. He found me an underground casino that would be possible to visit before opening time, but I had to promise not to talk to anyone, and he couldn't guarantee that I could take photographs. When he saw that I really wanted to take photographs, he said that he could work it out. Leonardo was the man, all right. Why shouldn't it be true? There'd been gaming houses in Mexicali since 1909. He described so well how it would be that I could almost see it. Soon a note was waiting for me at the Hotel Chinesca:

The tour would cost me fifty dollars, and I had to pay in advance. Leonardo went first to give the password; he'd be back in two minutes. I waited for him in the pitch-dark alley on the edge of the Río Nuevo; the moon resembled an orange darkly pitted by cyanide fumigation injury, and I waited and waited for admission to that splendid underground world that Leonardo had promised me.

To my rescue came Professor Yolanda Sánchez Ogás, lifelong resident of Mexicali (born in 1940), historian, anthropologist, and author of *Bajo el Sol de Mexicali* and *A La Orilla del Río Colorado: Los Cucapá,* both of which she sold me out of the closet of her house. The first time I asked her about Chinese tunnels, she said that she didn't know anything about them but would find out. The next time I saw her she calmly said: I went into the tunnels. That entire area under La Chinesca has a subterranean level. As for the casino, I know there *was* one, but right now I don't think so. But under the volleyball court many *Chinos* live.

Have you seen them living there?

No, but I have heard. And I met an old man who lived all his life under Restaurant Ocho.

## Rats and Cockroaches

Next morning in Callejón Chinesca the proprietors of the watch stores and clothing stores were already rolling up their gratings. We were looking for the Restaurant Jing Tung. Nobody in the street had ever heard of it. But that didn't mean it wasn't there. Yolanda led us to the Hotel Cecil, which I'm told was the labor of love of a Chinese named Cecil Chin. We went upstairs. Yolanda said that there had once been a tunnel with bars, casinos, and a restaurant.

This is all new, said the manager, gesturing around him. When they constructed this hotel in 1947, the tunnel was already there. There used to be an entrance on the first floor.

Can we go into the tunnel? I asked.

The manager wearily spread his hands. It's closed, he said. He didn't care to nourish any myths.

Across the street from the Cecil, in another roofed passageway called Pasajes Prendes, there was an ancient barbershop whose owner's white hair resembled his ribbed and whitewashed concrete ceiling, and he said: No, you walked in from the street, and the restaurant was on the left by the bar, and it had really big chairs and a piano, and there was a man who played the piano. They took the piano away many years ago. In the tunnel there was a store, and right here in front there was a butcher shop aboveground. The hotel was finished in April of '47, and there was nothing here before, he said, beaming through his round glasses. Oh, he was happy, smiling, talking about the past.

So what's in the tunnels now? I asked.

Pure trash.

His single customer, who was tub-shaped, chimed in: And rats!

Yolanda said nothing. I knew that she hated rats.

I went down there, said the customer, and it's all trash. Rats, cockroaches, because of the humidity . . .

A woman over here had a store, said the barber. There is still an entrance over there, and it's full of water. There was a cantina below. Cecil Chin owned the cantina. The whole building, there's tunnels all over the place. Anyone could go in. It was public property.

Were there casinos below?

No, there were never any casinos.

I thought there was a casino under the Callejón.

There could have been, said the barber happily. There was a barbershop, a shoe store, a bowling alley, pool tables . . .

I think there are some places where people get together to play cards, said Yolanda.

The tubby man, who was a foreman, shrugged and said: There are tunnels all through here, and also on Juárez and Reforma. It's like a labyrinth.

As the fan slowly rotated along the edge of the mirror, they talked happily about the old days *when they were all killing each other.*

Around '46 a lot of this was burned, said the barber. Slowly he reached up to turn on the auxiliary ceiling fan. The first of these buildings caught on fire, in '45 or '46, a lot of Chinese died. The second fire, nobody was inside. That was in '91. That second fire was so big that they came from Calexico and El Centro to put it out. And by the way, it seems to me that there used to be a tunnel under the Hotel Imperial. There used to be a cantina . . .

There still is, but not underneath, said the fat man.

Were there ever any opium dens? I asked.

The barber said: I worked in the Hotel Cecil for six years. I started in '49 as a waiter. Then I became a manager of the laundry department. When I was up there washing clothes, I saw the Chinese people smoking opium. There was a basketball court, and under there were six or seven Chinese men with a big pipe, passing it around. The pipe was as long as my arm!

Another old man had come in to get his hair cut, and he said: Yeah, I was there then, too. They were up all night smoking and gambling. They were playing *baraja* for a lot of money. That happened in the tunnels. I am seventy-six, and I was born here.

Were there prostitutes in the tunnels?

No, that was above.

Did anyone live in the tunnels?

Over in this part, in the Chinesca, sure.

Can we see the place where the water is? I asked.

A woman named Inocencia has the key. I never had the key.

We thanked the barber and wished him good business. As he was saying goodbye to us, he remarked, very sadly: There really aren't any businesses here anymore. It's all boutiques. All the Americans come here to buy medicines.

And I knew that he would have loved to go back in time, even just for a day, to wander in the tunnels when they were crammed with life, glamour, commerce, and vice.


## My First Tunnel

Near the Hotel Capri there was a certain clothing business owned by an elderly Mexican who knew Yolanda quite well. Behind the counter, next to the water closet, there was a metal door, which the man unlocked, inviting us into a concrete room, where clothes hung on a line. The man lifted up a trapdoor, and I saw stairs. Yolanda had her flashlight, and Terrie, my translator, was carrying the other flashlight, which we had bought an hour earlier for just this occasion. Smiling, the man stood aside.

Yolanda wanted me to go first, because she was afraid of the rats, so I did, and she came after me into that sweltering darkness, gamely half-smiling with her pale, sweat-drenched shirt unbuttoned almost to the breast and her head high and sweat shining on her cheekbones and sparkling in her short gray hair and her kind proud eyes alertly seeking just as the straight white beam of her flashlight did, cutting through the darkness like a knife. Terrie's flashlight was very steady. Where were we? The humidity was almost incredible. Dirt and darkness, flaring pillars composed my immediate impression. Lumber heaps leaped up as pale as bone piles under those twin beams of battery-powered light. I saw no rats. How stifling it was! Graffiti'd beams ran overhead, higher than I would have expected but still in arm's reach, and wire hangers with flaring underparts hung like the skeletal outlines of headless women. I glimpsed the folding X-frames of something, a table, and a metal wheel of protruding spokes. Beneath the heavy rectangular archways, the tunnel went on and on. Quite evidently it was much vaster than the store above it, even allowing for the fact that everything is always larger in darkness. Somewhere ahead of us, skeletal perspective lines approached one another palely within the ceiling darkness; the place where they lost themselves seemed to be a hundred feet away and was probably ten. I thought I could see a squarish passage. The floor was littered with trash and broken chairs and empty cardboard boxes. Here gaped an open safe. I picked my way as carefully as I could; for all I knew, ahead of me there might be an uncovered well that would lead straight to death in cheesy black currents of the Río Nuevo, which, thank God, I couldn't smell at the moment. Yolanda and Terrie were out of sight; they were in other worlds; I could see only one or the other of their flashlight beams. I felt almost alone. Chamber after chamber went on, connected by squarish archways. A palish blotch on the black wall gazed at me; my mind was beginning its usual game of dreaming up faces. Drumming and music came down to me from somewhere up above. The old Mexican who owned the place had said that he thought there had been a casino down here, and when I heard that music I could almost imagine it.

It might well be that the quality of the tunnels that haunted so many of us was quite simply their *goneness.* When I imagine them, my ignorance allows them to be what they will. Before we knew how hot the surface of Venus is, we used to be able to write beautiful science fiction stories of swamps and green-skinned Venusians. I could almost see myself descending the stairs into this place in the years when the electric lights still worked. Sometime between the first and second fires it might have been perfect down here. Having smoked opium in Thailand, I could imagine that one of these chambers might have had mats on the floor where I could have lain, watching the opium smoke rise sweetly from my pipe between inhalations. And from Thailand I also remembered Chinese men in black trousers, shiny black shoes, and white dress shirts; at an open-to-the-street restaurant in Chinatown, with stainless-steel tables and white tile walls, we were all drinking delicious sweet chrysanthemum juice the color of urine, and the handsomest man of all leaned on his elbow and gazed dreamily over his crossed fingers. Was this how the Chinese would have dressed when they went underground to drink, gamble, and womanize in Mexicali? Or would they have possessed nothing but the rough cotton clothes of the *braceros*?

There might have been a piano player here as there had been at Cecil Chin's, and when he paused to take a drink of Mexicali Beer, I would have heard all around me the lovely bone-clicks of mah-jongg. One hot summer day in the Chinese city of Nan-ning, I wandered through a park of lotus leaves and exotic flowers to a pagoda where ancient women sat, drowsily, happily playing mah-jongg amidst the scent of flowers, and that excellent sound of clicking tiles enchanted me; I was far from home, but that long slow summer afternoon with the mah-jongg sounds brought me back to my own continent and specifically to Mexicali, whose summer tranquillity never ends.

I remember a lady who smiled when she was dancing naked, a sweet smile of black eyes and glowing white teeth; she seemed so hopeful, so enthusiastic, so "sincere," if that word makes any sense between two strangers, and she was smiling right at me! She held my hand; that's right, she held my hand all the way to the hotel; I kissed her plump red lips and sucked on them as much as I wanted; she kissed me back. *Caliente!* the men in the street said approvingly. Afterward we walked hand in hand back to the dance hall, and all the men applauded. She was Mexican, not Chinese, and the place where she'd rented me her illusion of love lay several blocks beyond the edge of the Chinesca; all the same, it was she whom I now thought of in that tunnel whose revelry had turned to lumber and broken chairs; those click-clacking mah-jongg tiles in Nan-ning,

the laughter and preposterously exaggerated moans of that prostitute, the sensations of opium intoxication in Thailand — these
were the buried treasures that my flashlight beam sought in the
Chinese tunnels of Mexicali, my memories, my happy dissipations,
let's say my youth. No wonder I'd wanted to believe Leonardo
the "tour guide"! Waiting for nothing in the hot thick night, with
the ducklike quacking of a radio coming from one of the tin walls
of that alley, that evil sand-paved alley overlooking Condominios
Montealbán, I was already a citizen of this darkness; I was a spider
luxuriously centered in the silk web of my own fantasies.

## The Tunnel Letters

Next came the Restaurant Victoria, a tranquil paradise of coolness
and reliably bland food (the Dong Cheng was better) where the
waitresses were the only ones who hurried; the customers, who
were mostly Mexican, lived out the hours with their sombreros or
baseball caps on, lingering over their rice; here I had tried and
failed on several prior occasions to find out if there might be any
tunnels in the neighborhood. But it was just as my father always
said, *it's not what you know, it's who you know,* and I knew Yolanda,
who happened to be here, and who knew Miguel, the Chinese
owner, a slender youngish man with jet-black hair who'd come here
from Canton two decades before. He led us through the restaurant
— white ceiling, white incandescent lights, white tables, at one of
which a fat old lady and a young girl, both Chinese, sat slowly eating while the television emitted music that was sad and dramatic
and patriotically Mexican. The white walls gave way to pinkish
bathroomlike tiles as we passed beneath the rapidly whirling white
fans and admired from afar the Chinese-captioned painting of the
red sun floating on a turquoise sea — and through the swinging
doors he led us, straight into the kitchen, where the Mexican cook
and the Chinese dishwasher goggled at us; turning right, we came
into a long narrow courtyard and entered a detached two-story
building with what appeared to be an ancestral shrine just within
the entrance. To the right, next to a shopping cart full of stale
burned bread and a hand mill to grind the bread to flour for gravy,
wide stairs descended.

This tunnel was less dark, uncluttered, and more self-contained.

Indeed, it disappointed me at first; it appeared to be little more than a concrete cellar. Then I noticed that a five-socketed chandelier crouched on the ceiling like a potbellied spider, four of its sockets encased in ornate floral doughnuts, the fifth a bare metal bell. The ceiling itself comprised fancy-edged blocks like parquet flooring. But some blocks were stained or charred and some were moldy and some were entirely missing, leaving rectangles of darkness peering down from behind the rafters. It was a wide chamber that could have held many people, especially if they'd lived together like cigarettes. What had they done here? Had they gambled or simply banqueted? Had this place been an opium den? A tub held old Chinese porcelain bowls with floral designs. Then there were several dark and empty side-chambers.

The Victoria was in Miguel's estimation sixty years old, maybe eighty. Since we were in the heart of the Chinesca, this tunnel would have possibly already been here but so what, and how could I possibly speculate anyhow? On my second visit to this tunnel I saw a few more traces of fire, and I also found what might or might not have been a trapdoor in the concrete floor of the first chamber; it would not budge. In the dark room beneath some beds was a stack of bedframes. *Muchas prostitutas!* suggested one of my guides.

At the extreme end of the farthest room, another passageway had been bricked up. I asked Miguel how much it would cost me to have that obstruction broken down and then sealed up again when I had seen whatever there was to see. Smiling, he replied that there was no need for that; all I had to do was ask the pastor of the Sinai Christian Center down the street to let me into *his* tunnel.

When we turned back to the middle chamber we saw a desk, and we approached it without any great expectations since it was not so many steps away from the entrance to this place; all we had to do was turn around and we could see the supernaturally bright daylight of Mexicali burning down into the stairwell. I remember that a spiderweb as wide as a hammock hung on the wall; I remember how dismally humid it was in that place; I could almost believe Mr. Auyón, who'd claimed that of course the Chinese never lived underground, because that would have been too uncomfortable. In other words, I couldn't help but assume this desk to be a counterpart of the first tunnel's Sentry model 1230 safe, which sat upon the skeleton of a table that might once have had a glass top, lording it over broken beams and pipe lengths. Dust and filth speckled the top of the safe; behind rose a partly charred concrete wall. The door gaped open. Inside was nothing but dirt.

But as it turned out, under the Restaurant Victoria, in that roll-top desk with a writing surface of wood slats now beginning to warp away from one another just enough to let the darkness in between them, lay a hoard of letters, some of them rat-gnawed, all of them smelly, moldy, and spiderwebbed. Yolanda Ogás was standing against the wall whose pale sea-waves of stains were as fanciful as the serpent plumes of painted Chinese dragons; Miguel bent over the desk, fingering the old letters that had been crammed into blackened drawers for who knows how long. The darkness was hot, wet, and slightly rotten. Then he rose and turned away with indifference.

Miguel was a nice man, and he gave me permission to borrow the letters. When I chatted with him upstairs, in the richly glowing shade of the Restaurant Victoria, looking out through the lingerie-translucent curtains and the double glass doors with the red ideograms on them, the white rectangles of the street walls, and dried-blood-colored gratings of other Chinese businesses, the world one-third occluded by angle-parked cars and trucks, I found that he didn't want to talk, because he'd been here for only twenty years, which, he reminded me, *wasn't long enough to voice an opinion.* He referred us to the Chinese Association. There were actually either twenty-six or twenty-eight of those, but he meant the Chinese Association whose head was a certain Mr. Auyón.

The tunnel letters brought to life the time when there was light in the partly stripped chandelier, when that ceiling whose fanciness has long since been gutted into occasional waffle-pits of darkness was still whole, when the stacked tables were still laid out for reading, drinking, arguing, and gambling, a time before the walls were stained and the ceiling squares dangled down like laundry on the line. Here is one, an undated message from a wife in China to her husband in Mexico; perhaps he brought it downstairs to ask his Tong brothers what he could possibly do:

*Everything goes well at home, except that my father-in-law cannot understand why there is no letter from you. Father-in-law questioned money sent via Hong*

*Kong via Rong-Shi, and Rong-Shi denied receiving money. We borrowed money
from neighbors. Father-in-law is not in good health. Please send money home.
Also, when you send money home, do not send money via Rong-Shi, but addressed to . . .*

*Thinking of you. The way I miss you is heavy and long; however, the paper is too
short to carry the feelings.*

## Days of Ivory

I've never really heard about the tunnels. The tunnels don't exist. Meanwhile, I kept going into tunnels. Half a dozen times I had the experience of descending below a Mexican-owned boutique or pharmacy, asking the owner where another tunnel might be, getting
referred to this or that shop a door or three away, going to this or
that shop's proprietor, and being told: There are no tunnels here.
Sometimes they'd say: There is a tunnel but I don't have a key. The
boss has the key. How long are you here until? Tuesday? Well, the
boss will be in San Diego until Tuesday. One lady assured me that
the tunnels were a myth; another said that her establishment's tunnel was being rented out as a storage space and she didn't have
the key; a third, who'd operated her business in the Chinesca for
twenty-two years, assured me that there had never been any tunnels
in the Chinesca. Of course, with every passing year the tunnels did
come that much closer to a state of nonexistence. Restaurant Nineteen, one of the oldest in Mexicali, was abandoned half a decade
ago and in the early summer of 2003 had already been for three
months reincarnated as a pool hall, with blue-felted billiard tables
imported from Belgium. The Mexican owner, who wore blue to
match his tables, was actually less interested in billiards than in
carambola, which employs only three balls. He'd bought the building outright from the Chinese. He'd remodeled extensively and
knew that there had never been any tunnels. I asked if I could visit
his basement, but he didn't hear me. I asked again but he still
didn't hear me. Yolanda Ogás, Beatriz Limón, and José Lopez from
Jalisco were there; we each ordered a Clamato juice with real clams
in it, and when he brought me the bill (I was the gringo; I always
paid) it came to thirty-five dollars. He had one young Chinese customer who came to play; perhaps through him I could reach his fa-

ther. The big fire? Yes, everyone still talked about that. He believed that it had happened in 1985; that had been when *those Chinese came running everywhere;* he didn't know where they'd run from. He couldn't care less about the past, except in one respect: He sighed for the days when cue balls were still made out of real ivory.

> *Dear Ging Gei. In response to your letter, we understand your situation. I asked Bak Gei to go to Wong Gei for the money Bak Gei had asked for to lend his friend for medical bills since Wong Gei owes your brother Bak Sei money. If you do not know who Wong Gei is, please go to Chung Wei for further clarification. — 1924*

## Creation Myths

Do you want to know how they started? Clare Ng told me how she and her daughter Ros went down to Condominios Montealbán as I had asked them to do, trying to find tunnels or at least to ask about tunnels, and she told it like this: *It was nighttime, and it was that big apartment down there, and we saw some Chinese woman who was fetching water for the vegetables down there, and in the beginning she was scared to talk. The husband has been there for ten years and she has been there only for three years. I asked how do you like it, and she said just since my husband is here I like it; that is the only reason. The daughter does not speak Spanish yet. So we were there, and they opened their hearts. They told us it was many many years ago, and too hot. These Chinese people cannot take the heat, so they decide to live underground in the tunnel. There was a big fire, and everything was burned. They don't live there anymore, but they still keep some things there. They say there's still a casino down there. Maybe it is kind of secret.*

That was one version. But since Chinese tunnels are involved, no version is definitive. When I asked Steve Leung where the tunnels had come from, he first advised me to meet a certain Professor Auyón, then, when I continued to question him, he said that "mainly they was made by the Mexicans, actually." The Mexicans had made the tunnels. Mr. Leung said the Mexicans had copied the Chinese, who dug tunnels to smuggle their people across the border, and made tunnels for smuggling drugs. Mr. Leung said that the Chinese at one time had casinos underground but that they were closed because of pressure from the Mexican government. *It is still a corrupt government, definitely, but it is more elegant now;*

*it used to be you didn't need much connection as long as you got the money.*
*Now you need the connection too.*

## Women on Black Velvet

I remember tunnels that pretended to be cellars, and real cellars, and other tunnels of various sorts. I remember a plywood door partially ajar with two blood-dark ideograms painted on it, a hasp, a slender padlock. I remember cylindrical holes in the floor with locking hatch covers; these were the old Chinese safes. I remember how the palings of one tunnel wall resembled bamboo poles packed together, and around the top of them ran a stained metal collar. Then over a gap hung a torn ceiling, with strings and wires dangling down. The floor was a forest of paint buckets, toilets without tanks, cardboard, and upended chairs.

Late in the evening the sun caught the orangeness on the backward Restaurant Victoria lettering on the white window curtains, and the pleats of the curtains began sweating yellow and gold. A man on a crutch slowly hobbled out, and a boy held the door for him. For a long time I could see him creeping along outside, with backward Chinese lettering superimposed across his journey. The girls were already working across the street in the doorway of the Hotel Nuevo Pacifico; I counted six of them. Señor Daniel Avila, who'd worked at a certain supermarket for forty years and now owned a butcher shop, said that his son had once clerked at the Pacifico and that he had found tunnels but was never allowed to go inside them.

In your opinion, what is down there? I asked him.

He laughed and said: Secrets.

He took me down into his snow-white cellar tunnels, which had once been Chinese tunnels, and assured me that in a tunnel that had once connected with the tunnels under the supermarket and perhaps still did, there had been a cantina with paintings of naked women on black velvet; he knew for a fact that the paintings were still there, though he wasn't sure what condition they might be in. He was positive that the Chinese still lived underground just across the street. He couldn't say exactly where their tunnel was, because they entered at night *like rats.*

In that wonderfully Mexican way he had, he made everything

seem possible; any time now I was going to descend through the floor of a pharmacy or watch-repair store and hear piano music; I'd smell opium; I'd hear laughter and the click of mah-jongg tiles.

He knew a woman who trusted him and who could help me, but the next time I saw him he was more doubtful, and the time after that he was in a hurry to go to the cemetery for the Day of the Dead.

## A Chinese Lived and Died Here

To the supermarket that Daniel Avila had mentioned there sometimes came a Mexican caretaker who requested that I not use his name. He had worked long and faithfully for the Chinese owner, who had recently died and whose memory he adored. The children did not care to operate it anymore, and goods sat decaying on the shelves. Really it was no supermarket anymore but the shell of a supermarket. His job was to air the place out. He proudly said: This is one of the first stores that the Chinese opened in Mexicali.

After some persuasion the Mexican took me inside and through the double red curtains to the back, past an elevator cage (one of the first elevators in Mexicali, he announced loyally), and then we went downstairs into a white corridor. He said to me: This passageway originally went all the way to the cathedral on Reforma.

Aboveground it would have been a good fifteen-minute walk to that cathedral.

With his hand on his hip, thinking for a while amidst the humming electric whine of the lights, he finally said that the last time any Chinese had lived down here was in 1975.

Why did they stay in the tunnels?

They didn't have their papers, so they hid here. Around 1970 was the big fire. A lot of them came out, *with long beards!* I saw them. All old people! Many went back to China.

He pointed down into a cylindrical hole like many that I had seen in other tunnels, and he said: The Chinese didn't keep their money in the bank but in the wall. Here you would have had a safe, but it is full of water.

The tunnel went on and on, wide and humid, with salt-white stains on the walls. Huge beams spanned the ceiling. It was very well made.

Pointing to a square tunnel that went upward into darkness, he said: An emergency exit. This is how they came out during the fire.

I asked him why robbers and gangsters didn't live down here. He said it was because Mexicans are kind of timid. They think there are ghosts here. I have been working with the Chinese since I was twenty-seven. Now I am sixty. I myself believe in ghosts.

We reentered one of the middle chambers. The floor was stained white. The Mexican said the Chinese had slept in rows on small wooden beds. I asked if I could see one of the tunnels where they slept. All that has disappeared, he said. Then he took me upstairs to the boss's office.

The fire started with a man who sold tamales, the Mexican was saying. It burned right down to here, and he pointed off the edge of the roof. This whole street was cantinas back in 1955. There was a lot of conflict, delinquency, prostitution. It was like an old cowboy town, he said longingly.

I asked him again to show me the cantina where the velvet paintings are. And so he took me to the street behind the supermarket, in an alley I should say, a narrow dark place that smelled of the Río Nuevo and of birds, and on the far side of this there was a wall in which was set a white grating; when the Mexican unlocked this, the recess within was square, and within that stood another door. He had to go back to the supermarket to find the right key ring for that one. Laughingly he said: The Chinese have a lot of doors and a lot of keys.

This was all a cantina, he added with a sudden sadness. Pedro Infante sang here. Like Frank Sinatra.

He unlocked the inner door and pulled it open, a task that took most of his strength. Here at street level ran a very dark high-ceilinged space that seemed to have been gutted or perhaps was never finished; there were many wooden pallets, and he explained that illegal things had been stored here. What kind of illegal things? I wanted to know. Oh, butter and rice, he said hastily.

Dark stairs led down into black water; that was the cantina where the black-velvet paintings were. He said that it would take three weeks to pump it out, and he wasn't sure about the price. Three weeks later I was back, and he said that the pump had broken; he stood frowning with folded arms and said that the old Chino who would have shown me more had refused; I could tell that he wanted me to go away and never come back. But that was three weeks later; right now we still had an everlasting friendship ahead of us, and so after the flashlight finished glimmering on the stinking black tunnel in the cantina of the velvet paintings, he took me up a crazy flight of wooden steps through the darkness to a concrete cell with three windows that looked down into that chamber of illegal butter and rice.

A Chinese lived and died here, he said.

There had been a stove, he told me, but the stove was gone. The dresser was still there. The bed was gone.

It was a ghastly, lonely place.

He was silent for a while. The place was so hot and humid that it was difficult to breathe. The Mexican said slowly: Our race is like Italians. We like to party. But they are very strange. Look down, and you can see that tunnel; it's full of water . . .

Where does it go?

They say that that one also goes to the cathedral, but I don't know.

We descended the stairs, happy to get out of that eerie place, and we went back out to the street, and he locked the inner door and the outer door. In the doorway of the abandoned supermarket he said: When I started working here, fifteen or twenty people lived below.

You mean, where you first took me?

Yes. They never left.

He pointed to another building and said: When the fire came, this is where the Chinese came out, the old ones with the beards . . .

## Once Upon a Time in the Chinesca

Once upon a time in the Chinesca I peered in through the closed cracked window of the store that sold sombreros; there was supposed to be a tunnel underneath, but the owner had assured Yolanda and me that he'd never heard of anything like that. I looked in and everything was dim; how had I advanced my knowledge of tunnels? Now it was already six-thirty, and a few steps from me the fat lady was locking the white-painted, dirt-tinted gates of a roofed alley for the night. Sweet dreams to the store that sold communion dresses! A pleasant rest to the barbershop! There went the white number ninety-nine bus, crowded with standees; a man wheeled a dolly load of boxes down the gray sidewalk; a female radio voice was babbling cheerily from a store, and beneath that Mexican *carnicería,* which was very old, there presumably lay secrets dormant or active.

There was the old, low Restaurant Dong Cheng (Comida China Mexicana), where from time to time for half a dozen years now I've dropped in to get a beer or a half-order of fried rice, which was always as comfortingly large as a fat lady's breast. No matter how hungry I was, it was inexhaustible. Then a white fence stretched across a vacant lot, a palm tree behind; there was a parking lot, more Chinese restaurants, the Hotel Nuevo Pacifico, which is famed for its beautiful whores, many of whom are Chinese or half-Chinese; this was the Chinesca.

Once upon a time, in a certain street whose name I have already mentioned, not far from the sign where it said BILLARES and JAGUAR and unsurprisingly near to the ironwork letters that spelled out CHEE HOW OAK TIN, there was a gate, and a Mexican woman pointed to it and said to me: All the Chinese go there.

Do you think I can go inside?

They won't let you.

Why?

She shrugged. Who knows? A lot of Chinese come out of there to work. At night they come back here. Everybody says they live underground.

We were nearly at the basketball court, which was also the volleyball court that Yolanda had told me was the place beneath which the Chinese supposedly lived.

Every day that I passed by, I glanced at the CHEE HOW OAK TIN gate, but it was always closed until one morning in November when it wasn't; nakedly interpreter-less, I went in, and there was a Mexican standing in the courtyard. I gave him twenty dollars and said to him: *Por favor, señor, dónde está un subterráneo?* He laughed at me. He could speak English perfectly well. He told me not to tell anyone his name or where the tunnel was, but he could let me know that it was less than three doors from there. And it wasn't even a real *subterráneo,* only a *sótano,* a cellar, on whose floor a man in a blanket was sleeping; he was old and Chinese and might have been drunk; he did have a beard, though not as long as in the Mexicans' stories; a bag of clothes lay beside him; perhaps I should have photographed him, but it didn't seem very nice to steal a picture of a sleeping man. It all happened in a moment. Now I knew at least that people still slept in the tunnels; the myths were true; there remained secrets and subterranean passages, just as there used to be once upon a time in the Chinesca.

## The Red Handprints

Smiling a little grimly or more probably just anxiously, the Mexican girl held the candle jar out before her. From an oval decal on the side of this light, the Virgin of Guadalupe protected her. Although her family had owned the boutique overhead for several years, she had never dared to go down here, because of her fear of ghosts. Behind her, the other girl struck a match; a whitish-yellow glob of light suddenly hurt my eyes. I looked up and glimpsed a faraway ceiling's parallel beams, which might have been wood or concrete. Then the match went out. I went down and down. Suddenly the flashlight picked out something shiny-black: water. I thought then that it might be impossible to explore that tunnel, that the water might be ten feet deep or more. When I was in high school in Indiana, I'd once gone spelunking with some friends in a cave that required several hundred feet of belly-crawl with our noses almost in the mud and the backs of our heads grazing against rock; sometimes when it rained, fools like us were trapped and drowned. As I peered down into that Chinese tunnel, the feelings that I had had in that cave came back to me. And yet when I'd reached the bottom step and the flashlight split the darkness a trifle deeper, I could already see pale islands of dryness. Moreover, the floor appeared to be flat. So I stepped down into the wetness, and it came nowhere near the top of my shoe. Another step and another; that black water could have been a hundred miles deep the way it looked, but so far it wasn't. As always, my concern was that there might be a deep pit I couldn't see. I remembered helping a man from the Hudson's Bay Company drag a boat across weak sea-ice, which broke under me without warning; that was how I took my first swim in the Arctic Ocean. This memory proved as inapplicable as the first. With pettish, trifling steps I made my way, and presently so did the others. Soon the flashlight picked out the end of the pool; aside from a snake of darkness that narrowed and dwindled like the Colorado River, the rest of that tunnel was dry.

We were under Avenida Reforma. The two dark-haired *mejicanas* said they believed that Chinese had lived in this wide, high-ceilinged chamber. Always that pair stayed close together, often forming a right angle as they gazed or tried to gaze at something, usually close to the wall, whose blocks rewarded their candle's nourishment with paleness. Behind the stairs were three more huge rooms. At the end of the farthest, diagonal bars blocked us from the darkness's continuation.

The two *mejicanas* said that they thought this tunnel went all the way to the Restaurant Victoria, which would have been several city blocks from here. Shuffling with my careful old man's steps, I came across a mysterious square well of black water that might have been one foot deep or a hundred. Had I been a drainage engineer, I might have known what it was. Instead, I thought of Edgar Allan Poe.

The older girl, whose name was Karina, shyly said she'd heard that at one time people tried to kill the Chinese, so they came down here and hid. The other girl had already begun to feel nervous and declined to tell me her name.

Each concrete pillar in every niche had many shelves of dark spiderwebs. Receding rectangular arches of paleness made me feel as if I were inside some monster's rib cage. Perhaps everything was reinforced so well on account of earthquakes.

In the large chamber immediately under the stairs, we discovered an odd cabinet that was really a thick hollow wooden beam subdivided into shelves and compartments, with empty darkness above and below its dust — no, it actually had three sides, which went from floor to ceiling; it was simply that some of the back's slats had been pried off; on the back, in a niche whose ceiling was peg-board, someone had taped three pictures of space shuttles beside an image of the Virgin of Guadalupe, who presided with clasped hands and almost-closed eyes over the two plastic flowers that her admirer had also taped to that wall; and then below the cabinet the Chinese tunnel went on to its barren bricked-up end.

The nameless woman had already gone almost to the top of the stairs, and my flashlight caught the impossibly white cylinders of her ankles almost out of sight, while Karina, holding the candle, stood sideways on two steps, gazing at me with her dark eyes. Her wet sandal-prints on the stairs were almost as dark as her eyes. I remember her standing there and looking at me, looking at the darkness I remained in, and I will always wonder what she was thinking. Then she ascended the stairs and was gone.

I returned to that framework of bars from floor to ceiling; the tunnel kept going, but only rats and water could get through. Then I searched the niche behind the stairs.

On one whitewashed wall the flashlight suddenly picked out human handprints made in red; at first I thought it might be blood, but an experiment made with the rusty water on the floor proved that these handprints were part of a far less sinister game. Dashiell Hammett never wrote this.

The question of how vast the tunnels had been and still were preoccupied me. Old photographs seem to tell us how far they could have extended: In 1925, for instance, when Mexicali finally got its Chinese consulate, Avenida Reforma resembled a long, wide, well-ploughed field of dirt, with little square wooden houses going up behind a rail fence; Avenida Madero was much the same. How could there have been any subterranean passages here? But evidently these views must have been taken far from the heart of things, perhaps even as far as the future cathedral on Reforma; for here's a vista of the *edificio ubicado* on Reforma at Azueta *en zona "la chinesca," circa 1920:* A sign for the Mexicali Cabaret, pricked out in lightbulbs or wires, rises into the dirty-white sky above a two-story corner block of solid brick, fronted by squarish-arched arcades. Why *wouldn't* there have been Chinese tunnels there? Here's Chinese New Year, 1921: Two young boys, uniformed like soldiers or policemen, clasp hands atop a great float upon whose faded legend I can just barely make out the word CHINA; flowers, perhaps made of paper, bestrew the scene; behind them comes another float like a tall rectangular sail; an automobile's round blank eyes shine beneath it; a crowd of Chinese men and boys, their faces washed out by sun and time, gaze at us; everything is frozen, grainy, blurry, lost. Where are they? I don't know. And however many tunnels I ultimately entered, I would never be able to learn how many more remained. I tried to shine my feeble light as deep down into the past as I could, but I couldn't even see the bottom step of the tunnel's entrance.

SIMON WINCHESTER

# Welcome to Nowhere

FROM *National Geographic Adventure*

IT WAS A BLAZING TROPICAL morning in the middle of nowhere. I was on a rusting, salt-stained Russian tramp steamer beating slowly up toward England across the Doldrums, and for reasons
long forgotten I was in a desperate hurry to get home. We were
making no more than eight knots that day, which meant that I'd
not see the cranes of any European port for the better part of three
more weeks. And out there on those hot, high seas — I was on my
way back from Antarctica — it was unutterably tedious.

The radar on the bridge showed the Atlantic Ocean entirely
empty — except, that is, for the tiny speck of Ascension Island,
which lay otherwise invisible forty miles off our starboard bow. It
was then, in a sudden moment of realization, that I remembered
something. On Ascension Island there was an airfield, and jet
planes flew there, to and from London. If I played my cards right, I
could get myself out of here.

I promptly got on the ship's radio, asking if anyone over on Ascension could hear me. At first, nothing — just the hissing white silence of dead ocean air. But I called and I called, and eventually,
quite faintly at first, there came over the ether a British voice. Yes, it
said, he was the duty harbor master. What did I need? I told him I
wanted to get on the next Royal Air Force flight to Britain, and so
could I land on Ascension and try and wangle my way aboard?

Yes, he replied, after a momentary muffled conversation with
someone else, provided that I was able to jump when told to do so,
because the Atlantic rollers were making landing at Ascension per-
ilous that day. And since there was a northbound plane due to arrive in two days, I might also be able to find a seat and get myself to

London in double-quick time. "Ask your captain to steer toward Ascension," the man said, "and when half a mile off, tell him to put you ashore in the whaler. If you're fit," he said with what sounded like a sinister chuckle, "you ought to be able to make it."

Half a day's slow sailing later, the enormous dark pyramid of Ascension rose up ahead of us — a midocean volcano, half a mile high, its summit brushed with green foliage and a patch of dark cloud, the slopes and the spreading base iron-gray and seemingly as lifeless as the moon. A few sorry-looking buildings were dotted here and there, and there was a cluster of radar domes and antennas and a gathering of Quonset huts around the airport's single runway.

A grinning Russian sailor who said he had been here once before, and who the captain assured me "knew the form," lowered me into his whaler, and we motored swiftly across the chop to a tiny gap in the Ascension seawall, a gap in which I could see a narrow set of steps rising slimily from the waves. Enormous swells and rollers crashed over these steps at regular intervals, completely immersing them, then draining away again in a rush of wild white water and fronds of streaming weed. There was a slime-covered rope fastened to a doubtful-looking and very corroded stanchion. The Russian told me that all I had to do was wait for the interval between swells, leap onto the highest step I could manage — the higher I managed, the less slippery the steps, he said, laughing — and clutch the rope as tightly as I could.

Well, I'm here today, and so the scheme must have worked. All I remember is a welter of confused green water, the precipitous dipping and rising of our whaler's bow, the word "now!" suddenly screamed behind me, my feet and hands scrambling for a hold, the wet length of rope tightening under my weight, the onrushing of the next wave knocking me off balance but the rope holding, holding — and then my furious dash upward until I was at last on a dry step. My bag, hurled with great force by the Russian way down below, landed beside me, followed by the yell of *"Dosvidanya!"*

And then, quietly, almost like a gentle whisper, came another voice.

"Do let me be the first to welcome you to the British territory of Ascension Island," it said. "My name is Nicholas Turner. I am the vicar here. And this is my wife, Ann."

I turned, and indeed there was, quite unexpectedly, a cleric — a young fresh-faced clergyman very obviously of the Church of England, dressed in white shorts and a tropical shirt, but with the telltale clerical collar. He was short, fair-haired, very pinkish, precise, rimlessly bespectacled.

The Reverend Nicholas Turner, vicar of Saint Mary's, wore an expression that morning of a sincerely concerned kindliness — as did his wife, who looked rather like him, only she was larger and somewhat gawky in a sundress of an old-fashioned chintz print, such that unkind souls might say she looked a little like a small, animated sofa. The pair could not have been anything other than English, two expatriates doing their level best to find suitable employment during the languid hours of faraway tropical heat. Meeting me, I guessed, was part of what they might have called their pastoral duties, ensuring that all was well with their flock on this tiny outpost of what remained of Britain's empire, here in the outermost reaches of an otherwise unpopulated stretch of ocean.

I shook hands, and Nicholas suggested that I step along toward their house. It was a five-hundred-yard walk to Saint Mary's vicarage, a walk that took us past the old fever hospital and the former lazaretto for African lepers, and past the nineteenth-century barracks that had housed Royal Marines who were stationed on Ascension to make sure that Napoleon stayed put in his permanent post-Waterloo exile on Saint Helena, a few hundred miles to our southeast.

It was far too hot that day, and there was no one about — just a few donkeys, now wild animals plaguing the island just like the feral cats the locals had tried to eliminate some years before. The donkeys chewed the wing mirrors off the cars, and everybody loathed them.

We walked past the tiny modern bungalow where the administrator worked — no colonial governor was warranted on so small a dependency as this, said Reverend Nicholas. Then, in a low voice, he explained that most administrators were men who had "rather failed to make an impression" during their careers in Britain's diplomatic service.

It was the only unkind thing I ever heard Nicholas say, though it was evident that neither he nor Ann seemed much to like their posting. Nicholas had been preaching quite happily, thank you, in a church in Leeds when orders had appeared one Monday in the mail, suggesting that he might like to take over the Church of Saint Mary's of the High Seas in the Dependency of Ascension. It was a five-year job; there were no more than a thousand people on the island, most of them Saint Helenians working on contract for the air base, or else secretive expatriates working among the fields of antennas, performing hush-hush work for one of the American spy agencies.

"They call the Saint Helenians 'Saints,'" said Nicholas as he opened his garden gate. "So I imagine they don't really need us, do they?" He chuckled mildly at his own drollery. "So Ann and I have rather little to do — and we see almost no one. Which is why we were so pleased when they said you were stopping by. You are more than welcome to have lunch, and then please stay with us until the plane comes in tomorrow night."

Inside there was a salad waiting for me and a glass of cold beer. "I expect you'll be very happy with that," he said, and he winked at his wife conspiratorially, as if a drink at lunch was somehow mildly sinful.

And so I stayed with them for the rest of that day and night, chatting and indulging in what passes for Ascension tourism — which means, primarily, climbing Green Mountain, then going for a swim in the dewpond at the summit. From the mountaintop, if the clouds part for long enough, it is possible to see a hundred miles in all directions, and the ocean — looking like an unblemished sheet of hammered pewter — stretched empty to every horizon. It was so lonely that I almost shuddered.

During the night, the southbound air force jet had come in, on its way down to the Falkland Islands, and so the following morning we had English newspapers and magazines. I had been in the Southern Ocean for the better part of the previous four months and knew little of the goings-on up north; and now, reading all about it, so much seemed so blessedly irrelevant. Ann was happy, though, and spent her day in the garden contentedly buried in the *Daily Mail* and the *Tatler,* lobbing pebbles at any donkeys that tried to eat her sandwiches.

Once she looked up from her reverie and spoke to me. She had a surprise for me later that night, she said with a smile. The northbound plane, which Nicholas had managed to get me a seat on, was due in a little before two in the morning. Perhaps, Ann said, if we all took a siesta — something not too difficult to achieve in a place that was hot, lonely, and exceptionally boring — we could all arrange to go down to the airfield together, and they would see me off. I protested that there was really no need, but they seemed to want to. They apparently had something planned.

I must have slept until ten. It was quite dark when I awoke, and the house was alive with a curiously expectant air. Downstairs I found Nicholas and Ann dressed in mufti — no dog collar or chintz, but swimming costumes instead — and packing up a picnic basket. "Well done, waking now," said Nicholas cheerfully. "We thought we'd go off on an expedition. We'll take you to the best white-sand beach on the island — and when we're there I think we'll see something rather special.

"And by the way — I think Ann said something about a surprise? Well, they came on the jet from England. Fresh strawberries and Devonshire cream! We've not had them for a year! And you've probably gone without such things for ages. So let's take them down to the sea, right away!"

And so, after I had changed into my trunks, we set off in their rickety old Morris Minor — the car that they and their predecessors had all inherited from a vicar back in the sixties — and we swept slowly around the island until we turned off and bumped down through a rocky defile and along to a tiny beach, glinting pure white under a fast-rising moon.

As the moon rose, the soft and sugary sand took on an appearance just like snow — the sea beyond it black, its waves crashing rhythmically on the shore; the rocks behind, black also; and in between them this postcard-size field of the purest white shell powder, illuminated by the immense, pale moon, and with a clear sky filled with a blizzard of stars.

Ann unpacked the hamper, and she laid out dishes of strawberries and a jug of cream on the blanket, together with three glasses and a bottle of cool white wine. To sharpen our appetite, and to delay the pleasure of the food, we ran down to the sea and swam for a while, then lay floating beyond the surf, the water warm and velvet soft, and we gazed up at the sky, looking for shooting stars. After fifteen minutes or so Nicholas looked at his watch. "Back to the beach!" he cried. "The show starts soon."

I had no idea what he meant, but the three of us walked back up to where we had left our things and sat back and toasted one another with Vouvray and ate the soft fruit and the cool cream and joked with one another that we were, as Nicholas and Ann must have known, in some anteroom to heaven. And then Nicholas cried out.

"Look!" he said, and pointed down to the waves crashing onto the beach. "Quiet!"

I saw it in an instant. It quite startled me. A huge, dark shape was lumbering slowly out of the white water and was heading, inching, up the beach. First one emerged, then another, and another — until there were maybe fifteen of them, moving slowly and almost painfully up the sloping sand, like wounded soldiers of an invasion force. One of them approached within three feet of us — so close, I could see exactly what it was.

A green turtle. I had heard about them — green turtles, living on Brazil's Atlantic coast and yet choosing, due to some quirk of nature, to lay their eggs 1,400 miles away on this tiny island in the middle of their ocean. And this, precisely, was what each one of these huge, magnificent beasts was doing.

The lady closest to us turned ponderously around so that she was facing the sea, then used her back flippers to scoop out a cavity in the sand. Once it was three feet or so deep, she quieted herself and concentrated, until, with a strangely, unforgettably intimate sound of chelonian parturition, she expelled a clutch of at least a hundred eggs into the hole. I craned myself up quietly and saw the eggs as they lay glistening wetly in the moonlight, until their patient mother shoveled sand back on top of them, to protect them and keep them dry. She seemed utterly exhausted from the effort, quite drained, and for a few understandable moments she rested, until, with what in a man would have been a superhuman effort of will, she hoisted herself back down the slope, battered her weary way through the raging surf, and began her long, slow, eggless swim back home again, all the way to Brazil.

For more than an hour the three of us watched, transfixed. Occasionally I could see that Nicholas was watching me, just to make certain that I was as enraptured as he had been when first he saw the animals. Ann spoke softly as she poured another glass of wine. "Aren't we just the luckiest people?" she said. "Isn't this a privilege?"

But that wasn't the half of it. There was more. For at almost the same moment as she asked this rhetorical question, she shivered. I could see her skin was suddenly covered with goose bumps. She drew a beach towel around her shoulders. And I felt it, too — a sudden coldness in the air, as though a cloud had materialized from the tropical sky and blanketed everything in its chill.

But it wasn't a cloud. As I looked up at the moon I could see that the shadow of the Earth was now steadily sweeping across its face, and the whole world was darkening again, being turned back to black as this portion of our planet experienced a total lunar eclipse. Suddenly the white sand went dark. I could no longer see Nicholas or Ann. Only the glow of the distant runway lights spoke of civilization nearby. Only those lights, and the stars, broke the blackness of the night.

As I looked at the stars, I noticed something else: In the eastern sky, rising above the dark where the horizon had been, was a bright object that, once I could see it properly, was undeniably a comet. A famous, swept-tailed comet, blazing for thousands of miles out in some distant part of the solar system, and now only properly visible because the air was so clear here and the local world was so inkily black. It was splendid, unbelievably so.

A few moments later, the moon came out of the Earth's shadow and the brilliance of the stars faded a little, and the comet became barely visible once again. But just then it had been visible, and I, moreover, had seen it.

And it was in that instant I realized that in this astonishing grand conjunction — of new friendship, of tropical warmth, of strawberries and cream, and cool white wine, of white sand and sea swimming, and of Brazilian turtles, an eclipse of the moon, and the rising of a comet — was perhaps the greatest wealth of experience any one individual could ever know in one moment. I was at that instant blessed beyond belief, beyond all understanding. And that state of grace had all come about purely and simply because one man and one woman — the Reverend Nicholas Turner and his comfortable wife, Ann, who had been perfect strangers to me until then — had decided to offer me, for one unrewarded moment, no more and no less than their kindness.

And yet of course their kindness was rewarded, and more handsomely than is conceivable. For neither they nor I will ever be able to forget it. Virtue is its own reward, I thought, a reward written here for eternity on this tiny, unremembered island.

Then the mood altered, as it always must, for after a few minutes two brilliant searchlights appeared low on the horizon, and they grew steadily brighter every passing second. For a moment I thought it was the comet again, but Nicholas jumped up. He had seen it before. "Your plane," he announced. "We'd better hurry."

My jet landed the next morning at an air base in the Cotswolds, and I decided on a whim that on my way down to London, I would stop in and see my Oxford tailor. So at about ten o'clock I was standing in the fitting room, and before he slipped a new jacket on me, he asked me to unroll my shirtsleeves. As I did so, a cascade of the purest white sand fell from the folds, onto the carpet. I apologized, but the tailor said it was no trouble and asked, more out of politeness than serious inquiry, whether I could tell him where it had come from. Ascension Island, I said, and proceeded to tell him the story.

He listened patiently, and then, putting away his chalk and looping his tape around his neck, he said, "You know, you are a very, very lucky man indeed. Lucky to be in such a place. Lucky to see such things. And luckiest of all to meet such very kind people. I envy you. Everyone must envy you. Wherever would you be — have you ever wondered — without all their kindness and without all this luck?" As he opened the door for me, he put his hand briefly on my shoulder. And then I walked off into the rain.

# Contributors' Notes

**Tim Bascom**'s memoir about growing up in Ethiopia, *Chameleon Days,* won the 2005 Bakeless Literary Prize from Breadloaf Writing Conference and will be published in the summer of 2006. He has published a novel, *Squatters' Rites,* and a critical study of Christianity in U.S. culture, *The Comfort Trap.* His essays have won the Missouri Review Editor's Prize in Essay and the Florida Review Editor's Prize in Nonfiction. Bascom, who is a graduate of the nonfiction writing program at the University of Iowa, lives in Newton, Iowa, where his wife is priest at St. Stephen's Episcopal Church. They have two grade-school-age sons, Connor and Luke.

**Madison Smartt Bell** is the author of eleven novels, including *The Washington Square Ensemble; Waiting for the End of the World; Straight Cut; The Year of Silence; Save Me, Joe Louis; Ten Indians;* and *Master of the Crossroads.* His novel *Soldier's Joy* received the Lillian Smith Award in 1989. *All Soul's Rising* was a finalist for the 1995 National Book Award and the 1996 PEN/Faulkner Award. The final volume of his Haitian trilogy, *The Stone That the Builder Refused,* was published in 2004. Bell has also published two collections of short stories: *Zero db* and *Barking Man.* Since 1984, he has taught at Goucher College, along with his wife, the poet Elizabeth Spires.

**Tom Bissell** was born in Escanaba, Michigan, in 1974. After graduating from Michigan State University, he taught English in Uzbekistan as a Peace Corps volunteer and then worked for W. W. Norton and Henry Holt as a book editor. He is the author of *Chasing the Sea,* a travel narrative; *God Lives in St. Petersburg,* a short-story collection; and (with Jeff Alexander) *Speak, Commentary,* a collection of fake DVD commentaries. He is a contributing editor for *Harper's Magazine* and a regular contributor to *The Believer.* His work has appeared in *The Pushcart Prize Anthology XXIX, The Best American*

*Travel Writing 2003, The Best American Science Writing 2004,* and *The Best American Short Stories 2005,* among other publications. He is currently working on a nonfiction book about Vietnam, entitled *The Father of All Things* (from which "War Wounds" is drawn), teaches in Bennington College's low-residency MFA program, and lives in New York City.

**William E. Blundell** is a writer and teacher of writing, working mainly with newspaper and magazine writers and editors. He is the author of *The Art and Craft of Feature Writing,* originally published in 1988 and still in wide use among journalists and educators. Blundell spent thirty years at the *Wall Street Journal* as a reporter, editor, and national correspondent. His awards include the American Society of Newspaper Editors Award for feature writing, the Meyer Berger Award from Columbia University for metropolitan reporting, and the Scripps Howard Public Service Award for coverage of the Equity Funding insurance scandal.

**J. Michael Fay** has spent his life as a naturalist. After graduating from the University of Arizona in 1978, he spent six years in the Peace Corps as a botanist in national parks in Tunisia and the savannas of the Central African Republic. He then went on to work at the Missouri Botanical Garden, first to do a floristic study on a mountain range on Sudan's western border, then ending up doing doctoral research on the western lowland gorilla. It was at this time that he first entered the deep forests of central Africa, where he's worked for the past two decades. Fay has surveyed large forest blocks and worked to create and manage the Dzanga-Sangha and Nouabale-Ndoki parks in the Central African Republic and Congo. In 1996, Fay started flying a small airplane low over the forests of Congo and Gabon and realized that there was a vast, intact forest corridor that spanned these two countries from the Oubangui to the Atlantic Ocean. In 1997, he decided to walk the entire corridor, more than two thousand miles, systematically surveying trees, wildlife, and human impacts on twelve uninhabited forest blocks. This project, called the Megatransect, brought the world's attention to the last pristine blocks of forest in central Africa and their need for protection. This work has led to a historic initiative by the Gabonese government to create a system of thirteen national parks. Fay hosted Colin Powell on a forest walk in Gabon after the secretary of state's announcement to support the Congo Basin with tens of millions of dollars for national park creation and management. Fay has worked for the past fourteen years for the Wildlife Conservation Society of the Bronx and is the Conservation Fellow at the National Geographic Society. In 2004, he embarked on a project that took him from South Africa to Portugal, over eight months, in a small Cessna aircraft. His objective was to look at humanity in relation to ecosystems and how both are faring on the continent, and he took more than 100,000 documentary photographs on this trip. Fay has currently been in southern Tchad and Sudan and will use his data to urge Congress to provide more support for natural resource management throughout the continent of Africa.

**Ian Frazier** writes essays and longer works of nonfiction. His books include *Great Plains, Family, Coyote V. Acme, On the Rez, Dating Your Mom*, and most recently *The Fish's Eye*. He lives in New Jersey.

**Jim Harrison** is the author of four collections of novellas, seven novels, seven collections of poetry, and a collection of nonfiction. He has been awarded a National Endowment for the Arts grant and a Guggenheim Fellowship. His work has been published in twenty-two languages.

**William Least Heat-Moon** is the author of two best-selling travel classics, *Blue Highways* and *PrairyErth: A Deep Map*. His most recent book is *River-Horse: A Voyage Across America*. Born William Trogdon, Least Heat-Moon found his pen name early on, when his scoutmaster father, of Osage descent, christened himself "Heat Moon," William's brother "Little Heat Moon," and William "Least Heat Moon." He lives in Columbia, Missouri.

**Peter Hessler** is a native of Columbia, Missouri, and has lived in China since he was sent there as a Peace Corps volunteer in 1996. During his time in the Peace Corps, he taught English literature at a small college in Fuling, a town on the Yangtze. *River Town*, his 2001 book, was about that experience. Since 1999, he has been based in Beijing as a freelance writer and now writes for *The New Yorker* and *National Geographic*. His second book, *Oracle Bones*, will be published in early 2006.

**Jack Hitt** is a contributing writer for the *New York Times Magazine, Harper's Magazine*, and the public radio program *This American Life*.

**Pam Houston** is the author of two collections of linked short stories, *Cowboys Are My Weakness*, which was the winner of the 1993 Western States Book Award and has been translated into nine languages, and *Waltzing the Cat*, which won the Willa Award for Contemporary Fiction. Her stories have been selected for volumes of *The Best American Short Stories*, the O. Henry Awards, and the Pushcart Prize, and her story "The Best Girlfriend You Never Had" appeared in *The Best American Short Stories of the Century*. A collection of autobiographical essays about travel and home, *A Little More About Me*, was published in 1999, and her first novel, *Sight Hound*, was published in 2005. She is the Director of Creative Writing at the University of California, Davis. When she is not in Davis, she lives in Colorado at nine thousand feet above sea level near the headwaters of the Rio Grande.

**Ben Ryder Howe,** an editor at the *Paris Review* and former deli owner in Brooklyn, grew up in Panama before the handover of the canal. He has written for *Outside* and the *Atlantic Monthly* and reported from Colombia and El Salvador. He lives on Staten Island.

**Tom Ireland,** a native New Yorker, moved to the Southwest in 1971 to live in the mountains and practice sitting meditation. He has worked as a builder, rancher, and animal trainer and since 1985 has been an editor with the Museum of New Mexico and Smithsonian Books. His books include *Mostly Mules,* the account of a journey by mule; Our *Love Is Like a Cake,* a true-life romance in post-Soviet Poland, written with an NEA grant; and *Birds of Sorrow: Notes from a River Junction in Northern New Mexico,* an essay collection.

**Mark Jenkins** writes the monthly adventure column "The Hard Way" for *Outside.* He is the author of three books: *Off the Map,* detailing a coast-to-coast, 7,500-mile crossing of Siberia by bicycle; *To Timbuktu;* and *The Hard Way,* a volume of collected works from *Outside.* Jenkins has been an editor at *Men's Health, Backpacker, Adventure Travel,* and *Cross Country Skier,* and his work has appeared in *Bicycling, Condé Nast Traveler, Playboy, GQ,* and many other publications. His story "Ghost Road" appeared in *The Best American Travel Writing 2004.* He lives in Laramie, Wyoming, with his wife and two children and is currently at work on his second volume of collected essays.

**Murad Kalam**'s first novel, *Night Journey,* was a finalist for the PEN/Hemingway Award. His fiction and essays have appeared in *Harper's Magazine,* the *New York Times Magazine,* the *Daily Telegraph, Granta, Prize Stories: The 2001 O. Henry Awards,* and *Outside.* He lives outside of Washington, D.C., with his wife and is at work on his second novel, set in Cairo.

**Charles Martin Kearney** traveled in Central Asia and the Middle East in the late 1970s and eventually settled in Israel's Golan Heights during the early days of the undeclared war in Lebanon. The three chapters that appear here under the title "Maps and Dreaming" are an edited excerpt from his nonfiction manuscript, *The Logic of Maps and Dreaming,* which chronicles his travels from Athens to New Delhi with a blue-eyed blond American woman named Suzanne, who asked him to accompany her as her bodyguard. Their story moves from the first days of a long journey to their struggles with near-fatal bouts of typhoid in Afghanistan to encounters with gun smugglers in the Khyber Pass to their dramatic escape from Pakistan during a military coup. The memoir begins and ends in a military hospital in Safad, Israel, where Kearney was treated for typhoid and where he lived among wounded Israeli soldiers, Lebanese Christian militiamen, and veiled Bedouin women wailing for their husbands.

**Thomas Keneally** has won international acclaim for his novels *Schindler's List* (the basis for the movie and winner of the Booker Prize), *The Chant of Jimmie Blacksmith, Confederates, Gossip from the Forest, The Playmaker, A River Town,* and most recently *The Tyrant's Novel.* His nonfiction includes *The Great Shame* and a short biography of Abraham Lincoln. He lives in Sydney, Australia.

**Bucky McMahon** is a freelance adventure writer who, when not lost at sea, can be found high and dry hoeing weeds in his vegetable garden near Tallahassee, Florida. He is permanently at work on a confusing novel, a gigantic wood sculpture, and a cartoon book based on his dreams. An earlier story for *Esquire* was included in *The Best American Sports Writing 2001.*

**John McPhee** was born in Princeton, New Jersey, and was educated at Princeton University and Cambridge University. His writing career began at *Time* and led to his long association with *The New Yorker,* where he has been a staff writer since 1965. He is the author of twenty-six books, including *A Sense of Where You Are* (1965), *Oranges* (1967), *The Pine Barrens* (1968), *The Survival of the Bark Canoe* (1975), *Coming into the Country* (1977), *La Place de la Concorde Suisse* (1984), *The Control of Nature* (1989), and most recently *Founding Fish* (2002). Both *Encounters with the Archdruid* (1972) and *The Curve of Binding Energy* (1974) were nominated for National Book Awards in the category of science. *Annals of the Former World* was awarded the Pulitzer Prize in 1999.

**Robert Young Pelton** has made a career of bypassing the media, border guards, and the military and penetrating many of the world's terrorist, rebel, and paramilitary organizations in his goal of getting to the heart of the story. He is best known for his classic underground guide, *Robert Young Pelton's The World's Most Dangerous Places,* now in its fifth edition. His travels have taken him inside the siege of Groznyy in Chechnya, the battle of Qala-I-Jangi in Afghanistan, and the rebel campaign to take Monrovia in Liberia. Pelton has been kidnapped by right-wing death squads in Colombia, survived a plane crash in Indonesia and a head-on motorcycle accident in Peru, and gracefully endured numerous detainments and attacks. In addition to *National Geographic Adventure*, Pelton has worked for Discovery Channel, ABC News, *60 Minutes*, CNN, and other major media networks. His television work includes a world-exclusive interview of the American Taliban, John Walker Lindh. His other books include *Come Back Alive*, *The Adventurist* (his autobiography), and *Three Worlds Gone Mad*. He is currently writing a book about mercenaries and private contractors, as well as a young teen book based on his early childhood.

**David Quammen** travels on assignment for various magazines, most often to jungles, deserts, and swamps. His accustomed beat is the world of field biology, ecology, evolutionary biology, and conservation, though he also occasionally writes about travel, history, and outdoor sports. His work has appeared in *Harper's Magazine, National Geographic*, the *Atlantic, National Geographic Adventure, Outside*, the *New York Times Book Review*, and other journals. His books include *The Song of the Dodo, Monster of God*, and a spy novel, *The Soul of Viktor Tronko*. He lives in Montana with his wife (Betsy Gaines, a conservationist), their large furry dog, and a modest supply of cats.

**Kira Salak** is a contributing editor for *National Geographic Adventure* and was selected by the National Geographic Society for one of its 2005 Emerging Explorers Awards. She is the author of *The Cruelest Journey: Six Hundred Miles to Timbuktu* and *Four Corners: A Journey into the Heart of Papua New Guinea* (chosen by the *New York Times Book Review* as a notable travel book of the year). In 2004, Salak won the PEN Award in Journalism, as well as the Lowell Thomas Travel Journalism gold award for environmental reporting. Her work has appeared in *National Geographic, National Geographic Adventure, Travel + Leisure, The Best American Travel Writing 2002, 2003, 2004*, and *Best New American Voices*. Salak holds a Ph.D. in English from the University of Missouri in Columbia.

**Seth Stevenson** is a frequent contributor to *Slate*, where he writes on travel, culture, sports, and business. His writing has also appeared in the *New York Times Magazine, Newsweek, New York Magazine*, and *Rolling Stone*, among other publications. A graduate of Brown University, he currently lives in Washington, D.C.

**William T. Vollmann** was born in California in 1959. His most recent books are *Europe Central* and *Rising Up and Rising Down*, a multivolume treatise on the moral calculus of violence. His other books include *The Atlas, The Rainbow Stories, Butterfly Stories, Whores for Gloria*, and *The Royal Family*. A book on Copernicus is forthcoming in 2006.

**Simon Winchester**'s latest book, *A Crack in the Edge of the World,* about the 1906 San Francisco earthquake, comes out in October 2005. A former geologist, Winchester's other books include the best-selling *The Professor and the Madman* and *The Map That Changed the World.* Winchester, who is British, divides his time between a flat in New York and a farm in the Berkshires.

# Notable Travel Writing of 2004

## Selected by Jason Wilson

Roger Angell
La Vie En Rose. *The New Yorker,* February 16 & 23.

Tara Bahrampour
Eritrea Emerges. *Travel + Leisure,* September.
Richard Bangs
First into Libya. *Slate.com,* June 10.
Tom Bissell
Truth in Oxiana. *Agni,* Number 60.
William Booth
Heavy Metal. *Washington Post Magazine,* March 7.
Alexia Brue
Homer Bound. *Lexus,* Number 3.
Elinor Burkett
In Central Asia, an American Professor Finds Hostility Spiked with Cynicism. *The Chronicle of Higher Education,* April 23.

Sara Corbett
Rick Steves's Not-So-Lonely Planet. *New York Times Magazine,* July 4.

Alice DuBois
Yawning in the Uffizi. *New York Times,* September 19.

Elisabeth Eaves
Dancing in Spanish: Flamenco in Seville. *Slate.com,* December 6–10.
Theresa Everline
Letter from Cairo. *Yale Review,* April.

Laura Fraser
An Affair to Remember. *Gourmet,* January.

STEVE FRIEDMAN
Down and Out in Krasnaya Polyana. *Ski,* October.

J. MALCOLM GARCIA
Curfew. *Virginia Quarterly Review,* Spring.
Relief: Afghanistan, 2001. *Post Road.*
DON GEORGE
Every Journey Is a Pilgrimmage. *Yoga Journal,* March/April.
WILLIAM GEORGIADES
Adventures in Journalism: World Traveler. *mediabistro.com,* November 10.
ELIZABETH GILBERT
A Wine Worth Fighting For. *GQ,* September.
SAMANTHA GILLISON
Far Papua. *Condé Nast Traveler,* December.
PETER GODWIN
City of Hope, City of Fear. *National Geographic,* April.
KEVIN GRAY
Heart of Darkness. *Details,* May.

TOM HAINES
Seeking heaven in the stubborn earth. *Boston Globe,* September 26.
God wills, the desert provides. *Boston Globe,* October 31.
The calmer passage. *Boston Globe,* November 28.
Degrees of separation. *Boston Globe,* December 19.
CHRISTOPER HITCHENS
Afghanistan's Dangerous Bet. *Vanity Fair,* November.
AMANDA HESSER
Just off India, Kissed by Europe. *New York Times,* October 13.

PICO IYER
In the Realm of Jet Lag. *New York Times Magazine,* March 7.

ALDEN JONES
The Answer Was No. *Gulf Coast,* Summer/Fall.
ANNIE JACOBSEN
Terror in the Skies, Again? *Women's Wall Street,* July 18 & 21.

DAVE KUEHLS
Kenya Calling. *Runner's World,* January.
DEAN KING
The Cruelest Journey. *National Geographic Adventure,* February.
WENDY KNIGHT
The Burden of War. *WorldHum.com,* November 5.

CHRISTOPHER MCDOUGALL
Trekking to a Forgotten Paradise. *Esquire,* June.
TIM MCGIRK
Tracking the Ghost of bin Laden. *National Geographic,* December.

BILL THOMAS
Party Line. *Washington Post Magazine,* September 19.
JUNE THOMAS
Manchester, So Much to Answer For, *Slate.com,* August 30–September 3.
GUY TREBAY
True Hawaii. *Travel + Leisure,* November.

BILL VAUGHN
A Jug of Wine (More Jugs of Wine) et Moi. *Outside,* October.
FRANK VIVIANO
The Rebirth of Armenia. *National Geographic,* March.

STEPHEN WALKER
A Ghost in the Jungle. *New York Times,* August 8.
GENE WEINGARTEN
Fear Itself. *Washington Post Magazine,* August 22.
LAWRENCE WRIGHT
The Kingdom of Silence. *The New Yorker,* January 5.

# THE B·E·S·T AMERICAN SERIES®

## THE BEST AMERICAN SHORT STORIES® 2005

Michael Chabon, guest editor, Katrina Kenison, series editor. "Story for story, readers can't beat the *Best American Short Stories* series" (*Chicago Tribune*). This year's most beloved short fiction anthology is edited by the Pulitzer Prize–winning novelist Michael Chabon and features stories by Tom Perrotta, Alice Munro, Edward P. Jones, Joyce Carol Oates, and Thomas McGuane, among others.

0-618-42705-8 PA $14.00 / 0-618-42349-4 CL $27.50

## THE BEST AMERICAN ESSAYS® 2005

Susan Orlean, guest editor, Robert Atwan, series editor. Since 1986, *The Best American Essays* has gathered the best nonfiction writing of the year and established itself as the premier anthology of its kind. Edited by the best-selling writer Susan Orlean, this year's volume features writing by Roger Angell, Jonathan Franzen, David Sedaris, Andrea Barrett, and others.

0-618-35713-0 PA $14.00 / 0-618-35712-2 CL $27.50

## THE BEST AMERICAN MYSTERY STORIES™ 2005

Joyce Carol Oates, guest editor, Otto Penzler, series editor. This perennially popular anthology is sure to appeal to crime fiction fans of every variety. This year's volume is edited by the National Book Award winner Joyce Carol Oates and offers stories by Scott Turow, Dennis Lehane, Louise Erdrich, George V. Higgins, and others.

0-618-51745-6 PA $14.00 / 0-618-51744-8 CL $27.50

## THE BEST AMERICAN SPORTS WRITING™ 2005

Mike Lupica, guest editor, Glenn Stout, series editor. "An ongoing centerpiece for all sports collections" (*Booklist*), this series has garnered wide acclaim for its extraordinary sports writing and topnotch editors. Mike Lupica, the *New York Daily News* columnist and best-selling author, continues that tradition with pieces by Michael Lewis, Gary Smith, Bill Plaschke, Pat Jordan, L. Jon Wertheim, and others.

0-618-47020-4 PA $14.00 / 0-618-47019-0 CL $27.50

## THE BEST AMERICAN TRAVEL WRITING 2005

Jamaica Kincaid, guest editor, Jason Wilson, series editor. Edited by the renowned novelist and travel writer Jamaica Kincaid, *The Best American Travel Writing 2005* captures the traveler's wandering spirit and ever-present quest for adventure. Giving new life to armchair journeys this year are Tom Bissell, Ian Frazier, Simon Winchester, John McPhee, and many others.

0-618-36952-X PA $14.00 / 0-618-36951-1 CL $27.50

# THE B·E·S·T AMERICAN SERIES®

## THE BEST AMERICAN SCIENCE AND NATURE WRITING 2005

Jonathan Weiner, guest editor, Tim Folger, series editor. This year's edition presents another "eclectic, provocative collection" (*Entertainment Weekly*). Edited by Jonathan Weiner, the author of *The Beak of the Finch* and *Time, Love, Memory*, it features work by Oliver Sacks, Natalie Angier, Malcolm Gladwell, Sherwin B. Nuland, and others.

0-618-27343-3 PA $14.00 / 0-618-27341-7 CL $27.50

## THE BEST AMERICAN RECIPES 2005–2006

Edited by Fran McCullough and Molly Stevens. "Give this book to any cook who is looking for the newest, latest recipes and the stories behind them" (*Chicago Tribune*). Offering the very best of what America is cooking, as well as the latest trends, time-saving tips, and techniques, this year's edition includes a foreword by celebrated chef Mario Batali.

0-618-57478-6 CL $26.00

## THE BEST AMERICAN NONREQUIRED READING 2005

Edited by Dave Eggers, Introduction by Beck. In this genre-busting volume, best-selling author Dave Eggers draws the finest, most interesting, and least expected fiction, nonfiction, humor, alternative comics, and more from publications large, small, and on-line. With an introduction by the Grammy Award–winning musician Beck, this year's volume features writing by Jhumpa Lahiri, George Saunders, Aimee Bender, Stephen Elliott, and others.

0-618-57048-9 PA $14.00 / 0-618-57047-0 CL $27.50

## THE BEST AMERICAN SPIRITUAL WRITING 2005

Edited by Philip Zaleski, Introduction by Barry Lopez. Featuring an introduction by the National Book Award winner Barry Lopez, *The Best American Spiritual Writing 2005* brings the year's finest writing about faith and spirituality to all readers. This year's volume gathers pieces from diverse faiths and denominations and includes writing by Natalie Goldberg, Harvey Cox, W. S. Merwin, Patricia Hampl, and others.

0-618-58643-1 PA $14.00 / 0-618-58642-3 CL $27.50

HOUGHTON MIFFLIN COMPANY  www.houghtonmifflinbooks.com